Film Scripts Three

Film ScriptsThree

Charade
the Apartment
the Misfits

Edited by

GEORGE P. GARRETT
University of South Carolina

O.B. HARDISON, JR.
The Folger Shakespeare Library

JANE R. GELFMAN

IRVINGTON PUBLISHERS, INC.
NEW YORK

Distributed by
SAMUEL FRENCH TRADE
HOLLYWOOD, CALIFORNIA

Acknowledgments:
The Apartment Published by permission of Billy Wilder, I.A.L. Diamond, and The Mirisch Corporation.
The Misfits by Arthur Miller, Copyright ©1957 by Arthur Miller Reprinted by permission of The Viking Press, Inc.
Charade Copyright 1962 by Universal Pictures, Co., Inc., and Stanley Donen Films, Inc. All Rights Reserved. Screenplay by Peter Stone and Marc Behm.

First Irvington edition 1989
Copyright ©1972 by Meredith Corporation

Distributed by
Samuel French Trade,
7623 Sunset Blvd., Hollywood, CA 90046

Library of Congress Cataloging-in-Publication Data

Film scripts/edited by George P. Garrett, O.B. Hardison, Jr.,
    Jane R. Gelfman.
        p.   cm.
    Reprint. Originally published: New York: Appleton-Century-Crofts, 1971-
    ISBN 0-8290-2277-5 (v. 3): $19.95.—
    ISBN 0-8290-2278-3 (v. 4): $19.95
        1. Motion picture plays. I. Garrett, George P., 1929-
II. Hardison, O.B. III. Gelfman, Jane R.
PN1997.A1G25   1989
791.43'75—dc19   89-2004
                                                        CIP

10 9 8 7 6 5 4 3 2

Production and design:
The Bramble Company, Ashley Falls, Massachusetts
Cover design: Peter Ermacora and Larry Bramble

Printed in the United States of America

Contents

Acknowledgments

Many people have been helpful at all stages in the task of assembling the material for *Film Scripts*. Obtaining scripts and unravelling the complexities of rights and permissions would have been impossible without the generous assistance, aid, and counsel of many of the writers and artists directly involved in the making of these pictures. Some others, whose work is not represented here, but whose interest in the book and enthusiasm for the idea behind it led them to act to make this book possible, deserve the special thanks of the editors. The editors are especially grateful for the encouragement and efforts of Michael Franklin, President of the Writers Guild of America, West, to Samuel Gelfman of the United Artists, to the distinguished producer-directors Robert Wise and Samuel Goldwyn, Jr., and to Gillon Aitken of Anthony Sheil Associates Ltd. (London).

Introduction

The first movie in the modern sense of the word was made by the Thomas A. Edison laboratories and shown in the unlikely location of West Orange, New Jersey, on October 6, 1889. It was produced by the marriage of Edison's sprocket-controlled motion picture camera with the new nitrocellulose film developed by George Eastman of Rochester, New York. Because the early Edison movies had to be viewed individually, through a peephole exhibiting device, they remained curiosities. During the early 1890s attempts were made by Major Woodville Latham, Louis and Auguste Lumière, Thomas Armat, and others to wed Edison's films to the magic lantern to permit film showings for large audiences. Armat's projector was put in regular use at Koster and Bial's music hall in New York City on April 23, 1896. In spite of a series of ills, including a disastrous fire in a Paris theater that killed some 180 spectators, legal battles by Edison over foreign patent rights, and various attempts to regulate the new industry by monopoly control, motion pictures flourished. The final step in the emergence of the modern film industry was taken by Edwin S. Porter, an Edison cameraman, in 1903. Dissatisfied with the vaudeville acts and sporting events that were the staple of early film, Porter made a narrative film crowding as many thrills as possible onto a standard thousand-foot reel. *The Life of an American Fireman* was sufficiently successful to justify a second effort, which emerged as *The Great Train Robbery* (1903). This film was the first commercially important narrative movie. When it opened in 1905 in a theater specifically designed for film showing and dubbed the *nickelodeon* on the basis of the five-cent admission price,

1

the film industry was fairly launched on its amazing twentieth-century career.

For the first decade of the new century the movie industry was dominated by eastern producers (the Motion Picture Patents Company licensed by Edison). A group of independents using French equipment soon arose to challenge the monopoly of Edison's "movie trust." Partly as a result of competition, the independents moved to Southern California, where labor was cheap, the terrain varied, and the climate mild, an important consideration at a time when almost all movies were made outdoors. In 1911 the Nestor film company, under David Horsley, leased a studio site on Sunset Boulevard in Hollywood, and by the end of the year some fifteen companies had followed suit.

During the decade from 1910 to 1920, Hollywood became the film capital of the world. Cecil B. De Mille, Jesse Lasky, Samuel Goldwin, D. W. Griffith, Charlie Chaplin, Douglas Fairbanks, Sr., and a host of others came to Hollywood during this period and were to remain dominant for years to come, some, like De Mille and Goldwin, until after World War II. It was during this decade that movies found their audience. Regarded by intellectuals as crude popular entertainment, they quickly became the cultural staple for the unwashed millions. As success strengthened the financial position of the theater owners and Hollywood studios, movies challenged the supremacy of almost every form of popular entertainment—fiction, Victorian stage melodrama, and vaudeville—except sports. An awkward symbiosis, in some ways closer to an armed truce than peaceful coexistence, eventually developed between Hollywood and the legitimate theater, but movies badly upset the economy of stage drama. Touring companies were broken up. Smalltown theaters were everywhere converted into moving picture houses. Only the large cities—eventually, only New York—continued to support a vital stage drama. Many of the refugees from legitimate drama, of course, later found their way to Hollywood.

During the twenties and thirties movies reigned supreme in the mass entertainment field, and Hollywood was the undisputed center of world cinema. After World War I, while Europe's picture-making capacity was disrupted, the American industry quickly, and with little additional cost, peddled prints of its films abroad. By 1925, American films had captured 95 percent of the British market, 70 percent of the French, and 68 percent of the Italian; elsewhere the situation was much the same.[1]

The "Hollywood approach" was the hard sell. Hollywood producers based their work on what paid off at the box office, not on what film directors or critics claimed would make great art. They gave the public what the public wanted—slick photography, fast-paced plots, action for the men, and tear-soaked sentiment for the ladies. "Eventually two kinds of film

---

[1] Thomas H. Guback, *The International Film Industry: Western Europe and America Since 1945* (Bloomington: Indiana University Press, 1969), pp. 8–9; supporting references here omitted.

would dominate the screen: the peep show and the chase. As primitive tribes described them to Hortense Powdermaker, 'kiss-kiss' and 'bang-bang' stories are right for the screen." [2]

So successful was Hollywood that after 1915, the date of D. W. Griffith's *Birth of a Nation*, the film industry in England, France, Germany, and Italy never offered serious competition. But, in spite of Hollywood's unchallenged position in America as well as Europe through the twenties and thirties, the market at home still accounted for most of its income.[3] As the world's screen capital, it could afford to be as provincial and inward-looking as the country itself. To accommodate ever-larger audiences, enormous cathedrals or palaces of film were built in the major cities. The forerunner of these citadels was Mitchell Mark's Strand, opened in New York in 1914, with a seating capacity of 3,000. In the twenties the cathedral/palaces rivalled in glitter and luxury the fabled opera houses of Paris, Vienna, and Milan. The Roxy Theater in New York, for example, cost some $8,000,000 and had a seating capacity of over 6,000. But every small town had its moviehouse of some sort, and throughout America, Saturday night became almost synonymous with "going to the movies." Meanwhile, in addition to satisfying the popular craving for entertainment, movies created something like an American equivalent of European royalty. The star system fed the public on dreams of glamour, embodied in such popular idols as Theda Bara, Lillian Gish, Rudolph Valentino, Greta Garbo, William S. Hart, and others, whose exploits were followed obsessively not only on the screen but also in the gossip columns of newspapers and in the screen magazines that were by-products of the star system.

The introduction of sound in 1928 greatly increased the range of artistic effects possible in movies. At the same time it created a group of artistic problems that are still unresolved in the 1970s. Sound tended to nationalize movies. The silents spoke the universal language of visual imagery. Their few subtitles could easily be translated into French, Thai, Hindustani, or what have you, with no leakage of meaning. Talkies, however, relied heavily on rapidly spoken dialogue and often on fairly subtle vocal nuances. This was particularly true in their early years when directors tended to stress sound at the expense of image simply because sound was new, and when many Broadway plays—together with many actors— were translated bodily from the legitimate stage to film. To sell such films abroad it was necessary either to add subtitles or to dub in native-language dialogue. Neither expedient was satisfactory. Subtitles are a poor substitute for the spoken word. They can never translate more than a fraction of what is spoken in fast dialogue. And, of course, they make the unwarranted as-

[2] Roy Huss and Norman Silverstein, *The Film Experience: Elements of Motion Picture Art* (New York: Dell, 1969), p. 15; citing Hortense Powdermaker, *Hollywood: The Dream Factory* (Boston: Little, Brown, 1950), p. 14.
[3] Guback, p. 9.

sumption that the audience is literate! Dubbed dialogue, while better than subtitles, is also awkward. The actors who do the dubbing are usually poorly paid hacks. The dialogue itself is often crudely translated. Perhaps most distressing, the words on the sound track seldom correspond to the lip movements of the actors on the screen, a situation that undercuts, if it does not destroy, the dramatic illusion. Thus, in spite of the growing international character of the film industry, the serious viewer still suffers an annoying distortion and dislocation if he must experience, say, Michelangelo Antonioni's *L'Eclisse* (1961), which is set in contemporary Rome, under the amplification of an English-language sound track. Equally disturbing, on the other hand, is an encounter with the same director's *Blow-up* (1967), which is set in London of today, in any tones other than those of British English.

More fundamental, sound brought with it the unanswerable question of whether movies are a visual or a verbal art. The accident of limited technology forced the directors of the silent era to concentrate on the visual aspect of film. They explored a remarkable range of techniques for telling stories visually. In the opinion of many students of film, sound caused a regression in film technique that lasted until after World War II. Sound made it too easy to tell a story. Cinematic techniques that were commonplace to producers like Griffith and actors like Chaplin were replaced by stale devices imported from Broadway along with playscripts and actors. Not until after World War II, when a new breed of filmmakers formed by the realities of invasion, military defeat, and economic collapse made its vision felt, was Hollywood shaken out of its complacency.

While Hollywood continued to dominate world cinema between the two world wars, Europeans did produce many films that gained international attention either for their intrinsic qualities or innovative techniques. Sergei Eisenstein, the great Russian director, is a towering figure both in the art of making films and of analyzing principles of cinematography. Several of his films, notably *Potemkin* (1925), *Alexander Nevsky* (1938), and *Ivan the Terrible* (1944-46), have had worldwide influence. The silent, *The Cabinet of Dr. Caligari* (1919), by the Austrian director Robert Wiene, remains a classic of expressionism in the theater adapted to film while *The Blue Angel* (1930), a talking picture directed by Josef von Sternberg and starring Marlene Dietrich and Emil Jannings, remains a classic of harsh realism, social and psychological, which was inspired by the disillusionment that pervaded Germany in the last years of the Weimar Republic. Among the French, René Clair produced charming, socially cutting, film fantasies like *À nous la liberté* (1932) and *The Ghost Goes West* (1938); and Marcel Pagnol revealed with tender luminosity in *La Femme de boulanger* (1938) and a trilogy—*Marius* (1929), *Fanny* (1931), and *César* (1936)—complexities of feeling among the petty bourgeoisie of provincial France.

But it was not until 1945, following World War II, that European cinema began to challenge Hollywood and the economic situation for American producers began to change completely. In such films as Rossellini's *Open City* (1945), De Sica's *Shoe Shine* (1946), and his *Bicycle Thief* (1948), Italian filmmakers achieved sensitive but unsentimental renderings of the physical and emotional realities of German occupation, American liberation, and the struggle to rebuild a peacetime society with habits and outlooks conditioned by years of learning how to survive only from moment to moment. This new spirit of filmmaking, *cinéma vérité* (or direct cinema), came as a refreshing new perspective for American audiences when experienced against their own long exposure to Hollywood's vision, subsidized by our government, of a world at war. The newsreel-like verisimilitude of scenes shot on location where local inhabitants played the lesser roles was a radical break with the controlled and insulated environment of the sound studio and its professional actors.

This new and less-expensive procedure opened the door for shooting other films—from British comedies to Scandinavian psychocinedramas—out-of-doors. As the impressionists liberated painting during the last quarter of the nineteenth century by taking their canvases out of the studio and into the fields and streets, European directors led a similar revolution in filmmaking out of necessity after World War II. *Cinéma vérité* also restored to the directors some of the preeminence they had enjoyed during the silent era. They thus opened the way for such meditative, director-dominated films as *8½*, *Last Year at Marienbad* (1962), *Juliet of the Spirits* (1964), and *Blow-up*. French cinema has also been influential, though perhaps experimental, beginning with the postwar classic *Les enfants du Paradis* and extending through the *nouvelle vague* movement of the 1960s. Many isolated but major contributions have also come from Japanese and Scandinavian filmmakers, most notably Akira Kurosawa and Ingmar Bergman.

During the sixties British and American filmmakers began to draw on continental techniques. *A Hard Day's Night* (1964) is a brilliant English contribution which manages the difficult task of carrying its unorthodox techniques so lightly that they seem entirely natural expressions of the dominant tone of exuberant, uninhibited play. In the United States, as the photographic industry produced less cumbersome and expensive cameras and more light-sensitive film, a new kind of movie, one of *personal statement*, emerged. "Underground"—or "independent" as most of them preferred to be called—filmmakers could dissent "radically in form, or in technique, or in content, or perhaps in all three" from the offerings of commercial cinema, and all for an outlay of about a thousand dollars.[4] In the fifties

---

[4] Sheldon Renan, *An Introduction to the American Underground Film* (New York: Dutton, 1967), p. 17.

and sixties a subculture whose important personages included Stan Brakhage, Kenneth Anger, Stan VanDerBeek, and Andy Warhol established themselves as the heirs of an earlier generation of avant-gardists and experimentalists such as Jean Cocteau (*Le sang d'un poète*, 1930) and Luis Buñuel (*Un chien andalou*, 1928).

The response of the major American studios to the new freedom has been slow, but there are signs of change, principally in the form of more flexible use of visual strategies—jump-cuts, flash cuts (forward or backward), slow and accelerated motion, form cuts, zoom-freezes, and the like. *Petulia* (1968), *The Graduate* (1967), *The Wild Bunch* (1969), and *The Landlord* (1970) are excellent films which illustrate this tendency, and they doubtless indicate the direction of much future development. Whatever the case, the pressure on Hollywood to experiment is constant, especially (and ironically) from the screen of commercial television, which feeds heavily on Hollywood's past to keep its viewers awake and watching between plugs for automobiles, beer, and carpets. To compete, the motion picture industry, which is increasingly worldwide in every respect, must either seek a different audience from television or offer the average addict of the tube a positive inducement to leave his living room with its easy chair, ash tray, and nearby supply of cold beer for the privilege of spending from two to five dollars for a *new* movie.

The future of commercial filmmaking is now being shaped by pressures from several, and often conflicting, directions. In terms of revenues for a new feature film "just four countries in Western Europe—the United Kingdom, Italy, France, and West Germany—can yield almost half of the domestic [i.e., United States] gross for a film." [5] Indeed, as early in the postwar years as 1953, Hollywood producers conceded, through Eric Johnston, their industry spokesman, that "9 out of 10 United States films cannot pay their way on the domestic market alone." Simultaneously with greater dependence on foreign markets, other important economic shifts have occurred at home and abroad. Moviegoing in the United States, as reflected in average weekly attendance at theaters, is "but slightly more than half the 1941 figure, while population growth in the intervening years has stretched the imbalance." [6] Even though admission prices have risen steeply, they do not offset the loss of volume. In addition, the suppression of the "block-booking" system by forced separation of Hollywood's production facilities from its distribution outlets through action of the federal government (1948) early deprived major Hollywood studios of assured domestic showcases for each of their products, whatever their individual cinematic or other merits.

Since then, a number of forces are at work to push and shove the world's film capital into its future. Increasingly, "one centrally located, fully equipped permanent facility" makes little economic sense because

5 Guback, p. 4.
6 Guback, p. 3.

of high labor costs in the United States when compared with the rest of the world; access to remote corners of the world for airborne men and equipment becomes ever easier; an improved technology offers better and more portable cameras and more sophisticated editing equipment as well as film stock that is both more sensitive to light and less sensitive to extremes in climate; a new generation of filmmakers are as concerned about experimenting with the technical and psychological aspects of the medium as they are in exploring a variety of social themes; major studios are steadily absorbed by vast financial conglomerates which, though sensitive to costs and attentive to balance sheets, are insensitive to Hollywood's traditions and indifferent to established patterns of production.[7]

In addition to all of these pressures, American capital investment, starting in the early 1950s, has gone abroad and offered to national film industries, which welcomed aid from the United States, financial backing of production costs and the guarantees of an international distribution system for completed films. In two decades the rest of the world has, for better or worse, increasingly lost its independence. In other words, the internationalization of the film industry under American auspices has inevitably meant the diminishing of "chances for diversity and different points of view." Film, however, which is "not only a business commodity but a vehicle of communication . . . , is important not only for what it says but for what it does not say. The boundaries of human experience . . . expand or contract on the basis of what people have presented to them."[8]

The purpose of this thumbnail sketch of the history of film is not to outline or even block out a subject whose dimensions are so large that they are still partly unexplored. Rather, it is to document the basic contention of the present anthology: that film is not *an* art form of the twentieth century, it is *the* art form of the twentieth century. If sculpture was the glory of Periclean Greece, architecture of Augustan Rome, painting of Renaissance Italy, and drama of Elizabethan England, cinema has been both the major contribution of America to world culture and the dominant mode of world culture itself for the last fifty years.

In its brief history, the film has assimilated the photograph variously filtered and focused, motion near and far, sound from one or several directions, color in all of its subtle gradations, screens of great breadth both indoors and out, and lenses that give a visceral feeling of depth and movement. Within these expanding dimensions, filmmakers have elaborated techniques of transition and dislocation from frame to frame which dissolve rigidities of time and space as its audiences know them in everyday life. As a result, the tension achievable in film between order and chaos, between control and chance—which lies at the heart of every art regardless

[7] "Movies Leaving 'Hollywood' Behind," *The New York Times* (May 27, 1970), p. 36.
[8] Guback, pp. 203, 4; see also pp. 94–95.

of its media—is more dynamic and capable of greater complexity than in any other art. Film is far from exhausting its possibilities for artistic triumphs.

In the years since World War II a new medium and industry, television, has emerged not only to challenge established patterns of filmmaking and moviegoing but also to create intricate and reciprocal relations with cinema. Even a partial profile of the mutual impact of film and television on each other would take us too far afield from our primary concern, feature films and their scripts. But certain aspects, some of which we have already discussed, should be noted in passing. The advent of television in the United States has coincided with a reduction in selected subjects, especially newsreels and weekly serials, at moviehouses and their reintroduction in contemporary forms on home screens. Television has also relied heavily on films of the thirties through the sixties from its sister industry in order to sustain the commercial messages of its own advertisers. And, in the postwar years, while the large Hollywood production companies have redefined themselves—lost their chains of tied moviehouses, dismantled their sound stages, and dissolved the star system—commercial television has formed three major networks with affiliated stations across the country, fostered its own production facilities, and created its own stellar personalities—the hosts of its talk, news, and variety shows. At the present time, the internationalism that the film industry has gradually achieved since 1945 is only just becoming possible for television, thanks in part to the broadcast potential of transmission satellites.

The place of film in twentieth-century culture can be demonstrated in another, equally dramatic way. The average nineteenth-century child was illiterate. He was effectively isolated from the culture of the dominant class. As he matured, his entertainment, when he could afford it, consisted of dance-hall reviews, vaudeville, and, occasionally, a melodrama by Dion Boucicault or one of his imitators. Conversely, middle- and upper-class children were brought up on books. They were introduced to the world of art through the printed page. As adults they consumed a constant fare of novels, some good, most bad or indifferent. Theater and opera were significant, but the novel formed the core of the cultural life of the literate population. The modern child, by contrast, is exposed to the visual world of movies and television long before he can read. There is no class distinction in this exposure. It is experienced equally by rich and poor, and it becomes more rather than less intense as the typical modern child matures. College students read more than the general public, but it has been estimated that in the United States a typical freshman has seen twenty movies for every book he has read—and this does not include an average of some 15,000 hours of exposure to television by age 18! [9] After college, the student tends

[9] *Man and the Movies*, ed. W. R. Robinson (Baton Rouge: Louisiana State University, 1967), pp. 3–4.

to fall back into habits like those of the population in general, which means that he reads less, while his consumption of movies and television remains constant or increases. Clearly, film and television now form the cultural medium in which twentieth-century men—from the illiterate to the affluent —are immersed.

The consequences of the dominance of film and television as twentieth-century culture media have often been discussed. Marshall McLuhan feels we are being (or have been) pushed abruptly into a new phase of world culture, the post-Gutenberg era. Sounds and images, rather than printed words, shape our imaginative apprehension of the surrounding world. Sounds and images are not only far richer than printed words, they are also less "linear"—less dominated by the sequential logic of the sentence or paragraph or chapter—less constrained by the need to avoid redundancy or contradiction, and far more accessible since they do not assume literacy. McLuhan's theories imply that the printed word may be growing archaic: that some day the reading of printed books may be an antiquarian pursuit, a little like reading books written in Greek and Latin.

Whatever the future of the printed word, today's educational curricula are shaped around it to a degree that seems exaggerated on the secondary level and nearly obsessive on the college and university level. The higher-education establishment does obeisance to the printed word as devoutly as primitive tribes worship the idols of gods. While harmless in the area of the physical sciences, this behavior is questionable in the area of the humanities. Our literature departments boast of their concern for relevance—for significant examination of every aspect of modern culture. They actively encourage the study of modern fiction, modern poetry, modern drama, and modern criticism. Yet a Martian, after taking the "modern lit." curriculum at a typical American college, might emerge with no other knowledge of cinema than the vague realization that from time to time earthlings of the twentieth century went (probably furtively) to certain entertainments called movies. He might realize that plays and novels were occasionally made into movies, but he would have no inkling of the influence that movies have had on twentieth-century drama and fiction. At best, he would conclude that movies were a minor diversion appealing chiefly to the lower classes, the illiterate, the vulgar, the naive, the deviant.

Granted that film is the cultural medium characteristic of our age, that its neglect has been unfortunate, and that a proper understanding of its values and achievements would enrich studies of twentieth-century fiction, drama, and poetry, not to mention studies of modern psychology and sociology—the question remains: how does one study film?

In general, three approaches to film are possible: the technical, the historical, and the aesthetic. The technical is perhaps the most common one. Presently, some 850 courses on film are being taught at American colleges. The majority are technical in orientation. They are usually taught in departments of radio-television-film, of drama, and of speech, by individuals who are interested in how films are made.[10] Their common feature is their stress on making films—on script writing, photography, film acting, and film direction and editing. They are valuable, but they tend to be professionally oriented. In other words, they are primarily for those who hope to find a career (or, at least, an avocation) in film. They bear the same relation to the study of film that courses in creative writing bear to courses in literature and literary criticism, with the difference that, being much more technical, they are more numerous and less standardized in content.

No one who is interested in film can afford to be ignorant of the technical side of filmmaking, but the limitations of the technical approach should be recognized. One does not need to know how to write a novel in order to appreciate a good one once it is written: to respond to it, to observe its artistry, its literary relations, its form, and its thematic and historical significance. The same holds true for the study of film. Most films are made to be appreciated by audiences who could not care less about how they are made. Occasionally we have a technical *tour de force* like *The Cabinet of Doctor Caligari,* Cocteau's *Orpheus* (1949), or *Blow-up;* but the sheer cost of making a major film means that all but a few experimental directors use technique functionally—a point equally illustrated by Alfred Hitchcock's thrillers and Ingmar Bergman's meditative studies of the human psyche. Hitchcock and Bergman are both masters of film technique, and their technique is always part of their expression. Never present for its own sake, it serves as the medium of our vision, and, while we are members of an audience, we need be no more conscious of it *as technique* than the botanist examining plant cells is conscious of the complex arrangement of lenses that makes his observations possible.

The historical approach to film is also well-defined. Like the technical approach, it offers a valuable, even essential, body of information to the student. Although less common than the technical approach, it appears widely in the curriculum in the form of courses on "The History of Film," "The Silent Film Era," and the like. Historical courses are organized on analogy to the standard courses in the history of literature. Like the "surveys of English lit.," they tend to emphasize chronology, biography, and historical context, and to concentrate on early landmarks—the silent era—rather than later achievements. Their limitation is intrinsic to their approach. They are necessarily oriented toward history rather than toward the achievement of individual films.

The battle begun in the 1930s between historical scholars and the new critics of literature has given way to a generally peaceful coexistence. We recognize that there were (and are) important verities on both sides. In general, however, the basic contentions of the new critics have been established. We accept the idea that the study of literature is primarily a study

[10] *Film Study in Higher Education,* ed. D. C. Stewart (Washington, D.C.: American Council on Education, 1966), pp. 164–67.

of works of literature, not of dates, genres, influences, or biographies. This is why the old-fashioned sophomore literature survey has been replaced at most schools by courses in literary appreciation or literary masterpieces.

Surely, the same principles should apply to the study of film. It should be oriented toward our interest in ourselves and the culture within which the self is defined. The emphasis should be on individual films. Their artistic and cultural significance, rather than their technique or relation to the history of film, should receive first priority. Beyond that, if the films are considered in chronological order, the approach will take on an historical coloring; if they are considered by genres like the Western, the thriller, or the social documentary, the coloring will be formalist; if they are approached in terms of theme, the coloring will be sociological, philosophical, or theological. Some such coloration is inevitable and proper. It supplements the aesthetic approach, as long as it does not threaten to compromise examination of individual films.

To examine a film with the same care and thoroughness as a novel or a poem is difficult. The authoritative text of a film is the master print on which all prints made for commercial distribution are based. In the first place, the master print is never available. All films that are shown commercially and for educational purposes are later prints, and these are often edited silently to conform to local censorship laws, time requirements, and the like. Since many master prints have been lost, the later prints now available may or may not be edited versions, and for many early films, there is no way of knowing what the original really was.

Such bibliographical problems need not concern the average viewer. He can assume that the print of the film which he sees is reasonably close to the master print unless warned otherwise. His problem is of a different order. It stems from the fact that films are dynamic. They move. And as they move they convey more information than the human mind can retain. An experienced critic can pick up an impressive amount of detail from a single viewing of a film, but even the best observer has his limits and they are soon reached. The viewer of a film is the witness of a complex but significant series of events. We know how fallible even the most intelligent witnesses can be from the conflicting testimony that is always generated by a sensational public event. A vivid case in point is provided by the assassination of President Kennedy. We have to recognize the same propensity to error in ourselves. Yet the study of film demands accurate recall not only of what happened but what was said, how it was said, and—film being visual as well as verbal—how it was conveyed in images. That is, we certainly need to know that the hero married the heroine in the last reel. Depending on the aspect of the film that catches our interest, we may also need to know whether or not the butler was wearing gloves, whether the father drove a Ford or a Chevrolet, whether the heroine's costume in the first reel was red to foreshadow the sunset in the last, or whether there was a cut, a fade, or a dissolve from the chapel to the mountains. Moreover, if we wish to discuss our observations, we need some means of verifying them. If we disagree on the color of the heroine's costume, for example, the only way to decide who is right is to go to the film or an authoritative substitute.

Apparently, the ideal way of solving this problem is through movie archives and a viewing machine like the movieola, which permits the observer not only to see the film but to stop the action on a given frame, reverse it, and begin again. Comprehensive film archives would make it possible to document discussions of film in the same way that discussions of poems and novels are documented. An archive would have the further advantage of allowing interested critics to view films as often as necessary to refine and extend their observations.

But this solution, though ideal, is at present impracticable. No archive can accommodate the large numbers of individuals interested in film, and even if it could, the constant use of films quickly destroys them. A much more practical solution is to coordinate viewing of films with reading of scripts. Unlike reels of film, a script is easily portable; it can be read anywhere; it resists wear; notes can be written in its margins; and it is not "time bound," that is, it does not move continuously forward. If the critic comes to the last scene and wants to compare it to the first, he can simply turn back. Although a film can be reversed, the process is time-consuming, particularly if it has to be repeated several times.

Evidently, if film is to be studied as a cultural form in something of the same way that we study poetry, fiction, and drama, the script is a necessary adjunct to viewing the film. Note that it is an adjunct, not a replacement. A faithful copy of the master print must remain the final, authoritative text for the public at large. Normally, however, it is seen only once. At best it can be seen two or three times since rental schedules are fixed and viewing facilities (not to mention the time of the viewer) are limited. The script, which can be read as preparation for viewing the film, can also be annotated while the memory of the film is still fresh, reviewed easily and conveniently as often as needed, and can serve as documentation in resolving doubts about the filmmaker's intentions.

Note, too, that the importance here assigned the script does not imply that film is primarily verbal. The relative importance of image and word is a question in film aesthetics that will probably be debated as long as the question of what Aristotle meant by catharsis. The only assertion being made here is that if film is to be given its proper place in the study of modern culture, then viewing must be supplemented by use of scripts. In fact, a shooting script of the sort included in the present anthology often contains comments and revisions that call attention to effects that might otherwise be missed.

A final word may be useful concerning the scripts selected for the present volume. Silent films are not represented because they had no scripts in the modern sense of the term. Foreign films are excluded because they necessarily lead to awkward—usually misleading—compromises. Anyone who has read a translated script will be aware that its dialogue usually bears little relation to the dialogue in the film. The translator who provides subtitles works directly from the original shooting script, but within the economies of space and time in the footage. Many foreign films today are shown with dubbed-in dialogue. The alternative to a translation is thus a script transcribed from the English dialogue of a dubbed-in sound track. Such a script is next to worthless since the quality of the acting—the tonality, expression, gestures, and the like—was dictated by the nature of the *original* dialogue as well as the linguistic and cultural inheritance of the director and actor, not the words chosen by the English-language editor because they happen to fit the lip movements on the screen.

The scripts selected are entirely from the period between 1945 and 1970. The complicated legal status of prewar scripts makes permission to print difficult to obtain, and, evidently, many shooting scripts have been lost because they were not thought to have any intrinsic value. This limitation is not, however, without advantages. Hollywood's most vital periods were the silent era and the period following World War II. Postwar films are generally more serious in theme, more flexible in technique, and, of course, more directly relevant to contemporary life than their prewar forerunners. Since this anthology is intended for the study of film as an art form rather than the history or technique of film, the basis of the selection has been the quality and intrinsic interest of the film itself. Each selection attracted the serious attention of reviewers and critics when it originally appeared; and each still repays thoughtful critical analysis. Given the abundance and excellence of English and American films during the period covered, no more than a sampling of them can be offered. But an effort has been made to represent the more important types—comedy, satire, costume-movie, social criticism, psychological study, thriller, and fantasy— as well as the more important ways in which a story comes to the screen— from a novel or short story, from a drama, from television, and from an original screen play. Although every reader will inevitably miss several of his favorites, the editors believe that each film selected has a legitimate claim for inclusion.

Most of the scripts are shooting scripts; that is, they represent the written version of a story as it was available to director, actors, and cameraman before and during the making of the film itself. Because shooting scripts differ from dramatic scripts, a brief discussion of their characteristics will be helpful.

Place and Use of the Script

The true text of any film is the film itself, or, more strictly speaking it is the final negative, called the *master film,* from which all prints are made.

The relationship between a shooting script and a finished film is complex and depends upon a large number of variables, mostly upon the intentions and practices of the director. Some of the most outstanding directors, Alfred Hitchcock, for example, work with most explicit and detailed scripts and follow the script with much the same precision as a builder does the blueprints of an architect. (Hitchcock, of course, always works very closely with his writer at every step of the way in preparing his own kind of script.) Other directors prefer a loosely defined scenario so that they have a maximum amount of margin for revision and improvisation during the shooting stage. Some cineasts believe, quite wrongly, that many contemporary pictures are made without scripts. In general, this is simply not true, although the form of the script may vary widely from neatly bound scripts to pencilled scribblings done moments before shooting or even during the shooting of a scene. Granted the powerful aesthetic influence of *cinéma vérité* in our time, which some critics see as a new development in the medium and others as a return to the classical purity of improvisation that characterized the making of many of the greatest silent films, the fully developed script remains a key step in the creation of most films.

To be sure, a certain kind of film, increasingly popular and becoming well-known, dispenses with the rigidities of conventional plot and conventional story line, in favor of working out, directly before the camera, improvisations, ad lib dialogue, and even events or happenings. A conventional script obviously serves little or no purpose in such a scheme. In addition, as the old, arbitrary lines of distinction between fiction and nonfiction, fable and fact, continue to break down, even the feature-length documentary film will be affected by this new creative energy. The work of the American filmmaker Fred Wiseman is an excellent example. Using his team of cameramen to record actual people engaged in actual events, he might once have been called a documentary filmmaker, and judged by old-fashioned standards and classifications. Today he is regarded simply as a filmmaker. His *Titicut Follies* (1967), *High School* (1968), *Law and Order* (1969), and *Hospital* (1970) are, indeed, documentaries taken on the scene at particular times and places and using real people, not actors. Yet these films are also examples of advocacy reporting, designed to make strongly felt social and political points. He exercises the filmmaker's art in choosing to film the events that support his views and feelings and also in the most careful editing of the film to make "reality" coincide with his personal vision. He is thus as much a deliberate fabulator as any other filmmaker, an honest and engaged artist for whose work the old distinctions between "fiction" and "nonfiction" are largely irrelevant. But his method, at least in these films, precludes the use of any ordinary script.

Allowing for notable exceptions, however, it is still generally true that all feature films intended to be shown to audiences in theaters have a script. They may differ in form and format. The script may exist in many copies, available and known to all concerned, or it may be the private property of only a few key figures in the production process. But there is almost always a script, and that script precedes the making of the film.

The process of filmmaking and the unique nature of the medium are such that a script may be considered as raw material for the finished product. It helps to initiate the process of making, serves as a guide to director, actors, and technicians, and is then finally, to a greater or lesser degree, expendable. To the student of cinema, however, a script can be of real value. Close reading of it, in conjunction with an attentive viewing of the film, will demonstrate a great deal, which otherwise might be difficult to learn, about the nature of this twentieth-century art form. And such a procedure can offer substance for the purposes of query, discussion, and debate, the give-and-take and discovery that is learning.

The primary value of using shooting scripts in the study of films is that this method reflects honestly the first critical phase in the process of filmmaking. Although the outlines have been publicly available for a full half-century and have changed only slightly and very gradually during all that time, the process of making pictures is surprisingly little known. Or, when known, it is all too often ignored. Critics and reviewers are, for their own reasons, frequently indifferent to the process of making; or, what is perhaps less defensible, sometimes imply a very different sort of process than the one actually followed by the makers of films. Audiences, even some of the most appreciative and sophisticated, are frequently unfamiliar with the basics of the craft. This ignorance may be partially advantageous; for films, perhaps more than any other art form, depend almost as much upon sleight-of-hand, upon the magicians's art, for their effect upon the viewer as they do upon what is literally shown and seen. Often what is not shown, but is instead evoked in and imagined by the audience, is as viable as what is really shown. Good film shows us a great deal, but we perceive more than what is shown. From Eisenstein to Hitchcock to McLuhan and including the young filmmakers and cinema buffs around the world, directors and producers of films as well as critics and scholars of the art have sought to define theoretically and to name and classify the elements that combine to create the aesthetic effects of film. Their explorations, especially those of the makers of films, are a fascinating subject for research and study and are extremely important in the cultivation of a finer cinematic sensibility. The views of these men, although not to be ignored or slighted, in theory and practice, are far from definitive, whether they be interpreted singly or in any combination. The rules of the game, as even a slight reading of items listed in the bibliography will show, keep changing. One of the surest signs of vitality is the resistance of film art to every attempt at definitive classification, even the most subtle and persuasive. A rudimentary knowledge and general familiarity with the basic steps in the process of making a film should, however, at least serve to increase one's sense of appreciation, to refine one's taste and judgment rather than strip the cinematic experience of its human magic.

And that is the aim of this collection of scripts: to give the reader a means of seeing how films evolve from words to something else and, ideally, something much more than a script, namely, a complex of images, arranged in careful sequence, supported by sound and by music, dramatized by actors, and controlled by the intelligence and sensibility of a director.

Although most scripts are much transformed in the sequential processes of shooting and editing, the ideal of filmmakers, from producer to prop man, is to translate the script into the language and idiom of cinematography and to realize in doing so the script's full potential. This goal is an elusive one at best because of the nature of the process of making films and the many variables involved. All of the artists, craftsmen, and technicians who work at the making of a picture bring to it both skill and creativity. Each is a maker who seeks by his own skills to create something new and good. But even the best results have never given us "perfect" films, only truly fine films whose magic succeeds in spite of their imperfections.

A film script, even when published with care to reflect in detail the copy provided by the film's proprietors, is at best a verbal outline, a blueprint of what one sees and experiences in viewing a film. It is in no way a substitute for the actual experience of seeing a clear, unbutchered print of the film. But as an aid to memory, it helps us recall what we have already experienced as an ordering of meaningful sights and sounds.

Although the script writer is a valuable contributor to the total experience of a film, he is only one of many. Insofar as a single controlling sensibility unifies the entire process and experience, it is always that of the director. The director, of course, cannot possibly do everything himself or know in detail everything necessary to make a moving picture. But he, in the last analysis, is held responsible for all that happens or fails to happen. In recent years, especially with the decline of the large corporate producers in Hollywood, we have come to perceive this fact more clearly. The director's name rather than that of the producer or his imprint is the one we associate with a film in allotting praise or blame. In a very real sense the French critics of our time have been more accurate than innovative in naming the director of a picture its *auteur*. No full and easy analogy, however, quite explains the role of the director. His function is at once that of quarterback, orchestra conductor, building contractor, trail boss, company commander, and, sometimes, lion tamer—the latter image amusingly exploited by Fellini in 8½. The director rules, benevolently or despotically, over a little kingdom. The writer, though absolutely essential to the process and especially to the beginning of it, remains his majesty's loyal servant.

This book contains several sorts of film scripts in a variety of formats. Most are final shooting scripts, that is, examples of the very form which director, cast, and crew worked with when a film first went into production. In many cases additions and deletions and rearrangements and revisions of material take place during the period of shooting the film and, again, during the period of editing the film. Freedom and flexibility are basic characteristics of the creative process of filmmaking. The possibilities for revision are always present when a scene is being filmed, and equally so in the cutting room and laboratory as the film is being edited and polished into its finished form. The final shooting script is the first part of the production process, but it should be remembered that even in this form a script has usually been through many stages already and has been much revised.

Two scripts in this entire collection are not precisely final shooting scripts: those of *Henry V* (1944) and *The Pumpkin Eater* (1964). Each of these British scripts is designated, in British film terminology, as a *release screenplay*. That is to say, each has been more or less adjusted to conform as closely as possible to the edited film, its basic camera angles and shots, its frames and footage. These screenplays, in comparison with final shooting scripts, offer a fuller description of sound and music devices, present many more separate camera shots, and include such elements of the finished and released film as the full title and credits. Necessity requires the inclusion of these release screenplays; for, unlike their American counterparts, it is not the custom of British production companies to preserve copies of the earlier versions of scripts on file. We are most fortunate, however, thanks to the writers themselves, to have obtained rare versions of the shooting scripts of *A Hard Day's Night* (1964) and *Darling* (1965) for this collection. Yet even these release screenplays are somewhat different from and fall short of what is generally known as the *final* official form of a film script—the *combined continuity*. Created by a specialist (usually designated as *script girl*) who follows the shooting and editing of a film from beginning to end, based entirely upon the completed and commercially released form of the film, with all of the separate camera shots listed and all details of footage and running time of individual shots and scenes, etc., carefully recorded, a combined continuity is at once a sort of chart or graph of a finished film and the very last *word* of the film. Close as these two British release screenplays are to what is seen in the films, they are not combined continuities; and differences exist between them and the films. The alert student will note slight changes in each of them.

All of the other scripts in this collection are final shooting scripts. If the release screenplay comes near the end of the process of filmmaking, a final shooting script represents a true beginning. It is the demarcation point—many filmmakers would call it "the point of no return," the place where the production of the film really begins. From there on it goes first before the cameras, then, perhaps most crucially of all, into the movieola of

the film editor to be cut and arranged before the finished film is to be projected upon a screen. Next to the director the film editor has, in a literal
and physical sense, more control over what will be seen by an audience
than anyone engaged in the making of a picture. The director remains responsible for the results and thus supervises the editing process closely.
Some directors are engaged in the cutting and editing of a film in all details. Others prefer to give their film editor considerable freedom and to
act in a critical capacity, viewing sections of the film in the projection room
and offering general advice, suggestions, and criticism as, bit by bit, the
whole film is put together. (Sometimes the screenwriter is called upon to
participate at this stage as well.) The film editor, of course, is a highly
professional craftsman, often an experienced artist in his own right. How
he works with the director and others, and how much the actual labor is
overseen and divided is a subtle matter involving diplomacy, tact, and
personal relationships. Theoretically, in any event, the director has the
last word in this area and is held responsible for the quality of the editing.

The Process of Filmmaking

In the beginning someone has an idea for making a picture. Once this
"someone" was almost always a producer. Now, increasingly, it is a director,
a writer, or occasionally a star who initiates the process. As witnessed by
the scripts in this collection, the idea, the source of original inspiration for
a movie, may come from almost anywhere—a novel or short story, a play
for stage or television, another film old or new, something from the newspapers or magazines, or something that has captured an artist's attention
and can lead to an original screenplay. However the idea may begin, it
soon becomes a *property*. This term, though unfortunate in its connotations,
is almost universally used by filmmakers and is used in a neutral rather than
a pejorative sense. In any case, the original desire and intention to create a
film becomes a matter of real property when a producer involves himself
by means of an option or outright purchase of film rights.

   Enter the writer (if he has not arrived already) to set about building
a story and writing a script. Whether the picture is an adaptation or an
original screenplay, as soon as a producer is involved, commerce begins to
make its claims. The making of all pictures to be shown in theaters, where
audiences buy tickets of admission, is an elaborate (and sometimes lucra-
tive) business as well as an art. Each year the cost of making films increases. The producer must be able to raise the capital necessary to make
the film from one or more sources. Perhaps, under ideal circumstances
and blessed with a reputation for success, he can tentatively arrange the
financing, sign options with leading actors and the right director, and
gather the essential elements of the crew on the strength of the property

alone. But sooner or later, and usually sooner, he will need a script to present to both potential backers and key coworkers before any firm commitments can be made, contracts signed, and a budget and production schedules devised. The writer thus comes in early. If he is lucky he stays late and sees the picture through production.

A very large number of projects, begun with high hopes and much enthusiasm, never reach the point of a workable script, one that is satisfactory to everyone who must be satisfied. A large percentage of properties never become films. And a very large number of the films we see have had more than one screenwriter and many preliminary versions and drafts of the script. Only writers whose material is actually used in the film receive *film credit,* even though a number of writers may have worked on the property earlier.

For simplicity and assuming ideal circumstances, let us imagine one writer working on a script. It should also be understood that though the stages described here are customary and conventional, they vary considerably according to the experience and reputation of the writer and his personal relationship with the producer and the director. Usually the writer will first produce a brief *synopsis* that is basically a literary outline of how he proposes to deal with the story in cinematic terms. If this proves satisfactory, he then writes a *treatment,* a much longer and detailed development of the synopsis, an extended outline of the potential script. The treatment is still more or less literary in form, descriptive rather than dramatic, though it may very well include some individual scenes done in dramatic form and with some dialogue.

Many filmmakers find the treatment a vital stage in the development of script into film. A commonplace among filmmakers says, "If it isn't in the script, it won't be in the picture." What is not meant, of course, by this aphorism is the picture's style, direction, cinematography, cutting, or any matter of filmmaking technique. What is meant is what has always concerned writers as storytellers—structure, character, motivation, tone, etc. Some filmmakers themselves apply this rule of thumb to the treatment and swear that if a script—and hence the film—takes a wrong turn, the flaw can be found in the treatment.

Following the treatment comes the *first draft screenplay,* now employing one of the conventional formats used for film scripts. These forms, as you will see, have slight differences, but there are some general things that apply to all the shooting scripts in this collection. A script is broken down into separate units. Usually, though not always, these are numbered sequentially, and are called *master scenes.* These units may be many or relatively few in number, depending on the detail called for in order to help the translation of dialogue and action as written into camera frames, angles, depth-of-field, transitions, sound, etc. Compared to continuities all scripts are sparse in this kind of explicit direction. A master scene is, then, simply a single dramatic unit at a single location or setting. Within this unit any number of shots and camera angles may be used to shoot many feet of film—versions of the same scene from a variety of angles and points of view. Though the method is changing, the traditional one still employed by most directors requires that all actions in a given master scene be shot at least five times (sometimes the number can be as high as twelve) in order to insure proper *coverage* of the scene. The purpose here is not only to allow for different readings on the part of actors or, say, different lighting conditions, but to provide the director and the film editor with enough footage of the same basic dramatic unit so that they may cut and splice with a maximum of freedom and choice. In the cutting, which comes later, they may well use and juxtapose frames and pieces from all the separate versions of a photographed master scene. This rule does not apply easily, of course, to scenes (or entire films) based upon spontaneity and improvisation.

In addition to specifying a sequence of master scenes and calling for certain specific camera angles in the cinematography of a film, the writer may or may not specify the use of certain kinds of transitions from one unit to the next. Transitions from one scene to the next, from one piece of film to the next, are the concern of the editor. It is not properly a part of the writer's job to tell director, cameraman, or editor how to do theirs; nor will they heed his suggestions to the disadvantage of the film or the inhibition of their own talents. There are a number of reasons, however, why a writer will offer some directions, camera angles, and transitions in his script. First, he will do so in order to make clear a point within his proper area of concern—a story or plot point, a bit of characterization, a structural device, or, perhaps, an occasional suggestion as to the rhythm of a scene or sequence of shots. For the rhythm of a film is intricately wedded to its dramatic structure. Unless elapsed time, for example, is being used functionally for suspense, as in *High Noon* (1952), film is not concerned with what we call "real" time. Instead one has a sense of continual present, a sense that is created by the rhythm of the film. Context may make two scenes of approximately the same footage seem radically different. One may appear slow and lyrical whereas the other may seem jagged, jazzy, and quick. With a full awareness that his views are largely speculative suggestions and may frequently be ignored, the writer is within his rights in dealing with these elements. His views may give director, cameraman, or editor a clearer idea of the intent and inner quality of the script. He will be at fault only in persuading himself that his own visualization of the finished film ought to be binding on the director, actors, and technicians.

There is also another value in the writer's use of at least a few technical devices in his script. Although the script is mainly intended to lead towards the creation of the film, it must be read by a great many people, some very knowledgeable in cinematic technique, others less so. In addition to being examined by the cast and crew, the script is read by bankers and financial backers, by lawyers and talent agents and casting agents, by potential distributors, sometimes even by the owners of theaters, and by publishers and journalists, etc. And each of these readers must be given a sense of the finished film, enough detail to imagine, however, vaguely, the style, form, and content of the film itself. Whether or not the details are ever used as they are indicated in a shooting script depends upon many things, but clearly one function of the script writer, though it is secondary, is to produce a readable film script.

The writer writes his first draft screenplay and the drafts and versions that follow with the criticism, encouragement, and, to an increasing degree as he comes closer to the final shooting script, the collaboration of others who will be making the picture.

The *production manager* worries about the budget, tries to eliminate what seem to him unnecessary scenes and characters wherever possible. And he arranges his own *sequence* for the shooting of the picture, a sequence designed to use talent, sets, material, etc., as efficiently as possible. Almost all pictures made these days, anywhere is the world, are shot *out of sequence* because of the enormous expense of making films. The actual sequence of production and shooting thus hardly ever parallels the sequential structure of the script. Major parts, the leads, have the whole script to study and, with the help of the director, can, even out of proper order, build a character. The minor actors with bit parts are frequently given only *sides,* that is, those specific pages of the script which involve them. They are thus much more dependent on the director. Producer, director, actors, production manager, cameraman, editor, art director, set dresser, and even the prop man, these and many more all have legitimate interests and concerns, and they may exert a considerable influence before the final shooting script is ready.

Once the picture goes into production, collaboration is increased both because more people are involved at that stage and because of the necessity of meeting a fairly strict schedule, within the terms of a fixed budget. If the writer continues on the job, working through the period of production, he will make many changes on the spot to fit unforeseen circumstances. If he does not, there will be changes anyway. Like the diagram of a football play, the script, though well-conceived and planned, does not always work out on the ground exactly as anticipated.

Revision and repeated possibilities for revising, changing, and rearranging occur in every stage of the filmmaking process. Everyone involved has to make constant choices. With liberty to choose and change comes an increased responsibility. For often the choices that must be made are not clear-cut, not between good and bad, but, like many political choices, are decisions between imperfect options for the sake of expediency and in hope and faith that results may serve to justify what is finally decided.

Hence, everyone involved in the making of a film, and not least of these the writer, must always allow for the unexpected and for the possibility of change throughout the entire production. Even then, with the production finished and "in the can," the possibilities of change and (sometimes) improvement remain. Many films are slightly revised following their first previews. Some are revised even later, after their initial premiere openings and in response to reviews. One of the most famous of American filmmakers, the late Irving Thalberg (who served as the model for the producer in F. Scott Fitzgerald's last and unfinished novel, *The Last Tycoon*) is frequently quoted as describing the filmmaking process: "Pictures are not made, they are remade."

Sometime after the final shooting script is finished, the picture goes into actual production, following the shooting schedule. There are rehearsal periods (and, usually, subsequent changes) sometimes before the shooting begins, and always on the set during daily shooting. Scene by scene, the material to be shot is rehearsed until the director is ready to photograph the scene. Then, with everything in place, lighting arranged, camera and sound equipment ready to record, there is the *take*. There may be many takes before the director is satisfied and signifies that a particular take is a *print*. As the shooting schedule progresses the director and editor are regularly viewing the prints called *rushes* or *dailies* as they are delivered from the photographic laboratory. Always bearing in mind their aim of assembling the best possible scenes, they study the prints to decide if it is necessary (and possible) to reshoot sequences that seem to have failed.

When the shooting schedule has been completed and most of the cast and crew are gone, then the stage of full-scale editing commences. It is an intense time which, by traditional rule of thumb, is at least equal to the time spent shooting. All the prints must now be assembled into a single form, a sort of rough draft of the film called the *work print* or *rough cut*. Some figures will give an indication of the magnitude of the task facing the editor and the director. The average feature film runs approximately ninety minutes or, in footage, 8,100 feet of film. It is not unusual for the director and editor to have at least 200,000 feet of prints to work with, from which the film must be composed. And it is also common to have on hand another 100,000 feet of film which represent prints put aside in reserve but not yet discarded during the daily viewing of the rushes. These reserve prints are called *bolds*.

Now the director and editor begin the task of composing and arranging all of this material, through constant revision, into the order and form of the rough cut. When the rough cut is ready, the director can for the first time know with some degree of accuracy how long his film, in its present stage, runs. It is not uncommon for a rough cut to be very long indeed, sometimes an hour or even several hours too long for a feature film. When this is the case, a process of cutting back and simplifying begins. In editing, whole scenes from the script can be shortened or, in some cases, ruthlessly eliminated as being, in terms of the context of the entire picture, no longer necessary. Whole scenes and even larger blocks of script material can be easily rearranged. Both sequence and structure are relatively flexible again.

When the director and the producer are satisfied with the work print, more work still remains to be done. Although this custom is changing, the services of the *composer* are called upon at this late stage. He views the work print, studies the script, then writes music for the picture, which is arranged, performed, and recorded. The contribution of music to the total experience of the film can be enormous. From the beginning, even before the advent of sound, when pianos accompanied the silent pictures in theaters, music has been an integral part of the aesthetic experience of movies. The full implications and possibilities of the use of music in support of and conjunction with all the elements of the film are only now being systematically explored and understood. At least it is clear to all that composer and musicians make a really major creative contribution to the totality of a film.

With the music ready and recorded and all the various sound effects (for example, the ringing of a doorbell, traffic noise, a jet passing overhead, train and boat whistles, etc.) on hand, then, music, dialogue and sound effects are *mixed* by a careful and complicated electronic process to become the *sound track*, a permanent part of the *negative* and, thus, of the *composite print* made from it. At that point the film is done, the picture is finished and ready to be previewed and put into release.

From this oversimplified account of the making of a film several basic generalizations can be drawn:

(a) Filmmaking is complex and collaborative to an extent beyond any of our other media or art forms.

(b) The writer has a critical part to play in the collaboration, for he makes what is at once a blueprint for and the raw material of the finished film. But nonetheless his part is only one among many.

(c) The script is only the first tentative draft text of the film. The extent to which it is followed, closely or freely, literally or with much embellishment, depends on many variable factors.

(d) The effect of the finished film as experienced by an audience is simultaneous, a happening in which all the individual parts, done separately and in bits and pieces, come together at once. Only in the film, and to a lesser extent in the shooting script from which it evolved, is this unity possible.

(e) The making of pictures is a process allowing for many stages of revision, for an extraordinary number of choices to be made. Choices, even bad choices, are exercises of reason. Filmmaking becomes, by definition, one of the most rational art forms man has known. The writer shares in this process, and there is a reason for everything in his script. But in the end, since a film must evoke emotional and imaginative responses from the audience, all the reasons of the makers of the film become means to an end, tools to accomplish a task.

Perhaps the finest picture concerned with the process of filmmaking is Fellini's 8½, in which the protagonist is a gifted director trying to make a picture. Although he fails in his intention, he does succeed in creating the picture we have seen. At the end, the next-to-last scene of the film, the director and his writer sit in a lonely car and the writer, most reasonably, tells him all of the reasons why he has failed. The writer's arguments are irrefutable. Except . . . except precisely at that point a mind reader, a kind of magician who had appeared much earlier in the film, reappears and summons the director to come and do his proper job. The characters from all of the story's episodes reappear at once and, following the instructions of the director, come together hand in hand in a beautiful dance. As they fade out and we are left to confront a dark screen, the truth brightens at the last: out of all the confusion and chaos of this collaborative enterprise, out of all the choices and reasons, good and bad, comes something marvelous, a kind of magic. All the craft of filmmaking conspires to strive towards what Alexander Pope called "a grace beyond the reach of art."

Films are the art form of our tribe, our modern cave paintings. To study the script and to see the film is only the beginning, a preliminary stage in acquiring a finer appreciation of the medium and a greater refinement of taste and judgment. It is fitting and proper to begin where the filmmakers begin, with the script, and to retrace, partly by the evidence and partly by educated surmises, their journey to the final destination of the finished film.

Film Terms in Context

The grammar and syntax of film are not verbal. In the complete cinematic experience words play a part, a very small part, in the form of dialogue. And words are important in the creation of film, beginning with the written script. But when creators, critics, and scholars speak of the *language* of film they are very seldom referring to words. Rather they are speaking of all aspects of cinematic technique as they apply to the making of films and as they are part of the aesthetic experience of the finished film. Though the language of film is essentially nonverbal, a *vocabulary* for film exists to describe the steps taken in the making of films and the effects of films upon appreciative viewers.

The terminology associated with film is complex at its best and esoteric at its worst. It is often confusing to the uninitiated when it is not apparently contradictory. A classic example is the word *montage*. Originally it was the French filmmaker's technical term for the entire process of editing. Great Russian theorists and filmmakers, notably Lev Kuleshov, Vsevolod Pudovkin, and Eisenstein, pioneers of film art, took over the term and changed its meaning. It replaced for them what they had earlier called *the American cut* and was used more strictly to describe both their theory and practice of the art of rapid cutting. (See below for definition of a *cut*.) Because the art and critical theory of these men, and others who followed, have been extremely influential and remain so today, their definitions and classifications of montage are widely used. At the same time, however, American filmmakers incorporated the term montage to describe a very different thing, and their definition is also current and is sometimes called for in scripts. They used the word to describe a series of shots rapidly *dissolving* (see below) over each other. Today the word is used in either sense. Its meaning depends upon context.

The shifting values of montage, both denotative and connotative, are typical of many words in the glossary of film. Context tends to make meaning clear even when there is disagreement about the precise definition. Critics and reviewers, looking at films from the point of view of the effect of the experience of viewing, use their own words and definitions, some of these used exclusively in this critical language. Scholars and specialists in the history of film art are often inclined to use other words, or to use more common words within the limits of special connotation. Makers of films, usually quite aware of both these "dialects," have another vocabulary to describe the technical details of making. They can communicate to each other easily enough, even across the barriers of national language, as witnessed by the fact that in our time international pictures made by multi-lingual casts and crews are not a novelty. A great many terms in the film-maker's lexicon are thus more or less meaningless to all those outside of the craft. Fortunately, an appreciative student of film art need not master a very large vocabulary of technical terms at the outset to speak to the basic aspects of scripts or finished films. From an understanding of some of the elementary terms and experience with the things they signify, the student of film can go on to increase his knowledge and refine his understanding through reading the work of outstanding historians, critics, and filmmakers.

In recent years, precisely the years covered by the volumes of *Film Scripts*, it has been the custom of filmmakers to hire writers of all kinds—dramatists, novelists, poets, journalists—to write screenplays. Most of these writers at least begin their association with filmmaking without any previous experience, except for the great, common, shared experience of movie-going. The days of great production studios, each with its building where a corps of full-time script writers was kept busy, are gone for good. A writer is generally hired to work on one particular project. The common experience of the beginner, frequently described by these writers in interviews and written accounts of their experience, has been doubt at the ability to master the form of the medium, a doubt followed by a sense of surprise and relief that the fundamentals of the vocabulary of filmmaking are not so complex as to demand years of expert experience.

The purpose here is to offer a limited glossary needed for the reading of these scripts and the viewing of the films which came from them. (A full glossary will be found in the back of the book.) Some terms have already been isolated and defined in the preceding section. Others are briefly defined and discussed below.

Those readers who wish to seek out deeper and more inclusive working definitions and examples, will find them in a number of readily accessible books.

(a) *The Filmviewer's Handbook* by Emile G. McAnany, S.J., and Robert Williams, S.J. (Glen Rock, N.J.: Paulist Press, 1965). The chapter entitled "The Language of Film" (pp. 42–69) offers excellent and precise definitions of many terms in a general introduction to the subject.

(b) *A Grammar of the Film* by Raymond Spottiswoode (Berkeley, Calif.: University of California Press, 1965). The chapter "Definitions" (pp. 42–53) offers some useful definitions, though some of his terminology is eccentric when seen beyond the context of this volume.

(c) *A Dictionary of the Cinema* by Peter Graham (New York: A. S. Barnes, 1964). Essentially a brief listing of people in films, this book does offer some definitions of film terms and, notably, some of the special terms used by British and European filmmakers.

(d) *People Who Make Movies* by Theodore Taylor (New York: Doubleday, 1967). Though intended for younger readers, this introduction is exceptionally clear and fine in its coverage of many parts of the filmmaking process. Basic terms, together with examples, are used throughout the text. A brief but accurate glossary is appended.

(e) *Behind the Screen: The History and Techniques of the Motion Picture* by Kenneth MacGowan (New York: Delacorte Press, 1965). This massive compendium of information gives examples and illustrations by a distinguished producer and deals with all aspects of picture-making. Pages 333–501, concerned in depth with technical aspects of filmmaking, present a great many useful terms with full, accurate definitions.

The scene as unit

The opening unit of the script *High Noon*, the first capitalized section, incorporating scenes 1–8 in a descriptive passage, is a useful example. Its format is conventional enough to be called standard.

1–8 EXT. OUTSKIRTS OF HADLEYVILLE—DAY

First, the numbering indicates that eight separate shorter "scenes" are here incorporated into one unit. This device, which is somewhat literary, is designed to make the script more readable at the outset, to set the tone and style before any reader contends with the difficulty of trying to visualize and imagine a large number of separate scenes, 426 in all, many of which are to be very short, individual shots. In the capitalized identification the abbreviation "EXT." establishes that the shooting of the scene is *exterior,* outdoors. The abbreviation "INT." would have established an *interior* location, a setting within some structure. Though this identification may seem so obvious as to be silly to the reader, it serves both a narrative purpose in the script and a technical purpose in making the film. A number of important members of the crew, for example the production manager and the cameraman, not to mention a host of minor functionaries, use this information at a quick glance in their preparation for a scene. Since a film can seldom be shot in the order and sequence of scenes found in the script, the production manager must devise a schedule in which exterior scenes, or nearby parts of them, can be used in a single shooting sequence. At the same time he must be ready not to lose a full day's shooting on account of weather. In the event of rain, for example, he has ready a *backup schedule,* or alternate shooting plan that uses interior sets. These sets must be in order and ready, lighting and sound facilities available, and other members of the cast alert to be called. The script and the schedule also give the cameraman and his crew or *unit* some of the basic information they need to work efficiently. Their equipment for outdoor shooting, the size and composition of the crew, will be different than for interior work.

Because the action of *High Noon* takes place within a small span of time and entirely by daylight, the convention "DAY" is not repeated after the initial heading. In other scripts, however, this traditional direction is frequently used, either regularly with each separate scene, wherever context requires it, or the information is necessary for the crew. Very often scenes supposedly set at night are photographed during the day since the illusion of darkness can be created by the use of appropriate lens and filters as well as by the type and the quality of the film. If the scene must in fact be shot at night, then the proper artificial illumination must be on hand.

Occasionally a more specific direction will be found, such as "DAWN," "TWILIGHT," or "DAY FOR NIGHT," the latter calling explicitly for the daylight shooting of a night scene. These notations tell the cameraman and his unit the kind of light qualities they must capture on film.

The scene

Generally, the breakdown of scenes, headed by the capitalized line and separated by space from other scenes, is determined not only by place, but also by the primary *setup* of the camera and other equipment necessary for shooting. Although all of this equipment cannot easily be displaced in most instances from one setting to another, within a single setting the camera is readily movable. A scene combines, therefore, the physical setting and the primary placement of camera and equipment. In all of the scripts different "scenes" occur from time to time within the larger scene. These separate units, which are part of the same setting and sequence of action, can be used to identify a new and specific setup or to isolate a particular kind of shot.

The filmmaking technique of Alfred Hitchcock is an exception to the rule. Hitchcock prepares, simultaneously with the preparation of the final shooting script, an elaborate and detailed series of sketches (rather like an oversize comic strip) visualizing the film-to-be scene by scene. These sketches are called *continuity sketches*. Script and continuity sketches together, and coordinated as to camera angles and shots, are the material upon which the production of the film is based. Many other directors use continuity sketches as a part of their working strategy, for at least parts of a film, as a guide to the shooting and editing of difficult scenes and transitions. (See "Editorial Terms" below.)

Camera shots

Many kinds of shots are possible, but basically all of them are variations upon a few standards.

Three are defined by proximity of the camera to the subject, whether literally by distance or by use of special lenses. These shots—*long, medium*, and *close*—are only relative and not specific measures. The long shot includes details of an entire setting. Its subject may be on the horizon, for example, a distant ship, the buildings of a city, an expanse of open country, or it may be as close as, say, fifty yards. In order to emphasize great distance, an *extreme long shot* is sometimes called for. A medium shot is of a distance to include, if necessary, a group of two or more people and at least part of the surroundings. A close shot, also called *closeup*, focuses closely on its subject in isolation. It may be of the face or hands of a character or of some single object. Close shots, of course, can be photographed quite separately, even at another time and place, and inserted later in the action of a sequence. For further definition close shots may be *extreme* or *tight* on the one hand or a *medium close shot*, which is indefinite in scope, but nearer at hand than a standard medium shot and at the same time not so tight as the standard closeup.

Two other shots, in which the proximity may vary, are usually included in the five basic shots. They are the *two-shot*, or *group shot* if more than two characters are involved, and the *over-shoulder* shot. The first, at whatever distance, focuses attention on two characters or the group. Sometimes the cameraman is asked in this context to center attention on one of the characters by *featuring* or *favoring*. The over-shoulder shot is, in fact, a variation of the two-shot or group shot; for, in the foreground is the back of the head of one character and in the background we see what the character sees.

Occasionally other kinds of shots are called for, which the context makes clear. For example, a *full shot* does not specify distance, merely that the shot should be fully inclusive of the subject.

In scripts the term *montage* is sometimes used to describe a shot. It then signifies a "series of rapid dissolves," which was mentioned earlier, and involves both cameraman and editor in its creation.

A *stock shot* is a shot or sequence not filmed specifically for the picture but taken from the stock of available footage of any given subject or event. A frequently used stock shot is that of a commercial jet taking off or landing.

A *process shot* is a shot in which actors in the foreground play out a scene in front of a screen that is itself filled with a photograph or movie. The most familiar conventional example occurs in traffic scenes. The characters are photographed in the shell of a stationary automobile while a film of traffic, visible through the rear window, gives the impression of movement and traffic. Process shots may also be used to give the impression of some background or setting far from the studio and set where the actors are being photographed.

Camera angles

In addition to the specific kind of shot sometimes explicitly called for in a script, camera angles may be stated. Just as in the case of shots, these suggestions by the writer will be actually followed by the director and cameraman only insofar as they are deemed valid and functional.

The camera may photograph from certain basic *angles* and, as well, it may shoot from a particular *point of view* (usually abbreviated POV). Point of view need not include the observing character, whose presence on the screen would constitute an over-shoulder shot. A character, for example, looks up; the next shot, made as if to represent what he sees, is of a buzzard in the sky.

Camera angles can be reduced to three principal types: a *regular* or standard angle, unnamed and unspecified since it is assumed to be taken from the camera as set up, straight up and down; a *high angle* (looking from above); and a *low angle* (looking up).

Occasionally the angle is assumed and the direction *shooting up* or *shooting down* is given. The high angle is sometimes simply described as a *high shot*.

Camera and movement

In shooting a camera may be either *fixed* or *moving*.

A fixed camera is set up at one spot. But a fixed camera can nevertheless be used to create a sense of movement or action.

The fixed camera can *tilt*, be moved upward or downward on its single axis while shooting.

And the fixed camera can *pan*. The word is a contraction of the original term used—*panoramic shot*. It is a pivotal movement, usually lateral, made by turning the camera on its axis from one side or part of a scene or setting to another.

Two other customary movements of a fixed camera are the *zoom* and the *whip*.

The zoom is achieved by lens adjustment during photographing so that, without any break, the camera may move (*zoom in*) to a quick closeup of a particular subject.

The whip is a variation on the pan. The camera, focused on one object in a scene, is suddenly and swiftly moved (whipped) to focus upon another subject.

But, since the earliest days, it has not been necessary to depend exclusively upon a fixed camera. The camera may be moved while shooting in what are called *moving* or *running* shots.

One method of moving the camera is by means of a *dolly*. Mounted upon a short set of tracks or a level platform with wheels, the camera can be moved along to follow action, and it can *pull back* from or *come in* on the action. A *crab dolly* is a small platform on wheels designed to move in any direction.

More extensive movement over a larger area than can be accomplished by dollying is achieved by mounting the camera on a platform on a car or truck or other moving vehicle for what are called *trucking* or *tracking* shots. A well-known example of extensive tracking, praised by some critics and censured by others, is to be seen in Olivier's direction of the Battle of Agincourt in *Henry V*.

Still another form of using a mobile camera is by means of the *crane* or *boom*. A small camera platform is set at the end of a long crane, and the crane may be moved up and down or laterally across a set.

Another basic photographic effect, increasingly popular in recent times, is most often described as the use of a *hand-held* camera. The term is most accurately used to differentiate the filmic qualities obtained by a small camera held in the hands while shooting from those created by a standard studio camera which is balanced, level, and set on its tripod, a dolly, or platform. Ironically, the results of the hand-held camera, rather like that of home movies, can be duplicated by more conventional (and more expensive) camera setups. Combined by laboratory work with grainy prints of high or low key, the camera work appears to be less smooth and even in the recording of subjects and action. What is deliberately achieved is a certain urgent and amateurish quality, associated in the minds of the contemporary audience with the verisimilitude of newsreels and documentaries and, as well, with the art films of certain prominent European directors in the immediate postwar years, the *réalismo* of Roberto Rossellini and Vittorio De Sica, for example. The effects of the hand-held camera seem more "realistic" however they are manufactured, and call attention to the cameraman's struggle and the immediacy of his work. Because of the artifice of film techniques, however, these effects may in fact be as "artificial" as those usually associated with only the highest standards of cinematography.

Editorial terms

The process of editing, which has already been mentioned, is highly technical and requires specialized study and experience. Some basic editorial techniques should, however, be understood by any student of film. One of these is the method of *transition* from one unit of film or larger sequence to another. Although the screenwriter must concern himself to some extent with the transitions, his part is marginal and limited to suggestions. For the editing of a film is exclusively the director's concern and that of his editor, or *cutter* as he is usually called by filmmakers.

There are essentially three kinds of transitions, with variations and, in some cases, different ways of accomplishing the same effect. The three forms of transition are the *cut*, the *dissolve*, and the *fade*.

The cut is, quite simply, a break or cut in the film. A sequence of images photographed from the same setup and angle is literally cut off, then spliced to another sequence. Cutting is, inevitably, continuous in a film, so frequent a pattern that we seldom notice it—unless it is the intention of the editor and the director that we should. The use of the word *cut* is somewhat confused by a number of other definitions of the term. For example, a cut may be used to describe a single strip of film. Many filmmakers call shots cuts, as in "Let's have a cut of the charging Indians here." And cut may mean *take out* or *add to*.

Professionals have no difficulty with this burden of possible meaning because context makes the particular case clear. But in terms of transitions, some examples may be in order. One of the most frequent cuts occurs when a character in an exterior setting starts to open a door to go into an unseen interior. We see him turn the handle of the door and start inside. The next shot will likely be a *reverse*, taken from within the interior set. The door is opening and he is coming in. Another common example of the conventional direct cut is frequently found when two characters are in conversation. At the outset we may see them both together in a two-shot. Then we cut back and forth from their separate faces as they speak to each other and react.

For the most part we do not consciously notice simple cuts. We imaginatively supply the missing connections and, so long as we are engaged in the viewing of the film, the action may seem smooth and continuous. Part of our reaction comes from experience and the habit of response; for the fundamentals of cutting have remained much the same since the days of D. W. Griffith. In *Birth of a Nation* he effectively used five-second shots, cut and joined together, in many places to establish a pattern for future editing.

Equally conventional is the use of the cut for a special effect in unexpected circumstances. An excellent example of the cut, used for humor, occurs in the fine Italian comedy *Big Deal on Madonna Street* (1959). Vittorio Gassman, arrested and awaiting trial, confidently reassures his weeping girl friend that he has an excellent lawyer and that the prosecution has no case against him. Nothing to worry about. From his smiling self-assurance there is a *direct cut* to a line of convicts, Gassman among them, marching doubletime around the yard of a penitentiary.

A *dissolve* or *lap dissolve* is a different sort of transition, sometimes called a *special effect* because it involves laboratory work. It is a process of superimposition by which one image gradually vanishes to be simultaneously replaced by another image without any perceptible fading of the light. The result is often a graceful sort of transition, traditionally used to indicate shifts of time and place without appearing to break the continuity of the film.

A variation on the dissolve is the *swish-pan*, a very swift dissolve which seems to be the result of camera movement, but is in fact a laboratory process.

A fade, used within the film as a transition, begins as a *fade out*. Both light and images fade into darkness and the screen goes (briefly) black. Following that a new image slowly *fades in*. Traditionally a fade acts as a definite break in the action of a film, somewhat analogous to the use of the curtain in the proscenium theater. It is also traditional to begin a script with the direction "Fade In" and to end it with "Fade Out."

There are a number of variations which can be used in lieu of a dissolve or fade. One is the *wipe*, in which the scene we are watching appears literally to be wiped away or erased from the screen, horizontally, vertically, or diagonally.

The *flip* is an effect in which a frame of film and its images appear to be flipped over like a card, either horizontally or vertically, to be replaced by another frame of images.

One of the oldest means of transition in the history of filmmaking, once widely used before the fade was possible, but still in use today, is the *iris*. As in fades, we *iris out* or *iris in*. The effect of irising out may occur in one of two ways. Either, within the frame, black seems to come from all sides diminishing the area of the image seen so that the image itself appears to recede or dwindle until it vanishes; or a single spot of black in the frame may appear to grow larger, going outward in all directions until the entire frame is dark. To iris in is to reverse the process.

The extent to which any of these editorial devices of transition—or, for that matter, the full variety of camera shots and angles—is employed depends, of course, on such things as current cinematic fashion and the nature and treatment of the subject of a script and a film. It also depends in large part upon the taste and aesthetic predilections of the director. On the one hand is Richard Lester, who opened up a full, rich bag of tricks, and most appropriately, to enliven *A Hard Day's Night*, whose shooting script gives very little indication of the style of the finished film. On the other hand is Billy Wilder; his scripts for *Some Like It Hot* (1959) and *The Apartment* (1960) are almost equally bare of explicit or suggested directions to cameraman or editor. Although Wilder is no stranger to the use of tricks, witness his *Sunset Boulevard* (1950), he has long been outspoken against depending too much on techniques to do the work of actors and directors. Kenneth MacGowan quotes him as saying: "If the scene is well directed from the point of view of its feelings, the camera can be set down, forgotten, and allowed to record." Wilder is, as ever, more careful than he seems at first glance. While he proposes limitations on the camera as writer-director, Wilder does not place limits upon the techniques of the editor.

Sound

Though sound as a part of motion pictures was technically possible much earlier, it did not become commercially feasible until the mid-1920s, and silent films continued to thrive until 1930. With the advent of sound as an integral part of the film art, this element became a part of the editor's general responsibility. In preparing the sound track, he has a number of technicians to help him. A *sound crew*, which works during the shooting of the picture, usually consists of a *mixer*, a *recordist*, and a *sound boom man*. Once the editing process begins a *sound effects editor* and a *music editor* are usually on hand in addition to a number of mixers who work on the final synchronization of all sounds and images in creating the composite print.

For a beginning, the editor has at his disposal the sound crew's original recordings taken during shooting. When synchronized with the rough cuts these recordings comprise the *wild track*. Where dialogue needs correction and better quality, which is often the case, the actors redo their lines in a controlled sound studio where *off-screen* or *voice over* dialogue is also added. This process of recording in synchronization with the film is called *dubbing* or *looping.* The opposite procedure, the deletion of sound effects or unwanted noises, is called *dialing out.*

The technical resources and possibilities of filmmaking, as even this brief glossary makes clear, are enormous. The greatest problem facing all of a film's creators is to choose among all of the possibilities the most efficient and most suitable means. The director, aided and advised by other artists, bears final responsibility for the choices made.

The writer's special responsibility is to create a script which, whatever its format, speaks to the needs of all the cast and crew, points directions by suggestion, and yet leaves each artist and technician free to create within the framework of his own competence. Within this context the technical terms of filmmaking should be understood. The value in application can be measured only by close viewing of films.

A Note on the Text of These Scripts

In preparing *Film Scripts* for publication, the editors have tried to present, as closely as is reasonable and possible, the version of each script acquired in the form in which it originally came to them. Because no two are precisely the same in all details, the special characteristics of each are mentioned in the appropriate headnote.

All of the American scripts included here are final shooting scripts. Some were more "finished" and "clean" than others; some contained pencilled revisions, made on the spot during the process of making.

In order to facilitate comparative study of word and image, the following conventions have been observed in reproducing facsimile versions of the scripts:

Deletions (of a passage, line, speech, direction, etc.) are indicated by asterisks plus any end punctuation.

New passages are underlined with dashes. Where there was a deletion involved this is likewise indicated by asterisks.

Deleted material is given in the form of annotation at the foot of the page. Large brackets have been placed around each continuous deletion. Small brackets are used to indicate changes in material that was later discarded.

The purpose here is not to provide a description or analysis of bibliographical changes; for the true bibliography of a film would chiefly be concerned with the text of the film—the master film and the prints made from it. But since revisions, even of the final shooting script, are parts of the process of making a film, these changes are indicated where evidence of them in the script was decipherable.

The most important revisions and changes, however, are manifest in the difference between the script and the finished film. The reader, who should also be a viewer, may wish to keep his own notes, perhaps in the margin of the text, on the basis of his own seeing of the film. This anthology can thus lead the reader/viewer to a better and more detailed understanding of the process of filmmaking. For, by having the script in handy and readable form, he not only has points of reference for testing his own memory of a screening but also, at least in a number of cases, a base line for questioning the possible function and purpose of some of the filmmaker's visions and revisions.

the Apartment

1960—A Billy Wilder Production; released
by United Artists
Director   Billy Wilder
Script   Billy Wilder and I. A. L. Diamond
Source   Original screenplay
Stars   Jack Lemmon, Shirley MacLaine, Fred MacMurray

In 1960 *The Apartment* walked off with five Academy Awards, including "Best Picture," "Best Directing," and "Best Screenplay." That fact, taken in conjunction with the virtually unanimous chorus of dismay and negative reviews by the establishment critics earlier, when the film was first released, may not have served to endear Wilder and all his works to these skeptical, suspicious ladies and gentlemen.

Meanwhile Wilder has gone on making pictures. Following *The Apartment* he has made *One, Two, Three* (1961), *Irma La Douce* (1963), *Kiss Me, Stupid* (1964), and *The Fortune Cookie* (1966). And the fate of these films, at least in the hands of the critics if not at the box office, is instructive as to the fashions of film criticism.

The story begins with *The Apartment*. *Newsweek*, over the years staunch in support of Wilder, and *Time* gave him good notice and report. *Time* decided that *The Apartment* was "a peerless comedy of officemanship." On the other hand, some of the chief powers were negative. Philip Hartung attacked it in *Commonweal* (July 8) and argued that it "vacillates between comedy and near-tragedy." John McCarten, for *The New Yorker*, disliked everything about the picture and concluded: "These are gray-flannel beatniks all right. If you want them, take them." Stanley Kauffmann liked some things, but criticized the script which, he wrote, "wanders from near-slapstick to the near-tragic, and the story is based on a tasteless gimmick."

Nevertheless *The Apartment* walked off with prizes and with a solid business success. When *One, Two, Three* appeared a year later, they were ready to change their tune about Wilder. The raves came tumbling down upon his head like confetti at a hero's triumph. *Time* called it a "wonderfully funny exercise in nonstop nuttiness. . . ." Brendan Gill wrote for *The New Yorker,* "By the time the picture is over, we are exhausted, but what has caused our exhaustion is laughter, and few of us will object to paying such a price for that." Kauffmann praised it. Dwight Macdonald suggested it was one of the best films of the year. From all sides the tune was changed, the words were affirmative. Even the statesman-historian-swimmer of those years, Arthur Schlesinger, Jr., taking time off from duties in Washington to write movie reviews for the now-defunct *Show,* compared Wilder to Mark Twain and said that *One, Two, Three* left him "helpless, spent, and gasping for breath." The establishment loved him.

There was, however, even then, a cloud on the horizon, a formidable one—Pauline Kael. The lady was not amused. She had been amused by *Some Like It Hot,* and she was willing to admit to a certain nostalgic fondness for the early *Double Indemnity* and for the "decadence of *Sunset Boulevard* which, in 1950, she had found a beneficial change after "oceans of rosewater, lilies of San Fernando Valley, and the scrubbed, healthy look." But she was not about to let either Billy Wilder or her colleagues off the hook. She took them all to task. The source of his humor they were all praising and the "real location" of the film was "the locker room where tired salesmen swap the latest variants of stale old jokes." She added that the sum of his wit and humor was about as delightful as "you-know-what hitting the fan." For her it all took a turn for the worse with *The Apartment,* which exemplifies "machine-tooled, commercial social consciousness. 'The old payola won't work any more' announces the hero of *The Apartment,* and even people who should know better are happy to receive the message."

By 1963 she and other skeptics had made their point; and when *Irma La Douce,* despite mixed notices, grossed almost ten million dollars to set an all-time record for comedy, the establishment deserted him, except for a few of the faithful, like *Newsweek. Kiss Me, Stupid* took a severe beating from the critics in 1964. And now, a few years later, Wilder is not even in the index of some of the most recent critical books. John Simon allots him part of a paragraph in *Private Screenings,* to offer his own definition of the "Billy Wilder formula: sophomoric misanthropy; machine-made cynicism; gags, gags, and more gags. . . ."

Speaking more or less for the new and now generation in *Landscape of Contemporary Cinema,* William David Sherman celebrates the "Swiftian vulgarity and misanthropy" of the later films. *Kiss Me, Stupid* and *The Fortune Cookie* are placed in grand contemporary company, and with them come Wilder's work. "Like the novels of Barth, Donleavy, Heller, Pynchon, Vonnegut and others," Sherman writes, "the screenplays of Wilder/Diamond offer laughter as the only possible response to the horror of the human condition."

The public, too, has something to say. The latest issue of *Movies on T.V.* gives *The Apartment* the full four-star rating.

The Script Billy Wilder is noted for his clean copy and very readable scripts. Unlike many other filmmakers, he does not at any point indicate or note revisions on a shooting script. Moreover, though the script is broken down into 151 master scenes, Wilder offers very little camera direction following the first few opening shots. Once under way, the script is uncluttered with directions and description. It is, therefore, easy to *read*. Since he participated in the writing, and since he was an experienced director planning from the outset to direct, he clearly did not feel it necessary to offer a full blueprint of all these details. Scenes 1–7 are unusual in that they adopt the standard method of television scripts, separating the video and the audio into parallel columns. Note how occasional gag lines appear in the description, beginning in the first scenes, evidently to set the tone of comedy for the *reader*. The overall sense of this script is one of authority. The characters, settings, and scenes are there. The rest, apparently, from Wilder's point of view, can only be seen in the finished film.

Credits Producer, Billy Wilder; Director, Billy Wilder; Screenplay, Billy Wilder and I. A. L. Diamond; Art Direction, Alexander Trauner; Music, Adolph Deutsch; Photography, Joseph LaShelle; Editor, Daniel Mandell.

Cast	C. C. Baxter:	Jack Lemmon
	Fran Kubelik:	Shirley MacLaine
	J. D. Sheldrake:	Fred MacMurray
	Mr. Dobisch:	Ray Walston
	Miss Olsen:	Edie Adams
	Margie MacDougall:	Hope Holiday
	Dr. Dreyfuss:	Jack Kruschen
	Mr. Kirkeby:	David Lewis
	Sylvia:	Joan Shawlee
	Karl Matuschka	Johnny Seven
	Mrs. Dreyfuss:	Naomi Stevens
	Mrs. Lieberman:	Frances Weintraub Lax
	The Blonde:	Joyce Jameson
	Mr. Vanderhof:	Willard Waterman
	Mr. Eichelberger:	David White
	The Bartender:	Benny Burt
	The Santa Claus:	Hal Smith

Awards   Five Academy Awards—"Best Picture," "Best Directing," "Best Screenplay," "Best Art Direction," and "Best Editing." The New York Film Critics honored it with their awards for "Best Picture," "Best Direction," and "Best Screenplay." The British Film Academy tendered the award to *The Apartment* for "Best Film From Any Source" and named Jack Lemmon "Best Foreign Actor." Shirley MacLaine received the "Best Actress" award from the Venice Film Festival.

THE APARTMENT

1. A DESK COMPUTER

BUD'S VOICE

A man's hand is punching out a series of figures on the keyboard.

On November first, 1959, the population of New York City was 8,042,783. If you laid all these people end to end, figuring an average height of five feet six and a half inches, they would reach from Times Square to the outskirts of Karachi, Pakistan. I know facts like this because I work for an insurance company --

2. THE INSURANCE BUILDING -- A WET, FALL DAY

It's a big mother, covering a square block in lower Manhattan, all glass and aluminum, jutting into the leaden sky.

-- Consolidated Life of New York. We are one of the top five companies in the country -- last year we wrote nine-point-three billion dollars' worth of policies. Our home office has 31,259 employees -- which is more than the entire population of Natchez, Mississippi, or Gallup, New Mexico.

3. INT. NINETEENTH FLOOR

Acres of gray steel desks, gray steel filing cabinets, and steel-gray faces under indirect light. One wall is lined with glass-enclosed cubicles for the supervisory personnel. It is all very neat, antiseptic, impersonal. The only human touch is supplied by a bank of IBM machines, clacking away cheerfully in the background.

I work on the nineteenth floor -- Ordinary Policy Department -- Premium Accounting Division -- Section W -- desk number 861.

4. DESK 861

Like every other desk, it has
a small name plate attached to
the side. This one reads C. C.
BAXTER.

BAXTER is about thirty,
serious, hard-working,
unobtrusive. He wears a
Brooks Brothers type suit,
which he bought somewhere on
Seventh Avenue, upstairs.
There is a stack of perforated
premium cards in front of him,
and he is totaling them on the
computing machine. He looks
off.

My name is C. C. Baxter -- C.
for Calvin, C. for Clifford --
however, most people call me
Bud.

I've been with Consolidated
Life for three years and ten
months. I started in the
branch office in Cincinnati,
then transferred to New York.
My take-home pay is $94.70 a
week, and there are the usual
fringe benefits.

5. ELECTRIC WALL CLOCK

It shows 5:19. With a click,
the minute hand jumps to
5:20, and a piercing bell
goes off.

The hours in our department are
8:50 to 5:20 --

6. FULL SHOT - OFFICE

Instantly all work stops.
Papers are being put away,
typewriters and computing
machines are covered, and
everybody starts clearing out.
Within ten seconds, the place
is empty -- except for Bud
Baxter, still bent over his
work, marooned in a sea of
abandoned desks.

-- they're staggered by floors,
so that sixteen elevators can
handle the 31,259 employees
without a serious traffic jam.
As for myself, I very often
stay on at the office and work
for an extra hour or two --
especially when the weather is
bad. It's not that I'm overly
ambitious -- it's just a way
of killing time, until it's all
right for me to go home. You
see, I have this little problem
with my apartment --

DISSOLVE TO:

7. STREET IN THE WEST
   SIXTIES -- EVENING

Bud, wearing a weatherbeaten Ivy League raincoat and a narrow-brimmed brown hat, comes walking slowly down the sidewalk. He stops in front of a converted brownstone, looks up.

I live in the West Sixties -- just half a block from Central Park. My rent is $84 a month. It used to be eighty until last July when Mrs. Lieberman, the landlady, put in a second-hand air conditioning unit.

The windows on the second floor are lit, but the shades are drawn. From inside drifts the sound of cha-cha music.

It's a real nice apartment -- nothing fancy -- but kind of cozy -- just right for a bachelor. The only problem is -- I can't always get in when I want to.

8. INT. THE APARTMENT -- EVENING

What used to be the upstairs parlor of a one-family house in the early 1900's has been chopped up into living room, bedroom, bathroom and kitchen. The wallpaper is faded, the carpets are threadbare, and the upholstered furniture could stand shampooing. There are lots of books, a record player, stacks of records, a television set (21 inches and 24 payments), unframed prints from the Museum of Modern Art (Picasso, Braque, Klee) tacked up on the walls.

Only one lamp is lit, for mood, and a cha-cha record is spinning around on the phonograph. On the coffee table in front of the couch are a couple of cocktail glasses, a pitcher with some martini dregs, an almost empty bottle of vodka, a soup bowl with a few melting ice cubes at the bottom, some potato chips, an ashtray filled with cigar stubs and lipstick-stained cigarette butts, and a woman's handbag.

MR. KIRKEBY, a dapper, middle-aged man, stands in front of the mirror above the fake fireplace, buttoning up his vest. He does not notice that the buttons are out of alignment.

                    KIRKEBY
                (calling off)
        Come on, Sylvia. It's getting late.

SYLVIA, a first baseman of a dame, redheaded and saftig, comes cha-cha-ing into the room, trying to fasten a necklace as she hums along with the music. She dances amorously up to Kirkeby.

                           KIRKEBY

          Cut it out, Sylvia. We got to get out
          of here.

He helps her with the necklace, then turns off the phonograph.

                           SYLVIA
          What's the panic? I'm going to have
          another martooni.

She crosses to the coffee table, starts to pour the remnants of
the vodka into the pitcher.

                           KIRKEBY
          Please, Sylvia! It's a quarter to nine!

                           SYLVIA
                    (dropping slivers of
                     ice into the pitcher)
          First you can't wait to get me up here,
          and now -- rush, rush, rush! Makes
          a person feel cheap.

                           KIRKEBY
          Sylvia -- sweetie -- it's not that --
          but I promised the guy I'd be out of here
          by eight o'clock, positively.

                           SYLVIA
                    (pouring martini)
          What guy? Whose apartment is this,
          anyway?

                           KIRKEBY
                    (exasperated)
          What's the difference? Some schnook
          that works in the office.

9. EXT. BROWNSTONE HOUSE -- EVENING

    Bud is pacing back and forth, throwing an occasional glance at
    the lit windows of his apartment. A middle-aged woman with a dog
    on a leash approaches along the sidewalk. She is MRS. LIEBERMAN,
    the dog is a scottie, and they are both wearing raincoats.
    Seeing them, Bud leans casually against the stoop.

                              MRS. LIEBERMAN
        Good evening, Mr. Baxter.

                              BUD
        Good evening, Mrs. Lieberman.

                              MRS. LIEBERMAN
        Some weather we're having. Must be
        from all the meshugass at Cape Canaveral,
                         (she is half-way
                         up the steps)
        You locked out of your apartment?

                              BUD
        No, no. Just waiting for a friend.
        Good night, Mrs. Lieberman.

                              MRS. LIEBERMAN
        Good night, Mr. Baxter.

She and the scottie disappear into the house. Bud resumes
pacing, his eyes on the apartment windows. Suddenly he stops --
the lights have gone out.

10. INT. SECOND FLOOR LANDING -- EVENING

     Kirkeby, in coat and hat, stands in the open doorway of the
     darkened apartment.

                              KIRKEBY
        Come on -- come on, Sylvia!

     Sylvia comes cha-cha-ing out, wearing an imitation Persian lamb
     coat, her hat askew on her head, bag, gloves, and an umbrella
     in her hand.

                              SYLVIA
        Some setup you got here. A real, honest-
        to-goodness love nest.

                              KIRKEBY
        Sssssh.

     He locks the door, slips the key under the doormat.

                              SYLVIA
                         (still cha-cha-ing)
        You're one button off, Mr. Kirkeby.

She points to his exposed vest. Kirkeby looks down, sees that
the buttons are out of line. He starts to rebutton them as they
move down the narrow, dimly lit stairs.

                    SYLVIA
          You got to watch those things. Wives
          are getting smarter all the time. Take
          Mr. Bernheim -- in the Claims
          Department -- came home one night
          with lipstick on his shirt -- told his
          wife he had a shrimp cocktail for lunch --
          so she took it out to the lab and had it
          analyzed -- so now she has the house
          in Great Neck and the children and the
          new Jaguar --

                    KIRKEBY
          Don't you ever stop talking?

11. EXT. BROWNSTONE HOUSE -- EVENING

Bud, standing on the sidewalk, sees the front door start to
open. He moves quickly into the areaway, almost bumping into
the ashcans, stands in the shadow of the stoop with his back
turned discreetly toward Kirkeby and Sylvia as they come down
the steps.

                    KIRKEBY
          Where do you live?

                    SYLVIA
          I told you -- with my mother.

                    KIRKEBY
          Where does she live?

                    SYLVIA
          A hundred and seventy-ninth street --
          the Bronx.

                    KIRKEBY
          All right -- I'll take you to the subway.

                    SYLVIA
          Like hell you will. You'll buy me a cab.

                    KIRKEBY
Why do all you dames have to live in
the Bronx?

                    SYLVIA
You mean you bring other girls up here?

                    KIRKEBY
Certainly not. I'm a happily married man.

They move down the street. Bud appears from the areaway,
glances after them, then mounts the steps, goes through the
front door.

12. INT. VESTIBULE -- EVENING

There are eight mailboxes. Bud opens his, takes out a magazine
in a paper wrapper and a few letters, proceeds up the staircase.

13. INT. SECOND FLOOR LANDING -- EVENING

Bud, glancing through his mail, comes up to the door of his
apartment. As he bends down to lift the doormat, the door of
the rear apartment opens and MRS. DREYFUSS, a jovial, well-fed,
middle-aged woman, puts out a receptacle full of old papers and
empty cans. Bud looks around from his bent position.

                    BUD
Oh. Hello there, Mrs. Dreyfuss.

                    MRS. DREYFUSS
Something the matter?

                    BUD
I seem to have dropped my key.
          (faking a little
           search)
Oh -- here it is.

He slides it out from under the mat, straightens up.

                    MRS. DREYFUSS
Such a racket I heard in your place --
maybe you had burglars.

                              BUD
          Oh, you don't have to worry about that
          -- nothing in here that anybody would
          want to steal . . .
                         (unlocking door
                          quickly)
          Good night, Mrs. Dreyfuss.

He ducks into the apartment.

14.   INT. APARTMENT -- EVENING

Bud snaps on the lights, drops the mail and the key on a small
table, looks around with distaste at the mess his visitors have
left behind. He sniffs the stale air, crosses to the window,
pulls up the shade, opens it wide. Now he takes off his hat and
raincoat, gathers up the remains of the cocktail party from the
coffee table. Loaded down with glasses, pitcher, empty vodka
bottle, ice bowl, and potato chips, he starts toward the kitchen.

The doorbell rings. Bud stops, undecided what to do with the
stuff in his hands, then crosses to the hall door, barely
manages to get it open. Mr. Kirkeby barges in past him.

                           KIRKEBY
          The little lady forgot her galoshes.

He scours the room for the missing galoshes.

                              BUD
          Mr. Kirkeby, I don't like to complain --
          but you were supposed to be out of
          here by eight.

                           KIRKEBY
          I know, Buddy-boy, I know. But those
          things don't always run on schedule --
          like a Greyhound bus.

                              BUD
          I don't mind in the summer -- but on
          a rainy night -- and I haven't had any
          dinner yet --

                           KIRKEBY
          Sure, sure. Look, kid -- I put in a
          good word for you with Sheldrake, in
          Personnel.

                        BUD
                    (perking up)
Mr. Sheldrake?

                        KIRKEBY
That's right. We were discussing our
department -- manpower-wise -- and
promotion-wise --
                    (finds the galoshes
                    behind a chair)
-- and I told him what a bright boy you
were. They're always on the lookout
for young executives.

                        BUD
Thank you, Mr. Kirkeby.

                        KIRKEBY
                    (starting toward the door)
You're on your way up, Buddy-boy.
And you're practically out of liquor.

                        BUD
I know. Mr. Eichelberger -- in the
Mortgage Loan Department -- last night
he had a little Halloween party here --

                        KIRKEBY
Well, lay in some vodka and some
vermouth -- and put my name on it.

                        BUD
Yes, Mr. Kirkeby. You still owe me
for the last two bottles --

                        KIRKEBY
I'll pay you on Friday.
                    (in the open doorway)
And whatever happened to those little
cheese crackers you used to have around?

He exits, shutting the door.

                        BUD
                    (making a mental
                    note)
Cheese crackers.

He carries his load into the kitchen.

The kitchen is minute and cluttered. On the drainboard are an
empty vermouth bottle, some ice-cube trays, a jar with one olive
in it, and a crumpled potato-chip bag.

Bud comes in, dumps his load on the drainboard, opens the
old-fashioned refrigerator. He takes out a frozen chicken
dinner, turns the oven on, lights it with a match, rips the
protective paper off the aluminum tray and shoves it in.

Now he starts to clean up the mess on the drainboard. He rinses
the cocktail glasses, is about to empty the martini pitcher into
the sink, thinks better of it. He pours the contents into a
glass, plops the lone olive out of the jar, scoops up the last
handful of potato chips, toasts an imaginary companion, and
drinks up. Then he pulls a wastebasket from under the sink.
It is brimful of liquor bottles, and Bud adds the empty vodka
and vermouth bottles and the olive jar. Picking up the heavy
receptacle, he carries it through the living room toward the
hall door.

15.   INT. SECOND FLOOR LANDING -- EVENING

The door of Bud's apartment opens, and Bud comes out with the
wastebasket full of empty bottles. Just then, DR. DAVID
DREYFUSS, whose wife we met earlier, comes trudging up the
stairs. He is a tall, heavy-set man of fifty, with a bushy
mustache, wearing a bulky overcoat and carrying an aged medical
bag.

                    DR. DREYFUSS
          Good evening, Baxter.

                    BUD
          Hi, Doc. Had a late call?

                    DR. DREYFUSS
          Yeah. Some clown at Schrafft's 57th
          Street ate a club sandwich, and forgot
          to take out the toothpick.

                    BUD
          Oh.
                    (sets down
                    wastebasket)
          'Bye, Doc.

                    DR. DREYFUSS
                 (indicating bottles)
Say, Baxter -- the way you're belting
that stuff, you must have a pair of
cast-iron kidneys.

                    BUD
Oh, that's not me. It's just that once
in a while, I have some people in for
a drink.

                    DR. DREYFUSS
As a matter of fact, you must be an
iron man all around. From what I
hear through the walls, you got
something going for you every night.

                    BUD
I'm sorry if it gets noisy --

                    DR. DREYFUSS
Sometimes, there's a twi-night double-
header.
                 (shaking his head)
A nebbish like you!

                    BUD
                 (uncomfortable)
Yeah. Well -- see you, Doc.
                 (starts to back
                  through door)

                    DR. DREYFUSS
You know, Baxter -- I'm doing some
research at the Columbia Medical Center
-- and I wonder if you could do us a favor?

                    BUD
Me?

                    DR. DREYFUSS
When you make out your will -- and
the way you're going, you should --
would you mind leaving your body to
the University?

                    BUD
My body? I'm afraid you guys would
be disappointed. Good night, Doc.

                            DR. DREYFUSS
        Slow down, kid.

He starts into the rear apartment as Bud closes the door.

16.   INT. APARTMENT -- EVENING

Bud, loosening his tie, goes into the kitchen, opens the oven,
turns off the gas. He takes a coke out of the refrigerator,
uncaps it, gets a knife and fork from a drawer, and using his
handkerchief as a potholder, pulls the hot aluminum tray out
of the oven. He carries everything out into the living room.

In the living room, Bud sets his dinner down on the coffee
table, settles himself on the couch. He rears up as something
stabs him, reaches under his buttocks, pulls out a hairpin. He
drops it into an ashtray, tackles his dinner. Without even
looking, he reaches over to the end table and presses the remote
TV station-selector. He takes a sip from the coke bottle, his
eyes on the TV screen across the room.

The picture on the TV set jells quickly. Against a background
of crisscrossing searchlights, a pompous announcer is making
his spiel.

                            ANNOUNCER
        -- from the world's greatest library
        of film classics, we proudly present --
                    (fanfare)
        Greta Garbo -- John Barrymore -- Joan
        Crawford -- Wallace Beery -- and
        Lionel Barrymore in --
                    (fanfare)
        GRAND HOTEL!

There is an extended fanfare. Bud leans forward, chewing
excitedly on a chicken leg.

                            ANNOUNCER
        But first, a word from our sponsor.
        If you smoke the modern way, don't
        be fooled by phony filter claims --

Bud, still eating, automatically reaches for the station-
selector, pushes the button.

A new channel pops on. It features a Western --
cockamamie Indians are attacking a stagecoach.

That's not for Bud. He switches to another station. In a
frontier saloon, Gower Street cowboys are dismantling the
furniture and each other.

Bud wearily changes channels. But he can't get away from
Westerns -- on this station, the U.S. Cavalry is riding to the
rescue. Will they get there in time?

Bud doesn't wait to find out. He switches channels again, and
is back where he started.

On the screen, once more, is the announcer standing in front of
the crisscrossing searchlights.

                    ANNOUNCER
     And now, Grand Hotel -- starring Greta
     Garbo, John Barrymore, Joan Crawford --
            (Bud is all eyes and
            ears again)
     -- Wallace Beery, and Lionel Barrymore.
     But first -- a word from our alternate
     sponsor.
            (unctuously)
     Friends, do you have wobbly dentures -- ?

That does it. Bud turns the set off in disgust.

The TV screen blacks out, except for a small pinpoint of light
in the center, which gradually fades away.

In the bathroom, Bud, in pajamas by now, is brushing his teeth.
From his shower rod hang three pairs of socks on stretchers. Bud
takes a vial from the medicine shelf, shakes out a sleeping pill,
washes it down with a glass of water. He turns the light off,
walks into the bedroom.

In the bedroom, the single bed is made, and the lamp on the night
table is on. Bud plugs in the electric blanket, turns the dial
on. Then he climbs into bed, props up the pillow behind him.
From the night table, he picks up the magazine that arrived in
the mail, slides it out of the wrapper, opens it. It's the new
issue of PLAYBOY. Bud leafs through it till he comes to the
piece de resistance of the magazine. He unfolds the overleaf,
glances at it casually, refolds it, then turns to the back of the
magazine and starts to read.

What he is so avidly interested in is the men's fashion section.
There is a layout titled WHAT THE YOUNG EXECUTIVE WILL WEAR,
with a sub-head reading The Bowler is Back. Illustrating
the article are several photographs of male models wearing
various styles of bowlers.

Bud is definitely in the market for a bowler, but somehow his
mind starts wandering. He turns back to the overleaf again,
unfolds it, studies it, then holds the magazine up vertically
to get a different perspective on the subject. By now the
sleeping pill is beginning to take effect, and he yawns. He
drops the magazine on the floor, kills the light, settles down
to sleep. The room is dark except for the glow from the dial
of the electric blanket.

Three seconds. Then the phone jangles shrilly in the living
room. Bud stumbles groggily out of bed, and putting on his
slippers, makes his way into the living room. He switches on
the light, picks up the phone.

>   BUD
>   Hello? -- Hello? -- yes, this is Baxter.

17.   INT. PHONE BOOTH IN A MANHATTAN BAR -- NIGHT

On the phone is a hearty man of about forty-five, nothing but
personality, most of it obnoxious. His name is DOBISCH.
Outside the booth is a blonde babe, slightly boozed, and beyond
there is a suggestion of the packed, smoky joint.

>   DOBISCH
>   Hiya, Buddy-boy. I'm in this bar on
>   Sixty-first Street -- and I got to thinking
>   about you -- and I figured I'd give you a
>   little buzz.

18.   BUD -- ON PHONE
>   BUD
>   Well, that's very nice of you -- but
>   who is this?

19.   INT. PHONE BOOTH

>   DOBISCH
>   Dobisch -- Joe Dobisch, in Administration.

20. BUD -- ON PHONE

                         BUD
                 (snapping to attention)
         Oh, yes, Mr. Dobisch. I didn't recognize
         your voice --

21. INT. PHONE BOOTH

                         DOBISCH
         That's okay, Buddy-boy. Now like I
         was saying, I'm in this joint on Sixty-
         first -- and I think I got lucky --
                 (glances toward blonde)
         -- she's a skater with the Ice Show --
                 (he chuckles)
         -- and I thought maybe I could bring
         her up for a quiet drink.

22. BUD -- ON PHONE

                         BUD
         I'm sorry, Mr. Dobisch. You know I
         like to help you guys out -- but it's
         sort of late -- so why don't we make it
         some other time?

23. INT. PHONE BOOTH

                         DOBISCH
         Buddy-boy -- she won't keep that long --
         not even on ice. Listen, kid, I can't
         pass this up -- she looks like Marilyn
         Monroe.

24. BUD -- ON PHONE

                         BUD
         I don't care if it is Marilyn Monroe --
         I'm already in bed -- and I've taken a
         sleeping pill -- so I'm afraid the answer
         is no.

25. INT. PHONE BOOTH

                          DOBISCH
                       (pulling rank)
              Look, Baxter -- we're making out the
              monthly efficiency rating -- and I'm
              putting you in the top ten. Now you don't
              want to louse yourself up, do you?

26. BUD -- ON PHONE

                            BUD
              Of course not. But -- how can I be
              efficient in the office if I don't get
              enough sleep at night?

27. INT. PHONE BOOTH

                          DOBISCH
              It's only eleven -- and I just want the
              place for forty-five minutes.

The blonde opens the door of the phone booth, leans in.

                          BLONDE
              I'm getting lonely. Who are you talking
              to, anyway?

                          DOBISCH
              My mother.

                          BLONDE
              That's sweet. That's real sweet.

Dobisch shuts the door in her face.

                          DOBISCH
                    (into phone again)
              Make it thirty minutes. What do you
              say, Bud?

28.   BUD
                       (a last stand)
              I'm all out of liquor -- and there's no
              clean glasses -- no cheese crackers --
              no nothing.

29. INT. PHONE BOOTH

                    DOBISCH
          Let me worry about that. Just leave
          the key under the mat and clear out.

30. INT. APARTMENT

                    BUD
              (into phone; resigned)
          Yes, Mr. Dobisch.

He hangs up, shuffles back into the bedroom.

                    BUD
              (muttering to himself)
          Anything you say, Mr. Dobisch -- no
          trouble at all, Mr. Dobisch -- be my
          guest --

He reappears from the bedroom, pulling his trousers on over his
pajama pants.

                    BUD
          -- We never close at Buddy-boy's
          -- looks like Marilyn Monroe --
              (he chuckles a la
              Dobisch)

Putting on his raincoat and hat, Bud opens the hall door, takes
the key from the table, shoves it under the doormat. His eyes
fall on the Dreyfuss apartment, and there is some concern on his
face. He picks up a pad and pencil from the table, prints
something in block letters. Tearing off the top sheet, he
impales it on the spindle of the phonograph, then walks out,
closing the door behind him. The note reads:

                NOT TOO LOUD
          THE NEIGHBORS ARE COMPLAINING

31. EXT. BROWNSTONE HOUSE -- NIGHT

Bud comes out the door, in slippered feet, pants and raincoat
over his pajamas. As he sleep-walks down the steps, a cab pulls
up in front of the house. Bud ducks discreetly into the areaway.

Mr. Dobisch, bareheaded, emerges cautiously from the cab.
Between the fingers of his hands he is carrying four long-stemmed
glasses, brimful of stingers. The blonde steps out, holding
his hat.

                       BLONDE
    This the place?

                       DOBISCH
    Yeah.
              (to cab driver)
    How much?

                       CABBIE
    Seventy cents.

Dobisch, his hands full of stingers, turns to the blonde,
indicates his pants pocket.

                       DOBISCH
    Get the money, will you?

The blonde plants the hat on top of his head, unbottons his
overcoat, reaches into his pants pocket. As she does so, she
jogs his elbow.

                       DOBISCH
    Watch those stingers!

The blonde has taken out Dobisch's money clip, with about a
hundred dollars in it.

                       DOBISCH
    Give him a buck.

The blonde peels a bill off, hands it to the cabbie, hangs on to
the rest of the roll just a second too long.

                       DOBISCH
    Now put it back, honey.
              (she does)
    Atta girl.

The cab drives off. Dobisch and the blonde start up the steps to
the house.

                       BLONDE
    You sure this is a good idea?

                    DOBISCH
Can't think of a better one.

                    BLONDE
               (holding door open
                for him)
I mean -- barging in on your mother --
in the middle of the night?

                    DOBISCH
               (edging past her
                with stingers)
Don't worry about the old lady. One
squawk from her, and she's out of a job.

In the areaway, Bud has overheard them, and it doesn't make him
any happier. He steps out on the sidewalk, shuffles down the
street.

32. INT. SECOND FLOOR LANDING -- NIGHT

The blonde and Dobisch, his hands full of stingers, come up to
Bud's door.

                    DOBISCH
Get the key, will you.

Automatically, she reaches into his pocket.

                    DOBISCH
Not there. Under the mat.

                    BLONDE
               (puzzled)
Under the mat?
               (picks up key)

                    DOBISCH
               (impatiently)
Open up, open up -- we haven't got
all night.

The blonde unlocks the door to the apartment, opens it.

                    BLONDE
               (suspiciously)
So this is your mother's apartment?

                              DOBISCH
          That's right. Maria Ouspenskaya.

                              BLONDE
                      (sticking her head in)
          Hiya, Ouspenskaya.

Dobisch nudges her inside with his knee, follows, kicks the
door shut behind him.

The landing is empty for a second. Then the door of the rear
apartment opens, and Dr. Dreyfuss, in a beaten bathrobe, sets out
a couple of empty milk bottles with a note in them. Suddenly,
from Bud's apartment, comes a shrill female giggle. Dr. Dreyfuss
reacts. Then the cha-cha music starts full blast.

                           DR. DREYFUSS
                      (calling to his wife,
                       off-scene)
          Mildred -- he's at it again.

Shaking his head, he closes the door.

33. EXT. CENTRAL PARK -- NIGHT

Bud, in raincoat and slippered feet, turns in off the street,
plods along a path in the deserted park. He stops at a damp
bench under a lamp post, sits. In the background, lights shine
from the towering buildings on Central Park South.

Bud huddles inside his raincoat, shivering. He is very sleepy
by now. His eyes close and his head droops. A gust of wind
sends wet leaves swirling across the bench. Bud doesn't stir.
He is all in.

                                             FADE OUT:

FADE IN:

34. INT. LOBBY INSURANCE BUILDING -- DAY

It's a quarter to nine of a gray November morning, and work-bound
employees are piling in through the doors. Among them is Bud,
bundled up in a raincoat, hat, heavy muffler and wool gloves, and
carrying a box of Kleenex. He coughs, pulls out a tissue, wipes
his dripping nose. He has a bad cold.

The lobby is an imposing, marbled affair, as befits a company
which last year wrote 9.3 billion dollars' worth of insurance.
There are sixteen elevators, eight of them marked LOCAL --
FLOORS 1-18, and opposite them eight marked EXPRESS -- FLOORS
18-37. The starter, a uniformed Valkyrie wielding a clicker, is
directing the flow of traffic into the various elevators.

Bud joins the crowd in front of one of the express elevators.
Also standing there is Mr. Kirkeby, reading the Herald-Tribune.

> BUD
> (hoarsely)
> Good morning, Mr. Kirkeby

> KIRKEBY
> (as if he just knew
> him vaguely)
> Oh, how are you, Baxter. They keeping
> you busy these days?

> BUD
> Yes, sir. They are indeed.
> (he sniffs)

The elevator doors open, revealing the operator. She is in her
middle twenties and her name is FRAN KUBELIK. Maybe it's the
way she's put together, maybe it's her face, or maybe it's just
the uniform -- in any case, there is something very appealing
about her. She is also an individualist -- she wears a carnation
in her lapel, which is strictly against regulations. As the
elevator loads, she greets the passengers cheerfully.

> FRAN
> (rattling it off)
> Morning, Mr. Kessel -- Morning, Miss
> Robinson -- Morning, Mr. Kirkeby --
> Morning, Mr. Williams -- Morning, Miss
> Livingston -- Morning, Mr. McKellway --
> Morning, Mr. Pirelli -- Morning, Mrs.
> Schubert --

Interspersed is an occasional "Morning, Miss Kubelik" from the
passengers.

> FRAN
> Morning, Mr. Baxter.

> BUD
> Morning, Miss Kubelik.

He takes his hat off -- he is the only one. The express is now
loaded.

                    STARTER
               (working the clicker)
          That's all. Take it away.

                    FRAN
               (shutting the door)
          Watch the door, please. Blasting off.

35. INT. ELEVATOR

Bud is standing right next to Fran as the packed express shoots
up.

                    BUD
               (studying her)
          What did you do to your hair?

                    FRAN
          It was making me nervous, so I chopped
          it off. Big mistake, huh?

                    BUD
          I sort of like it.

He sniffs, takes out a Kleenex, wipes his nose.

                    FRAN
          Say, you got a lulu.

                    BUD
          Yeah. I better not get too close.

                    FRAN
          Oh, I never catch colds.

                    BUD
          Really? I was looking at some figures
          from the Sickness and Accident Claims
          Division -- do you know that the average
          New Yorker between the ages of twenty
          and fifty has two and a half colds a year?

                    FRAN
          That makes me feel just terrible.

                    BUD
Why?

                    FRAN
Well, to make the figures come out even
-- since I have no colds a year -- some
poor slob must have five colds a year.

                    BUD
That's me.
               (dabs his nose)

                    FRAN
You should have stayed in bed this
morning.

                    BUD
I should have stayed in bed last night.

The elevator has slowed down, now stops. Fran opens the door.

                    FRAN
Nineteen. Watch your step.

About a third of the passengers get out, including Bud and Mr.
Kirkeby. As Kirkeby passes Fran, he slaps her behind with his
folded newspaper. Fran jumps slightly.

                    FRAN
               (all in the day's work)
And watch your hand, Mr. Kirkeby!

                    KIRKEBY
               (innocently)
I beg your pardon?

                    FRAN
One of these days I'm going to shut
those doors on you and --

She withdraws her hand into the sleeve of her uniform, and waves
the "amputated" arm at him.

                    FRAN
Twenty next.

The doors close.

36. INT. NINETEENTH FLOOR -- DAY

Kirkeby turns away from the elevator, and grinning smugly, falls
in beside Bud.

                    KIRKEBY
          That Kubelik -- boy! Would I like to
          get her on a slow elevator to China.

                    BUD
          Oh, yes. She's the best operator in
          the building.

                    KIRKEBY
          I'm a pretty good operator myself --
          but she just won't give me a tumble --
          date-wise.

                    BUD
          Maybe you're using the wrong approach.

                    KIRKEBY
          A lot of guys around here have tried it
          -- all kinds of approaches -- no dice.
          What is she trying to prove?

                    BUD
          Could be she's just a nice, respectable
          girl -- there are millions of them.

                    KIRKEBY
          Listen to him. Little Lord Fauntleroy!

Leaving Bud at the employees' coat-racks, Kirkeby heads toward
his office, one of the glass-enclosed cubicles. Bud hangs up
his hat and raincoat, stows away the gloves and muffler. Out of
his coat pocket he takes a plastic anti-histamine sprayer and a
box of cough drops, and still carrying the Kleenex, threads his
way to his desk. Most of the desks are already occupied, and the
others are filling rapidly.

Once seated at his desk, Bud arranges his medicaments neatly in
front of him. He takes a Kleenex out of the box, blows his
nose, then leaning back in his swivel chair sprays first one
nostril, then the other. Suddenly the piercing bell goes off --
the workday has begun. Being the ultra-conscientious type, Bud
instantly sits upright in his chair, removes the cover from his
computing machine, picks up a batch of perforated premium cards,
starts entering figures on his computer.

After a few seconds, he glances around to make sure that
everybody in the vicinity is busy. Then he looks up a number in
the company telephone directory, dials furtively.

> BUD
> (cupping hand over
> phone mouthpiece)
> Hello, Mr. Dobisch? This is Baxter,
> on the nineteenth floor.

37. INT. DOBISCH'S OFFICE -- DAY

It is a glass-enclosed cubicle on the twenty-first floor.
Through the glass we see another enormous layout of desks,
everybody working away. Dobisch is holding the phone in one
hand, running an electric shaver over his face with the other.

> DOBISCH
> Oh, Buddy-boy. I was just about to
> call you.
> (shuts off
> electric shaver)
> I'm sorry about that mess on the living
> room wall. You see, my little friend,
> she kept insisting Picasso was a bum --
> so she started to do that mural -- but I'm
> sure it will wash off -- just eyebrow pencil.

38. BUD -- ON PHONE

> BUD
> It's not Picasso I'm calling about. It's
> the key -- to my apartment -- you were
> supposed to leave it under the mat.

39. DOBISCH -- ON PHONE

> DOBISCH
> I did, didn't I? I distinctly remember
> bending over and putting it there --

40. BUD -- ON PHONE

> BUD
> Oh, I found a key there, all right --
> only it's the wrong key.

41.   DOBISCH -- ON PHONE

                      DOBISCH
      It is?
                (takes Bud's key
                out of his pocket)
      Well, how about that? No wonder I
      couldn't get into the executive washroom
      this morning.

42.   BUD -- ON PHONE

                      BUD
      And I couldn't get into my apartment --
      so at four a.m. I had to wake up the
      landlady and give her a whole song and
      dance about going out to mail a letter
      and the door slamming shut.

43.   DOBISCH -- ON PHONE

                      DOBISCH
      That's a shame. I'll send the key right
      down. And about your promotion --
                (leafs through report
                on desk)
      -- I'm sending that efficiency report
      right up to Mr. Sheldrake, in Personnel.
      I wouldn't be surprised if you heard
      from him before the day is over.

44.   BUD -- ON PHONE

                      BUD
      Thank you, Mr. Dobisch.

      He hangs up, feels his forehead. It is warm. Clipped to his
      handkerchief pocket are a black fountain pen and, next to it,
      a thermometer in a black case. Bud unclips the thermometer
      case, unscrews the cap, shakes the thermometer out, puts it under
      his tongue. He resumes work.

      A messenger comes up to his desk with an interoffice envelope.

                      MESSENGER
      From Mr. Dobisch.

                        BUD
               (thermometer in mouth)
     Wait.

He turns away from the messenger, unties the string of the
envelope, takes his key out, puts it in a coat pocket. From
a trouser pocket, he extracts Dobisch's key to the executive
washroom, slips it discreetly into the envelope, reties it,
hands it to the messenger.

                        BUD
               (thermometer in mouth)
     To Mr. Dobisch.

Puzzled by the whole procedure, the messenger leaves. Bud
now removes the thermometer from his mouth, reads it. It's
worse than he thought. He puts the thermometer back in the
case, clips it to his pocket, takes his desk calendar out of
a drawer, turns a leaf. Under the date WEDNESDAY, NOVEMBER 4
there is an entry in his handwriting -- MR. VANDERHOF. Bud
consults the telephone directory again, picks up the phone,
dials.

45. INT. VANDERHOF'S OFFICE -- DAY

     This is another glass-enclosed cubicle on another floor. MR.
     VANDERHOF, a Junior Chamber of Commerce type, is dictating to an
     elderly secretary who sits across the desk from him.

                        VANDERHOF
               Dear Mr. MacIntosh --
                    (phone rings and
                    he picks it up)
               Vanderhof, Public Relations. Oh, yes,
               Baxter. Just a minute.
                    (to secretary)
               All right, Miss Finch -- type up what
               we got so far.
                    (he waits till she
                    is out of the office;
                    then, into phone)
               Now, what is it, Baxter?

46. BUD -- ON PHONE

                              BUD
          Look, Mr. Vanderhof -- I've got you
          down here for tonight -- but I'm going
          to be using the place myself -- so I'll
          have to cancel.

47. VANDERHOF -- ON PHONE

                           VANDERHOF
          Cancel? But it's her birthday -- I
          already ordered the cake --

48. BUD -- ON PHONE

                              BUD
          I hate to disappoint you -- I mean,
          many happy returns -- but not tonight --

49. VANDERHOF -- ON PHONE

                           VANDERHOF
          That's not like you, Baxter. Just the
          other day, at the staff meeting, I was
          telling Mr. Sheldrake what a reliable
          man you were.

50. BUD -- ON PHONE

                              BUD
          Thank you, Mr. Vanderhof. But I'm
          sick -- I have this terrible cold -- and
          a fever -- and I got to go to bed right
          after work.

51. VANDERHOF -- ON PHONE

                           VANDERHOF
          Buddy-boy, that's the worst thing you
          can do. If you get a cold, you should
          go to a Turkish bath -- spend the night
          there -- sweat it out --

52. BUD -- ON PHONE

>   BUD
>   Oh, no. I'd get pneumonia -- and if I
>   got pneumonia, I'd be in bed for a
>   month -- and if I were in bed for a month --

53. VANDERHOF -- ON PHONE

>   VANDERHOF
>   Okay, you made your point. We'll just
>   have to do it <u>next</u> Wednesday -- that's
>   the only night of the week I can get away.

54. BUD -- ON PHONE

>   BUD
>   Wednesday -- Wednesday --
>   (leafing through
>   calendar)
>   I got somebody pencilled in -- let me
>   see what I can do -- I'll get back to you.

He hangs up, riffles through the directory, finds the number,
and with a furtive look around, dials again.

>   BUD
>   (into phone)
>   Mr. Eichelberger? Is this Mortgage
>   and Loan? I'd like to speak to Mr.
>   Eichelberger. Yes, it <u>is</u> urgent.

55. INT. EICHELBERGER'S OFFICE -- DAY

Also glass-enclosed, but slightly larger than the others. MR.
EICHELBERGER, a solid citizen of about fifty, is displaying some
mortgage graphs to three associates. A fourth one has answered
the phone.

>   ASSOCIATE
>   (holding out phone
>   to Eichelberger)
>   For you, Mel.

Eichelberger puts the charts down, takes the phone.

>   EICHELBERGER
>   Eichelberger here -- oh, yes, Baxter --

                              EICHELBERGER (cont.)
                         (a glance at his associates;
                          then continues, as though
                          it were a business call)
          What's your problem? -- Wednesday is
          out? -- oh -- that throws a little monkey
          wrench into my agenda -- Thursday?
          No, I'm all tied up on Thursday -- let's
          schedule that meeting for Friday.

56.   BUD -- ON PHONE

                              BUD
          Friday?
                         (checks calendar)
          Let me see what I can do. I'll get back
          to you.

      He hangs up, consults the directory, starts to dial a number.

57.   INT. KIRKEBY'S OFFICE -- DAY

      It's another of those glass-enclosed cubicles, on the nineteenth
      floor. Kirkeby is talking into a dictaphone.

                              KIRKEBY
          Premium-wise and billing-wise, we
          are eighteen percent ahead of last year,
          October-wise.

      The phone has been ringing. Kirkeby switches off the machine,
      picks up the phone.

                              KIRKEBY
          Hello? Yeah, Baxter. What's up?

58.   BUD -- ON PHONE

                              BUD
          Instead of Friday -- could you possibly
          switch to Thursday? You'd be doing me
          a great favor --

59.   KIRKEBY -- ON PHONE

                              KIRKEBY
          Well -- it's all right with <u>me</u>, Bud.
          Let me check. I'll get back to you.

He presses down the button on the cradle, dials Operator.

60. INT. SWITCHBOARD ROOM

     There is a double switchboard in the center, with nine girls on
     each side, all busy as beavers. In the foreground we recognize
     Sylvia, Kirkeby's date of last night.

                              SYLVIA
          Consolidated Life -- I'll connect you --
          Consolidated Life --

     The girl next to her turns and holds out a line.

                              SWITCHBOARD GIRL
          Sylvia -- it's for you.

     Sylvia plugs the call into her own switchboard.

                              SYLVIA
          Yes? Oh, hello -- sure I got home all
          right -- you owe me forty-five cents.

61. KIRKEBY -- ON PHONE

                              KIRKEBY
          Okay, okay. Look, Sylvia -- instead
          of Friday -- could we make it Thursday
          night?

62. SYLVIA -- AT SWITCHBOARD

                              SYLVIA
          Thursday? That's the Untouchables.
          -- with Bob Stack.

63. KIRKEBY -- ON PHONE

                              KIRKEBY
          Bob WHO? -- all right, so we'll watch
          it at the apartment. Big deal.

                        KIRKEBY (cont.)
                      (he hangs up, dials)
          Baxter? It's okay for Thursday.

64. INT. NINETEENTH FLOOR -- DAY

     Bud, at his desk, is on the phone.

                            BUD
          Thank you, Mr. Kirkeby.
                      (hangs up, consults
                      directory, dials)
          Mr. Eichelberger? It's okay for Friday.
                      (hangs up, consults
                      directory, dials)
          Mr. Vanderhof? It's okay for Wednesday.

     During this, the phone has rung at the next desk, and the
     occupant, MR. MOFFETT, has picked it up. As Bud hangs up --

                          MOFFETT
                      (into phone)
          All right -- I'll tell him.
                      (hangs up, turns to Bud)
          Hey, Baxter -- that was Personnel.
          Mr. Sheldrake's secretary.

                            BUD
          Sheldrake?

                          MOFFETT
          She's been trying to reach you for the
          last twenty minutes. They want you
          upstairs.

                            BUD
          Oh!

     He jumps up, stuffs the nose-spray into one pocket, a handful of
     Kleenex into the other.

                          MOFFETT
          What gives, Baxter? You getting
          promoted or getting fired?

                            BUD
                      (cockily)
          Care to make a small wager?

                         MOFFETT
        I've been here twice as long as you
        have --

                         BUD
        Shall we say -- a dollar?

                         MOFFETT
        It's a bet.

Bud snake-hips between the desks like a broken-field runner.

At the elevator, Bud presses the UP button, paces nervously. One
of the elevator doors opens, and as Bud starts inside, the doors
of the adjoining elevator open, and Fran Kubelik sticks her head
out.

                         FRAN
        Going up?

Hearing her voice, Bud throws a quick "Excuse me" to the other
operator, exits quickly and steps into Fran's elevator.

                         BUD
        Twenty-seven, please. And drive
        carefully. You're carrying precious
        cargo -- I mean, manpower-wise.

Fran shuts the doors.

65.   INT. ELEVATOR -- DAY

Fran presses a button, and the elevator starts up.

                         FRAN
        Twenty-seven.

                         BUD
        You may not realize it, Miss Kubelik,
        but I'm in the top ten -- efficiency-wise
        -- and this may be the day -- promotion-
        wise.

                         FRAN
        You're beginning to sound like Mr.
        Kirkeby already.

                            BUD
            Why not? Now that they're kicking me
            upstairs --

                            FRAN
            Couldn't happen to a nicer guy.
                    (Bud beams)
            You know, you're the only one around
            here who ever takes his hat off in the
            elevator.

                            BUD
            Really?

                            FRAN
            The characters you meet. Something
            happens to men in elevators. Must be
            the change of altitude -- the blood rushes
            to their head, or something -- boy, I
            could tell you stories --

                            BUD
            I'd love to hear them. Maybe we could
            have lunch in the cafeteria sometime --
            or some evening, after work --

        The elevator has stopped, and Fran opens the doors.

                            FRAN
            Twenty-seven.

    66. INT. TWENTY-SEVENTH FLOOR FOYER -- DAY

        It is pretty plush up here -- soft carpeting and tall mahogany
        doors leading to the executive offices. The elevator door is
        open, and Bud steps out.

                            FRAN
            I hope everything goes all right.

                            BUD
            I hope so.
                    (turning back)
            Wouldn't you know they'd call me on
            a day like this -- with my cold and
            everything --
                    (fumbling with his tie)
            How do I look?

                            FRAN
        Fine.
                        (stepping out of
                          elevator)
        Wait.

She takes the carnation out of her lapel, starts to put it in
Bud's buttonhole.

                            BUD
        Thank you. That's the first thing I ever
        noticed about you -- when you were still
        on the local elevator -- you always wore
        a flower --

The elevator buzzer is now sounding insistently. Fran steps
back inside.

                            FRAN
        Good luck. And wipe your nose.

She shuts the doors. Bud looks after her, then takes a Kleenex
out of his pocket, and wiping his nose, crosses to a glass door
marked J. D. SHELDRAKE, DIRECTOR OF PERSONNEL. He stashes the
used Kleenex away in another pocket, enters.

67.   INT. SHELDRAKE'S ANTEROOM -- DAY

       It is a sedate office with a secretary and a couple of typists.
       The secretary's name is MISS OLSEN. She is in her thirties,
       flaxen-haired, handsome, wears harlequin glasses, and has an
       incisive manner. Bud comes up to her desk.

                            BUD
        C. C. Baxter -- Ordinary Premium
        Accounting -- Mr. Sheldrake called me.

                          MISS OLSEN
        I called you -- that is, I tried to call
        you -- for twenty minutes.

                            BUD
        I'm sorry, I --

                          MISS OLSEN
        Go on in.

She indicates the door leading to the inner office. Bud squares
his shoulders and starts in.

68. INT. SHELDRAKE'S OFFICE -- DAY

Mr. Sheldrake is a $14,000 a year man, and rates a four-window
office.

It is not quite an executive suite, but it is several pegs above
the glass cubicles of the middle echelon. There is lots of
leather, and a large desk behind which sits MR. SHELDRAKE. He
is a substantial looking, authoritative man in his middle forties,
a pillar of his suburban community, a blood donor and a family
man. The latter is attested to by a framed photograph showing
two boys, aged 8 and 10, in military school uniforms.

As Baxter comes through the door, Sheldrake is leafing through
Dobisch's efficiency report. He looks up at Bud through a
pair of heavy-rimmed reading glasses.

                        SHELDRAKE
Baxter?

                        BUD
Yes, sir.

                        SHELDRAKE
                 (studying him)
I was sort of wondering what you looked
like. Sit down.

                        BUD
Yes, Mr. Sheldrake.

He seats himself on the very edge of the leather armchair
facing Sheldrake.

                        SHELDRAKE
Been hearing some very nice things
about you -- here's a report from Mr.
Dobisch -- loyal, cooperative,
resourceful --

                        BUD
Mr. Dobisch said that?

                         SHELDRAKE
And Mr. Kirkeby tells me that several
nights a week you work late at the office
-- without overtime.

                           BUD
                        (modestly)
Well, you know how it is -- things pile
up.

                         SHELDRAKE
Mr. Vanderhof, in Public Relations,
and Mr. Eichelberger, in Mortgage and
Loan -- they'd both like to have you
transferred to their departments.

                           BUD
That's very flattering.

Sheldrake puts the report down, takes off his glasses, leans
across the desk toward Bud.

                         SHELDRAKE
Tell me, Baxter -- just what is it that
makes you so popular?

                           BUD
I don't know.

                         SHELDRAKE
Think.

Bud does so. For a moment, he is a picture of intense
concentration. Then --

                           BUD
Would you mind repeating the question?

                         SHELDRAKE
Look, Baxter, I'm not stupid. I know
everything that goes on in this building
-- in every department -- on every
floor -- every day of the year.

                           BUD
                     (in a very small
                        voice)
You do?

                    SHELDRAKE
              (rises, starts pacing)
In 1957, we had an employee here, name
of Fowler. He was very popular, too.
Turned out he was running a bookie joint
right in the Actuarial Department --
tying up the switchboard, figuring the
odds on our I.B.M. machines -- so the
day before the Kentucky Derby, I called
in the Vice Squad and we raided the
thirteenth floor.

                    BUD
                 (worried)
The Vice Squad?

                    SHELDRAKE
That's right, Baxter.

                    BUD
What -- what's that got to do with me?
I'm not running any bookie joint.

                    SHELDRAKE
What kind of joint are you running?

                    BUD
Sir?

                    SHELDRAKE
There's a certain key floating around
the office -- from Kirkeby to Vanderhof
to Eichelberger to Dobisch -- it's the
key to a certain apartment -- and you
know who that apartment belongs to?

                    BUD
Who?

                    SHELDRAKE
Loyal, cooperative, resourceful C. C.
Baxter.

                    BUD
Oh.

                    SHELDRAKE
Are you going to deny it?

                         BUD
No, sir. I'm not going to deny it. But
if you'd just let me explain --

                      SHELDRAKE
You better.

                         BUD
                    (a deep breath)
Well, about six months ago -- I was
going to night school, taking this course
in Advanced Accounting -- and one of
the guys in our department -- he lives
in Jersey -- he was going to a banquet
at the Biltmore -- his wife was meeting
him in town, and he needed someplace to
change into a tuxedo -- so I gave him
the key -- and word must have gotten
around -- because the next thing I knew,
all sorts of guys were suddenly going to
banquets -- and when you give the key
to one guy, you can't say no to another --
and the whole thing got out of hand --
pardon me.

He whips out the nasal-spray, administers a couple of quick
squirts up each nostril.

                      SHELDRAKE
Baxter, an insurance company is founded
on public trust. Any employee who
conducts himself in a manner unbecoming --
                    (shifting into
                    a new gear)
How many charter members are there
in this little club of yours?

                         BUD
Just those four -- out of a total of 31,259
-- so actually, we can be very proud of
our personnel -- percentage-wise.

                      SHELDRAKE
That's not the point. Four rotten apples
in a barrel -- no matter how large the
barrel -- you realize that if this ever
leaked out --

                              BUD
          Oh, it won't. Believe me. And it's not
          going to happen again.   From now on,
          nobody is going to use my apartment --

In his vehemence he squeezes the spray bottle, which squirts
all over the desk.

                          SHELDRAKE
          Where is your apartment?

                              BUD
          West 67th Street. You have no idea what
          I've been going through -- with the
          neighbors and the landlady and the liquor
          and the key --

                          SHELDRAKE
          How do you work it with the key?

                              BUD
          Well, usually I slip it to them in the
          office and they leave it under the mat --
          but never again -- I can promise you that --

The phone buzzer sounds, and Sheldrake picks up the phone.

                          SHELDRAKE
          Yes, Miss Olsen.

69.   INT. SHELDRAKE'S ANTEROOM -- DAY

Miss Olsen is on the phone.

                          MISS OLSEN
          Mrs. Sheldrake returning your call --
          on two --

She presses a button down, starts to hang the phone up, glances
around to see if the typists are watching, then raises the
receiver to her ear and eavesdrops on the conversation.

70.   INT. SHELDRAKE'S OFFICE -- DAY

Sheldrake is talking into the phone.

                          SHELDRAKE
          Yes, dear -- I called you earlier --
          where were you? Oh, you took Tommy
          to the dentist --

During this, Bud has risen from his chair, started inching
toward the door.

                    SHELDRAKE
                (turning to him)
Where are you going, Baxter?

                    BUD
Well, I don't want to intrude -- and I
thought -- since it's all straightened
out anyway --

                    SHELDRAKE
I'm not through with you yet.

                    BUD
Yes, sir.

                    SHELDRAKE
                (into phone)
The reason I called is -- I won't be
home for dinner tonight. The branch
manager from Kansas City is in town
-- I'm taking him to the theatre --
Music Man, what else? No, don't
wait up for me -- 'bye, darling.
                (hangs up, turns
                 to Bud)
Tell me something, Baxter -- have
you seen Music Man?

                    BUD
Not yet. But I hear it's one swell
show.

                    SHELDRAKE
How would you like to go tonight?

                    BUD
You mean -- you and me? I thought
you were taking the branch manager
from Kansas City --

                    SHELDRAKE
I made other plans. You can have both
tickets.

                    BUD
Well, that's very kind of you -- only
I'm not feeling well -- you see, I have
this cold -- and I thought I'd go straight
home.

                         SHELDRAKE
          Baxter, you're not reading me. I told
          you I have plans.

                         BUD
          So do I -- I'm going to take four aspirins
          and get into bed -- so you better give
          the tickets to somebody else --

                         SHELDRAKE
          I'm not just giving those tickets, Baxter
          -- I want to swap them.

                         BUD
          Swap them? For what?

          Sheldrake picks up the Dobisch reports, puts on his glasses,
          turns a page.

                         SHELDRAKE
          It also says here -- that you are alert,
          astute, and quite imaginative --

                         BUD
          Oh?
                    (the dawn is breaking)
          Oh!

          He reaches into his coat pocket, fishes out a handful of Kleenex,
          and then finally the key to his apartment. He holds it up.

                         BUD
          This?

                         SHELDRAKE
          That's good thinking, Baxter.
          Next month there's going to be a shift
          in personnel around here -- and as far
          as I'm concerned, you're executive material.

                         BUD
          I am?

                         SHELDRAKE
          Now put down the key --
                    (pushing a pad
                    toward him)
          -- and put down the address.

Bud lays the key on the desk, unclips what he thinks is his
fountain pen, uncaps it, starts writing on the pad.

                    BUD
        It's on the second floor -- my name is
        not on the door -- it just says 2A --

Suddenly he realizes that he has been trying to write the address
with the thermometer.

                    BUD
        Oh -- terribly sorry. It's that cold --

                    SHELDRAKE
        Relax, Baxter.

                    BUD
        Thank you, sir.

He has replaced the thermometer with the fountain pen, and is
scribbling the address.

                    BUD
        You'll be careful with the record player,
        won't you? And about the liquor -- I
        ordered some this morning -- but I'm
        not sure when they'll deliver it --

He has finished writing the address, shoves the pad over to
Sheldrake.

                    SHELDRAKE
        Now remember, Baxter -- this is
        going to be our little secret.

                    BUD
        Yes, of course.

                    SHELDRAKE
        You know how people talk.

                    BUD
        Oh, you don't have to worry --

                    SHELDRAKE
        Not that I have anything to hide.

                                BUD
            Oh, no sir. Certainly not. Anyway,
            it's none of my business -- four apples,
            five apples -- what's the difference --
            percentage-wise?

                              SHELDRAKE
                            (holding out
                             the tickets)
            Here you are, Baxter. Have a nice time.

                                BUD
            You too, sir.

        Clutching the tickets, he backs out of the office.

                                                DISSOLVE TO:

        71. INT. LOBBY INSURANCE BUILDING -- EVENING

            It is about 6:30, and the building has pretty well emptied out
            by now. Bud, in raincoat and hat, is leaning against one of
            the marble pillars beyond the elevators. His raincoat is
            unbuttoned, and Fran's carnation is still in his lapel. He is
            looking off expectantly toward a door marked EMPLOYEES'
            LOUNGE -- WOMEN.

            Some of the female employees are emerging, dressed for the
            street. Among them are Sylvia and her colleague from the
            switchboard.

                              SYLVIA
            So I figure, a man in his position, he's
            going to take me to 21 and El Morocco --
            instead, he takes me to Hamburg Heaven
            and some schnook's apartment --

            They pass Bud without paying any attention to him. Bud has
            heard the crack, and looks after Sylvia, a little hurt. Then
            he glances back toward the door of the lounge, as it opens and
            Fran Kubelik comes out. She is wearing a wool coat over a
            street dress, no hat.

                              FRAN
                            (passing Bud)
            Good night.

                    BUD
              (casually)
     Good night.

She is about three paces beyond him when he suddenly realizes
who it is.

                    BUD
     Oh -- Miss Kubelik.
              (he rushes after her,
               taking off his hat)
     I've been waiting for you.

                    FRAN
     You have?

                    BUD
     I almost didn't recognize you -- this
     is the first time I've ever seen you in
     civilian clothes.

                    FRAN
     How'd you make out on the twenty-seventh
     floor?

                    BUD
     Great. Look -- have you seen The Music
     Man?

                    FRAN
     No.

                    BUD
     Would you like to?

                    FRAN
     Sure.

                    BUD
     I thought maybe we could have a bite to
     eat first -- and then --

                    FRAN
     You mean tonight?

                    BUD
     Yeah.

                          FRAN
          I'm sorry, but I can't tonight. I'm
          meeting somebody.

                          BUD
          Oh.
                    (a beat)
          You mean -- like a girl-friend?

                          FRAN
          No. Like a man.

She proceeds across the lobby toward the street entrance, Bud
following her.

                          BUD
          I wasn't trying to be personal -- it's
          just that the fellows in the office were
          wondering about you -- whether you
          ever --

                          FRAN

          Just tell 'em -- now and then.

                          BUD
          This date -- is is just a date -- or is
          it something serious?

                          FRAN
          It used to be serious -- at least I was --
          but he wasn't -- so the whole thing is
          more or less kaput.

                          BUD
          Well, in that case, couldn't you -- ?

                          FRAN
          I'm afraid not. I promised to have a
          drink with him -- he's been calling me
          all week --

                          BUD
          Oh, I understand.

He follows her out through the revolving doors.

72.   EXT. INSURANCE BUILDING -- EVENING

Fran and Bud come out.

> BUD
> (putting his hat on)
> Well, it was just an idea -- I hate to
> see a ticket go to waste --

> FRAN
> (stops)
> What time does the show go on?

> BUD
> Eight-thirty.

> FRAN
> (looks at her watch)
> Well -- I could meet you at the theatre
> -- if that's all right.

> BUD
> All right? That's wonderful! It's the
> Majestic -- 44th Street.

> FRAN
> Meet you in the lobby. Okay?

Bud nods happily, falls in beside her as she starts down the
street.

> BUD
> You know, I felt so lousy this morning
> -- a hundred and one fever -- then my
> promotion came up -- now you and I --
> eleventh row center -- and you said I
> should have stayed in bed.

> FRAN
> How _is_ your cold?

> BUD
> (high as a kite)
> What cold? And after the show, we
> could go out on the town --
> (does a little
> cha-cha step)
> I've been taking from Arthur Murray.

> FRAN
> So I see.

                              BUD
          They got a great little band at El Chico,
          in the Village -- it's practically around
          the corner from where you live.

                              FRAN
          Sounds good.
                        (a sudden thought)
          How do you know where I live?

                              BUD
          Oh, I even know who you live <u>with</u> --
          your sister and brother-in-law -- I
          know when you were born -- and where --
          I know all sorts of things about you.

                              FRAN
          How come?

                              BUD
          A couple of months ago I looked up your
          card in the group insurance file.

                              FRAN
          Oh.

                              BUD
          I know your height, your weight and your
          Social Security number -- you had mumps,
          you had measles, and you had your
          appendix out.

     They have now reached the corner, and Fran stops.

                              FRAN
          Well, don't tell the fellows in the office
          about the appendix. They may get the
          wrong idea how you found out.
                        (turning the corner)
          'Bye.

                              BUD
                        (calling after her)
          Eight-thirty!

     He watches her walk away, an idiot grin on his face. Despite
     what he told Fran, his nose is stuffed up, so he takes out the
     anti-histamine and sprays his nostrils. Then, carried away, he

squirts some of the stuff on the carnation in his buttonhole,
moves off in the opposite direction.

73. EXT. DOWNTOWN STREET -- EVENING

Fran comes hurrying along the street. She is late. Her
objective is a small Chinese restaurant, with a neon sign
reading THE RICKSHAW -- COCKTAILS -- CANTONESE FOOD. She starts
down a flight of steps leading to the entrance.

74. INT. CHINESE RESTAURANT -- EVENING

The bar is a long, narrow, dimly-lit room with booths along one
side. Beyond a bamboo curtain is the main dining room, which
does not concern us. The place is decorated in Early Beachcomber
style -- rattan, fish-nets, conch shells, etc.

The help is Chinese. At this early hour, there are only half a
dozen customers in the place -- all at the bar except for one
man, sitting in the last booth with his back toward camera.
At a piano, a Chinese member of Local 808 is improvising mood
music.

Fran comes through the door, and without looking around, heads
straight for the last booth. The bartender nods to her -- they
know her there. As she passes the piano player, he gives her a
big smile, segues into JEALOUS LOVER.

Fran comes up to the man sitting in the last booth.

                    FRAN
                (a wistful smile)
        Good evening, Mr. Sheldrake.

Sheldrake, for that's who it is, looks around nervously to make
sure no one has heard her.

                    SHELDRAKE
        Please, Fran -- not so loud.
                (he gets up)

                    FRAN
        Still afraid somebody may see us together?

                    SHELDRAKE
                (reaching for her coat)
        Let me take that.

                         FRAN
          No, Jeff. I can't stay very long.
                    (sits opposite him,
                    with her coat on)
          Can I have a frozen daiquiri?

                         SHELDRAKE
          It's on the way.
                    (sits down)
          I see you went ahead and cut your hair.

                         FRAN
          That's right.

                         SHELDRAKE
          You know I liked it better long.

                         FRAN
          Yes, I know. You want a lock to carry
          in your wallet?

     A waiter comes up with a tray: two daiquiris, fried shrimp,
     eggrolls, and a bowl of sauce.

                         WAITER
                    (showing all
                    his teeth)
          Evening, lady. Nice see you again.

                         FRAN
          Thank you.

     The waiter has set everything on the table, leaves.

                         SHELDRAKE
          How long has it been -- a month?

                         FRAN
          Six weeks. But who's counting?

                         SHELDRAKE
          I missed you, Fran.

                         FRAN
          Like old times. Same booth, same song --

                         SHELDRAKE
          It's been hell.

                              FRAN
                        (dipping shrimp)
-- same sauce -- sweet and sour.

                            SHELDRAKE
You don't know what it's like -- standing
next to you in that elevator, day after
day -- Good morning, Miss Kubelik --
Good night, Mr. Sheldrake -- I'm still
crazy about you, Fran.

                              FRAN
                        (avoiding his eyes)
Let's not start on that again, Jeff --
please. I'm just beginning to get over it.

                            SHELDRAKE
I don't believe you.

                              FRAN
Look, Jeff -- we had two wonderful
months this summer -- and that was it.
Happens all the time -- the wife and
kids go away to the country, and the
boss has a fling with the secretary --
or the manicurist -- or the elevator girl.
Comes September, the picnic is over --
goodbye. The kids go back to school,
the boss goes back to the wife, and
the girl --
                        (she is barely able
                         to control herself)
They don't make these shrimp like
they used to.

                            SHELDRAKE
I never said goodbye, Fran.

                              FRAN
                        (not listening)
For a while there, you try kidding
yourself that you're going with an
unmarried man. Then one day he keeps
looking at his watch, and asks you if
there's any lipstick showing, then rushes
off to catch the seven-fourteen to
White Plains. So you fix yourself
a cup of instant coffee -- and you sit

                    FRAN (Cont.)
        there by yourself -- and you think --
        and it all begins to look so ugly --

There are tears in her eyes. She breaks off, downs what's left
of the daiquiri.

                    SHELDRAKE
        How do you think I felt -- riding home
        on that seven-fourteen train?

                    FRAN
        Why do you keep calling me, Jeff? What
        do you want from me?

                    SHELDRAKE
                (taking her hand)
        I want you back, Fran.

                    FRAN
                (withdrawing her hand)
        Sorry, Mr. Sheldrake -- I'm full up.
        You'll have to take the next elevator.

                    SHELDRAKE
        You're not giving me a chance, Fran.
        I asked you to meet me because -- I
        have something to tell you.

                    FRAN
        Go ahead -- tell me.

                    SHELDRAKE
                (a glance around)
        Not here, Fran. Can't we go some
        place else?

                    FRAN
        No. I have a date at eight-thirty.

                    SHELDRAKE
        Important?

                    FRAN
        Not very -- but I'm going to be there
        anyway.

She takes out an inexpensive square compact with a fleur-de-lis pattern on it, opens it, starts to fix her face. The waiter comes up with a couple of menus.

> WAITER
> You ready order dinner now?

> FRAN
> No. No dinner.

> SHELDRAKE
> Bring us two more drinks.

CUT TO:

75. EXT. MAJESTIC THEATRE -- EVENING

It is 8:25, and there is the usual hectic to-do -- taxis pulling up, people milling around the sidewalk and crowding into the lobby. In the middle of this melee, buffeted by the throng, stands Bud, in raincoat and hat, looking anxiously for Fran.

CUT TO:

76. INT. CHINESE RESTAURANT -- EVENING

Fran and Sheldrake, in the booth, are working on the second round of drinks.

> SHELDRAKE
> Fran -- remember that last weekend
> we had?

> FRAN
> (wryly)
> Do I. That leaky little boat you rented
> -- and me in a black negligee and a life
> preserver --

> SHELDRAKE
> Remember what we talked about?

> FRAN
> We talked about a lot of things.

                         SHELDRAKE
          I mean -- about my getting a divorce.

                           FRAN
          We didn't talk about it -- you did.

                         SHELDRAKE
          You didn't really believe me, did you?

                           FRAN
                        (shrugging)
          They got it on a long playing record
          now -- Music to String Her Along By.
          My wife doesn't understand me -- We
          haven't gotten along for years -- You're
          the best thing that ever happened to me --

                         SHELDRAKE
          That's enough, Fran.

                           FRAN
                      (going right on)
          Just trust me, baby -- we'll work it
          out somehow --

                         SHELDRAKE
          You're not being funny.

                           FRAN
          I wasn't trying.

                         SHELDRAKE
          If you'll just listen to me for a minute --

                           FRAN
          Okay. I'm sorry.

                         SHELDRAKE
          I saw my lawyer this morning -- I
          wanted his advice -- about the best way
          to handle it --

                           FRAN
          Handle what?

                         SHELDRAKE
          What do you think?

                    FRAN
              (looking at him for a
              long moment -- then)
        Let's get something straight, Jeff --
        I never asked you to leave your wife.

                  SHELDRAKE
        Of course not. You had nothing to do
        with it.

                    FRAN
              (her eyes misting
              up again)
        Are you sure that's what you want?

                  SHELDRAKE
        I'm sure. If you'll just tell me that you
        still love me --

                    FRAN
                (softly)
        You know I do.

                  SHELDRAKE
        Fran --

He takes her hand, kisses it. The bar has been filling up,
and now two couples are seating themselves in a nearby booth.
One of the women is Miss Olsen.

                    FRAN
              (pulling her hand
              away gently)
        Jeff -- darling --

She indicates the other customers. Sheldrake glances over
his shoulder.

                  SHELDRAKE
        It is crowding up. Let's get out of here.

They rise. Sheldrake leaves some money on the table, leads
Fran toward the entrance. As they pass Miss Olsen's booth,
she turns around slowly, and putting on her glasses, looks
after them.

Sheldrake slips a bill to the piano player, who gives them a
big smile, slides into JEALOUS LOVER again. Retrieving his hat

and coat from the checkroom girl, Sheldrake steers Fran through
the door.

Miss Olsen watches them with a cold smile.

77.   EXT. CHINESE RESTAURANT -- EVENING

Fran and Sheldrake come up the steps.

                    SHELDRAKE
                (to a passing cab)
        Taxi!

It passes without stopping.

                    FRAN
        I have that date -- remember?

                    SHELDRAKE
        I love you -- remember?

Another taxi approaches. Sheldrake gives a shrill whistle,
and it pulls up. He opens the door.

                    FRAN
        Where are we going, Jeff? Not back
        to that leaky boat --

                    SHELDRAKE
        I promise.

He helps her into the cab, takes out of his coat pocket the
page from the pad on which Bud wrote the address of the
apartment.

                    SHELDRAKE
                (to cab driver)
        51 West Sixty-Seventh.

He gets in beside Fran, shuts the door. As the cab pulls
away, through the rear window the two can be seen kissing.

                                        CUT TO:

78.   EXT. MAJESTIC THEATRE -- EVENING

It's 9 o'clock, the lobby is deserted, and standing on the
sidewalk all by himself, is Bud. He takes a Kleenex out of
his pocket, blows his nose, stuffs the used Kleenex in
another pocket. He looks up and down the street, consults
his watch, decides to wait just a little longer.

FADE OUT:

FADE IN:

79. BAXTER'S DESK CALENDAR

The leaves are flipping over. Mr. Sheldrake seems to be
using The Apartment regularly -- for the name Sheldrake, in
Bud's handwriting, appears on the pages dated Monday, November
9, Thursday, November 12, Thursday, November 19, Monday,
November 23, and Monday, November 30. Mr. Sheldrake also
seems to be Baxter's only customer by now, since the other
leaves of the calendar are blank.

DISSOLVE TO:

80. INT. NINETEENTH FLOOR -- INSURANCE BUILDING -- DAY

It is a gloomy December morning, and hundreds of desk-bound
employees are bent over their paper work.

Bud Baxter, in raincoat and hat, is clearing out his desk. He
has piled everything on his blotter pad -- reference books,
papers, a fountain-pen set, pencils, paper clips and the
calendar. Watching him from the next desk is a dumbfounded
Moffett. Bud picks up the blotter pad with his stuff on it,
and as he moves past Moffett's desk, Moffett takes out a
dollar bill, drops it grudgingly on the loaded pad. Bud
flashes him a little grin, continues between the desks toward
the row of glass-enclosed offices housing the supervisory
personnel.

He comes up to an unoccupied cubicle. A sign painter is brushing
in some new lettering on the glass door -- it reads C. C. BAXTER,
Second Administrative Assistant. Bud studies the sign with a
good deal of satisfaction.

                    BUD
                (to painter)
          Would you mind -- ?

                        BUD (Cont.)
                     (the painter turns
                        around)
         C. C. Baxter -- that's me.

With an "Oh," the painter opens the door for him.

81.   INT. BAXTER'S OFFICE -- DAY

Bud enters his new office, deposits his stuff on the bare desk,
looks around possessively.   The small cubicle boasts one
window, carpeting on the floor, a filing cabinet, a couple of
synthetic-leather chairs, and a clothes-tree -- to Bud, it is
the Taj Mahal.   He crosses to the clothes-tree, removes his
hat and coat, hangs them up.   From OFF comes --

                     KIRKEBY'S VOICE
         Hi, Buddy-boy.

                     DOBISCH'S VOICE
         Congratulations, and all that jazz.

Bud turns. Kirkeby, Dobisch, Eichelberger and Vanderhof have
come into the office.

                        BUD
         Hi, fellas.

                     EICHELBERGER
         Well, you made it, kid -- just like we
         promised.

                     VANDERHOF
         Quite an office -- name on the door --
         rug on the floor -- the whole schmear.

                        BUD
         Yeah.

                     DOBISCH
         Teamwork -- that's what counts in an
         organization like this. All for one and
         one for all -- know what I mean?

                        BUD
         I have a vague idea.

Kirkeby signals to Vanderhof, who shuts the door. The four
charter members of the club start closing in on Bud.

                    KIRKEBY
Baxter, we're a little disappointed in
you -- gratitude-wise.

                    BUD
Oh, I'm very grateful.

                    EICHELBERGER
Then why are you locking us out, all
of a sudden?

                    BUD
It's been sort of rough these last few
weeks -- what with my cold and like that --

He has picked up the desk calendar, shoves it discreetly
into one of the drawers.

                    DOBISCH
We went to bat for you -- and now you
won't play ball with us.

                    BUD
Well, after all, it's my apartment --
it's private property -- it's not a public
playground.

                    VANDERHOF
All right, so you got yourself a girl --
that's okay with us -- but not every
night of the week.

                    KIRKEBY
How selfish can you get?
                    (to the others)
Last week I had to borrow my nephew's
car and take Sylvia to a drive-in in
Jersey. I'm too old for that sort of
thing -- I mean, in a Volkswagen.

                    BUD
I sympathize with your problem -- and
believe me, I'm very sorry --

                    DOBISCH
You'll be a lot sorrier before we're
through with you.

                              BUD
          You threatening me?

                              DOBISCH
          Listen, Baxter, we made you and we can
          break you.

He deliberately flips a cigar ash on Bud's desk.   At the same
time, the door opens, and Sheldrake comes striding in briskly.

                              BUD
          Good morning, Mr. Sheldrake.

The others swivel around.

                              SHELDRAKE
          Morning, gentlemen.
                    (to Bud)
          Everything satisfactory?   You like your
          office?

                              BUD
          Oh, yes, sir.   Very much.   And I want
          to thank you --

                              SHELDRAKE
          Don't thank me -- thank your friends
          here -- they're the ones who recommended
          you.

The four friends manage to work up some sickly smiles.

                              DOBISCH
          We just dropped in to wish him the best.
                    (quickly brushes cigar
                    ash off desk)

                              KIRKEBY
                    (as they move toward
                    the door)
          So long, Baxter.   We know you won't let
          us down.

                              BUD
          So long fellas.   Drop in any time.
          The door is always open -- to my
          office.

They leave.   Sheldrake and Bud are alone.

                    SHELDRAKE
I like the way you handled that. Well
how does it feel to be an executive?

                    BUD
Fine. And I want you to know I'll work
very hard to justify your confidence in me --

                    SHELDRAKE
Sure you will.
          (a beat)
Say, Baxter, about the apartment -- now
that you got a raise, don't you think we
can afford a <u>second</u> key?

                    BUD
Well -- I guess so.

                    SHELDRAKE
You know my secretary -- Miss Olsen --

                    BUD
Oh, yes. Very attractive. Is she --
the lucky one?

                    SHELDRAKE
No, you don't understand. She's a
busybody -- always poking her nose
into things -- and with that key passing
back and forth -- why take chances?

                    BUD
Yes, sir. You can't be too careful.

He glances toward the glass partitions to make sure that nobody
is watching.

                    BUD
I have something here -- I think it
belongs to you.

Out of his pocket he has slipped the compact with the fleur-de-
lis pattern we saw Fran use at the Rickshaw. He holds it out
to Sheldrake.

                    SHELDRAKE
To me?

                         BUD
I mean -- the young lady -- whoever
she may be -- it was on the couch when
I got home last night.

                       SHELDRAKE
Oh, yes. Thanks.

                         BUD
The mirror is broken.
               (opens compact,
                revealing crack
                in mirror)
It was broken when I found it.

                       SHELDRAKE
So it was.
               (takes the compact)
She threw it at me.

                         BUD
Sir?

                       SHELDRAKE
You know how it is -- sooner or later
they all give you a bad time.

                         BUD
               (man-of-the-world)
I know how it is.

                       SHELDRAKE
You see a girl a couple of times a week
-- just for laughs -- and right away she
thinks you're going to divorce your wife.
I ask you -- is that fair?

                         BUD
No, sir. That's very unfair -- especially
to your wife.

                       SHELDRAKE
Yeah.
               (shifting gears)
You know, Baxter, I envy you. Bachelor
-- all the dames you want -- no headaches,
no complications --

                    BUD
Yes, sir. That's the life, all right.

                  SHELDRAKE
Put me down for Thursday again.

                    BUD
Roger. And I'll get that other key.

Sheldrake exits. Bud takes the calendar out of the desk
drawer, makes an entry.

82. BAXTER'S DESK CALENDAR

Again the leaves are flipping over, and again we see Sheldrake's
name in Bud's handwriting -- booked for the following dates:
Monday, December 14, Thursday, December 17, Monday, December
21, Thursday, December 24.

                                        DISSOLVE TO:

83. INT. SWITCHBOARD ROOM -- DAY

Perched on top of the switchboard is a small decorated
Christmas tree, and the operators are dispensing holiday
greetings to all callers.

                  OPERATORS
Consolidated Life -- Merry Christmas --
I'll connect you -- Consolidated Life --
Merry Christmas -- I'm ringing --

In the foreground, Sylvia is engaged in a private conversation
of her own.

                   SYLVIA
              (into mouthpiece)
Yeah? -- YEAH? -- Where? -- You bet --

She tears off her headset, and turns to the other girls.

                   SYLVIA
Somebody watch my line -- there's a
swinging party up on the nineteenth
floor --

She scoots out the door. The other girls immediately abandon
their posts, and dash after her.

84.   INT. NINETEENTH FLOOR -- DAY

It's a swinging party, all right. Nobody is working. Several
desks have been cleared and pushed together, and on top of
this improvised stage four female employees and Mr. Dobisch,
with his pants-legs rolled up, are doing a Rockette kick
routine to the tune of JINGLE BELLS. Employees are ringed
around the performers, some drinking out of paper cups, others
singing and clapping in rhythm.

One of the cubicles has been transformed into a bar, and it is
jammed with people. Mr. Kirkeby and Mr. Vanderhof are pouring --
each has a couple of bottles of liquor in his hands, and is
emptying them into the open top of a water-cooler. But the
stuff is flowing out as fast as it flows in -- everybody is in
line with a paper cup waiting for a refill.

Bud comes shouldering his way out of the crowded cubicle,
holding aloft two paper cups filled with booze. Since his
promotion he has bought himself a new suit, dark flannel, and
with it he wears a white shirt with a pinned round collar, and
a foulard tie. He also has quite a glow on. Detouring past
necking couples, he heads in the direction of the elevators.

The doors of Fran's elevator are just opening, and the switchboard operators, led by Sylvia, come streaming out.

                    SYLVIA
               (to a colleague)
          -- so I said to him: Never again! --
          either get yourself a bigger car or a
          smaller girl --

As they head for the party, they pass Bud, who is approaching
the elevator with the two drinks. Fran is just closing the
elevator doors.

                    BUD
          Miss Kubelik.

The doors slide open again, and Fran looks out. Instead of
the customary carnation in the lapel of her uniform, she wears
a sprig of holly.

                    BUD
               (holding out one
                of the drinks)
          Merry Christmas.

                    FRAN
          Thank you.

                    FRAN (Cont.)
                  (takes drink)
I thought you were avoiding me.

                    BUD
What gave you that idea?

                    FRAN
In the last six weeks you've only been
in my elevator once -- and then you
didn't take your hat off.

                    BUD
Well, as a matter of fact, I was rather
hurt when you stood me up that night --

                    FRAN
I don't blame you. It was unforgivable.

                    BUD
I forgive you.

                    FRAN
You shouldn't.

                    BUD
You couldn't help yourself. I mean, when
you're having a drink with one man, you
can't just suddenly walk out on him
because you have another date with another
man. You did the only decent thing.

                    FRAN
Don't be too sure. Just because I wear
a uniform -- that doesn't make me a Girl
Scout.

                    BUD
Miss Kubelik, one doesn't get to be a
second administrative assistant around
here unless he's a pretty good judge of
character -- and as far as I'm concerned,
you're tops, I mean, decency-wise --
and otherwise-wise.
                  (toasting)
Cheers.

                    FRAN
Cheers.

They down their drinks. Bud takes the empty cup from her.

                    BUD
    One more?

                    FRAN
              (indicating elevator)
    I shouldn't drink when I'm driving.

                    BUD
    You're so right.

He reaches into the elevator, takes a cardboard sign off a
hook, hangs it on the elevator door. It reads USE OTHER
ELEVATOR.

                    BUD
    By the power vested in me, I herewith
    declare this elevator out of order.
              (leading her toward
              the party)
    Shall we join the natives?

                    FRAN
    Why not?
              (as they pass a
              kissing couple)
    They seem friendly enough.

                    BUD
    Don't you believe it. Later on there
    will be human sacrifices -- white-collar
    workers tossed into the computing
    machines, and punched full of those
    little square holes.

                    FRAN
    How many of those drinks did you have?

                    BUD
              (holding up
              four fingers)
    Three.

                    FRAN
    I thought so.

They have now reached the entrance to the bar, which is
overflowing with thirsty natives.

                              BUD
        You wait here.   I think I hear the sound
        of running water.

He leaves her outside the cubicle, and elbows his way through
the crowd toward the booze-filled water cooler.   Out of
another cubicle comes Miss Olsen, cup in hand.   She too has
had quite a few.   Seeing Fran, she walks up to her, with an
acid smile on her face.

                         MISS OLSEN
        Hi.   How's the branch manager from
        Kansas City?

                              FRAN
        I beg your pardon?

                         MISS OLSEN
        I'm Miss Olsen -- Mr. Sheldrake's
        secretary.

                              FRAN
        Yes, I know.

                         MISS OLSEN
        So you don't have to play innocent with
        me.   He used to tell his wife that I was
        the branch manager from Seattle --
        four years ago when we were having a
        little ring-a-ding-ding.

                              FRAN
        I don't know what you're talking about.

                         MISS OLSEN
        And before me there was Miss Rossi in
        Auditing -- and after me there was Miss
        Koch in Disability -- and just before you
        there was Miss What's-Her-Name, on
        the twenty-fifth floor --

                              FRAN
                    (wanting to get away)
        Will you excuse me?

                         MISS OLSEN
                    (holding her by
                    the arm)

MISS OLSEN (Cont.)
What for? You haven't done anything --
it's him -- what a salesman -- always
the last booth in the Chinese restaurant
-- and the same pitch about divorcing
his wife -- and in the end you wind up
with egg foo yong on your face.

Bud comes burrowing out of the crowded cubicle, balancing
the two filled paper cups, spots Fran.

BUD
Miss Kubelik.

Fran turns away from Miss Olsen.

FRAN
Well -- thank you.

MISS OLSEN
Always happy to do something for our
girls in uniform.

She moves off as Bud joins Fran, who is looking a little pale.

BUD
You all right? What's the matter?

FRAN
Nothing.
(takes the drink)
There are just too many people here.

BUD
Why don't we step into my office?
There's something I want your advice
about, anyway.
(leads her toward
his cubicle)
I have my own office now, naturally.
And you may be interested to know I'm
the second-youngest executive in the
company -- the only one younger is a
grandson of the chairman of the board.

85.   INT. BAXTER'S OFFICE -- DAY

Bud ushers Fran in, and is confronted by a strange couple
necking in the corner. He gestures them out, crosses to his
desk.

                    BUD
        Miss Kubelik, I would like your honest
        opinion. I've had this in my desk for
        a week -- cost me fifteen dollars -- but
        I just couldn't get up enough nerve to
        wear it --

From under the desk he has produced a hatbox, and out of the
hatbox a black bowler, which he now puts on his head.

                    BUD
        It's what they call the junior executive
        model. What do you think?

Fran looks at him blankly, absorbed in her own thoughts.

                    BUD
        Guess I made a boo-boo, huh?

                    FRAN
              (paying attention again)
        No -- I like it.

                    BUD
        Really? You mean you wouldn't be
        ashamed to be seen with somebody in
        a hat like this?

                    FRAN
        Of course not.

                    BUD
        Maybe if I wore it a little more to the
        side --
              (adjusting hat)
        -- is that better?

                    FRAN
        Much better.

                    BUD
        Well, as long as you wouldn't be ashamed
        to be seen with me -- how about the three
        of us going out this evening -- you and
        me and the bowler -- stroll down Fifth
        Avenue -- sort of break it in --

                              FRAN
          This is a bad day for me.

                              BUD
          I understand. Christmas -- family and
          all that --

                              FRAN
          I'd better get back to my elevator. I
          don't want to be fired.

                              BUD
          Oh, you don't have to worry about that.
          I have quite a bit of influence in Personnel.
          You know Mr. Sheldrake?

                              FRAN
                         (guardedly)
          Why?

                              BUD
          He and I are like this.
                         (crosses his fingers)
          Sent me a Christmas card. See?

He has picked up a Christmas card from his desk, shows it to
Fran. It is a photograph of the Sheldrake clan grouped around
an elaborate Christmas tree -- Mr. and Mrs. Sheldrake, the two
boys in military school uniforms, and a big French poodle.
Underneath it says:

                    SEASON'S GREETINGS
                    from the SHELDRAKES
                Emily, Jeff, Tommy, Jeff Jr.,
                       and Figaro.

                              FRAN
                         (studying the card
                          ruefully)
          Makes a cute picture.

                              BUD
          I thought maybe I could put in a word
          for you with Mr. Sheldrake -- get you
          a little promotion -- how would you
          like to be an elevator starter?

                              FRAN
          I'm afraid there are too many other
          girls around here with seniority over me.

                              BUD
          No problem. Why don't we discuss it
          sometime over the holidays -- I could
          call you and pick you up -- and we'll
          have the big unveiling --
                         (touching the brim
                         of his bowler)
          -- you sure this is the right way to
          wear it?

                              FRAN
          I think so.

                              BUD
          You don't think it's tilted a little too
          much --

Fran takes her compact out of her uniform pocket, opens it,
hands it to Bud.

                              FRAN
          Here.

                              BUD
                         (examining himself
                         in the mirror)
          After all, this is a conservative firm --
          I don't want people to think I'm an
          entertainer --

His voice trails off. There is something familiar about the
cracked mirror of the compact -- and the fleur-de-lis pattern
on the case confirms his suspicion. Fran notices the peculiar
expression on his face.

                              FRAN
          What is it?

                              BUD
                         (with difficulty)
          The mirror -- it's broken.

                              FRAN
          I know. I like it this way -- makes
          me look the way I feel.

The phone has started to ring. Bud doesn't hear it. He closes
the compact, hands it to Fran.

                              FRAN
          Your phone.

                              BUD
          Oh.
                         (picks up phone
                          from desk)
          Yes?
                         (throws a quick
                          look at Fran)
          Just a minute.
                         (covers mouthpiece;
                          to Fran)
          If you don't mind -- this is sort of
          personal.

                              FRAN
          All right.   Have a nice Christmas.

     She exits, closing the door.   Bud takes his hand off the
     mouthpiece.

                              BUD
                         (every word hurts)
          Yes, Mr. Sheldrake -- no, I didn't
          forget -- the tree is up and the Tom
          and Jerry mix is in the refrigerator --
          yes, sir -- same to you.

     He hangs up, stands there for a moment, the bowler still on
     his head, the noise from the party washing over him.   He slowly
     crosses to the clothes-tree, picks up his coat -- a new, black
     chesterfield.   With the coat over his arm, he starts out of
     the office.

86.   INT. NINETEENTH FLOOR -- DAY

     The party has picked up tempo.   On top of the desks, Sylvia is
     doing a mock strip tease -- without taking any clothes off.
     There is hollering, drinking and clapping all around her.

     Bud moves past the floor show, paying no attention.   Kirkeby
     spots him, detaches himself from the cheering section around
     Sylvia.

                              KIRKEBY
          Where you going, Buddy-boy?   The
          party's just starting.

                      KIRKEBY (Cont.)
                  (catching up with him)
        Listen, kid -- give me a break, will
        you -- how about tomorrow afternoon?
        I can't take her to that drive-in again --
        the car doesn't even have a heater --
        four o'clock -- okay?

Bud ignores him, continues walking through the ranks of empty
desks.

                                                DISSOLVE TO:

87. INT. CHEAP BAR -- COLUMBUS AVENUE IN THE SIXTIES -- EVENING

It is six o'clock, and the joint is crowded with customers having
one for the road before joining their families for Christmas
Eve. There are men with gaily wrapped packages, small trussed-up
Christmas trees, a plucked turkey in a plastic bag. Written
across the mirror behind the bar, in glittering white letters,
is HAPPY HOLIDAYS. Everybody is in high spirits, laughing it
up and toasting each other.

Everybody except Bud Baxter. He is standing at the bar in his
chesterfield and bowler, slightly isolated, brooding over an
almost empty martini glass. The bartender comes up, sets down
a fresh martini with an olive on a toothpick, takes his payment
from a pile of bills and coins lying in front of Bud. Bud
fishes out the olive, adds it to a half a dozen other impaled
olives neatly arranged in fan shape on the counter. He is
obviously trying to complete the circle.

A short, rotund man dressed as Santa Claus hurries in from the
street, and comes up to the bar beside Bud.

                      SANTA CLAUS
                  (to bartender)
        Hey, Charlie -- give me a shot of
        bourbon -- and step on it -- my sleigh
        is double parked.

He laughs uproariously at his own joke, nudges Bud with his
elbow. Bud stares at him coldly, turns back to his martini.
The laughter dies in Santa Claus' throat. He gets his shot of
bourbon, moves down the bar to find more convivial company.

Standing near the end of the curved bar is a girl in her middle
twenties wearing a ratty fur coat. Her name is MARGIE
MACDOUGALL, she is drinking a Rum Collins through a straw, and
she too is alone. From a distance, she is studying Bud with
interest. On the bar in front of her is a container of straws in
paper wrappers. She takes one of them out, tears off the end of
the paper, blows through the straw -- sending the wrapper
floating toward Bud. The paper wrapper passes right in front of
Bud's nose. He doesn't notice it.

Margie, undaunted, lets go with another missile.

This time the wrapper lands on the brim of Bud's bowler. No
reaction. Another wrapper comes floating in, hits Bud's cheek.
He never takes his eye off his martini.

Margie leaves her place, and carrying her handbag and her empty
glass, comes up alongside Bud. Without a word, she reaches up and
removes the wrapper from Bud's bowler.

                    MARGIE
          You buy me a drink, I'll buy you some
          music.
                    (sets the glass down)
          Rum Collins.

Not waiting for an answer, she heads for the juke box. Bud
looks after her noncommittally, then turns to the bartender.

                    BUD
          Rum Collins.
                    (indicating martini
                    glass)
          And another one of these little mothers.

At the juke box, Margie has dropped a coin in and made her
selection. The music starts -- ADESTE FIDELES. She rejoins
Bud at the bar just as the bartender is putting down their
drinks in front of them. Bud removes the new olive, adds it
to the pattern on the counter in front of him. They both
drink, staring straight ahead. For quite a while, there is
complete silence between them.

                    MARGIE
                    (out of nowhere)
          You like Castro?
                    (a blank look from Bud)
          I mean -- how do you feel about Castro?

                         BUD
What is Castro?

                         MARGIE
You know, that big-shot down in Cuba --
with the crazy beard.

                         BUD
What about him?

                         MARGIE
Because as far as I'm concerned, he's
a no-good fink. Two weeks ago I wrote
him a letter -- never even answered me.

                         BUD
That so.

                         MARGIE
All I wanted him to do was let Mickey
out for Christmas.

                         BUD
Who is Mickey?

                         MARGIE
My husband. He's in Havana -- in jail.

                         BUD
Oh. Mixed up in that revolution?

                         MARGIE
Mickey? He wouldn't do nothing like
that. He's a jockey. They caught him
doping a horse.

                         BUD
Well, you can't win 'em all.

They sit there silently for a moment, contemplating the
injustices of the world.

                         MARGIE
                    (to herself)
'Twas the night before Christmas
And all through the house
Not a creature was stirring --
Nothing --

MARGIE (Cont.)
No action --
Dullsville!
(drinks; to Bud)
You married?

BUD
No.

MARGIE
Family?

BUD
No.

MARGIE
A night like this, it sort of spooks you
to walk into an empty apartment.

BUD
I said I had no family -- I didn't say
I had an empty apartment.

They both drink.

CUT TO:

88.   INT. BUD'S APARTMENT -- EVENING

The living room is dark, except for a shaft of light from the
kitchen, and the glow of the colored bulbs on a small Christmas
tree in front of the phony fireplace.

Hunched up in one corner of the couch is Fran, still in her
coat and gloves, crying softly. Pacing up and down is
Sheldrake. His coat and hat are on a chair, as are several
Christmas packages. On the coffee table are an unopened
bottle of Scotch, a couple of untouched glasses, and a bowl
of melting ice.

SHELDRAKE
(stops and faces Fran)
Come on, Fran -- don't be like that.
You just going to sit there and keep
bawling?
(no answer)
You won't talk to me, you won't tell
me what's wrong --

                    SHELDRAKE (Cont.)
                  (a new approach)
Look, I know you think I'm stalling you.
But when you've been married to a
woman for twelve years, you don't just
sit down at the breakfast table and say
"Pass the sugar -- and I want a divorce."
It's not that easy.
                  (he resumes pacing:
                  Fran continues
                  crying)
Anyway, this is the wrong time. The
kids are home from school -- my in-laws
are visiting for the holidays -- I can't
bring it up now.
                  (stops in front of her)
This isn't like you, Fran -- you were
always such a good sport -- such fun
to be with --

                    FRAN
                  (through tears)
Yeah -- that's me. The Happy Idiot --
a million laughs.

                    SHELDRAKE
Well, that's more like it. At least you're
speaking to me.

                    FRAN
Funny thing happened to me at the office
party today -- I ran into your secretary
-- Miss Olsen. You know -- ring-a-ding-
ding? I laughed so much I like to died.

                    SHELDRAKE
Is that what's been bothering you --
Miss Olsen? That's ancient history.

                    FRAN
I was never very good at history. Let
me see -- there was Miss Olsen, and then
there was Miss Rossi -- no, she came
before -- it was Miss Koch who came
after Miss Olsen --

                    SHELDRAKE
Now, Fran --

                              FRAN
          And just think -- right now there's some
          lucky girl in the building who's going to
          come after me --

                              SHELDRAKE
          Okay, okay, Fran. I deserve that.
          But just ask yourself -- why does a man
          run around with a lot of girls? Because
          he's unhappy at home -- because he's
          lonely, that's why -- all that was before
          you, Fran -- I've stopped running.

Fran has taken a handkerchief out of her bag and is dabbing her
eyes.

                              FRAN
          How could I be so stupid? You'd think
          I would have learned by now -- when
          you're in love with a married man, you
          shouldn't wear mascara.

                              SHELDRAKE
          It's Christmas Eve, Fran -- let's not
          fight.

                              FRAN
          Merry Christmas.

She hands him a flat, wrapped package.

                              SHELDRAKE
          What is it?

He strips away the wrapping to reveal a long-playing record.   The
cover reads: RICKSHAW BOY - Jimmy Lee Kiang with Orchestra.

                              SHELDRAKE
          Oh. Our friend from the Chinese
          restaurant. Thanks, Fran. We
          better keep it here.

                              FRAN
          Yeah, we better.

                              SHELDRAKE
          I have a present for you. I didn't
          quite know what to get you -- anyway
          it's a little awkward for me, shopping --

                    SHELDRAKE (Cont.)
                (he has taken out a
                money clip, detaches
                a bill)
        -- so here's a hundred dollars -- go out
        and buy yourself something.

He holds the money out, but she doesn't move.   Sheldrake slips
the bill into her open bag.

                    SHELDRAKE
        They have some nice alligator bags at
        Bergdorf's --

Fran gets up slowly and starts peeling off her gloves.
Sheldrake looks at her, then glances nervously at his wrist
watch.

                    SHELDRAKE
        Fran, it's a quarter to seven -- and I
        mustn't miss the train -- if we hadn't
        wasted all that time -- I have to get home
        and trim the tree --

Fran has started to remove her coat.

                    FRAN
        Okay.
                (shrugs the coat
                back on)
        I just thought as long as it was paid for --

                    SHELDRAKE
                (an angry step
                toward her)
        Don't ever talk like that, Fran!   Don't
        make yourself out to be cheap.

                    FRAN
        A hundred dollars?   I wouldn't call that
        cheap.   And you must be paying somebody
        something for the use of the apartment --

                    SHELDRAKE
                (grabbing her arms)
        Stop that, Fran.

                         FRAN
                       (quietly)
           You'll miss your train, Jeff.

Sheldrake hurriedly puts on his hat and coat, gathers up his
packages.

                       SHELDRAKE
           Coming?

                         FRAN
           You run along -- I want to fix my face.

                       SHELDRAKE
                 (heading for the door)
           Don't forget to kill the lights. See you
           Monday.

                         FRAN
           Sure. Monday and Thursday -- and
           Monday again -- and Thursday again --

                       SHELDRAKE
                 (that stops him in
                  the half-open door)
           It won't always be like this.
                 (coming back)
           I love you, Fran.

Holding the packages to one side, he tries to kiss her on the
mouth.

                         FRAN
                 (turning her head)
           Careful -- lipstick.

He kisses her on the cheek, hurries out of the apartment, closing
the door. Fran stands there for a while, blinking back tears,
then takes the long-playing record out of its envelope, crosses
to the phonograph. She puts the record on, starts the machine --
the music is JEALOUS LOVER. As it plays, Fran wanders aimlessly
around the darkened room, her body wracked by sobs. Finally
she regains control of herself, and picking up her handbag,
starts through the bedroom toward the bathroom.

In the bathroom, Fran switches on the light, puts her bag on the
sink, turns on the faucet. Scooping up some water, she washes
the smeared mascara away, then turns the faucet off, picks up a

towel. As she is drying her face, she notices in the pull-away
shaving mirror the magnified reflection of a vial of pills on
the medicine shelf. Fran reaches out for the vial, turns it
slowly around in her hand. The label reads: SECONAL - ONE AT
BEDTIME AS NEEDED FOR SLEEP.

Fran studies the label for a second, then returns the vial to
the shelf. She opens her handbag, takes out a lipstick. As
she does so, she sees the hundred dollar bill Sheldrake left in
the bag. Her eyes wander back to the vial on the medicine
shelf. Then very deliberately she picks up Bud's mouthwash
glass, removes the two toothbrushes from it, turns on the
faucet, starts filling the glass with water.

                                                  DISSOLVE TO:

89. INT. CHEAP BAR -- COLUMBUS AVENUE -- NIGHT

The joint is deserted now except for the Santa Claus, who is
leaning against the bar, quite loaded, and Bud and Margie
MacDougall, who are dancing to a slow blues coming from the
juke box. Bud is still in his overcoat and bowler, and Margie
is wearing her fur coat. The bartender is sweeping up the
place.

                          BARTENDER
                       (to Santa Claus)
               Drink up, Pop. It's closing time.

                          SANTA CLAUS
               But it's early, Charlie.

                          BARTENDER
               Don't you know what night this is?

                          SANTA CLAUS
               I know, Charlie. I know. I work for
               the outfit.

He polishes off his drink, walks out unsteadily. The bartender
approaches the dancers.

                          BARTENDER
               Hey, knock it off, will you? Go home.

Bud and Margie ignore him, continue dancing -- or rather
swaying limply cheek-to-cheek. The bartender crosses to the

juke box, pulls the plug out.   The music stops, but not Bud
and Margie -- they continue dancing.

                    BARTENDER
         O-U-T -- out!

He goes to the front of the bar, starts to extinguish the
lights.   Margie picks up her handbag from the bar, and Bud
downs the remains of his drink.

                    MARGIE
         Where do we go -- my place or yours?

                    BUD
              (peering at his watch)
         Might as well go to mine -- everybody
         else does.

He leads her through the dark bar toward the entrance.   The
bartender holds the door open for them as they go out.

                              DISSOLVE TO:

90.   EXT. BROWNSTONE HOUSE -- NIGHT

Bud and Margie come walking down the street.   As they reach
the house, Bud starts up the steps, but Margie continues along
the sidewalk.

                    MARGIE
         Poor Mickey -- when I think of him all
         by himself in that jail in Havana --
              (opening her handbag)
         -- want to see his picture?

                    BUD
              (from steps)
         Not particularly.

Margie, realizing her mistake, hurries back to join him.

                    MARGIE
         He's so cute -- five-foot-two -- ninety-
         nine pounds . . . like a little chihuahua.

They pass through the front door into the vestibule.

91. INT. STAIRCASE -- BROWNSTONE HOUSE -- NIGHT

Bud and Margie are mounting the stairs toward the apartment.

                    MARGIE
          Can I ask you a personal question?

                    BUD
          No.

                    MARGIE
          You got a girl-friend?

                    BUD
          She may be a girl -- but she's no
          friend of mine.

                    MARGIE
          Still stuck on her, huh.

                    BUD
          Stuck on her! Obviously, you don't
          know me very well.

                    MARGIE
          I don't know you at all.

                    BUD
          Permit me -- C. C. Baxter -- junior
          executive, Arthur Murray graduate, lover.

                    MARGIE
          I'm Mrs. MacDougall -- Margie to you.

Bud has taken the key out of his pocket, opened the door to his
apartment.

                    BUD
          This way, Mrs. MacDougall.

He ushers her in.

92. INT. APARTMENT -- NIGHT

It is exactly the way we left it. There is no sign of Fran,
except for the gloves she dropped on the coffee table earlier.
Bud switches on the light, shuts the door.

                            MARGIE
                       (looking around)
          Say, this is Snugsville.

                            BUD
                       (helping her out
                        of her coat)
          Mrs. MacDougall, I think it is only fair
          to warn you that you are now alone with
          a notorious sexpot.

                            MARGIE
                       (a gleam)
          No kidding.

                            BUD
          Ask anybody around here. As a matter
          of fact, when it's time for me to go --
          and I may go just like that --
                       (snaps his fingers)
          -- I have promised my body to the
          Columbia Medical Center.

                            MARGIE
                       (shuddering deliciously)
          Gee. Sort of gives you goose bumps
          just to think about it.

                            BUD
          Well, they haven't got me yet, baby.
          Dig up some ice from the kitchen and
          let's not waste any time -- preliminary-
          wise.

                            MARGIE
          I'm with you, lover.

She takes the bowl of melted ice Bud has handed her, disappears
into the kitchen. As Bud starts to remove his coat, he becomes
aware of a scratching noise from the phonograph. He crosses to
it, sees that the needle is stuck in the last groove of a
long-playing record.

Bud lifts the record off, examines it curiously, then puts it
aside and substitutes the cha-cha record. As the music starts,
he dances over to the coat-rack beside the door, hangs up his
chesterfield and bowler. He turns back into the room, still
dancing, suddenly spots Fran's gloves on the coffee table.

He picks up the gloves, looks around for some convenient
place to get rid of them. Moving over to the bedroom door,
he opens it, tosses the gloves toward the bed inside. He
shuts the door, starts to turn away, freezes in a delayed
reaction to something he saw inside. He quickly opens the
door again, looks.

Sprawled across the bed, on top of the bedspread, is Fran.
The light from the bathroom falls across her. She is fully
dressed, still in her coat, and apparently asleep.

Bud steps into the bedroom, closing the door behind him,
walks over to Fran.

                         BUD
          All right, Miss Kubelik -- get up. It's
          past checking-out time, and the hotel
          management would appreciate it if you
          would get the hell out of here.
                    (Fran doesn't stir)
          Look, Miss Kubelik, I used to like you
          -- I used to like you a lot -- but it's
          all over between us -- so beat it --
          O-U-T -- out!
                    (no reaction; he puts
                     a hand on her shoulder,
                     shakes her)
          Come on -- wake up!

She doesn't respond. But something falls out of her hand,
rolls across the bed. Bud picks it up, looks at it -- it is
his sleeping-pill vial, now uncapped and empty.

                         BUD
                    (a hoarse whisper)
          Oh, my God.

For a second he is paralyzed. Then he drops the vial, grabs
Fran, lifts her into a sitting position on the bed, shakes
her violently.

                         BUD
          Miss Kubelik! Miss Kubelik!

Fran's head droops to one side, like a rag doll's. Bud lets
go of her, rushes out.

In the living room, the phonograph is still cha-cha-ing away,
Bud dashes to the phone, picks it up. Then it occurs to him
that he doesn't know whom to call and he hangs up. Out of the
kitchen comes Margie, with a bowlful of ice cubes.

                    MARGIE
          I broke a nail trying to get the ice-tray
          out. You ought to buy yourself a new
          refrigerator.

Bud, not listening, runs past her to the hall door and out.

                    MARGIE
               (calling after him)
          I didn't mean right now.

93. INT. SECOND FLOOR LANDING -- NIGHT

Bud arrives at the door of the Dreyfuss apartment, starts
ringing the doorbell and pounding with his fist.

                    BUD
          Dr. Dreyfuss! Hey, Doc!

The door opens, and Dr. Dreyfuss stands there sleepily,
pulling on his beaten bathrobe.

                    BUD
               (words tumbling over
                each other)
          There's a girl in my place -- she took
          some sleeping pills -- you better come
          quick -- I can't wake her up.

                    DR. DREYFUSS
          Let me get my bag.

He disappears from the doorway.

                    BUD
          Hurry up, Doc.

Bud turns and runs back into his apartment.

94. INT. APARTMENT -- NIGHT

Margie has settled herself comfortably on the couch, and is
fixing the drinks. The cha-cha music is still going. Bud
comes flying in, heads for the bedroom.

>   MARGIE
>   Hey -- over here, lover.

Bud stops in his tracks, suddenly aware of her.

>   MARGIE
>   What's all this running around? You're
>   going to wear yourself out.

Bud strides over to her purposefully, yanks her up to her
feet.

>   MARGIE
>   Not so rough, honey.

>   BUD
>   (taking the glass out
>   of her hand)
>   Good night.

>   MARGIE
>   Good night?

>   BUD
>   (thrusting the fur coat
>   at her)
>   The party's over.

>   MARGIE
>   What's the matter? Did I do something
>   wrong?

>   BUD
>   (easing her toward door)
>   It's an emergency -- see you some other
>   time.

Dr. Dreyfuss comes hurrying in, carrying his medical bag. He
stops, bewildered by the sound of music and the sight of a
wide-awake girl in the apartment.

>   BUD
>   Not this one --
>   (pointing to the bedroom)
>   -- in there, Doc.

Dr. Dreyfuss proceeds into the bedroom.

> MARGIE
> Say, what's going on here, anyway?

> BUD
> Nothing.
>> (propelling her
>> toward the door)
> Just clear out, will you?

> MARGIE
>> (pointing back)
> My shoes.

Bud reaches under the coffee table, where she left her shoes, retrieves them.

> MARGIE
>> (bitterly)
> Some lover you are. Some sexpot!

Bud shoves the shoes at her, takes a bill out of his wallet, hands it to her.

> BUD
> Here -- find yourself a phone booth and call your husband in Havana.

> MARGIE
> You bet I will. And when I tell him how you treated me, he'll push your face in.
>> (he shoves her through
>> the open door)
> You fink!

Bud slams the door shut, starts toward the bedroom. Halfway there, he becomes aware that the cha-cha record is still on. He detours to the phonograph, switches it off, continues into the bedroom.

In the bedroom, the overhead light is on, and Dr. Dreyfuss is working on the unconscious Fran. He has removed her coat, and is shining a flashlight into her eyes, examining her pupils. Bud approaches the bed worriedly.

> BUD
> She going to be all right, Doc?

                    DR. DREYFUSS
        How many pills were in that bottle?

                    BUD
        It was half-full -- about a dozen or so.
        You going to have to take her to the
        hospital?

Dr. Dreyfuss ignores him. Out of his medical bag, he takes
a stomach tube with a rubber funnel at the end. Then he
starts to lift Fran off the bed.

                    DR. DREYFUSS
        Help me, will you?

Between them, they get Fran into an upright position.

                    DR. DREYFUSS
        Into the bathroom.

They half-carry, half-drag Fran's limp form toward the bathroom.

                    BUD
        What are you going to do, Doc?

                    DR. DREYFUSS
        Get that stuff out of her stomach -- if
        it isn't too late. You better put some
        coffee on -- and pray.

Bud starts away as Dr. Dreyfuss takes Fran into the bathroom.

Bud loses no time getting into the kitchen. He fills an
aluminum kettle with water, strikes a match, lights the gas
burner, puts the kettle on. Then he takes a jar of instant
coffee and a chipped coffee mug out of the cupboard, shakes
an excessive portion of coffee into the mug, sticks a spoon
in it. He watches the kettle for a moment, mops his brow with
a handkerchief, then starts back toward the bedroom.

Bud crosses the bedroom to the half-open door of the bathroom,
looks in anxiously. From inside come the sounds of a coughing
spasm and running water. Bud turns away, undoes his tie and
collar, paces the bedroom floor. Something on the night
table attracts his attention -- resting against the base of
the lamp is a sealed envelope. Bud picks it up -- on it, in
Fran's handwriting, is one word, JEFF. He turns the letter
over in his hand, trying to decide what to do with it.

Dr. Dreyfuss emerges from the bathroom, carrying a pale, still
unconscious Fran. Bud quickly conceals the suicide note behind
his back.

>   DR. DREYFUSS
> Bring my bag.

He lugs Fran into the living room. Bud stashes the letter in
his back pocket, picks up the medical bag, follows them.

In the living room, Dr. Dreyfuss lowers Fran into a chair.
Her chin falls to her chest. Dreyfuss takes the bag from Bud,
fishes out a hypodermic syringe, draws 2 cc's from a bottle
of picrotoxin.

>   DR. DREYFUSS
> Roll up her right sleeve.

Bud does so. Dr. Dreyfuss hands the hypodermic to Bud,
searches for a spot for the injection.

>   DR. DREYFUSS
> Nice veins.

He swabs the spot with alcohol, takes the hypodermic back from
Bud.

>   DR. DREYFUSS
> Want to tell me what happened?

>   BUD
> I don't know -- I mean -- I wasn't here
> -- you see -- we had some words earlier
> -- nothing serious, really -- what you
> might call a lovers' quarrel --

>   DR. DREYFUSS
>   (making off-scene
>   injection)
> So you went right out and picked yourself
> up another dame.

>   BUD
> Something like that.

>   DR. DREYFUSS
> You know, Baxter, you're a real cutie-
> pie -- yes, you are.

Bud just stands there, taking it. Fran stirs slightly, and
from her parched lips comes a low moan. Dr. Dreyfuss grabs
her by the hair, lifts her head up.

> DR. DREYFUSS
> If you'd come home half an hour later,
> you would have had quite a Christmas
> present.

With his free hand, Dr. Dreyfuss slaps Fran viciously across
the face. Bud winces. Dreyfuss, still holding Fran by the
hair, takes a box of ammonia ampules out of his bag. He
crushes one of the ampules in his hand, passes it under her
nose. Fran tries to turn her head away. Dreyfuss slaps her
again, hard, crushes another ampule, repeats the process.

Bud is watching tensely. From the kitchen comes the whistle
of the boiling kettle, but Bud pays no attention.

> DR. DREYFUSS
> Get the coffee.

Bud hurries into the kitchen. He turns off the gas, pours
the boiling water into the mug with the instant coffee, stirs
it. From off, come the sounds of more slapping and some
moaning. Bud carries the coffee out.

In the living room, Dr. Dreyfuss is working another ammonia
ampule under Fran's nose. Her eyes start fluttering. Dreyfuss
takes the coffee mug from Bud, forces it between Fran's lips,
pours coffee into her mouth. Fran resists instinctively, half
the coffee dribbling over her chin and dress, but Dr. Dreyfuss
keeps at it.

> DR. DREYFUSS
> Let's get some air in here. Open the
> windows.

Bud complies promptly -- pulls up the shades, opens the
windows wide.

> DR. DREYFUSS
> (putting the empty
> mug down)
> What's her name?

> BUD
> Miss Kubelik -- Fran.

                    DR. DREYFUSS
                 (to Fran, slowly)
     Fran, I'm a doctor. I'm here because
     you took too many sleeping pills. Do
     you understand what I'm saying?
                 (Fran mutters
                  something)
     Fran, I'm Dr. Dreyfuss -- I'm here to
     help you. You took all those sleeping
     pills -- remember?

                    FRAN
                 (mumbling groggily)
     Sleeping pills.

                    DR. DREYFUSS
     That's right, Fran. And I'm a doctor.

                    FRAN
     Doctor.

                    DR. DREYFUSS
     Dr. Dreyfuss.

                    FRAN
     Dreyfuss.

                    DR. DREYFUSS
                 (to Bud)
     Get more coffee.

Bud picks up the mug, leaves.

                    DR. DREYFUSS
                 (to Fran)
     Tell me again -- what's my name?

                    FRAN
     Dr. Dreyfuss

                    DR. DREYFUSS
     And what happened to you?

                    FRAN
     I took sleeping pills.

                    DR. DREYFUSS
     Do you know where you are, Fran?

                    FRAN
              (looking around
               blankly)
    No.

                         DR. DREYFUSS
        Yes, you do. Now concentrate.

                         FRAN
    I don't know.

    Bud is coming back with the coffee.

                         DR. DREYFUSS
                    (pointing to Bud)
        Do you know who this is?
                    (Fran tries to focus)
        Look at him.

                         FRAN
    Mr. Baxter -- nineteenth floor.

                         BUD
    Hello, Miss Kubelik.

                         DR. DREYFUSS
                    (to Bud)
        Mister -- Miss -- such politeness!

                         BUD
                    (to Dr. Dreyfuss,
                     discreetly)
        Well -- we work in the same building
        -- and we try to keep it quiet --

                         FRAN
                    (to Bud, puzzled)
        What are you doing here?

    Bud throws Dr. Dreyfuss a look, as if to say that Fran's mind
    still wasn't functioning properly.

                         BUD
                    (to Fran)
        Don't you remember? We were at
        the office party together --

                         FRAN
    Oh, yes -- office party -- Miss Olsen --

                                 BUD
        That's right.
                        (to Dr. Dreyfuss;
                        improvising rapidly)
        I told you we had a fight -- that's what
        it was about -- Miss Olsen -- you know
        -- that other girl you saw --

                                 FRAN
                        (still trying to figure
                        out Bud's presence)
        I don't understand --

                                 BUD
        It's not important, Fran -- the main
        thing is that I got here in time -- and
        you're going to be all right --
                        (to Dr. Dreyfuss)
        -- isn't she, Doc?

                                 FRAN
                        (closing her eyes)
        I'm so tired --

                                 DR. DREYFUSS
        Here -- drink this.

        He forces her to swallow some coffee.

                                 FRAN
                        (pushing the mug away)
        Please -- just let me sleep.

                                 DR. DREYFUSS
        You can't sleep.
                        (shaking her)
        Come on, Fran -- open your eyes.
                        (to Bud)
        Let's get her walking. We've got to
        keep her awake for the next couple of
        hours.

        They lift her from the chair, and each draping one of her arms
        over his shoulder, they start to walk her up and down the
        room.

                                 DR. DREYFUSS
                        (urging Fran on)
        Now walk, Fran. One, two, three, four

                          DR. DREYFUSS (Cont.)
          -- one, two, three, four -- that's the
          idea -- left, right, left, right -- now we
          turn -- one, two, three, four --

At first, Fran's feet just drag along the floor between them.
But gradually, as Dr. Dreyfuss' voice continues droning
hypnotically, she falls into the rhythm of it, repeating the
words after him and putting her weight on her feet.

                          DR. DREYFUSS
          Left, right, left, right -- walk, walk,
          walk -- one, two, three, four -- turn --
          left, right, left, right -- now you got it --

                                              DISSOLVE TO:

95.   INT. THE APARTMENT -- DAWN

Through the bedroom window comes the first faint light of
dawn. Fran has been put to bed by an exhausted Dr. Dreyfuss.
She is in her slip, and Dreyfuss is just drawing the blanket
over her. Her eyes are closed, and she is moaning fitfully.
Watching from the doorway is Bud, in shirtsleeves now,
weary and dishevelled.

                          DR. DREYFUSS
          She'll sleep on and off for the next
          twenty-four hours. Of course, she'll
          have a dandy hangover when she wakes
          up --

                          BUD
          Just as long as she's okay.

                          DR. DREYFUSS
                    (massaging his calves)
          These cases are harder on the doctor
          than on the patient. I ought to charge
          you by the mile.

They have now moved out into the living room, where the
overhead light and the Christmas tree bulbs are still on.

                          DR. DREYFUSS
          Any of that coffee left?

                            BUD
     Sure.

He goes into the kitchen. Dr. Dreyfuss takes a small notebook
with a fountain pen clipped to it out of his bag, sinks down
on the couch.

                       DR. DREYFUSS
     How do you spell her last name?

                            BUD
                       (from kitchen)
     Kubelik -- with two k's.

                       DR. DREYFUSS
     What's her address?
                       (no answer from Bud)
     Where does she live?

Bud appears from the kitchen, stirring the coffee powder in a
cup of hot water.

                            BUD
                       (apprehensive)
     Why do you want to know, Doc? You
     don't have to report this, do you?

                       DR. DREYFUSS
     It's regulations.

                            BUD
                       (setting the coffee down)
     She didn't mean it, Doc -- it was an
     accident -- she had a little too much to
     drink and -- she didn't know what she
     was doing -- there was no suicide note
     or anything -- believe me, Doc, I'm not
     thinking about myself --

                       DR. DREYFUSS
                       (sipping the hot coffee)
     Aren't you?

                            BUD
     It's just that she's got a family -- and
     there's the people in the office -- look,
     Doc, can't you forget you're a doctor
     -- let's just say you're here as a
     neighbor --

                    DR. DREYFUSS
                  (a long look at Bud)
        Well, as a doctor, I guess I can't prove
        it <u>wasn't</u> an accident.
                  (closes notebook)
        But as your neighbor, I'd like to kick
        your keester clear around the block.
                  (indicating coffee)
        Mind if I cool this off?

He uncaps the bottle of Scotch, pours a large slug into his
coffee.

                        BUD
        Help yourself.

                    DR. DREYFUSS
                  (taking a big gulp of
                   the spiked coffee)
        I don't know what you did to that girl
        in there -- and don't tell me -- but
        it was bound to happen, the way you
        carry on. Live now, pay later.
        Diner's Club!
                  (another swig)
        Why don't you grow up, Baxter? Be a
        <u>mensch</u>! You know what that means?

                        BUD
        I'm not sure.

                    DR. DREYFUSS
        A mensch -- a human being! So you
        got off easy this time -- so you were
        lucky --

                        BUD
        Yeah, wasn't I?

                    DR. DREYFUSS
                  (finishing coffee)
        But you're not out of the woods yet,
        Baxter -- because most of them try it
        again!
                  (picks up bag,
                   starts toward door)
        You know where I am if you need me.

He walks out, closing the door after him. Bud dejectedly turns
off the overhead light, kicks out the plug of the Christmas
tree lights, trudges into the bedroom.

Fran is fast asleep. Bud picks up her dress, gets a hanger,
drapes the dress over it, hangs it from the door. An early
morning chill has invaded the room, and Bud switches on the
electric blanket to keep Fran warm. Then he slumps into a
chair beside the bed, looks at Fran compassionately. The
light on the dial of the electric blanket glows in the grayish
room. Bud just sits there, watching Fran.

                                             FADE OUT:

FADE IN:

96.   INT. STAIRCASE -- BROWNSTONE HOUSE -- DAY

Mrs. Lieberman, followed by her dog, is climbing the stairs
to Bud's apartment, puffing asthmatically. She seems quite
angry as she arrives at the door and rings the bell. There is
no answer. She starts knocking impatiently.

                    MRS. LIEBERMAN
          Mr. Baxter. Open up already!

Finally the door opens a crack, and Bud peers out. He looks
like a man who has slept in his clothes -- rumpled, bleary-
eyed, unshaven.

                    BUD
          Oh -- Mrs. Lieberman.

                    MRS. LIEBERMAN
          So who did you think it was -- Kris
          Kringle? What was going on here last
          night?

                    BUD
          Last night?

                    MRS. LIEBERMAN
          All that marching -- tramp, tramp,
          tramp -- you were having army maneuvers
          maybe?

> BUD
>
> I'm sorry, Mrs. Lieberman -- and I'll
> never invite those people again.

> MRS. LIEBERMAN
>
> What you get from renting to bachelors.
> All night I didn't sleep ten minutes -- and
> I'm sure you woke up Dr. Dreyfuss.

> BUD
>
> Don't worry about Dr. Dreyfuss -- I
> happen to know he was out on a case.

> MRS. LIEBERMAN
>
> I'm warning you, Mr. Baxter -- this is
> a respectable house, not a honky-tonky.
> > (to the dog)
> Come on, Oscar.

Bud watches her start down the stairs with the dog, withdraws
into the apartment.

97. INT. THE APARTMENT -- DAY

Bud closes the door, crosses toward the bedroom, looks
inside. Fran is asleep under the electric blanket, breathing
evenly. He tries to shut the bedroom door, but it won't
close completely because Fran's dress, on a hanger, is hooked
over the top. He goes to the phone, picks it up, dials the
operator.

> BUD
> > (his voice low)
> Operator, I want White Plains, New
> York -- Mr. J. D. Sheldrake --
> > (an added thought)
> -- make it person to person.

98. INT. LIVING ROOM -- SHELDRAKE HOUSE -- DAY

The decor is split-level Early American. There is a huge
Christmas tree and a jumble of presents, open gift boxes,
and discarded wrappings.

Sheldrake and his two sons, TOMMY and JEFF JR., are squatting
on the floor, testing a Cape Canaveral set the kids got for

Christmas. Sheldrake is in a brand new dressing gown, with a
manufacturer's tag still dangling from it, and the boys are in
pajamas and astronaut's helmets. As for the Cape Canaveral
set, it is a miniature layout of block-houses, launching pads,
and assorted space-missiles. Tommy has his finger on the
button controlling one of the rockets.

> SHELDRAKE
> (counting down)
> 7-6-5-4-3-2-1 -- let her rip!

Tommy presses the button, and a spring sends the rocket
toward the ceiling. Just then, the phone in the entrance
hall starts ringing.

> JEFF JR.
> I'll get it.

He hurries to the phone.

> TOMMY
> Hey, Dad -- why don't we put a fly in
> the nose cone and see if we can bring it
> back alive?

> SHELDRAKE
> It's a thought.

> TOMMY
> Maybe we should send up two flies -- and
> see if they'll propagate in orbit.

> SHELDRAKE
> See if they'll what?

> TOMMY
> Propagate -- you know, multiply -- baby
> flies?

> SHELDRAKE
> Oh -- oh!

> JEFF JR.
> (coming back from
> the phone)
> It's for you, Dad. A Mr. Baxter.

> SHELDRAKE
> (getting up)
> Baxter?

JEFF JR.
Person to person.

Sheldrake heads quickly for the phone.

TOMMY
(to Jeff Jr.)
Come on -- help me round up some flies.

In the entrance hall, Sheldrake picks up the phone, turns
his back toward the living room, speaks in a low voice.

SHELDRAKE
Hello? -- yes -- what's on your mind,
Baxter?

99. BUD -- ON PHONE

BUD
I hate to disturb you, but something
came up -- it's rather important -- and
I think it would be a good idea if you
could see me -- at the apartment -- as
soon as possible.

100. SHELDRAKE -- ON PHONE

SHELDRAKE
You're not making sense, Baxter.
What's this all about?

101. BUD -- ON PHONE

BUD
I didn't want to tell you over the phone --
but that certain party -- you know who I
mean -- I found her here last night --
she had taken an overdose of sleeping pills.

102. SHELDRAKE -- ON PHONE

SHELDRAKE
What?

From the stairway beyond him comes:

                              MRS. SHELDRAKE'S VOICE
        What is it, Jeff? Who's on the phone?

Sheldrake turns from the phone. Halfway down the stairs is
Mrs. Sheldrake, in a quilted house robe.

                              SHELDRAKE
                           (a nice recovery)
        One of our employees had an accident
        -- I don't know why they bother me with
        these things on Christmas Day.
                           (into phone)
        Yes, Baxter -- just how serious is it?

Out of the corner of his eye, he watches Mrs. Sheldrake come
down the stairs, pass behind him on the way to the living
room.

103.   BUD -- ON PHONE

                              BUD
        Well, it was touch and go there for a
        while -- but she's sleeping it off now.

He glances through the half-open door toward the sleeping
Fran.

                              BUD
        I thought maybe you'd like to be here
        when she wakes up.

104.   SHELDRAKE -- ON PHONE

                              SHELDRAKE
        That's impossible.
                           (an apprehensive look
                            toward the living room)
        You'll have to handle this situation
        yourself -- as a matter of fact, I'm
        counting on you --

105.   INT. THE APARTMENT -- DAY

                              BUD
                           (into phone)
        Yes, sir -- I understand.

                    BUD (Cont.)
                (taking Fran's letter
                 out of his pocket)
      She left a note -- you want me to open
      it and read it to you?
                    (a beat)
      Well, it was just a suggestion -- no, you
      don't have to worry about that, Mr.
      Sheldrake -- I kept your name out of it --
      so there'll be no trouble, police-wise or
      newspaper-wise --

As Bud continues talking on the phone, Fran, in the bedroom,
opens her eyes, looks around vaguely, trying to figure out
where she is. She sits up in bed, winces, holds her head in
her hands -- she has a fierce hangover.

                    BUD
                (into phone)
      -- you see, the doctor, he's a friend of
      mine -- we were very lucky in that
      respect -- actually, he thinks she's my
      girl -- no, he just jumped to the conclusion
      -- around here, I'm known as quite a
      ladies' man --

In the bedroom Fran, becoming aware of Bud's voice, crawls
out of bed and holding on to the furniture, moves unsteadily
toward the living room door.

                    BUD
                (into phone)
      -- of course, we're not out of the woods
      yet -- sometimes they try it again -- yes
      sir, I'll do my best -- it looks like it'll
      be a couple of days before she's fully
      recovered, and I may have a little problem
      with the landlady --

Behind him, Fran appears in the bedroom doorway, barefooted and
in her slip. She leans groggily against the door post, trying
to focus on Bud and to concentrate on what he's saying.

                    BUD
                (into phone)
      -- all right, Mr. Sheldrake, I'll keep her
      in my apartment as long as I can -- any
      sort of message you want me to give her?

                   -- well, I'll think of something -- goodbye,
          Mr. Sheldrake.

He hangs up the phone slowly.

                              FRAN
                        (weakly)
          I'm sorry.

Bud turns around, sees her standing there on rubbery legs.

                              FRAN
          I'm sorry, Mr. Baxter.

                              BUD
          Miss Kubelik --
                        (hurries toward her)
          -- you shouldn't be out of bed.

                              FRAN
          I didn't know -- I had no idea this was
          your apartment --

                              BUD
                        (putting his arm
                         around her)
          Let me help you.

He leads her back into the bedroom.

                              FRAN
          I'm so ashamed. Why didn't you just
          let me die?

                              BUD
          What kind of talk is that?
                        (he lowers her into
                         the bed)
          So you got a little over-emotional --
          but you're fine now.

                              FRAN
                        (a groan)
          My head -- it feels like a big wad of
          chewing gum. What time is it?

                              BUD
          Two o'clock.

                              FRAN
                    (struggling to her feet)
            Where's my dress? I have to go home.

Her knees buckle. Bud catches her.

                              BUD
            You're in no condition to go anywhere --
            except back to bed.

                              FRAN
            You don't want me here --

                              BUD
            Sure I do. It's always nice to have
            company for Christmas.

He tries to put her back to bed. Fran resists.

                              BUD
            Miss Kubelik, I'm stronger than you are --

                              FRAN
            I just want to go brush my teeth --

                              BUD
            Oh -- of course. I think there's a new
            toothbrush somewhere.

He crosses to the bathroom, takes a plaid robe off the hook on
the back of the door, hands it to Fran.

                              BUD
            Here -- put this on.

In the bathroom, he finds an unused toothbrush in a plastic
container. His eyes fall on his safety razor. With a glance
toward the bedroom, he unscrews the razor, removes the blade,
drops it in his shirt pocket. Then he empties the blades from
the dispenser, puts those in his pocket. Now he notices a
bottle of iodine on the medicine shelf, stashes that in another
pocket, just as Fran appears in the doorway wearing the robe.

                              BUD
                    (handing her the toothbrush)
            Here. How about some breakfast?

                              FRAN
            No -- I don't want anything.

                              BUD
               I'll fix you some coffee.

He crosses the bedroom, heading for the kitchen, stops.

                              BUD
               Oh -- we're all out of coffee -- you
               had quite a lot of it last night --

He thinks for a moment, hurries toward the hall door.

106.   INT. SECOND FLOOR LANDING -- DAY

Bud comes out of his apartment, leaving the door half open, heads
for the Dreyfuss apartment. He rings the bell, peers down over
the banister to make sure Mrs. Lieberman isn't snooping around.
Mrs. Dreyfuss opens the door.

                              BUD
               Mrs. Dreyfuss, can I borrow some
               coffee -- and maybe an orange and a
               couple of eggs?

                         MRS. DREYFUSS
                         (contemptuously)
               Eggs he asks me for. Oranges. What
               you need is a good horse-whipping.

                              BUD
               Ma'am?

                         MRS. DREYFUSS
               From me the doctor has no secrets.
               Poor girl -- how could you do a thing
               like that?

                              BUD
               I didn't really do anything -- honest --
               I mean, you take a girl out a couple of
               times a week -- just for laughs -- and
               right away she thinks you're serious --
               marriage-wise.

                         MRS. DREYFUSS
               Big shot! For you, I wouldn't lift a
               finger -- but for her, I'll fix a little
               something to eat.

She slams the door in his face.   Bud starts back to his
apartment.

107.   INT. THE APARTMENT -- DAY

Fran enters shakily from the bedroom, looks around for the
phone, locates it, picks it up.   As she starts dialing, Bud
comes in from the hall.

                    BUD
          Who are you calling, Miss Kubelik?

                    FRAN
          My sister -- she'll want to know what
          happened to me.

                    BUD
                 (alarmed)
          Wait a minute -- let's talk this over first.
                 (hurries up to her,
                  takes the receiver away)
          Just what are you going to tell her?

                    FRAN
          Well, I haven't figured it out, exactly.

                    BUD
          You better figure it out -- exactly.
          Suppose she asks you why you didn't
          come home last night?

                    FRAN
          I'll tell her I spent the night with a friend.

                    BUD
          Who?

                    FRAN
          Someone from the office.

                    BUD
          And where are you now?

                    FRAN
          In his apartment.

                    BUD
          His apartment?

                         FRAN
     I mean -- her apartment.

                         BUD
     What's your friend's name?

                         FRAN
     Baxter.

                         BUD
     What's her first name?

                         FRAN
     Miss.
                    (she is impressed with
                    her own cleverness)

                         BUD
     When are you coming home?

                         FRAN
     As soon as I can walk.

                         BUD
     Something wrong with your legs?

                         FRAN
     No -- it's my stomach.

                         BUD
     Your stomach?

                         FRAN
     They had to pump it out.

                         BUD
                    (hanging up the phone)
     Miss Kubelik, I don't think you ought to
     call anybody -- not till that chewing gum
     is out of your head.
                    (leads her into bedroom)

                         FRAN
     But they'll be worried about me -- my
     brother-in-law may be calling the police --

                         BUD
     That's why we have to be careful -- we

                    BUD (Cont.)
don't want to involve anybody -- after
all, Mr. Sheldrake is a married man --

                    FRAN
Thanks for reminding me.

She pulls away from him, starts to get into bed.

                    BUD
               (contritely)
I didn't mean it that way -- I was just
talking to him on the phone -- he's very
concerned about you.

                    FRAN
He doesn't give a damn about me.

                    BUD
Oh, you're wrong. He told me --

                    FRAN
He's a liar. But that's not the worst part
of it -- the worst part is -- I still love him.

The doorbell rings.

                    BUD
Must be Mrs. Dreyfuss --
               (starts into living room)
-- remember the doctor -- from last
night -- that's his wife.

He opens the hall door. Mrs. Dreyfuss brushes past him with a
tray full of food.

                    MRS. DREYFUSS
So where is the victim?
               (Bud indicates
                the bedroom)
Max the Knife!

She sweeps into the bedroom, Bud tagging along.

                    MRS. DREYFUSS
               (to Fran)
Nu, little lady, how are we feeling today?

                              FRAN
          I don't know -- kind of dizzy.

                              MRS. DREYFUSS
          Here. The best thing for dizzy is a
          little noodle soup with chicken -- white
          meat -- and a glass tea.

She sets the tray down on Fran's lap.

                              FRAN
          Thank you. I'm really not hungry.

                              MRS. DREYFUSS
          Go ahead! Eat! Enjoy!

She hands her the soup spoon, turns to Bud.

                              MRS. DREYFUSS
          You wouldn't have such a thing as a
          napkin, would you?

                              BUD
          Well, I have some paper towels --

                              MRS. DREYFUSS
          Beatnik! Go to my kitchen -- third
          drawer, under the good silver, there is
          napkins.

                              BUD
          Yes, Mrs. Dreyfuss.

He starts out with a worried backward glance toward the two.
Fran is just sitting there, the spoon in her hand, not touching
the soup.

                              MRS. DREYFUSS
          So what are you waiting for -- a singing
          commercial?

                              FRAN
          I can't eat.

Mrs. Dreyfuss takes the spoon from her, starts to feed her.

                              MRS. DREYFUSS
          You <u>must</u> eat -- and you must get
          healthy -- and you must forget him.

                         MRS. DREYFUSS (Cont.)
Such a fine boy he seemed when he first
moved in here -- clean and cut -- a
regular Ivy Leaguer. Turns out he is
King Farouk. Mit the drinking -- mit
the cha-cha -- mit the no napkins. A
girl like you, for the rest of your life
you want to cry in your noodle soup?
Who needs it! You listen to me, you
find yourself a nice, substantial man --
a widower maybe -- and settle down --
instead of nashing all those sleeping
pills -- for what, for whom? -- for
some Good Time Charlie?
                    (sees Bud approaching
                     with napkin)
Sssh!

                         BUD
                    (gaily)
One napkin, coming up.
                    (hands it to Fran)
I wish we had some champagne to wrap
it around.

                         MRS. DREYFUSS
                    (to Fran)
What did I tell you?

                         BUD
                    (uncomfortable)
Look, Mrs. Dreyfuss, you don't have to
wait around. I'll wash the dishes and --

                         MRS. DREYFUSS
You wash 'em, you break 'em. I'll come
back for them later.
                    (to Fran)
If he makes trouble, give me a yell.

She exits.

                         FRAN
She doesn't seem to like you very much.

                         BUD
Oh, I don't mind. As a matter of fact,
I'm sort of flattered -- that anybody

                          BUD (Cont.)
          should think a girl like you -- would do
          a thing like this -- over a guy like me.

                          FRAN
                    (glancing at night table)
          Oh. Did you find something here -- an
          envelope -- ?

                          BUD
          Yes, I've got it.
                    (takes envelope out
                    of back pocket)
          Don't you think we'd better destroy it?
          So it won't fall into the wrong hands -- ?

                          FRAN
          Open it.

Bud tears open the envelope, takes out Sheldrake's hundred
dollars.

                          BUD
          There's nothing here but a hundred
          dollar bill.

                          FRAN
          That's right. Will you see that Mr.
          Sheldrake gets it?

                          BUD
                    (shrugging)
          Sure.

He puts the money in his pocket.

                          FRAN
                    (holding out tray)
          Here -- take this, will you?

Bud relieves her of the tray, sets it down.

                          BUD
          You want me to move the television set
          in here?
                    (Fran shakes her head)
          You play gin rummy?

                    FRAN
          I'm not very good at it.

                    BUD
          I am. Let me get the cards.

                    FRAN
          You don't have to entertain me.

Bud opens the bureau drawer, takes out a deck of cards, a score
pad, and a pencil.

                    BUD
          Nothing I'd like better -- you know
          togetherness. Guess what I did last
          Christmas. Had an early dinner at
          the automat, then went to the zoo, then
          I came home and cleaned up after Mr.
          Eichelberger -- he had a little eggnog
          party here. I'm way ahead this year.

He pulls a chair up to the bed, starts to shuffle the cards.

                    BUD
          Three across, spades double, high deals.
                    (they cut)
          Eight -- ten.
                    (he starts to deal)

                    FRAN
                    (pensively)
          I think I'm going to give it all up.

                    BUD
          Give what up?

                    FRAN
          Why do people have to love people,
          anyway?

                    BUD
          Yeah -- I know what you mean.
                    (flips over down card)
          Queen.

                    FRAN
          I don't want it.

                              BUD
        Pick a card.

She does, and they start playing.

                              FRAN
        What do you call it when somebody keeps
        getting smashed up in automobile accidents?

                              BUD
        A bad insurance risk?

                              FRAN
                         (nodding)
        That's me with men. I've been jinxed
        from the word go -- first time I was ever
        kissed was in a cemetery.

                              BUD
        A cemetery?

                              FRAN
        I was fifteen -- we used to go there to
        smoke. His name was George -- he
        threw me over for a drum majorette.

                              BUD
        Gin.

He spreads his hand. Fran lays her cards down, and Bud adds
them up.

                              BUD
        Thirty-six and twenty-five -- that's
        sixty-one and two boxes.
                         (enters score on pad)

                              FRAN
        I just have this talent for falling in love
        with the wrong guy in the wrong place at
        the wrong time.

                              BUD
                         (shuffling)
        How many guys were there?

                              FRAN
                         (holding up four fingers)
        Three. The last one was manager of a

                              FRAN (Cont.)
finance company, back home in Pittsburgh
-- they found a little shortage in his
accounts, but he asked me to wait for
him -- he'll be out in 1965.

                         BUD
                    (pushing the deck
                     toward her)
Cut.

                         FRAN
                    (she does, and he
                     starts dealing)
So I came to New York and moved in
with my sister and her husband -- he
drives a cab. They sent me to
secretarial school, and I applied for a
job with Consolidated - but I flunked the
typing test --

                         BUD
Too slow?

                         FRAN
Oh, I can type up a storm, but I can't
spell. So they gave me a pair of white
gloves and stuck me in an elevator --
that's how I met Jeff --
                    (her eyes mist up, and
                     she puts her cards down)
Oh, God, I'm so fouled up. What am I
going to do now?

                         BUD
You better win a hand -- you're on a blitz.

                         FRAN
Was he really upset when you told him?

                         BUD
Mr. Sheldrake? Oh, yes. Very.

                         FRAN
Maybe he <u>does</u> love me -- only he doesn't
have the nerve to tell his wife.

                         BUD
I'm sure that's the explanation.

                        FRAN
      You really think so?

                        BUD
      No doubt about it.

                        FRAN
                  (a thoughtful beat, then)
      Can I have that pad and the pencil?

                        BUD
                  (handing her score
                   pad and pencil)
      What for?

                        FRAN
      I'm going to write a letter to <u>Mrs.</u>
      Sheldrake.

                        BUD
      You <u>are</u>?

                        FRAN
      As one woman to another -- I'm sure
      she'll understand --

                        BUD
      Miss Kubelik, I don't think that's such
      a good idea.

He gently takes the pad and pencil away from her.

                        FRAN
      Why not?

                        BUD
      Well, for one thing, you can't spell.
      And secondly -- if you did something
      like that -- you'd hate yourself.

                        FRAN
                  (fighting back tears)
      I don't like myself very much anyway.

                        BUD
      Pick up your cards and let's go.

                        FRAN
      Do I have to?

> BUD
> You bet. I got a terrific hand.

Fran, her eyes drooping sleepily, picks up her cards, makes a discard.

> BUD
> You sure you want to throw that card?

> FRAN
> Sure.

> BUD
> Gin.

He removes the cards from her hand, starts to add them up.

> BUD
> Fifty-two and twenty-five -- that's
> seventy-seven -- spades is double --
> a hundred and fifty-four -- and four
> boxes -- you're blitzed in two games.

He enters the score on the pad. As he starts to shuffle again, he notices that Fran has slid down on the pillow, and that her eyes are closed -- she is asleep.

Bud rises, adjusts the blanket over her. He stands there looking at her for a moment, runs his hand over his chin. Realizing he needs a shave, he crosses to the bathroom.

In the bathroom, Bud washes his face, squirts some shaving cream into his hand, starts to apply it.

108. EXT. BROWNSTONE HOUSE -- DAY

A Volkswagen draws up to the curb in front of the house. Kirkeby gets out on the street side, Sylvia squeezes herself out through the other door. Kirkeby raises the front hood of the Volkswagen, reaches into the luggage compartment, takes out a cardboard bucket with a bottle of champagne on ice. Together, he and Sylvia start up the steps of the house, Sylvia already cha-cha-ing in anticipation.

109. INT. APARTMENT -- DAY

In the bathroom, Bud has just finished lathering his face when
the doorbell rings. He starts into the bedroom.

                         BUD
                 (muttering to himself)
        All right -- all right, Mrs. Dreyfuss.

He glances at the sleeping Fran, picks up the tray, carries
it into the living room, pulling the bedroom door closed behind
him. But it doesn't shut completely, because of Fran's dress
hooked over the top.

Bud crosses to the hall door, opens it. Outside are Kirkeby,
with the champagne bucket, and Sylvia.

                         KIRKEBY
        Hi, Baxter.

                         BUD
                 (blocking the door)
        What do you want?

                         KIRKEBY
        What do I -- ?
                 (to Sylvia)
        Just a minute.

He pushes his way into the apartment past Bud.

                         BUD
        You can't come in.

                         KIRKEBY
                 (closing the door
                  behind him)
        What's the matter with you, Buddy-boy?
        I made a reservation for four o'clock,
        remember?

He heads for the coffee table, sets the champagne down. Bud
shoots a quick glance toward the bedroom door, gets rid of
the tray.

                         BUD
        Look, you can't stay here. Just take
        your champagne and go.

                    KIRKEBY
Baxter, I don't want to pull rank on you
-- but I told the lady it was all set --
you want to make a liar out of me?

                    BUD
Are you going to leave, Mr. Kirkeby,
or do I have to throw you out?

As Bud spins him around, Kirkeby notices the dress on the
bedroom door.

                    KIRKEBY
Buddy-boy, why didn't you say so?
            (indicating dress)
You got yourself a little playmate, huh?

                    BUD
Now will you get out?

110.   INT. SECOND FLOOR LANDING -- DAY

Outside the door of Bud's apartment, Sylvia is cha-cha-ing
impatiently. Up the stairs comes Dr. Dreyfuss, in his overcoat
and carrying his medical bag.

                    SYLVIA
            (knocking on the door)
Hey, come on, what are we waiting for?
Open up, will you?

She continues cha-cha-ing. Dr. Dreyfuss has unlocked the door
to his apartment, and is watching Sylvia, appalled by the fact
that Baxter seems to be at it again. He starts inside.

                    DR. DREYFUSS
            (calling)
Mildred -- !

He shuts the door behind him.

                    SYLVIA
            (knocking on Baxter's
            door)
What's holding things up?

111.   INT. APARTMENT -- DAY

Kirkeby looks toward the door in response to Sylvia's knocking.

                      KIRKEBY
        Say, why don't we have ourselves a
        party -- the four of us?

                      BUD
        No!

He forces Kirkeby toward the hall door. Kirkeby, glancing
past him through the partly open door of the bedroom, catches
sight of Fran asleep in bed.

                      KIRKEBY
              (grinning smugly)
        Well, I don't blame you. So you hit the
        jackpot, eh kid -- I mean, Kubelik-wise?
              (Bud opens the door,
               gestures him out)
        Don't worry. I won't say a word to anybody.

112.   INT. SECOND FLOOR LANDING -- DAY

Kirkeby comes backing out the door of Bud's apartment, minus
the champagne bucket.

                      KIRKEBY
        Stay with it, Buddy-boy!
              (Bud shuts the door
               on him)
        Come on, Sylvia.

                      SYLVIA
        What gives?

                      KIRKEBY
        A little mixup in signals. Let's go.

                      SYLVIA
        Go where?

                      KIRKEBY
              (leading her toward
               stairs)
        What's your mother doing this afternoon?

                      SYLVIA
        She's home -- stuffing a turkey.

                         KIRKEBY
          Why don't we send her to a movie --
          like Ben-Hur?

                         SYLVIA
          That's fine. But what are we going to
          do about Grandma and Uncle Herman
          and Aunt Sophie and my two nieces --

113. INT. APARTMENT -- DAY

      Bud comes into the bedroom. As he heads for the bathroom,
      Fran stirs slightly, opens her eyes.

                         FRAN
          Who was that?

                         BUD
          Just somebody delivering a bottle of
          champagne. Like some?

                         FRAN
                  (shaking her head)
          Would you mind opening the window?

      She turns off the electric blanket as Bud crosses to the
      window, pushes it up. Then a thought strikes him, and he
      looks at Fran suspiciously.

                         BUD
          Now don't go getting any ideas, Miss
          Kubelik.

                         FRAN
          I just want some fresh air.

                         BUD
          It's only one story down -- the best you
          can do is break a leg.

                         FRAN
          So they'll shoot me -- like a horse.

                         BUD
                  (approaching the bed)
          Please, Miss Kubelik, you got to promise
          me you won't do anything foolish.

FRAN

Who'd care?

BUD

I would.

FRAN
(sleepily)

Why can't I ever fall in love with somebody
nice like you?

BUD
(ruefully)

Yeah. Well -- that's the way it crumbles,
cookie-wise. Go to sleep.

Fran closes her eyes. Bud returns to the bathroom, picks up
his razor, starts to shave. But something seems to be wrong
with the razor -- and unscrewing it, he realizes that there
is no blade. Sheepishly, he takes out the blade he hid in his
shirt pocket, inserts it in his razor, screws it shut. Then
he resumes shaving.

FADE OUT:

FADE IN:

114.   INT. SHELDRAKE'S ANTEROOM -- DAY

It is the morning after Christmas, and Miss Olsen and the
other girls are just settling down to work. Sheldrake, in
hat and coat, approaches from the elevators, comes through
the glass doors.

SECRETARIES
(ad lib)

Good morning, Mr. Sheldrake.

SHELDRAKE
(ignoring them)

Miss Olsen, will you come into my
office, please?

He strides into the inner office. Miss Olsen picks up her
stenographic pad, follows him in.

115.   INT. SHELDRAKE'S OFFICE -- DAY

Sheldrake is removing his hat and coat as Miss Olsen comes in,
shuts the door behind her.

> MISS OLSEN
> Did you have a nice Christmas?

> SHELDRAKE
> Lovely. You were a big help.

> MISS OLSEN
> Me?

> SHELDRAKE
> Thank you for giving that little pep talk
> to Miss Kubelik at the office party.

> MISS OLSEN
> (dropping her business-
> like mask)
> I'm sorry, Jeff. You know I could never
> hold my liquor --

> SHELDRAKE
> But I thought you could hold your tongue.

> MISS OLSEN
> It won't happen again.

> SHELDRAKE
> You bet it won't. I'll arrange for you to
> get a month's severance pay --
> (she looks at him,
> uncomprehending)
> That's right, Miss Olsen. I'm letting
> you go.

> MISS OLSEN
> (quietly)
> You let me go four years ago, Jeff. Only
> you were cruel enough to make me sit out
> there and watch the new models pass by.

> SHELDRAKE
> I'd appreciate it if you'd be out of here
> as soon as you can.

> MISS OLSEN
> (formal again)
> Yes, Mr. Sheldrake.

She turns and walks out of the office, shutting the door.
Sheldrake looks after her for a moment, then goes to his
desk, picks up the phone, dials the operator.

> SHELDRAKE
> (into phone)
> This is Mr. Sheldrake. I'd like Mr.
> Baxter's home telephone number --
> that's C. C. Baxter, in Ordinary
> Premium Accounting --

116. INT. SHELDRAKE'S ANTEROOM -- DAY

Miss Olsen has put on her coat, and is going through her desk
drawers, cleaning out her personal belongings -- nail polish,
emery boards, an extra pair of glasses, etc. As she stows
them away in her handbag, one of the buttons on the telephone
lights up. Miss Olsen hesitates for a second, then with a
quick look around, she pushes the button down, carefully picks
up the receiver, listens in.

117. INT. SHELDRAKE'S OFFICE -- DAY

Sheldrake is dialing the last two digits of a telephone number.
After a moment, someone answers.

> SHELDRAKE
> Hello, Baxter? Jeff Sheldrake. Can
> you talk?

118. INT. THE APARTMENT -- DAY

Bud, wearing slacks, a shirt open at the neck, and a cardigan
sweater, is at the phone.

A pillow and a blanket on the living room couch indicate where
he spent the night.

> BUD
> (looking off)
> Yes, she's in the shower -- she's
> coming along fine, considering.

119. SHELDRAKE -- ON PHONE

                    SHELDRAKE
        Good. Is there anything you need --
        -- money -- ?

120. BUD -- ON PHONE

                    BUD
        No, thank you, Mr. Sheldrake. As a
        matter of fact, I've got some money for
        you -- a hundred dollars --

121. SHELDRAKE -- ON PHONE

                    SHELDRAKE
        Oh.
                    (a beat)
        Well, if there's anything I can do for
        you --

122. BUD -- ON PHONE

                    BUD
        For me? I don't think so. But I was
        hoping maybe you could do something
        for her --

123. SHELDRAKE -- ON PHONE

                    SHELDRAKE
        Like what? Put yourself in my place,
        Baxter -- how can I help her -- my
        hands are tied --

124. INT. APARTMENT -- DAY

        Fran now appears in the bedroom, wearing the plaid robe, and
        toweling her damp hair.

                    BUD
                    (into phone)
        Well, at least you can talk to her --
        let me put her on -- and please be gentle --

        He puts the receiver down, crosses toward the bedroom door.

                              BUD
            There's a call for you --

                              FRAN
                         (approaching)
            For me?

                              BUD
            -- Mr. Sheldrake.

                              FRAN
            I don't want to talk to him.

                              BUD
            I think you should. I have to run down
            to the grocery anyway -- all that's left
            around here is one frozen pizza --
                         (takes raincoat and
                          old hat from hanger)
            I'll be right back -- okay?

        Fran nods, watches him go out. Then she glances toward the
        phone, which is off the hook. Reluctantly she advances toward
        it, picks it up.

                              FRAN
                         (into phone)
            Hello, Jeff.
                         (a long beat)
            Yes, I'm all right.

    125. SHELDRAKE -- ON PHONE

                              SHELDRAKE
            Fran, why did you do it? It's so childish
            -- and it never solves anything -- I ought
            to be very angry with you, scaring me
            like that -- but let's forget the whole thing
            -- pretend it never happened -- what do
            you say, Fran?
                         (no answer)
            Fran --

    126. INT. SHELDRAKE'S ANTEROOM

        Miss Olsen, glued to the phone, is listening intently.

127. SHELDRAKE -- ON PHONE

                    SHELDRAKE
          Are you there, Fran?

128. FRAN -- ON PHONE

                    FRAN
          Of course I'm not here -- because the
          whole thing never happened -- I never
          took those pills -- I never loved you --
          we never even met -- isn't that the way
          you want it?

129. SHELDRAKE -- ON PHONE

                    SHELDRAKE
          There you go again -- you know I didn't
          mean it that way, Fran. Just get well --
          do what the nurse tells you -- I mean
          Baxter -- and I'll see you as soon as I
          can. Bye, Fran.
                    (he hangs up)

130. INT. SHELDRAKE'S ANTEROOM -- DAY

     Miss Olsen hangs up the phone, sits there for a moment,
     weighing what she has overheard. Then she makes a decision,
     picks up the phone again, dials a number. As she waits for
     an answer, she glances toward Sheldrake's office.

                    MISS OLSEN
                    (into phone)
          Hello, Mrs. Sheldrake? This is Miss
          Olsen -- fine, thank you -- Mrs.
          Sheldrake, I was wondering if we could
          have lunch together? -- well, I don't
          know how important it is, but I think
          you might find it educational -- it
          concerns your husband -- all right, one
          o'clock, at Longchamp's, Madison and
          59th.

     She looks up as the door to the inner office opens and Sheldrake
     comes out. He stops when he sees that Miss Olsen is still
     there.

                              MISS OLSEN
                          (hanging up phone)
              Don't worry, I'm on my way.
                          (she rises)
              I was just making a personal call.

She opens her handbag, takes out a coin, puts it down on the
desk.

                              MISS OLSEN
              Here's a dime.

She marches out through the glass doors toward the elevators
as Sheldrake stands there, watching her.

                                                    DISSOLVE TO:

131. EXT. BROWNSTONE HOUSE -- DAY

      Bud comes down the street, carrying a large brown paper bag
      overflowing with groceries. He goes up the steps of the house
      and through the front door.

132. INT. STAIRCASE AND SECOND FLOOR LANDING -- DAY

      As Bud starts up the stairs, with the groceries, Mrs. Lieberman
      comes hurrying down toward him.

                              MRS. LIEBERMAN
                          (breathlessly)
              Oh, Mr. Baxter -- I'm glad you're here
              -- I was just going to get the passkey.

                              BUD
              What for?

                              MRS. LIEBERMAN
              I thought I smelled gas coming from your
              apartment.

                              BUD
              Gas?

      He races up the stairs two at a time, fumbling frantically for
      his key. Reaching the door of his apartment, he unlocks it,
      dashes in.

133. INT. THE APARTMENT -- DAY

Bud comes bursting through the door. The living room is empty,
and the bedclothes have been removed from the couch.

>   BUD
>   (calling)
>   Miss Kubelik!

He dumps the bag of groceries on a table, rushes into the
kitchen. The burner has been turned on under the kettle, but
there is no flame, and gas is hissing from the vents. Bud
snaps it off, starts out again.

>   BUD
>   Miss Kubelik!

Meanwhile Fran has appeared from the bathroom, and is approaching
the bedroom door. She is still in her robe, and is holding a
double sock-stretcher with one of Bud's socks on it. Bud,
rounding the corner from the kitchen at full speed, collides
with Fran in the bedroom doorway. He grabs her arm with obvious
relief.

>   BUD
>   Are you all right?

>   FRAN
>   Sure.
>   (sniffs)
>   What's that funny smell?

>   BUD
>   Gas.
>   (indicating kitchen)
>   Didn't you turn it on?

>   FRAN
>   Yes. I was boiling some water to get
>   the coffee stains out of my dress.

>   BUD
>   (accusingly)
>   You turned it on -- but you didn't <u>light</u> it.

>   FRAN
>   Are you supposed to?

                              BUD
          In <u>this</u> house, you're supposed to.

                              FRAN
          Oh.

Bud starts to take off his hat and coat, notices the sock-stretcher
in her hand.

                              BUD
          What are you doing with that?

                              FRAN
          I was washing my stockings, so I
          decided I might as well do your socks.

                              BUD
          Thank you.

                              FRAN
          It's very curious -- I could only find
          three and a half pair.

                              BUD
          Well, things are a little disorganized
          around here.

He carries the bag of groceries into the kitchen, Fran trailing
after him. During the following, he removes the contents of
the bag -- bread, eggs, bacon, spaghetti, ground round,
frankfurters, and assorted canned goods -- sets them out on
the drainboard.

                              FRAN
          I'd say. What's a tennis racquet doing
          in the kitchen?

She produces the racquet from behind the stove.

                              BUD
          Tennis racquet? Oh, I remember --
          I was cooking myself an Italian dinner.
                    (Fran looks at him
                     oddly)
          I used it to strain the spaghetti.

                              FRAN
                    (thinking it over)
          Why not?

                         BUD
As a matter of fact, I'm a pretty good
cook -- but I'm a lousy housekeeper.

                         FRAN
Yes, you are.
                   (indicating the
                    living room)
When I was straightening up the couch,
you know what I found? Six hairpins,
a lipstick, a pair of false eyelashes,
and a swizzle stick from the Stork Club.

                         BUD
                   (shrugging)
It's just that I'm the kind of guy who
can't say no -- I don't mean to girls --
I mean --

                         FRAN
You mean to someone like Mr. Sheldrake.

                         BUD
I guess so.

                         FRAN
I know so. He's a taker.

                         BUD
A what?

                         FRAN
Some people take, some people get took
-- and they know they're getting took --
and there's nothing they can do about it.

                         BUD
I wouldn't say that --
                   (trying to change
                    the subject)
What would you like to have for dinner?
There's onion soup and canned asparagus --

                         FRAN
I really ought to be getting home. My
family will be flipping by now.

She starts into the living room. Bud follows her.

                              BUD
          You can't leave yet. The doctor says it
          takes forty-eight hours to get the stuff
          out of your system.

                              FRAN
                          (wistfully)
          I wonder how long it takes to get someone
          you're stuck on out of your system? If
          they'd only invent some kind of a pump
          for that --

     She sits on the arm of a chair.

                              BUD
          I know how you feel, Miss Kubelik.
          You think it's the end of the world --
          but it's not, really. I went through
          exactly the same thing myself.

                              FRAN
          You did?

                              BUD
          Well, maybe not <u>exactly</u> -- I tried to
          do it with a gun.

                              FRAN
          Over a girl?

                              BUD
          Worse than that -- she was the wife of
          my best friend -- and I was mad for her.
          But I knew it was hopeless -- so I
          decided to end it all. I went to a pawnshop
          and bought a forty-five automatic and drove
          up to Eden Park -- do you know Cincinnati?

                              FRAN
          No, I don't.

                              BUD
          Anyway, I parked the car and loaded the
          gun -- well, you read in the papers all the
          time that people shoot themselves, but
          believe me, it's not that easy -- I mean,
          how do you do it? -- here, or here, or
          here --

                    BUD (Cont.)
               (with cocked finger,
               he points to his
               temple, mouth and chest)
-- you know where I finally shot myself?

                    FRAN
Where?

                    BUD
               (indicating kneecap)
Here.

                    FRAN
In the knee?

                    BUD
Uh-huh. While I was sitting there,
trying to make my mind up, a cop stuck
his head in the car, because I was
illegally parked -- so I started to hide
the gun under the seat and it went off --
pow!

                    FRAN
               (laughing)
That's terrible.

                    BUD
Yeah. Took me a year before I could
bend my knee -- but I got over the girl
in three weeks. She still lives in
Cincinnati, has four kids, gained twenty
pounds -- she sends me a fruit cake
every Christmas.

                    FRAN
               (suddenly suspicious)
Are you just making that up to make me
feel better?

                    BUD
Of course not. Here's the fruit cake.
               (shows it to her
               under Christmas tree)
And you want to see my knee?
               (starts to raise
               pant-leg)

                              FRAN
            No, thanks. The fellows in the office may
            get the wrong idea how I found out.

                              BUD
            So let 'em. Look, I'm going to cook
            dinner for us. We'll have the fruit
            cake for dessert. You just sit there and
            rest. You've done enough for one day.

                              FRAN
                           (smiling)
            Yes, nurse.

      Bud starts happily into the kitchen.

                                                    DISSOLVE TO:

134. INT. LOBBY INSURANCE BUILDING -- DAY

      It is mid-afternoon, and traffic is light. A Yellow Cab has
      pulled up in front of the entrance, and the driver, a stockily-
      built young man in a leather jacket and cap, gets out and comes
      through the revolving doors into the lobby. His name is KARL
      MATUSCHKA, and he is Fran's brother-in-law. As he cases the
      elevators, the starter comes up to him.

                              ELEVATOR STARTER
            Can I help you?

                              MATUSCHKA
            I'm looking for one of the elevator girls
            -- Miss Kubelik.

                              ELEVATOR STARTER
            So am I. She didn't report this morning.

                              MATUSCHKA
            She didn't. Where can I get some
            information -- who's in charge here?

                              ELEVATOR STARTER
            That comes under General Office
            Administration. See Mr. Dobisch,
            twenty-first floor.

                              MATUSCHKA
            Thanks.

He steps into an elevator, the doors of which are just closing.

135. INT. DOBISCH'S OFFICE -- DAY

Dobisch is sitting behind his desk, lighting a cigar. Kirkeby, who has dropped in for a little visit, is perched on the edge of the desk.

                    KIRKEBY
          -- so yesterday afternoon I take Sylvia
          up to the apartment, and guess who he's
          got stashed away in the bedroom?

                    DOBISCH
          Who?

                    KIRKEBY
          Kubelik.

                    DOBISCH
          No kidding. Buddy-boy and Kubelik
          having themselves a little toot!

                    KIRKEBY
          Toot? It's more like a lost weekend.
          Neither of them showed up for work today.

                    DOBISCH
          A.W.O.L.?

                    KIRKEBY
          What gripes me is the two of them were
          guzzling my champagne while Sylvia and
          I wound up at the Guggenheim Museum.

The glass door opens and Matuschka comes in.

                    MATUSCHKA
          Mr. Dobisch?

                    DOBISCH
          Yeah.

                    MATUSCHKA
          My name is Karl Matuschka -- my sister-
          in-law, she runs one of the elevators
          here -- Fran Kubelik.

                          KIRKEBY
                    (exchanging a glance
                     with Dobisch)
     Miss Kubelik?

                          MATUSCHKA
     You know her?

                          DOBISCH
     Of course. There may be a lot of
     employees here -- but we're one big
     happy family.

                          MATUSCHKA
     Well, she lives with us -- and my wife,
     she's getting a little nervous -- on
     account of Fran hasn't been home for
     two days.

                          KIRKEBY
                    (another look at Dobisch)
     That so.

                          MATUSCHKA
     Anyway, we was wondering if somebody
     in the office would know what happened
     to her.

                          DOBISCH
     I see.
                    (to Kirkeby)
     What do you think, Al? Can we help the
     man?

                          KIRKEBY
                    (after a pregnant pause)
     Why not? We don't owe Buddy-boy
     anything.

                          DOBISCH
     Yeah. What's Buddy-boy done for us
     lately?

                          MATUSCHKA
                    (scowling)
     Who is Buddy-boy?

                                        DISSOLVE TO:

136. INT. THE APARTMENT -- EVENING

Buddy-boy is bending over a hot stove, preparing an Italian
dinner. He takes a saucepan of spaghetti off the fire, and
picking up the tennis racquet with the other hand, pours the
spaghetti on top of the racquet strings. Then he turns on
the faucet, runs water over the spaghetti. With the combined
technique of Brillat-Savarin and Pancho Gonzales, he gently
agitates the racquet, letting the water drain off the spaghetti.
As he works, he hums a theme from Tschaikowsky's Capriccio
Italien.

Fran walks in, still in her robe.

                    FRAN
          Are we dressing for dinner?

                    BUD
          No -- just come as you are.

                    FRAN
                 (watching him)
          Say, you're pretty good with that racquet.

                    BUD
          You ought to see my backhand.
                 (dumping spaghetti
                  into platter)
          And wait till I serve the meatballs.
                 (demonstrates)

                    FRAN
          Shall I light the candles?

                    BUD
          It's a must -- gracious-living-wise.

As Fran starts into the living room, Bud begins to ladle meat
sauce onto the spaghetti, humming operatically.

In the living room, the small table has been set for two, and
prominent on it is the champagne bottle that Mr. Kirkeby left
behind, still in its cardboard bucket, but freshly iced. As
Fran lights the candles, she notices the napkins on the table,
peels a price tag off the corner of one of them.

                    FRAN
          I see you bought some napkins.

                           BUD
          Might as well go all the way.

He carries the platter of spaghetti and meat sauce in from the
kitchen, sets it on the table, sprinkles some cheese on it.
Then he crosees to the coffee table, where a full martini
pitcher stands in readiness, fills a couple of glasses. Fran
seats herself at the table.

                           BUD
          You know, I used to live like
          Robinson Crusoe -- shipwrecked
          among eight million people. Then
          one day I saw a footprint in the sand
          -- and there you were --
                     (hands her martini)
          It's a wonderful thing -- dinner for two.

                           FRAN
          You usually eat alone?

                           BUD
          Oh, no. Sometimes I have dinner with
          Ed Sullivan, sometimes with Dinah Shore
          or Perry Como -- the other night I had
          dinner with Mae West -- of course, she
          was much younger then.
                     (toasting)
          Cheers.

                           FRAN
          Cheers.

They drink.

                           BUD
          You know what we're going to do after
          dinner?

                           FRAN
          The dishes?

                           BUD
          I mean, after that?

                           FRAN
          What?

                              BUD
          You don't have to if you don't want to --

                              FRAN
          I don't?

                              BUD
          We're going to finish that gin game.

                              FRAN
          Oh.

                              BUD
          So I want you to keep a clear head.

The doorbell rings. Carrying his martini glass, Bud crosses
to the door, starts to open it.

                              BUD
          Because I don't want to take advantage
          of you -- the way I did yesterday in bed.

By now the door is open, and Bud is speaking to Fran over his
shoulder. He turns, finds himself face to face with Karl
Matuschka, who is standing grimly in the doorway.

                              MATUSCHKA
          Baxter?

                              BUD
          Yes?

Matuschka shoves him roughly aside, strides past him toward
Fran, who has risen to her feet.

                              MATUSCHKA
          What's with you, Fran -- did you forget
          where you live?

                              FRAN
                    (to Bud)
          This is my brother-in-law, Karl Matuschka.

                              BUD
                    (friendly)
          How do you do, Mr. Matuschka?

                          MATUSCHKA
                    (pushing Bud away;
                      to Fran)
          Okay, get your clothes on.   I got the
          cab downstairs.

                             BUD
          Now, wait a minute.   I know what you're
          thinking -- but it's not as bad as it looks --

                          MATUSCHKA
                    (shoving him away)
          It's none of my business what you do,
          Fran -- you're over twenty-one --
          but your sister happens to think you're
          a lady.

                             BUD
          All we were going to do is eat and wash
          the dishes --

                          MATUSCHKA
                    (grabbing him)
          Look, Buddy-boy -- if there wasn't
          a lady present, I'd clobber you.

                            FRAN
                    (separating them)
          All right, Karl -- I'll get dressed.

          She exits into the bedroom, removing her dress from the door,
          and closing it.   Matuschka leans against the wall beside the
          hall door, eyeing Bud truculently.   Bud raises a finger to
          remonstrate with him -- then breaks into a nervous, ingratiating
          smile.

                             BUD
          Care for a martini?   Champagne?
                    (Matuschka continues
                      glaring at him)
          How about a little spaghetti with meat
          sauce?   Made it myself.
                    (Matuschka just scowls)
          Your sister-in-law sure is terrific --
                    (realizes his mistake;
                      switching abruptly)
          Must be murder driving a cab in New
          York -- I mean, with all that cross-
          town traffic --

He gestures with the martini glass, spilling the contents over
his shirtfront. Through the partly open hall door, Dr. Dreyfuss
sticks his head in.

                    DR. DREYFUSS
     Hi, Baxter.

He steps into the apartment, passing Matuschka without seeing
him.

                    DR. DREYFUSS
     How's the patient?

                    BUD
                  (quickly)
     Oh, I'm fine, Doc.

                    DR. DREYFUSS
     Not you -- Miss Kubelik.

                    MATUSCHKA
                  (stepping forward)
     What's the matter with Miss Kubelik?

                    BUD
     Oh, this is Mr. Matuschka -- he's Miss
     Kubelik's -- he's got a cab downstairs --

                    MATUSCHKA
                  (to Dreyfuss)
     Fran been sick or something?

Dr. Dreyfuss looks at Bud.

                    BUD
     No, no -- just had a little accident.

                    MATUSCHKA
                  (to Dreyfuss)
     What does he mean, accident?

                    DR. DREYFUSS
     Well, these things happen all the time --

                    MATUSCHKA
     What things?
                  (grabbing Dreyfuss)
     Say, what kind of doctor are you, anyway?

                              BUD
                          (hastily)
               Oh, not that kind. He just gave her a
               shot and pumped her stomach out --

          Behind them, the bedroom door has opened, and Fran comes out,
          wearing her coat over her dress.

                              MATUSCHKA
               What for?

                              FRAN
                          (coming up)
               Because I took some sleeping pills.
               But I'm all right now -- so let's go.

                              MATUSCHKA
               Why did you take sleeping pills?

                              BUD
                          (promptly)
               On account of me.

                              MATUSCHKA
                          (whirling on him)
               You?

                              BUD
               Who else?

          Matuschka lashes out with a left to Bud's jaw, and while he is
          off balance, catches him with a right to the eye. Bud falls
          back against the Christmas tree, which topples with a crash.
          Fran pulls Matuschka away from him.

                              FRAN
               Leave him alone, Karl.

          She kneels beside Bud.

                              FRAN
                          (tenderly)
               You fool -- you damn fool.

                              MATUSCHKA
               Come on, Fran.

                              FRAN
               Goodbye, Mr. Baxter.

She kisses him on the cheek, rises, starts toward the door.

                    FRAN
        Goodbye, Doctor.

She follows Matuschka out. Bud looks after her, starry-eyed.

                    DR. DREYFUSS
        I don't want to gloat, but just between
        us, you had that coming to you.
                (tilts Bud's chin up,
                examines his eye)
        Tch, tch, tch. Are you going to have
        a shiner tomorrow. Let me get my bag.
                (he starts out)

                    BUD
                (calling after him)
        Don't bother, Doc. It doesn't hurt a bit.

He is on Cloud Nine.

                                        FADE OUT:

FADE IN:

137. INT. NINETEENTH FLOOR -- DAY.

Bud is coming from the elevators toward his office. He is
wearing his chesterfield, bowler, and a pair of dark glasses.
He opens the office door, starts in.

138. INT. BUD'S OFFICE -- DAY

Bud crosses directly to the phone, removes his glasses --
revealing a swollen left eye. He dials a number.

                    BUD
                (into phone)
        Mr. Sheldrake's office? This is
        C. C. Baxter. Would you please tell
        Mr. Sheldrake I'd like to come up and
        see him? It's rather important.
        Will you call me back, please?

He hangs up, takes off his hat and coat, deposits them on the

clothes-tree. Then he paces around the office, rehearsing a
speech out loud.

> BUD
> Mr. Sheldrake, I've got good news for
> you. All your troubles are over. I'm
> going to take Miss Kubelik off your hands.
> > (nods to himself
> > with satisfaction)
> The plain fact is, Mr. Sheldrake, that
> I love her. I haven't told her yet, but
> I thought you should be the first to know.
> After all, you don't really want her, and
> I do, and although it may sound presumptuous,
> she needs somebody like me. So I think it
> would be the thing all around --
> > (the phone rings and
> > he picks it up)
> -- solution-wise.
> > (into phone)
> Yes? I'll be right up.

He hangs up, crosses to the door, opens it.

> BUD
> (to himself)
> Mr. Sheldrake, I've got good news for
> you --

Putting on his dark glasses, he heads for the elevators, still
talking to himself.

139.   INT. NINETEENTH FLOOR -- DAY

Kirkeby and Dobisch are just stepping out of an elevator when
Bud approaches. They grin smugly when they see that he is
wearing dark glasses.

> KIRKEBY
> Hi, Buddy-boy. What happened to you?

> DOBISCH
> Hit by a swinging door? Or maybe a
> Yellow Cab?

Bud pays no attention, walks right past them into the elevator,
still muttering to himself. The doors close.

                         KIRKEBY
                    (as they move away
                     from the elevators)
              That guy really must've belted him.

                         DOBISCH
              Yeah, he's punchy. Talking to himself.

140. INT. TWENTY-SEVENTH FLOOR FOYER -- DAY

      The elevator doors open.

                         ELEVATOR OPERATOR
              Twenty-seven.

      Bud steps out. As he heads for Sheldrake's office, he
      continues rehearsing his speech.

                         BUD
              You see, Mr. Sheldrake, those two days
              she spent in the apartment -- it made me
              realize how lonely I'd been before. But
              thanks to you, I'm in a financial position
              to marry her -- if I can ever square things
              with her family.

      He opens the door to Sheldrake's anteroom.

141. INT. SHELDRAKE'S OFFICE -- DAY

      Sheldrake is pacing in front of his desk. A couple of suitcases
      are standing in a corner of the room. The intercom buzzes, and
      Sheldrake presses the lever down.

                         SECRETARY'S VOICE
              Mr. Baxter is here.

                         SHELDRAKE
              Send him in.

      A beat, then the door opens, and Bud marches in determinedly.

                         BUD
              Mr. Sheldrake, I've got good news
              for you --

                    SHELDRAKE
And I've got good news for you, Baxter.
All your troubles are over.

                    BUD
            (reacting to the echo)
Sir?

                    SHELDRAKE
I know how worried you were about Miss
Kubelik -- well, stop worrying -- I'm
going to take her off your hands.

                    BUD
            (stunned)
You're going to take her off <u>my</u> hands?

                    SHELDRAKE
That's right.
            (indicating suitcases)
I've moved out of my house -- I'm going
to be staying in town, at the Athletic Club.

                    BUD
You left your wife?

                    SHELDRAKE
Well, if you must know -- I fired my
secretary, my secretary got to my wife,
and my wife fired me. Ain't that a kick
in the head?

                    BUD
Yeah --

                    SHELDRAKE
Now what was your news, Baxter?

                    BUD
            (recovering with
             difficulty)
It's about Miss Kubelik -- she's all
right again -- so she went back home.

                    SHELDRAKE
Swell. And don't think I've forgotten
what you did for me.

                         SHELDRAKE (Cont.)
                     (opens door to
                      adjoining office)
          This way, Baxter.

Bud advances slowly toward the door.

142. INT. ADJOINING OFFICE -- DAY

      It is a slightly smaller and less lavish edition of Sheldrake's
      office. Sheldrake ushers Bud through the door, points to the
      chair behind the desk.

                         SHELDRAKE
          Sit down. Try it on for size.

Bud obeys like an automaton, lowers himself into the chair.

                         SHELDRAKE
          You like?
                     (indicating office)
          It's all yours.

                         BUD
          Mine?

                         SHELDRAKE
          My assistant, Roy Thompson, has been
          shifted to the Denver office, and you're
          taking his place.
                     (no reaction from Bud)
          What's the matter, Baxter? You don't
          seem very excited.

                         BUD
          Well, it's just that so many things have
          been happening so fast -- I'm very pleased
          -- especially for Miss Kubelik. Now that
          I've gotten to know her better, I think
          she's the kind of girl that definitely ought
          to be married to somebody --

                         SHELDRAKE
          Oh, sure, sure. But first the property
          settlement has to be worked out -- then
          it takes six weeks in Reno -- meanwhile,
          I'm going to enjoy being a bachelor for a
          while.

                              SHELDRAKE (Cont.)
                            (starts back toward
                              his own office)
              Oh, by the way, you can now have lunch
              in the executive dining room --

                                  BUD
              Yes, sir.

He removes his dark glasses reflectively.

                               SHELDRAKE
              That's just one of the privileges that
              goes with this job. You also get a nice
              little expense account, the use of the
              executive washroom --
                            (breaks off, peers
                            at Bud's face)
              Say, what happened to you, Baxter?

                                  BUD
              I got kicked in the head, too.

                               SHELDRAKE
              Oh?

With a shrug, he exits into his own office, closing the door
behind him. Bud sits there, unconsciously bending the glasses
in his hand until they suddenly snap in two. Bud glances
down at the two broken halves, as though surprised by his own
violence, tosses them onto the desk.

                                                   DISSOLVE TO:

143.   INT. LOBBY INSURANCE BUILDING -- EVENING

We are close on the building directory. Listed under PERSONNEL is
J. D. SHELDRAKE, Director, and just below that a man's hand is
inserting the name C. C. BAXTER in the slot marked Asst. Director.
The lettering is complete except for the final R.

Camera pulls back to reveal the sign painter we saw earlier,
working on the directory. Watching him is Bud. He is wearing
his chesterfield and bowler, and still has a slight welt under
his left eye. It is after six o'clock, and there is very little
activity in the lobby.

Fran, wearing her coat over street clothes, approaches from
the direction of the elevators, stops when she sees Bud.

> FRAN
>
> Good evening, Mr. Baxter.

Bud turns to her in surprise, removes his bowler.

> BUD
>
> Oh, Miss Kubelik. How do you feel?

> FRAN
>
> Fine. How's your eye?

> BUD
>
> Fine.

There is a moment of constraint between them.

> FRAN
>
> How's everything at the apartment?

> BUD
>
> Nothing's changed. You know, we never
> finished that gin game --

> FRAN
>
> I know.
> (a beat)
> I suppose you heard about Mr. Sheldrake -- ?

> BUD
>
> You mean, leaving his wife? Yeah. I'm
> very happy for you.

> FRAN
>
> I never thought he'd do it.

> BUD
>
> I told you all along. You see, you were
> wrong about Mr. Sheldrake.

> FRAN
>
> I guess so.

> BUD
>
> For that matter, you were wrong about
> me, too. What you said about those who
> take and those who get took? Well, Mr.

                         BUD (Cont.)
Sheldrake wasn't using me -- I was
using him. See?
                (indicating his name
                 on directory)
Last month I was at desk 861 on the
nineteenth floor -- now I'm on the
twenty-seventh floor, panelled office,
three windows -- so it all worked out
fine -- we're both getting what we want.

                         FRAN
Yes..
                (looks at her watch)
You walking to the subway?

                         BUD
No, thank you.
                (fumbling)
I -- well, to tell you the truth --
                (glancing around lobby)
-- I have this heavy date for tonight --

He points off toward the newsstand. Standing there is a tall,
attractive brunette, obviously waiting for someone. Fran
looks off in the indicated direction.

                         FRAN
Oh.

                         BUD
Aren't you meeting Mr. Sheldrake?

                         FRAN
No. You know how people talk. So I
decided it would be better if we didn't
see each other till everything is settled,
divorce-wise.

                         BUD
That's very wise.

                         FRAN
Good night, Mr. Baxter.

                         BUD
Good night, Miss Kubelik.

Fran walks toward the revolving door. Bud watches her for a
moment, then strides briskly across the lobby toward the
newsstand. He goes right past the waiting brunette, stops in
front of a rack of pocket books, examines the merchandise.
A man now comes out of a phone booth, joins the waiting
brunette, and they go off together. Bud picks out a couple
of paperbacks, pays the clerk behind the counter. Stuffing
a book into each coat pocket, he moves slowly toward the
revolving doors.

                                                    DISSOLVE TO:

144.   INT. SHELDRAKE'S OFFICE -- DAY

Sheldrake is swiveled around sideways behind his desk, with a
bootblack kneeling in front of him, shining his shoes.
Reaching for the intercom, Sheldrake presses down one of the
levers.

                        SHELDRAKE
            Baxter -- would you mind stepping
            in here for a minute?

                        BAXTER'S VOICE
            Yes, Mr. Sheldrake.

The bootblack finishes the second shoe with a flourish, gathers
up his equipment. Sheldrake tosses him a half dollar.

                        BOOTBLACK
            Much obliged.

He exits into the anteroom as the door of the adjoining office
opens and Bud comes in, carrying several charts. There is no
trace left of his black eye.

                        BUD
                (putting charts on desk)
            Here's the breakdown of figures on
            personnel turnover. Thirty-seven
            per cent of our female employees
            leave to get married, twenty-two
            per cent quit because --

                        SHELDRAKE
                (breaking in)
            You're working too hard, Baxter. It's
            New Year's Eve -- relax.

                              BUD
          Yes, sir.

                              SHELDRAKE
          I suppose you'll be on the town tonight
          -- celebrating?

                              BUD
          Naturally.

                              SHELDRAKE
          Me, too. I'm taking Miss Kubelik out
          -- I finally talked her into it --

                              BUD
          I see.

                              SHELDRAKE
          The only thing is I'm staying at the
          Athletic Club -- and it's strictly stag --
          so if you don't mind --

                              BUD
          Don't mind what?

                              SHELDRAKE
          You know that other key to your apartment
          -- well, when we had that little scare
          about Miss Kubelik, I thought I'd better
          get rid of it quick -- so I threw it out the
          window of the commuter train.

                              BUD
          Very clever.

                              SHELDRAKE
          Now I'll have to borrow your key.

                              BUD
          Sorry, Mr. Sheldrake.

                              SHELDRAKE
          What do you mean, sorry?

                              BUD
          You're not going to bring anybody up
          to my apartment.

> SHELDRAKE

I'm not just bringing <u>anybody</u> -- I'm
bringing Miss Kubelik.

> BUD

<u>Especially</u> not Miss Kubelik.

> SHELDRAKE

How's that again?

> BUD
> (flatly)

No key!

> SHELDRAKE

Baxter, I picked you for my team
because I thought you were a bright
young man. You realize what you're
doing? Not to me -- but to yourself.
Normally it takes years to work your
way up to the twenty-seventh floor --
but it takes only thirty seconds to be
out on the street again. You dig?

> BUD
> (nodding slowly)

I dig.

> SHELDRAKE

So what's it going to be?

Without taking his eyes off Sheldrake, Bud reaches into his
pocket, fishes out a key, drops it on the desk.

> SHELDRAKE

Now you're being bright!

> BUD

Thank you, sir.

He turns abruptly, starts back into his own office.

145. INT. BUD'S NEW OFFICE -- DAY

Bud comes in, shutting the door behind him, stands rooted to the
spot for a moment. Then he takes some pencils out of his breast
pocket and drops them into a container on the desk, closes his
account book, slams a couple of open file drawers shut.

As he crosses to the clothes closet, the connecting door opens
and Sheldrake comes in, key in hand.

                    SHELDRAKE
          Say, Baxter -- you gave me the wrong
          key.

                    BUD
          No I didn't.

                    SHELDRAKE
                 (holding it out)
          But this is the key to the executive washroom.

                    BUD
          That's right, Mr. Sheldrake. I won't
          be needing it -- because I'm all washed
          up around here.

He has taken his chesterfield and bowler out of the closet,
and is putting the coat on.

                    SHELDRAKE
          What's gotten into you, Baxter?

                    BUD
          Just following doctor's orders. I've
          decided to become a mensch. You know
          what that means? A human being.

                    SHELDRAKE
          Now hold on, Baxter --

                    BUD
          Save it. The old payola won't work any
          more. Goodbye, Mr. Sheldrake.

He opens the door to the anteroom, starts out.

146. INT. SHELDRAKE'S ANTEROOM -- DAY

Bud comes out of his office, carrying his bowler, strides
past the secretaries and through the glass doors to the foyer.
An elevator is just unloading, and beside it a handyman is
cleaning out one of the cigarette receptacles. Bud crosses
to the elevator, and as he passes the handyman, he jams his
bowler on the man's head -- surrendering his crown, so to

speak. The elevator doors close. The handyman straightens
up, looks around in bewilderment.

                                                    DISSOLVE TO:

147. INT. THE APARTMENT -- NIGHT

Bud is in the process of packing. In the middle of the living
room are several large cardboard cartons filled with his
possessions. The art posters are off the walls, the bric-a-brac
has been removed from the shelves, and Bud is stowing away
the last of his books and records. He crosses to the fireplace,
opens one of the drawers in the cabinet above it, takes out
a forty-five automatic. He holds the gun in the palm of his
hand, studies it appraisingly. The doorbell rings. Bud snaps
out of his reverie, drops the gun into one of the cartons,
goes to the door and opens it. Standing outside is Dr.
Dreyfuss, with a plastic ice bucket in his hand.

                         DR. DREYFUSS
               Say, Baxter -- we're having a little
               party and we ran out of ice -- so I was
               wondering --

                         BUD
               Sure, Doc.

                         DR. DREYFUSS
                         (stepping inside)
               How come you're alone on New Year's
               Eve?

                         BUD
               Well, I have things to do --

                         DR. DREYFUSS
                         (noticing cartons)
               What's this -- you packing?

                         BUD
               Yeah -- I'm giving up the apartment.

He goes into the kitchen, opens the refrigerator, starts to
pry out the ice-cube trays.

                         DR. DREYFUSS
               Where are you moving to?

                              BUD
      I don't know. All I know is I got to
      get out of this place.

                         DR. DREYFUSS
      Sorry to lose you, Baxter.

                              BUD
      Me? Oh, you mean my body. Don't
      worry, Doc -- it'll go to the University
      -- I'll put it in writing --

He dumps the ice cubes, still in their trays, into the bucket
Dr. Dreyfuss is holding. Then he pulls Kirkeby's unopened
bottle of champagne out of the refrigerator.

                              BUD
      Can you use a bottle of champagne?

                         DR. DREYFUSS
      Booze we don't need. Why don't you
      join us, Baxter? We got two brain
      surgeons, an ear, nose and throat
      specialist, a proctologist, and three
      nurses from Bellevue.

                              BUD
      No, thanks -- I don't feel like it.
      Look, Doc -- in case I don't see you
      again -- how much do I owe you for
      taking care of that girl?

                         DR. DREYFUSS
      Forget it -- I didn't do it as a doctor --
      I did it as a neighbor.
                    (stopping in doorway)
      By the way, whatever happened to her?

                              BUD
                    (airily)
      You know me with girls. Easy come,
      easy go. Goodbye, Doc.

                         DR. DREYFUSS
      Happy New Year.

Bud closes the door, returns to the kitchen, brings out a box
of glassware and the tennis racquet. As he starts to deposit

the racquet in a carton, he notices a strand of spaghetti
clinging to the strings. He removes it gently, stands
there twirling the limp spaghetti absently around his finger.

                                              CUT TO:

148.   INT. CHINESE RESTAURANT -- NIGHT

It is five minutes before midnight, New Year's Eve. Sitting
alone in the last booth is Fran, a paper hat on her head, a
pensive look on her face. There are two champagne glasses on
the table, and the usual noisemakers, but the chair opposite
her is empty. Above the general hubbub, the Chinese pianist
can be heard playing. After a moment, Fran glances off.

Threading his way through the merrymakers crowding the bar
and overflowing from the booths is Sheldrake. He is in dinner
clothes, topped by a paper hat. Reaching the last booth, he
drops into the chair facing Fran.

                     SHELDRAKE
          Sorry it took me so long on the phone.
          But we're all set.

                     FRAN
          All set for what?

                     SHELDRAKE
          I rented a car -- it's going to be here
          at one o'clock -- we're driving to
          Atlantic City.

                     FRAN
          Atlantic City?

                     SHELDRAKE
          I know it's a drag -- but you can't find
          a hotel room in town -- not on New Year's
          Eve.

                     FRAN
                (a long look at
                 Sheldrake)
          Ring out the old year, ring in the new.
          Ring-a-ding-ding.

                         SHELDRAKE
         I didn't plan it this way, Fran -- actually,
         it's all Baxter's fault.

                         FRAN
         Baxter?

                         SHELDRAKE
         He wouldn't give me the key to the
         apartment.

                         FRAN
         He wouldn't.

                         SHELDRAKE
         Just walked out on me -- quit -- threw
         that big fat job right in my face.

                         FRAN
                  (a faint smile)
         The nerve.

                         SHELDRAKE
         That little punk -- after all I did for
         him! He said I couldn't bring anybody
         to his apartment -- especially not Miss
         Kubelik. What's he got against you,
         anyway?

                         FRAN
                  (a faraway look in her eye)
         I don't know. I guess that's the way it
         crumbles -- cookie-wise.

                         SHELDRAKE
         What are you talking about?

                         FRAN
         I'd spell it out for you -- only I can't
         spell.

The piano player is consulting the watch on his upraised left
arm. He drops the arm in a signal, and the lights go out. At
the same time, he strikes up AULD LANG SYNE.

All over the dimly lit room, couples get to their feet,
embracing and joining in the song.

In the last booth, Sheldrake leans across the table, kisses Fran.

                          SHELDRAKE
     Happy New Year, Fran.

Fran's expression is preoccupied. Sheldrake faces in the
direction of the pianist, and holding his glass aloft, sings
along with the others.

As AULD LANG SYNE comes to an end, the place explodes noisily
-- there is a din of horns, ratchets, and shouted greetings.
The lights come up again.

In the last booth, Sheldrake turns back toward Fran -- but she
is no longer there. Her paper hat lies abandoned on her
vacated chair.

                          SHELDRAKE
     Fran --
               (looking around)
     -- where are you, Fran?

He rises, cranes his neck, trying to spot her in the crowd.

                                              DISSOLVE TO:

149. EXT. BROWNSTONE HOUSE -- NIGHT

     Fran, a coat thrown over the dress she was wearing at the
     Rickshaw, comes down the street almost at a run. There is a
     happy, expectant look on her face. She hurries up the steps
     of the house and through the front door.

150. INT. STAIRCASE AND SECOND FLOOR LANDING -- NIGHT

     Fran mounts the stairs eagerly. As she reaches the landing and
     heads for Bud's apartment, there is a loud, sharp report from
     inside.

     Fran freezes momentarily, then rushes to the door.

                          FRAN
          Mr. Baxter!
               (pounding on door)
          Mr. Baxter! Mr. Baxter!

     The door opens and there stands Bud, the bottle of champagne he
     has just uncorked still foaming over in his hand. He stares at
     Fran unbelievingly.

                              FRAN
                    (sagging with relief)
          Are you all right?

                              BUD
          I'm fine.

                              FRAN
          Are you sure? How's your knee?

                              BUD
          I'm fine all over.

                              FRAN
          Mind if I come in?

                              BUD
                    (still stunned)
          Of course not.

151.   INT. THE APARTMENT -- NIGHT

       Fran comes in and Bud shuts the door. The room is the same as
       we left it, except for an empty champagne glass standing on the
       coffee table.

                              BUD
          Let me get another glass.

       He goes to one of the cartons, takes out a champagne glass
       wrapped in newspaper, starts to unwrap it.

                              FRAN
                    (looking around)
          Where are you going?

                              BUD
          Who knows? Another neighborhood --
          another town -- another job -- I'm on
          my own.

                              FRAN
          That's funny -- so am I.
                    (Bud, pouring champagne,
                    looks up at her)
          What did you do with the cards?

                              BUD
                    (indicating carton)
          In there.

Fran takes the deck of cards and the gin rummy score pad out
of the carton, settles herself on the couch, starts to shuffle
the cards expertly.

                    BUD
          What about Mr. Sheldrake?

                         FRAN
          I'm going to send him a fruit cake every
          Christmas.

Bud sinks down happily on the couch, and Fran holds out the
deck to him.

                         FRAN
          Cut.

Bud cuts a card, but doesn't look at it.

                    BUD
          I love you, Miss Kubelik.

                         FRAN
                    (cutting a card)
          Seven --
                    (looking at Bud's card)
          -- queen.

She hands the deck to Bud.

                    BUD
          Did you hear what I said, Miss Kubelik?
          I absolutely adore you.

                         FRAN
                    (smiling)
          Shut up and deal!

Bud begins to deal, never taking his eyes off her. Fran
removes her coat, starts picking up her cards and arranging
them. Bud, a look of pure joy on his face, deals -- and
deals -- and keeps dealing.

And that's about it. Story-wise.

                                        FADE OUT.

                    THE END

the Misfits

1961—Seven Arts Productions; released
by United Artists
Director   John Huston
Script   Arthur Miller
Source   Original screenplay
Stars   Clark Gable, Marilyn Monroe, Montgomery Clift

At the beginning *The Misfits* looked to be a sure winner. It had an original script by Arthur Miller, winner of the Pulitzer Prize for theater (for *Death of a Salesman*, 1949); two New York Drama Critics' Circle Awards; and many other honors for his work in the theatre in such plays as *All My Sons*, *The Crucible*, and *A View From the Bridge*. He was at the peak of his career and reputation. *The Misfits* had the celebrated and honored director (who had also written and acted for films) whose credits included such films as the brilliant documentary from World War II, *The Battle of San Pietro* (1944), and feature films including *The Maltese Falcon* (1941), *The Treasure of Sierra Madre* (1947), *Key Largo* (1948), *The Asphalt Jungle* (1950), *The Red Badge of Courage* (1951), *The African Queen* (1951, with a script by James Agee), *Moulin Rouge* (1952), and the zany classic *Beat the Devil* (1954). He was a "legend" in the industry, and the legend had been at once exposed and made more widespread by Lillian Ross' devastating accounting, in *Picture*, of the making of *The Red Badge of Courage*.

   The Misfits had an impeccable cast of stars—Clark Gable, at the top of the heap; Miller's wife, Marilyn Monroe, "sex-goddess" and ready for her twenty-eighth feature film; the young and rising, intense and erratic Montgomery Clift.

Small wonder that the producer, Frank Taylor, matter-of-factly told a reporter for *Time,* "This is an attempt at the ultimate motion picture."

When the film was released, expectations were high indeed, perhaps too high; for the response of the reviewers was disappointment. "The premise is promising," Stanley Kauffmann wrote in *The New Republic.* But he concluded that *The Misfits* is finally unsuccessful both in its treatment of its subject and as a use of the film form. Roger Angell of *The New Yorker* called it "a dramatic failure of considerable dimensions," and defined it as "false and fundamentally uninteresting." *Time* was not hesitant in the least, opening with: "*The Misfits* is a dozen pictures rolled into one. Most of them, unfortunately, are terrible." *Newsweek* called it (perhaps in ironic echo of Frank Taylor's remark) "ultimately disappointing" and sought to suggest a reason—"Because its heart is not in the movies at all. *Misfits* is a writer's picture, philosophical and static—and it is a tribute to cast and director that they keep its true nature enjoyably hidden most of the way through." Even Bosley Crowther of the *New York Times* decided that "characters and theme do not congeal. There is a lot of absorbing detail in it, but it doesn't add up to a point." The anonymous critic of the *Daily News,* "Kate Cameron," was an exception, celebrating it on almost patriotic grounds: "After the long drought of vital American pictures one can now cheer, for *The Misfits* is so distinctly American nobody but an American could have made it."

Although a critical failure and not the great box-office success anticipated, *The Misfits* has survived both as a challenge to critical curiosity and for special historical reasons. It was, after all, to be the last completed picture of both Clark Gable and Marilyn Monroe. Interest in both these stars, as well as the late Montgomery Clift, continues and grows. And gradually the terms of critical appraisal are changing. Alexander Walker finds no difficulty in isolating the essential theme of the picture. In *Sex in the Movies,* he writes, "Please Don't Kill Anything is the message of the film: it is also the title of a story Arthur Miller once wrote for his wife." Michael Conway and Mark Ricci put it in more dramatic terms in *The Films of Marilyn Monroe.* "It is," they write, "a poignant conflict between a man and a woman in love, with each trying to maintain individual characteristics and preserve a fundamental way of life."

Perhaps *The Misfits* was much simpler in design than the critics could comprehend. Perhaps it was, in the sense of timing, premature. It failed at the time, but its final record is not complete.

The Script   The script bears the notation "Revised – September 1959," but is otherwise almost entirely clean of any changes or revisions. This script is not broken down into numbered master scenes. Except in a few spots, the conventions of separating the units—for example, the exterior and interior scenes and the camera setups and locations, are ignored. The script moves along, depending upon description and dialogue. Perhaps most noteworthy are bits and pieces of psychology of characterization indicated in description and in parentheses for crucial lines of dialogue, presented by Arthur Miller. These are rare in film scripts and indicate the distinguished playwright's awareness of the importance of the actors and his desire to control with some precision the exact nuances inherent in an action or a line of dialogue.

Credits Producer, Frank E. Taylor; Director, John Huston; Screenplay, Arthur Miller; Art Direction, Stephen Grimes; Music, Alex North; Photography, Russell Metty and Wimpy Rex; Editor, George Tomasini.

Cast		
	Gay Langland:	Clark Gable
	Roslyn Taber:	Marilyn Monroe
	Perce Howland:	Montgomery Clift
	Isabelle Steers:	Thelma Ritter
	Guido Delinni:	Eli Wallach
	Old Man in Bar:	James Barton
	Church Lady:	Estelle Winwood
	Roslyn's Husband:	Kevin McCarthy
	Young Boy in Bar:	Dennis Shaw
	Charles Steers:	Philip Mitchell
	Old Groom:	Walter Ramage
	Young Bride:	Peggy Barton
	Fresh Cowboy in Bar:	J. Lewis Smith
	Susan (at railroad station):	Marietta Tree
	Bartender:	Bobby LaSalle
	Man in Bar:	Ryall Bowker
	Ambulance Attendant:	Ralph Roberts

THE MISFITS

It is a little before nine o'clock of a weekday morning. The Camera
opens facing the beginning of an active main street in a medium-sized
town. Ahead and stretched above the street is a big banner on which
we read, "WELCOME TO RENO, THE BIGGEST LITTLE CITY IN THE WORLD."
The sun is shining.

The Camera moves ahead with a slight jerk -- we are inside a vehicle
but do not turn to see the driver. Through the windshield we see
the great neon signs of the gambling clubs -- all of them lit. We
are in traffic and in a moment halt at a corner for a light. Jazz
music is coming from our vehicle's radio.

Then, a very strained, polka-dot-dressed young girl carrying her
three-year-old daughter on her arm, comes up to the side window
of our vehicle. Both mother and child are dressed up and perspiring.
In an Oklahoma accent . . .

                         WOMAN
Am I headed right for the courthouse, Mister?

                         DRIVER'S VOICE
Straight on one block and then two left.

                         WOMAN
Thank you kindly. It's awfully confusin' here.

                         DRIVER'S VOICE
It sure is, Ma'm.

The Woman steps away and walks on and we can see her with her child
going along the sidewalk. Our vehicle moves now, but slowly in the
traffic, and we keep her in camera through our side window. The
jazz on the radio ends, and a hillbilly commentator is heard, while
we are still focused on the thin woman.

                         COMMENTATOR'S VOICE
Well, here's somethin' to think about while you're a-waitin' for
your vacuum-packed Rizdale Coffee to come to a boil. For the third
month a-runnin', we've beat out Las Vegas. Four hundred and eleven
divorces have been granted as of yesterday compared to 391 for
Vegas. No doubt about it, pardners, we are the Divorce Capital of
the World. And speakin' of divorce; would you like to cut loose

COMMENTATOR'S VOICE (Cont.)
of a bad habit? How about rootin' yourself out of that chair and
gettin' over to Haber's Drug Store and treat yourself to a good
night's sleep with good old Dream-E-Z?

As the above proceeds, the Camera has been enlarging its vision; in
a knot of people it has picked out another woman -- better dressed
than the first, perhaps haughty -- and utterly alone. Then another,
only a girl, but clearly in a hurry to an important moment; despite
the hour she is dressed up -- and her face strained. The street
becomes not merely populated, but from it has been selected the
women -- alone. We catch one through the window of a supermarket,
a grocery bag in one arm, yanking a slot machine handle with the
other. Another woman, suitcase in hand, is asking directions of a
cop. A couple-in-love is caught staring at bridal gowns in a store
window, beside which is a lawyer's shingle and the legend, "Divorce
Actions." Our Vehicle now turns off the busy main street, and we
are going down a tree-lined street, almost suburban, the houses very
small, some of them frayed and nearly poor. Here there is a peaceful,
almost somnolent quality of a hot Nevada day. As we turn . . .

COMMENTATOR'S VOICE
Now naturally we don't claim to provide you with any special type
of dream, friends. Dream-E-Z's only one of them names they made up
back East in ·New York. But it does work. I can rightly swear your
sleepless nights are over; you get that dream ready, and we'll give
you the sleep. Dream-E-Z's a real little bottle of rest, folks,
and relaxation, and peace. Put that burden down, Mother; Daddy? --
let yourself go. Dream-E-Z. Come on folks, let's get together
here . . . say it with me now like we always do . . . all
together . . .

(A mass of violins soars into a
music of wafting sleep)

Dream -- Eeeeee --- Zzzzzzeeeee . . .

The vehicle comes to a halt at the curb and the engine is shut off
and the radio with it.

Guido emerges from what we see now is a tow truck. He is cleanly
dressed in work pants and shirt. Referring to an address on a paper
in his hand, he goes up the stoop of a house, rings the bell.

As he waits, a gigantic passenger plane flies low over the house.
Guido looks up, and we see the mixture of expert appraisal and

longing in his eyes. The door at his back opens. Isabelle appears.
She is a sixty-year-old tomboy, rather timid, ready for humor,
incompetent, and slightly ashamed of herself. She is in a wrapper,
with straight bobbed hair in the manner of the twenties. She drinks,
and it is very early in the morning for her. She is sober now.

                        GUIDO
Mrs. Taber live here? I'm supposed to look at her car.

                        ISABELLE
Oh sure. You just wait right there . . .
                    (Glancing at her wrapper, then up
                    and down the street, giggling)
Oh, I guess it's all right.
                    (She descends past him down the
                    stoop. Now we see she has one arm
                    in a sling. HE follows)
They say things anyway. Now don't rush me, I just busted it and I'm
not going to do it again. I made up my mind. There now, where is
that car?
                    (She looks at driveway)
Oh, yes, it's in the garage. Follow me, just keep right behind me.
I hope you're going to be generous with her. I hope you're not the
kind to be miserly. She's a dear sweet person, Mrs. Taber.

                        GUIDO
Is that it?

They have halted, looking at a car which is sticking out of the
garage behind the house. It is a new shiny Cadillac convertible.
But every fender is smashed in, the trunk is warped, bumpers bent.

                        ISABELLE
Don't you be put off by appearances, young man. Keep your mind open.
As open as can be.

Guido walks along the car, opens the door, looks in at the speedometer,
then quickly sticks his head out, and incredulously . . .

                        GUIDO
Twenty-three miles!?

                        ISABELLE
Now you just pay attention. She only took one ride in it six weeks
ago and it's been sittin' there since.

ISABELLE (Cont.)
(Intimately)
You know the men in this town -- they kept runnin' in to her just to
start a conversation.

(GUIDO looks doubtful)

Bang, bang, bang! -- terrible! It was a divorce present from her
husband, don't y'know, so it's no great loss.

GUIDO
(He has bent over to look at a tire)
They giving presents for divorces now?!

ISABELLE
(With great innocence and feeling)
Why not! On the anniversary of our divorce, my husband has never
failed to send me a potted yellow rose, and it'll be nineteen years
July. The heart's a tricky little thing, young fella. Of course
he never paid me the alimony, but I wouldn't care to put a man out
anyway.

From above Roslyn's voice is heard calling, "Isabelle? Iz?" Isabelle
looks up at a screened window on the second floor.

ISABELLE
Coming right up, dear! I'm outside!
(To Guido)
Now you be your most generous self, 'cause she's got to start a new
life now, you know.

With which Isabelle starts into the back door of the house, favoring
her broken arm.

GUIDO
. . . You break your arm in the car?

ISABELLE
Oh no. I . . . my last roomer before Mrs. Taber -- we celebrated
her divorce and I . . . misbehaved.
(Suddenly ashamed and angry at her
position)
I'm just so sick and tired of myself!

Almost in tears she vanishes into the house. Guido looks up at the
screened window above; he can faintly hear Roslyn talking and for an
instant she passes close enough to the window screen for him to see
her outline, then she vanishes.

Guido goes down the driveway to his truck, leans over to pick up a
battery, and a Saint's medal swings out of his shirt and brushes
the battery pole and makes a quick vicious spark. He jumps back,
examines the medal, which is superimposed on a crucifix whose tip
has been charred. He puts it back in his shirt, carries the battery
up the driveway toward Roslyn's car, his black, questioning eyes
looking up toward the second floor.

Isabelle is opening the door of Roslyn's room on the second floor.

                          ISABELLE
It's after nine, dear girl!

She enters the room which is in chaos; bureau drawers hang open, the
bed is a mess, covered with letters, a few magazines, toilet articles,
hair curlers. From the closet Roslyn calls:

                          ROSLYN
I can't find it! Did you move it somewhere?

                          ISABELLE
It's the heat, dear -- I'm always losing things in hot weather!
What'd you lose?

Roslyn emerges from the closet, going straight to a bureau where
she turns things over, searching. She is well-brushed, in a light
print dress.

                          ROSLYN
My answers. I've got to have my answers!

                          ISABELLE
Oh my, your answers! What's that?

Isabelle spots a slip of paper sticking out of a mirror frame.

                              ROSLYN
There it is!   Here.   Ask me.

Isabelle sits on the bed with the slip of paper; Roslyn makes up her
face at the mirror as the catechism proceeds.

                              ISABELLE
Now let's see.   "Did your husband, Mr. Raymond Taber, act toward you
with cruelty?"

                              ROSLYN
Well . . . yes.

                              ISABELLE
Just say yes.

                              ROSLYN
Yes.

                              ISABELLE
"In what ways did his cruelty manifest itself?"

                              ROSLYN
He . . . How's it go again?

                              ISABELLE
          (Reading)
"He persistently and cruelly ignored my personal rights and wishes, and
resorted on several occasions to physical violence against me."

                              ROSLYN
He persistently and cruelly ignored my . . .
          (She breaks off, troubled)
Must I say that? It wasn't that way, exactly. I mean he just didn't
understand anything.

                              ISABELLE
You can't get a divorce for that reason. Just answer the questions
the way your lawyer wrote them and it'll all be over in five minutes.
He did beat up on you, didn't he?

                              ROSLYN
Yes, but he . . . People don't know what they're doing, Isabelle. It
wasn't only that he beat up on me . . . he just wasn't <u>there</u>. You
know what I mean? I mean you could touch him, but he wasn't there.

ISABELLE

Darling child, if that was grounds for divorce there'd be about
eleven marriages left in the United States. Now just repeat . . .

A car horn blows below. Isabelle hurries to the window. From the
driveway Guido talks up to her.

GUIDO

They'll call in their estimate from the office.

ROSLYN
(Going to the window, calling down)
Those bumps weren't my fault, you know!

Guido now sees Roslyn for the first time, still behind the window
screen, but more or less clearly. He is smiling, strangely embarrassed.

GUIDO

I'll recommend the best price I can, Miss. You can drive her now, I
put a battery in.

ROSLYN

Oh, I'll never drive that car again.

GUIDO

I'll give you a lift in my truck if you're leavin' right away.

ROSLYN

Swell! Two minutes!
(To Isabelle in the room)
Get dressed, Iz, you got to be my witness!

ISABELLE

This'll be my seventy-seventh time I've witnessed for a divorce. Two
sevens is lucky, darlin'.

ROSLYN

Oh, Iz, I hope!

Roslyn smiles, but fear and a puzzled consternation remain in her eyes.

We cut to the interior of the truck, Guido driving, Isabelle in the
middle, and Roslyn at the window studying her answers and reading her
lines to herself.

                                    GUIDO
I went to school for a while about a hundred miles from Chicago.

                                  ISABELLE
                    (ROSLYN returns to her memorizing)
Oh! You a college man?

                                    GUIDO
That was medical school.

                                  ROSLYN
                    (Turns curiously)
You a doctor?

                                    GUIDO
No, I got drafted. . . . And a couple of other things.   Going back East
right away?

                                  ROSLYN
                    (Shrugs)
I don't know.   All I could think about here was when my six weeks
would be up.

                                    GUIDO
Don't you have family back there?

                                  ROSLYN
No.   I don't have anybody.

                                    GUIDO
That's lucky.

                                  ROSLYN
Why is it lucky?

                                    GUIDO
I always prefer dealing with strangers.   Kinda leaves you free.

                                  ISABELLE
Spoken like a true Reno man!

                                    GUIDO
                    (As THEY chuckle)
Here's your courthouse.
                    (Brings car to a halt)
My name is Guido.   Guido Delinni.

ROSLYN
(Opening her door)
I'm Roslyn Taber . . . or rather . . . Well, I guess I'm still Roslyn
Taber.

GUIDO
If you're not leaving town right away I'd be glad to take you out and
show you the country. There's some beautiful country once you get
out of this town.

ROSLYN
Thanks anyway. I don't know what I'm going to do, though.

Roslyn gets out. Then, as Isabelle is sliding out . . .

ISABELLE
My name is Isabelle Steers.

GUIDO
(He laughs at her jibe)
Okay, Isabelle. You could come along if you like.

ISABELLE
That's a sweet afterthought! Oh you Reno men!
(She laughs and goes)

Guido stares out after them as they walk across the paved paths that
section the grass in front of the courthouse. Men on park-benches
look up at Roslyn as she passes; men turn as she goes by. The young
polka-dot woman carrying her baby is shaking hands with a lawyer on the
courthouse steps. They part. Gaunt-eyed, the woman passes Roslyn.

We truck in front of Roslyn and Isabelle as they approach the steps of
the court; Roslyn is rapidly going over her lines from her prompt
paper. Her anxiety is tight now.

ROSLYN
I can't memorize this; it's not the way it was.

ISABELLE
You take everything so seriously, dear! Just say it; it doesn't have
to be true. It's not a quiz show, it's only a court.

They start up the courthouse steps, and as Roslyn looks up after putting her paper away, she is stopped by what she sees. A man is descending the steps toward her. Well-built, tall, about thirty-eight, soft straw hat and a tie with a big design. His mind is constantly trying to tune in on the world but the message is never clear -- he feels self-conscious now, having to plead; he was successful early in life and this pleading threatens his dignity. He expects that the simple fact of his having come here will somehow convince his wife how guilty she is. But he will forgive her and she will idolize him again. He is Raymond Taber, her husband. He manages a hurt, embarrassed grin.

                         TABER
Just got off the plane. I'm not too late, am I?

She looks at him; a rising fear for herself holds her silent. He comes up to her.

                         ROSLYN
Don't, Raymond. Please, I don't want to hear anything.

                         TABER
          (Downing his resentment)
Give me five minutes, will you? After two years, five minutes isn't . . .

                         ROSLYN
          (With a climactic, quivering intensity)
I don't want to hear it. You can't have me, so now you want me. That's all. Please . . . I'm not blaming you. I just never saw it any different. I mean I don't <u>believe</u> in the whole thing.

                         TABER
Kid, I understand what . . .

                         ROSLYN
You don't understand it, because nobody understands it!
          (With her finger she presses his
          chest)
You aren't <u>there</u>, Raymond!
          (She steps back)
If I'm going to be alone, I want to be alone by myself. . . . I always was, anyway. Go back, Raymond -- you're not going to make me sorry for you any more.

She leaves him standing there in an impotent fury and goes to Isabelle who puts her arms around her; and Roslyn is inwardly quaking with sobs, but she will not cry, and they ascend the steps together.

We cut to Guido in his truck. From his viewpoint we see Roslyn going up the courthouse steps with Isabelle's arm comfortingly around her while the ex-husband furiously looks on. Guido sees that Isabelle is giving Roslyn a handkerchief to wipe away her tears as they disappear into the building.

Guido is staring in puzzlement, attracted and above all fascinated. He starts the truck and drives away.

Guido has come to a halt at the railroad tracks which cross Main Street. His eye catches a nearby man who is kissing a woman preparatory to putting her aboard the train. This is Gay. Guido calls to Gay who turns and yells back . . .

                    GAY
I been lookin' for you! Wait up for me!

We are close in now on Gay and the departing woman.

                    GAY
Good luck, now, Susan. I hope you find somebody you like real soon.

                    SUSAN
Promise you'll think about it, Gay. It's the second largest laundry in St. Louis.

                    GAY
I just ain't cut out for it, Susan. But thanks anyway.

          (CONDUCTOR calls "All aboard")

Best get aboard now . . .

                    SUSAN
Gay! How am I going to live without you! If I write to you will you answer?

                    GAY
Most likely. Now be a good sport and get aboard. Go ahead, Honey.
          (Gets her onto the step)
That's a girl! So long, Sue, it sure was pleasant!

        (The train moves and SHE stands
        appealingly weeping, as she disappears)

Gay ambles along the tracks and with Margaret, his dog, he gets into
the truck. Gay is weary and slumps in his seat.

                GUIDO

Which one was that?

                GAY

The laundry. One of the best things about knowin' a woman is sayin'
goodbye. Leaves things so restful.

The train clears the tracks and they drive.

        (HE spits out the window, sighs)

                GAY

She _was_ appreciative, though. . . . good sport.
        (Stretches)
I could sleep for about three days and a half and then rest up for a
month or two.

        (GUIDO smiles; it excites him)

What say we get out in the country, Guido? I was about to look you
up, soon as she left.

                GUIDO

I been thinking about it myself, but I don't know.

                GAY

Seems to me you been more than a month holdin' down that job. That's
just about your limit, fella.

                GUIDO

I'd like to get about five hundred before I take off this time. I'd
like to get a brand new engine.

                GAY

Why? That engine'll fly you anywhere. That's a good airplane you
got there, Guido.
        (With new vigor)
Pack yourself up tonight, and let's get out in those mountains! I
long for some fresh air and no damned people, male or female. . . .
Maybe we do a little mustangin' up there, what do you say?

Guido pulls up before a used-car lot. He is moved even as he speaks.

                         GUIDO
I just saw a hell of a lookin' woman, Gay. Sweet enough to eat.

They get out of the truck, Guido talking as they enter a small auto
repair shed.

                         GAY
          (Grinning; but he shows a certain
          respectful restraint)
Why, you old rabbit you -- I don't believe I _ever_ saw you worked up
over a woman! You know where she lives?

                         GUIDO
          (Idly spinning a gear with his
          finger, a deep uneasiness permeating
          his shy smile)
Yeah, but . . . I don't know, there's always so damn much useless talk
you gotta go through.

                         GAY
It ain't the talkin' I mind, it's buyin' the drinks. Whyn't you get
her to come out in the country? Things move ahead a lot faster out
there. Go ahead -- you gettin' awful moody, boy.

                         GUIDO
          (With an indecisive decision)
I'll meet you over the bar later, talk about it.

                         GAY
Good enough -- and let's go for mustangs soon, huh? You had enough
wages for this year -- you gonna git the habit you don't watch out.

                         GUIDO
See ya.

Gay ambles out of the shop, followed by the dog. We are left with a
disturbed dream in Guido's face.

We cut to a shot of the fast-moving river which flows under Main
Street; we see it from the railing bordering the street. It is near
noon. Roslyn and Isabelle are walking along and Isabelle stops.

                         ISABELLE
Throw in your ring.

                         ROSLYN
               (She looks at her wedding ring;
               puzzled)
Why?

                         ISABELLE
It's a custom. If you throw it in you'll never have a divorce
again.

               (ROSLYN hesitates, turning her ring)

There's more gold in that river than the Klondike. Go ahead, honey,
everybody does it.

                         ROSLYN
               (With a certain revulsion)
Did you do it?

                         ISABELLE
Oh no, I lost mine on my honeymoon, and I never got time to buy
another.

                         ROSLYN
Let's get a drink!

                         ISABELLE
That's my girl!

They go into a bar and sit at a table. Roslyn is suddenly grateful
for Isabelle's company.

                         ROSLYN
I don't know what I would've done without you, Iz. You're practically
the only woman who was ever my friend.
               (To the WAITER, who appears)
Scotch and ice.

                         ISABELLE
Rye and water.

The waiter goes. There is a pause. Roslyn looks around the near-empty
bar.

                              ISABELLE
Cheer up, dear, you're free!

                              ROSLYN
          (Smiles uncertainly)
I know, I just hate to fight with anybody, that's all. I hate it.
I mean, even if I win I lose. In my heart, you know?

          (WAITER brings drinks. THEY toast)

                              ISABELLE
To freedom, Roslyn!

                              ROSLYN
          (With more of resolve than free
          joy, she raises her glass)
Yes! To freedom.
          (ROSLYN drinks deeply, inhales)
You see, darling, it's just you're not used to it yet.

                              ROSLYN
That's just the trouble. . . . I am. I never had anybody, and here
I am again. And I feel like I walked all the way.

                              ISABELLE
Well you had your mother, though, didn't you?

                              ROSLYN
I guess she had me, but I never had her. She never knew how to do it,
you know? She meant well, I guess, but . . . I mean she'd go off with
a patient and . . . I guess to her a month wasn't so much longer than a
week, but to a kid it matters. A mother should show up when she
promises. . . . What are we talking about her for?
          (She drinks, again. Inhales)

                              ISABELLE
Your father sounds wonderful.

                              ROSLYN
Oh, I say so but I don't know. I just remember him when I was very
little. He'd come wherever we happened to be living and he'd fix
everything. Doorknobs, and the dripping faucets. And I used to stand
by his leg and just watch. And when everything got fixed . . . he
would take off.
          (Laughs)
People are always disappearing . . ! Once he picked me up and sat me
on the table, and I don't remember what he said, but I remember how it
felt, y'know? Holding my hands and talking to me. I can still feel
it. . . . I guess you just can't blame anybody.

                              ISABELLE
Oh, no, you can't blame anybody.

                              ROSLYN
                    (Suddenly reaches across and grasps
                    ISABELLE's hand)
You're a fine woman, Isabelle. You really are. I'm thankful to you.

                              ISABELLE
Oh, I'm nothin'; just an old ·first-wife -- town is full of 'em. I hope
you're not going to leave. 'Cause you might find yourself here.
'Cause the wonderful thing about this town is it's always full of
interesting strangers.

                              ROSLYN
That's all I've known, Isabelle. Interesting strangers.

                              ISABELLE
You could teach dancing here. There is a school, you know . . . make
nice money.

                              ROSLYN
I never worry about money -- I always made my way . . . What *is* there?
Does anybody know? I mean . . . the whole thing . . . is . . .

                    (Tears are springing into her eyes.
                    ISABELLE anxiously strokes her hand,
                    fearful Roslyn will sob)

                              ISABELLE
Oh, dear girl, I'm so sorry . . .

                              ROSLYN
I suddenly miss my mother. Isn't that the stupidest thing?
                    (She covers her face, but quickly
                    looks up, trying to smile)
Let's have another drink!
                    (She turns for the waiter and sees
                    Margaret, Gay's dog, sitting patiently
                    at the foot of the bar)
Oh, look at that dear dog! How sweet it sits there!

                              ISABELLE
Yeah, dogs are nice.

Now, looking again toward the dog, she and Isabelle see Gay placing a
glass of water before Margaret. Margaret drinks. Gay glances at the
two women, nods just for hello, and as he straightens up to turn back

to the bar, Guido enters, dressed in a clean shirt now and dress
trousers. Guido sees Roslyn and comes over as Gay starts to greet
him.

                              GUIDO
Oh, hello! How'd you make out?

                              ROSLYN
                    (Shyly)
Okay. It's all over.

                              GUIDO
                    (He nods, uncertain how to proceed,
                    and beckons GAY over in part as a
                    relief for his tension)
Like you to meet a friend of mine. This is Gay Langland. Mrs.
Taber . . .

                              GAY
                    (Realizing she is the one)
Oh! How de do.

                              GUIDO
                    (Of Isabelle, not remembering her
                    name)
And this is . . .

                              ISABELLE
Isabelle Steers.
                    (To Roslyn)
One thing about Western men, they do remember the name.

                    (THEY laugh. To Gay -- she loves
                    new people)

You look familiar, Mister. I think you called on a girl was living
in my house. About a year ago?

                              GAY
What street?

                              ISABELLE
Sutter.

                              GAY
Sutter? That's possible. Yeah, I believe I did call around Sutter.

                              ISABELLE
Whyn't you boys sit down?

                              GAY
Well, thank you. Sit down, Guido. Waiter? What're you girls drinkin'?

                              ISABELLE
Whiskey. We're celebrating the jail burned down.

                              GAY
          (To the Waiter)
Get four doubles.

                              GUIDO
I got you a good price on your car, I think. Boss'll be calling you
up later about it.

                              ROSLYN
Oh, thanks.
          (GUIDO's intensely searching stare
          forces her to Gay, to whom she says . . .)
You a mechanic too?

          (The WAITER serves the drinks)

                              ISABELLE
Him? He's a cowboy.

                              GAY
          (Grinning)
How'd you know?

                              ISABELLE
I can smell, can't I?

                              GAY
You can't smell cows on me.

                              ISABELLE
I can smell the look in your face, Cowboy.
          (She reaches across and laughs)
I love 'em, though! Nothin' like a cowboy! I had a cowboy friend . . .
          (She quickly sips)
He had one arm gone, but he was more with one arm than any man with two.
I mean like cooking . . .

          (THEY laugh)

I'm serious! He could throw a whole frying pan full of chops in the
air and they'd all come down on the other side. Of course, you're all
good-for-nothin' -- as you know.

                              GAY
Well, good-for-nothin' may not be much, but it's better than wages.

GUIDO

I suppose you're headin' back East now, huh?

ROSLYN

I don't know. I'm just trying to make up my mind.

GUIDO

I'd be sorry to see you go so soon.

GAY

She's probably got a business, or somethin' . . .

ROSLYN

(Surprised)
Me?! Why'd you think I had a business?

GAY

No reason. Just that you meet so many have a business back home,
or an office -- y'know, lady-lawyers, dentists, certified public
accountants, writers. You a writer?

ROSLYN

Me?! I didn't even finish high school!

GAY

(Wryly)
Well, that's real <u>good</u> news.

ROSLYN

(Laughs)
Why? -- don't you like educated women?

GAY

Oh, I don't mind 'em. But I've known some could ask so many questions
it dried out my mouth keepin' up with 'em. Always wantin' to know what
you're <u>thinkin'</u>. There sure must be a load of thinkin' goin' around
back East.

ROSLYN

Well . . . maybe they're trying to get to know you better.
(Wryly)
You don't mind that, do you?

GAY

I don't at all,
(Laughs)
. . . but did you ever get to know a man by askin' him questions?

                         ROSLYN
You mean, he's going to lie.

                          GAY
Well he might not -- but then again, he just might!

          (THEY laugh)

It's a little bit like a horse, ain't it? You can talk about him,
you can talk to him . . . but if you gonna know him you gotta get on
and ride.

                        ISABELLE
Till he throws you off.

                          GAY
Well, as the man said, that's the nature of the beast.

                         ROSLYN
And anyway, there's always another horse, isn't there?

                          GAY
          (With a certain sympathy toward her)
Yes, Ma'm, I guess there always is.

                        ISABELLE
And some are real nice too --- so let's get another drink!

                         ROSLYN
          (A relaxed pleasure stirring in her)
Sure, let's have some more!

                          GAY
Can't see a bit of harm in that.
          (Calls)
Fella? See if you can get us four more, will ya?
          (To Guido, relaxed and happy --
          trying to open the way)
How about it, Pilot? We takin' out of this town today?

                         GUIDO
          (Spurred to open his campaign -- and
          a little awkward)
You been out of Reno at all, Mrs. Taber?

                         ROSLYN
Well, I walked to the edge of town once and looked out, but -- it looks
like nothing's there.

                              GAY
That might just be where everything is.

                            ROSLYN
Like what?

                              GAY
The country.

                            ROSLYN
What do you do there?

                              GAY
Only thing you <u>can</u> do there -- live.

                            ROSLYN
          (To Guido)
You work here, though, don't you?

                            GUIDO
Just long enough to get back out there again. I quit just now.

                              GAY
You did?! That's the boy!
          (To Roslyn)
Whyn't you do yourself a favor? Take a ride out with us. It's only
fifty miles; we'd bring you back tonight.

                            ROSLYN
You have a farm or something?

                              GAY
Y'know, it's peculiar thing. When you tell people that you just live,
they don't know what you're talkin' about.

                            ROSLYN
          (Drawn in, she searches his eyes)
Well how can you . . . just live?

                              GAY
Well . . . you start by going to sleep. Next step is you get up when
you feel like it. Then you scratch yourself.

          (THEY chuckle)

Fry yourself some eggs, see what kind of day it is, throw a stone, ride
a horse, read the paper, visit, whistle, get some groceries . . . It'll
come to you soon as you get rid of the feelin' that somebody's chasin'
you or you gotta chase somebody else.

                              ROSLYN
                    (Her eyes meet his; he has challenged
                    her)
I know what you mean.

                              ISABELLE
Might be nice, dear, whyn't you go out for a ride?

                              GUIDO
If it hit you right I've got an empty house out there you could
have. . . . I don't live there myself, but it's yours if you want a
little rest before you go back. I'd rent it to you cheap, if you
wanted to stay a while.

                              ROSLYN
                    (Grinning)
Oh, is the last woman gone now?

                              GUIDO
                    (Flushing)
No! No kidding, I've never rented it before.
                    (With a sudden self-exposure that is
                    difficult for him)
I never offered it, before.

                              ROSLYN
Well thanks. I wouldn't stay there, but I <u>was</u> thinking of renting a
car and seeing what the country . . .

                              GUIDO
                    (Excitedly)
Gay's got a truck, or I could get my car.

                              ROSLYN
No. Then you'll have to drive me back.

                              GUIDO
Oh, I don't mind!

                              ROSLYN
No, I always . . . like my own. But thanks . . .
                    (A little flustered at having to
                    stand against him, she touches his
                    hand)
I mean I always like to . . . feel I'm on my own, y'know? Because I
always used to be, and I don't intend to be any different again. I'll
rent a car. Where can I?

GAY

Right now?

ROSLYN

Why not?

GAY
(Standing -- enthusiastically)
Okay! You sure don't waste your time, do you!

ROSLYN
(Standing, and with a laugh)
Always have! -- but not any more, if I can help it!

We cut to an endless vista of the bare, vacant Nevada hills. Now a
highway --- straight, white, lonely. Gay's battered truck is on it;
following behind, a three-year-old station wagon.

We shoot inside the station wagon. Roslyn is driving, Isabelle
beside her. Roslyn is constantly turning to stare out.

ROSLYN

What's behind those hills?

ISABELLE

Hills.

ROSLYN

What's that beautiful smell? It's like some kind of green perfume.

ISABELLE

Sage, darling.

ROSLYN

Is that sage! I always wondered what sage was! Oh, Isabelle -- it's
beautiful, isn't it?

ISABELLE

Oh, it's just bare, beat-up range country, honey.
(After a pause looking out)
I better tell you something about cowboys, dear.

ROSLYN
(Laughs warmly)
You really worry about me, don't you!

                              ISABELLE
You're too believing, dear.   Cowboys are the best men in the world.
I know.   Providin' you don't expect they're gonna be there tomorrow.
They're the last real men and as reliable as jackrabbits.

                              ROSLYN
                    (After a hesitation)
You think I'm reliable, Isabelle?

                              ISABELLE
I imagine with a man you'd be.

                              ROSLYN
Not always.
                    (Shyly)
In fact, mostly not, I think.   I mean I never stay when it comes time
to go, y'know?

                              ISABELLE
Well you probably never had anybody to be reliable <u>to</u>.

                              ROSLYN
Maybe I have, I don't know.   I've had some awful things said to me;
sometimes I wonder if maybe they're true, some of them.

                              ISABELLE
You haven't been understood yet, Roslyn.

                              ROSLYN
Is there such a thing?

                              ISABELLE
                    (Conceding . . .)
Well, it's supposed to be -- you read about it.

                              ROSLYN
I'd like to see it once.
                    (With sudden energy)
Let's enjoy ourselves today!   I just want to look at everything.   I'm
not going to care about a thing but seeing everything there is to see!

Cut to the truck.   Guido is driving.

                              GAY
Thanks for drivin', Guido.   I feel like a head full of cotton.

                    GUIDO
          (In his own world)
I couldn't hear what he said to her but . . .
          (Glances at Gay for corroboration)
He looked like <u>she</u> left <u>him</u>. The husband.

                    GAY
Most likely. Good-lookin' woman's harder to hold than money.

                    GUIDO
          (In his own inner, troubled world)
She's kind of hard to figure out, y'know? One minute she looks dumb
and brand new. Like a kid. But maybe he caught her knockin'
around. . . . What do you think? You know more about women than I
do. I kind of like her but I can't figure her.

                    GAY
Nobody knows nothin' about women, Pilot, and the man that says he
does, knows less. I just go with it, that's all, and if it don't
go, I go elsewhere. Let me take a nap now.
          (He curls up with his back to Guido.
          Slight pause)

                    GUIDO
She sure <u>moves</u>, doesn't she?

                    GAY
Mm, yeah. She's real prime.

Now the camera comes around and shoots Gay's face. Instead of being
asleep, as he seems to be, his eyes are open, and he is calculating.

Dissolve on Gay's face to a long shot of both vehicles moving along
the highway. Now the truck turns off and climbs a narrow, rock-strewn
trail into the side hills.

We now see Roslyn and Isabelle in the station wagon, bouncing up the
steep path. Roslyn is wide-eyed as the hills envelop them. There
is even a suggestion of trepidation in her, but above all she seems
to be moving into a newness.

The truck pulls up before Guido's former home. The building, a rather
modern, ranch-style affair, is still without some of its sheathing
boards, which lie in a pile on the ground with weeds twisting around
and through them. Beside the house is a concrete slab for a garage;
weeds are sprouting through its cracks. The house is at the head
of the trail. All get out. The men come to Roslyn, who gets out of

her car and looks at the house with a certain excitement. Guido is
taking a key packet out of his pocket.

                              ROSLYN
Why isn't it finished?

                              GUIDO
          (Cryptically)
It's weathertight. Come on in.

They follow him to the front door. He reaches up and unlocks --
there is no step yet. He hops up the two-and-a-half-foot rise and
reaches down and pulls her up, then Isabelle, then Gay hops up.

We scan the interior. The place is strangely somber. There is a
motley assortment of living-room furniture, a finished stone fireplace
going through the roof; Indian blankets are spread over some chairs
and the couch. Bare studs mark where the kitchen wall should be, and
the appliances seem to stand in the living room. Nevertheless,
Roslyn is somehow excited. Gay pulls coverings off the chairs to
show her how nice it all is, and looks in the kerosene can and reports
that it's almost full and she can start cooking right off. Roslyn
asks where the bedroom is, and Guido takes her to the door of the
only room with finished partitions, and with a heightened intensity
which she notices in him but cannot interpret, he opens the door and
they go in.

The bedroom is finished but rather bare, and over the double bed is a
photograph of Guido and his wife.

                              ROSLYN
Oh, it's nice! Who's that woman?

                              GUIDO
My wife. She died here.

                              ROSLYN
          (With shock)
Oh! . . .

                              GUIDO
She was due to have a baby. I was up setting the top stones into the
chimney, and . . . she screamed, and that was that.

                              ROSLYN
You don't live here, huh?

                              GUIDO
I stay at my sister's a couple miles away. It's a nice house, just
needs a little finishing. There's a view from every window. Look.

He takes her to a window. The trail descends to the highway, beyond
which is the endless, hill-pocked range and the horizon.

                              ROSLYN
Couldn't you call the doctor?

                              GUIDO
She didn't seem to be that sick. Then I got a flat and didn't have
a spare. . . . Everything just happened wrong. It does that sometimes.

                              ROSLYN
Oh, I know. Couldn't you live here again?

                              GUIDO
I could no more live here than I could in a grave.
          (He senses her sympathy, and to a
          certain degree, he cultivates it now)
We knew each other since we were seven years old, see.
          (He smiles at himself)
We got engaged when we were ten.

                              ROSLYN
Really? You should find another girl -- you'll make somebody a good
husband.

                              GUIDO
          (Calling on her evident sympathy)
I don't know. Being with anybody else, it just seems . . . wrong you
know? She wasn't _like_ other women. Stood behind me hundred percent;
uncomplaining as a tree.

                              ROSLYN
          (She senses an invidious comparison;
          she laughs lightly, and still in sympathy)
Maybe if you understood tree language you'd have got the doctor
sooner.
          (Quickly adding -- in view of his
          surprise)
I mean it's possible, y'know? I mean you shouldn't look for somebody
so perfect, because nobody _really_ is. They'll maybe _seem_ so but . . .
I mean no woman's like a tree, Guido . . . I mean, not _really_, you
know?

ROSLYN (Cont.)
(Suddenly striving for a gayety --
and pardon, she takes his arm, starting him out of the room)
Come!   Show me the rest of it! -- it's beautiful!

(THEY emerge into the living room
area. GAY is sprawled on the couch,
ISABELLE is holding up an Indian
blanket to examine it)

Isn't it beautiful here, Iz?

ISABELLE
It'd be perfect if somebody'd go out in the car and get the bottle of
whiskey I bought with my own money.

GUIDO
Hey, that's right!

(Glad for the reprieve, he hops down,
out the front door. ROSLYN wanders
about the room, touching things)

GAY
Glasses are in the kitchen, Isabelle --- I'm real tired.

ISABELLE
No, darling, you're just a cowboy; -- you fellas won't get up unless
it's rainin' down your neck.

(GAY laughs as SHE goes into the
kitchen area. HE turns and watches
ROSLYN, who has halted at a window
to look out. HE runs his eyes over
her back, her legs)

GAY
Too rough for you, Roslyn?

ROSLYN
Oh, I don't mind that. But it could've been fixed up beautifully.

GAY
Whyn't you go ahead and do it?

ROSLYN
(Looking about; shrugging)

Gay's interest is heightened; Isabelle feels a little ashamed and ineffectual; Guido is slightly frightened and drawn to her. And because there is no one here to receive her meaning as she intends it, she suddenly . . .

                    ROSLYN
Is there a phonograph or a radio?! Let's get some music!

                    GUIDO
There's no electricity.

                    ROSLYN
How about the car radio!

                    GAY
          (Surprised)
Now who'd've thought of that! Turn it on, Guido!

Guido excitedly rushes out, hopping down to the ground.

                    GAY
How about another drink, Roslyn . . . it'll keep the first one warm.

                    ROSLYN
I'd love it!

          (The car engine is heard starting
          outside)

                    ISABELLE
Think I'll make a sandwich! How about you people!

          (ISABELLE goes into the kitchen area.
          GAY, alone with ROSLYN, pours a drink
          into her glass, and quietly)

                    ROSLYN
Okay!

                    GAY
I hope you're going to stay here. Any chance?

                    ROSLYN
          (Her face filling with a sadness that
          approaches a self-abandonment -- thus,

                    ROSLYN (Cont.)
          she smiles)
Why? What difference would it make?

                    GAY
Might make all the difference in the world as time goes by.

                    ROSLYN
          (With the inner intensity of a searcher)
Why? You don't care about anything, do you?

               (Music is heard from out the door.
               The engine is shut off outside)

                    GAY
Sure do. Some things. But that don't mean it has to make a difference
to anybody else. Like to dance?

                    ROSLYN
Okay.

Gay takes her in his arms. He is a fair dancer. Guido enters, and is
rather caught in midair by this progress.

                    ROSLYN
          (Calling over Gay's shoulder to Guido)
Thanks, Guido! --- Iz, give Guido another drink! It's a very nice
house!

Isabelle comes out of the kitchen area. Guido goes around them and
forces an interest in stoking up the fire. In his face, seen in the
firelight, there is rapid, planning thought.

                    ISABELLE
          (Making sandwiches with one hand)
That's pretty good dancing, Cowboy!

                    GAY
          (To Roslyn)
I never danced this good in my life! -- What're you makin' my feet
do?

                    ROSLYN
          (She is getting quite high; her
          body is moving more freely)

ROSLYN (Cont.)
Just what you're going to do next. Relax. Join your partner, don't
fight her.

GAY
          (Drawing her closer)
<u>I</u> ain't fightin' her.

          (SHE breaks and tries to move him
          into a Lindy. HE does it awkwardly,
          but amazed at himself)

GUIDO
          (Excitedly)
What <u>are</u> you doing!

Guido and Isabelle are watching with intrigued smiles. Guido drinks
deeply now, a competitive tension rising in him.

ISABELLE
          (Aside, to Guido)
She taught dancing, y'know, before she was married.

GUIDO
No kiddin'! In a dance hall?

ISABELLE
Something like that, I guess.

The information tends to "place" Roslyn for Guido now. From his
viewpoint we see her now -- abandoned, her body suggestive. Guido
suddenly breaks in between her and Gay.

GUIDO
How about the landlord?
          (Lightly, to Gay)
Move over, boy, huh?

GAY
Just watch out for those pretty little feet there!

GUIDO
          (Looking at Roslyn, his eyes firing,
          his teeth set and glistening)
Oh, she knows how to get out of the way! Let's go!

ROSLYN (Cont.)

I'd love to, but I don't know what for. I always loved houses.
I never had one, but I love them.

GAY

Should've seen his wife -- she helped pour the cement, knocked in
nails. She was a real good sport.

ROSLYN
(Looking around)

And now she's dead. . . . Because he didn't have a spare tire.

GAY

Well, that's the way it goes.

(Their eyes meet; HERS are vaguely
hostile)

Often goes the other way, though; don't forget that.
(He smiles at her kindly)

ROSLYN
(She smiles back, closing her eyes
for an instant as though to shake off
her mood)

I know; I'm going to try to remember.

Guido jumps up into the room with a small bag of groceries and a
bottle. He looks at them and at Isabelle drying glasses on her
sling.

GUIDO

Nice to see people in here! Come on, folks, let's get a drink!
(Going to Isabelle)

I'll start the refrigerator -- it makes ice quick.

ISABELLE

Ice! --
(Calling through the open studs to
Roslyn)

We stayin' that long, Roslyn?

ROSLYN

I don't know . . .

                          GAY
          (He meets her eyes -- and he is referring
          to her resolve of a moment ago)
Sure! -- come on, there's no better place to be! And you couldn't
find better company either!

                        ROSLYN
          (She laughs)
All right!

                          GAY
That's it, sport!
          (Calling to the kitchen)
Turn on that ice, Guido-boy!

                    (ISABELLE comes in balancing a tray
                    and glasses, which GAY leaps up to
                    take -- and the bottle out of her
                    sling. He pours)

Let's get this stuff a-flowin' and make the desert bloom.

                        ISABELLE
Flow it slow -- we only got the one bottle.

                          GAY
          (Handing ROSLYN a drink)
There you are, now! Put that in your thoughts and see how you come
out.

                    (SHE laughs. GUIDO enters and takes
                    a glass)

                         GUIDO
Come on, sit down, everybody!

                    (ROSLYN sits on the couch, and
                    ISABELLE sits with her. THE TWO MEN
                    take chairs. GUIDO addresses Roslyn,
                    his sense of hope flying)

Say, I'm really glad you like this place!

                        ISABELLE
          (Raising her glass)
Well, here's to Nevada, the state of mind.

                              ROSLYN
          (As THEY chuckle)
State of <u>mind</u>?

                              ISABELLE
That's what they say, y'know. There's nothin' <u>in</u> this state -- the
whole thing is practically unnecessary. All they've got is an attitude.

                              GAY
What attitude?

                              ISABELLE
"Anything goes but don't complain if it went."
          (She laughs with them)

                              GAY
          (Laughs)
That's no lie! -- God!

                              ISABELLE
You want to lose your money, gamble it here; divorce? -- get it here;
extra atom bomb you don't need? -- just blow it up here and nobody
will mind in the slightest.

                              GUIDO
How come you never went back home, Isabelle? You came here for your
divorce, didn't you?

                              ISABELLE
          (She drinks, glances diffidently at
          Roslyn)
Tell you the truth, I wasn't beautiful enough to go home.

                              ROSLYN
Oh, Isabelle . . .

                              ISABELLE
It's true, darling. Beauty helps anywhere, but in Virginia it's a
necessity. You practically need it for a driver's license. I love
Nevada -- it's the state of confusion. Why, they don't even have
mealtimes here. Just eat any time. I never met so many people
didn't own a watch. Might have two wives at the same time, but no
watch.

               (ROSLYN, relaxing, is leaning her
               head back on the couch as THEY all
               chuckle. Their rhythm has become
               relaxed)

                    ROSLYN
How quiet it is here!

                    GAY
          (Sprawled out, sipping)
Sweetest sound there is.

          (Pause. Quiet. THEY sip their drinks)

                    GUIDO
There's an Indian store about five miles, --

          (ROSLYN looks at him quizzically)

-- if you wanted to shop. Groceries, everything.

                    GAY
          (Without any insinuation)
We'd be glad to come by and do your chores. If you liked.

                    ROSLYN
          (She drinks again, gets up. THEY
          watch as, in a closed world of her
          own, SHE wanders to the fireplace,
          then turns to the men, asking)
Could we have a fire?

                    GUIDO
Sure! It's a good fireplace!

Guido has sprung up and goes and piles wood into the fireplace. He
looks up at her, dares to smile, thankful for her command. She
smiles back.

Gay catches this silent exchange; and Roslyn looks up from Guido and
sees that Gay has been watching her. She smiles at him and he
replies with a certain new intensity in his gaze at her. She drops
her gaze and says to Isabelle . . .

                    ROSLYN
Maybe they know your friend.
          (To the Men)
You ever know a fellow named Andy?

                    GAY
Andy who?

                              ISABELLE
Stop it, darling, you can't go lookin' for a man.

                              GAY
What'd he, take off?

                              ISABELLE
Not exactly -- he just didn't come back.
          (She laughs at herself)
Andy Powell? You ever . . .

                              GAY
Sure! Fella with one arm. Call him Andy Gump sometimes?

                              ISABELLE
          (A little excitedly, she laughs)
That's him!

                              ROSLYN
          (Hopefully for Isabelle)
Where is he?

                              GAY
Saw him at the rodeo last month.

                              ROSLYN
          (To Gay)
Could you find him if you . . ?

                              ISABELLE
Now, stop, Honey! You know a man that wants a woman's going to come
and get her. And if he don't want her . . .

                              ROSLYN
But Isabelle, maybe he's just waiting and hoping you'll come and see
him! Maybe you don't have to be alone any more!

                              ISABELLE
Dear girl, you got to stop thinkin' you can change things . . .

                              ROSLYN
          (Driven on by a wider vision . . .)
But if you know what to do . . . I mean I don't know what to do, but
if I knew, I'd do it!

She suddenly finds the three of them looking at her in silence;
looking at her as though she had challenged them in some secret way.

Guido, with a clap of his hands, astounds them all by breaking into
a boogie Lindy. Roslyn immediately, and happily, accepts the
challenge. They come together, part, dance back to back, and he puts
her to her mettle.

                        GAY
Where in hell you learn that, Pilot!
          (To Isabelle)
I never knew him to dance at all!
          (Calling)
Where you been hiding, Pilot!

The number ends, and on the last beat Guido has her pressed close,
and in the silence she deftly, but definitely -- however smiling --
breaks his grip on her body, her expression striving to deny the easy
and slightly over-familiar victory in his eyes.

                        GAY
You two oughta put on a show! That's some goin', Roslyn!

                        ROSLYN
Wheeew!

Panting, getting high, she laughingly staggers to the door. Another
number starts from the radio. Guido goes to her, clasps her waist and
turns her around to him familiarly.

                        GUIDO
Come on, Honey, this is a good one.

                        ROSLYN
No, I had enough right now.

                        GUIDO
          (Thinking to press an advantage)
Come on, I haven't danced in years.

                        ROSLYN
Didn't your wife dance?

                        GUIDO
          (Unknowingly but definitely turning
          his back on the memory and the
          hallowed mourning)

GUIDO (Cont.)
Not like you. She had no . . . gracefulness.

ROSLYN
(She lets him lead her from the door
with his arm around her -- and through
a faint haze of alcohol, almost laughing)
And anyway she's dead.

Guido, struck with guilt and wounded by some aspersion on his fidelity
to a previously hallowed wife, tries to keep his grin and the gay
mood, but his eyes are resentful, and he halts. On the couch, Gay
and Isabelle are observing, eating sandwiches and drinking, sensing
something serious now.

GUIDO
(Trying to laugh at her)
What do you mean by that?

ROSLYN
(She stays close to him looking up
into his face)
Whyn't you teach her to be graceful?

GUIDO
You can't teach that.

ROSLYN
How do you know? I mean how do you know? I mean did you ever dance
that way with your wife?

GUIDO
Well she just couldn't make that kind of . . .

ROSLYN
You see? She died, and she never knew how you could dance! I mean it's
nobody's fault, but to a certain extent --
(She holds thumb and index finger a
half inch apart)
-- I mean just to a certain extent maybe you were strangers.

GUIDO
(Defensively; hardening)
I don't feel like discussing my wife.

                              ROSLYN
                    (She takes his arm -- the jazz is
                    going, she is high now)
Oh! I didn't mean to make you mad. I just meant that if you loved
her you could have taught her anything. Because we have to die,
we're really dying right now, aren't we? All the husbands and all
the wives are dying every minute, and they are not teaching one
another what they really know!
                    (Genuinely trying to plead with him)
You're such a nice man, Guido -- why are you so afraid?!
                    (She wipes her hair out of her eyes
                    to blot out the sight of his resentful
                    face, and suddenly . . .)
I want air!

                    (She goes quickly to the door and
                    starts to step out. GAY rushes from
                    the couch and catches her before she
                    goes down where the step is missing.
                    ISABELLE rushes right behind him.
                    GAY, holding her . . .)

                              GAY
You better lie down, girl.

                            ISABELLE
Come on, let's get back home. Heist her down, Cowboy.

                             ROSLYN
No, I'm all right, I'm all . . . !

                    (She starts once again to walk out
                    the door. GAY leaps down to the
                    ground and SHE falls into his arms
                    standing up. She looks into his
                    face, laughing in surprise at her
                    sudden drop)

How'd you get out here?

                            ISABELLE
                    (Calling from the threshold)
Get me down, Cowboy! Get in the car, Roslyn! -- we're goin' home!

Gay leaves Roslyn and goes and helps Isabelle down to the ground,
while Guido helps from within the house -- his eyes on Roslyn.
Roslyn, momentarily alone, looks about her. The radio jazz is still
playing. She flies into a warm, longing, solo dance among the

weeds, and coming to a great tree she halts, and then embraces it,
pressing her face against its trunk.

Guido, Isabelle, and Gay are watching in a group at the doorway of
the house, mystification on their faces. Gay breaks and strides
across the weeds to the tree, and gently tries to turn Roslyn's
shoulder, for her face is hidden under her arm. As soon as he touches
her she quickly turns and faces him and, astonishingly, her face is
bright and laughing. Gay starts to smile, but he is mystified.

                         ROSLYN
You were worried about me!

                         GAY
Well, I . . .

                         ROSLYN
Oh, that's so sweet!

                         GAY
How about we get you back now, huh?

                    (He puts his arm around her and SHE
                    lets herself be led to her station
                    wagon, which is parked beside Gay's
                    beat-up pickup truck. At the car's
                    open door, GAY turns to Guido, and
                    with some hesitation . . .)

I guess I'll drive them back to town, okay? Whyn't you take my
truck and I'll come by for it later tonight.

Guido glances at Roslyn, rebuffed, left out.

                         ROSLYN
No, don't leave Guido all alone. Isabelle, ride with him. He's
lonely. Go ahead, dear . . . ride with poor Guido.

She has gone to press Isabelle toward the truck, and with an apologetic,
even shamed smile at Guido, she gets into the station wagon.

In a long shot we see both vehicles descending the rocky trail to the
highway below, the truck ahead.

Inside the station wagon, Roslyn is sitting beside Gay, one leg tucked under, the other on the seat, her foot almost touching Gay's hip. She is in the momentary calm after a quick storm, staring out at the passing hills that rise from the roadside. She turns to look at Gay's profile; a calm seems to exude from him, an absence of uncertainty which has the quality of kindness.

                              ROSLYN
Where we going?

                              GAY
Take you home, I guess. Reno.

                              ROSLYN
I didn't mean to hurt his feelings. Did I hurt his feelings?

                              GAY
That's what feelings are for, I guess.
          (Grins)
You sure brought out the little devil in him -- surprised me. Takes
a lot of woman to do that to Guido.
          (He laughs)
He sure looked comical doin' that dance!
          (He laughs deeply)

They have arrived at the foot of the trail. The truck has entered the highway, turned, and moved off. Now Gay stops the car, looks left and right for traffic, and his eyes fall on Roslyn's, and she is looking at him searchingly, a residual smile lingering on her face.

                              GAY
You don't have a friend in the world, do you?

                              ROSLYN
          (Quietly)
No.

                              GAY
          (He runs his eyes along her leg up
          to her face)
Don't seem possible.

                              ROSLYN
Why?

                          GAY
               (Straightforwardly, with a genuine
               wonder)
You the most beautiful woman I ever looked at.
               (He grins)
I've said that before, but I never meant it. I mean it now.
You're . . . you're a real beautiful woman. It's . . . almost kind
of an honor sittin' next to you. You just shine in my eyes.

               (SHE laughs, surprised, soundlessly
               but for a child's high tinkle)

That's my true feelin', Roslyn.
               (He pulls up the brake and shifts around
               to face her, but not touching her)
I could be a good friend to you.

               (SHE is silent, watching him)

Nobody I ever met, and nobody I ever said goodbye to, ever owed me
anything. There's no better friend than that.
               (He takes her hand and is made happy
               by it)
You're even beautiful down into your hands.
               (He looks at her directly again)
I think a person's got to stop _goin'_, Roslyn. You ever watch a horse
out grazing? Every once in a while he raises up his head and just
stands still. You won't find a better place for that. I'm stayin'
at Guido's. I could come every day and do your chores. Get us a
couple of horses and ride through the country. Won't cost you
hardly nothin', either . . . I'd like to kiss you.
               (He draws her to him, he kisses her)
Like pressin' my face into a barrel of cream.

                          ROSLYN
               (HE tries to embrace her and SHE
               gently stops him)
I don't feel that way about you, Gay.

                          GAY
               (Pleased, somehow, he holds up her
               chin)
Well don't be discouraged, girl -- you might!

               (THEY both laugh. HE quickly puts
               the car in gear)

Suppose I take you back and you get your things, okay?
               (He drives onto the highway. Now
               urgently . . .)

                          GAY (Cont.)
Try it a week. See what happens! You got nowhere to go to, do you?

                          ROSLYN
No.

                          GAY
Well, then there's nothin' better than standin' still.

                          ROSLYN
Don't you have a home?

                          GAY
Sure. Never was a better one either.

                          ROSLYN
Where is it?

                          GAY
Right here.

                    (With his head he indicates the open
                    country. SHE looks out for a house,
                    but seeing only the vast land, she
                    turns back to his profile, his self-
                    containment -- and she turns back,
                    facing the desert and the hills,
                    trying to understand and to connect)

The camera holds on the panorama of the hills, but the light fails
rapidly and we dissolve on a darkening scene.

We open on another area; not the former valley where the highway runs,
but up in the hills, and the sun is newly risen, the light brightening
as we watch. At first the scene is pastoral, all beauty. Now we tilt
down to discover the conflict and rapacity beneath; we come closeup
upon a rabbit emerging from under a sage bush. A shadow passes over
it and tilting up we catch a hawk floating in the air above. Cut to
a butterfly lighting on a branch; then to a chameleon near it. The
chameleon's tongue flicks, the butterfly is taken. Even now birds
nearby are making a racket. We cut to a nest full of fledglings, the
parent bird agitated. It suddenly takes off. We shoot up. Three or
four birds are diving at the soaring hawk, bothering him to drive him
off.

The screaming of these birds accompanies the camera, at first it cuts
back to the fledglings, then pans across bushes and discovers Guido's
house close by. An open window faces us -- this is the side of the

house. We cut to the window and look in, the screaming of the birds
continuing.

Over the window sill we discover Roslyn asleep alone in the bed.
The screaming seems to be tensing her sleeping face; her fists are
closing. The shot widens as the door opens and Gay, fully dressed,
stands in the doorway looking down at her. From his viewpoint now,
the camera runs its fingers along the outlines of her body under the
sheet. Beside her head is his pillow, still dented. The picture of
Guido and his wife is gone from over the bed, only the book remaining.

His face is almost inspired with lust and desire. He happens to catch
his image in the mirror over the bureau. He smooths back his rumpled
hair, but the gesture is transformed -- he tautens the skin of his
neck, as though for a moment he felt the ending of his youth. But
as though to dispel this dark thought he quickly goes from the mirror
to her bedside and sits on his heels, his face a foot away from
hers. Now, again, his eyes glide over her, and he shows the feeling
of one who is both happy and troubled by the question of his possessing
a wonder.

While outside, the racket of the birds rises to a crescendo, he moves
his face in and kisses her. She instantly draws away, awakening.
And then she stares at him.

                         GAY
Welcome to the country.

                       ROSLYN
          (Softly)
Hi! -- I almost forgot where I was for a minute.

                         GAY
Well I didn't! I never knew a woman to look better in the morning
than she does at night.

               (ROSLYN softly laughs. HE kisses
               her gently, then . . .)

How in the world did any man ever let you go?

                       ROSLYN
          (Shrugs. And with a certain faint
          guilt . . .)
Not all of them exactly let me. . . . I'm a pretty good runner if I
have to. Boy, I'm hungry!

                         GAY
Come on out, I got a surprise.

He walks out of the room. She sits up, her face showing a pleasurable
anticipation, and she starts out of bed.

We cut to Gay at the stove turning over some eggs in a pan. Near
him is a kitchen table set for two. He turns and sees . . .

Roslyn in a terry cloth robe emerging from the bedroom doorway. She
looks about in surprise.

                         ROSLYN
You been <u>cleaning</u>?

          (HE smiles in reply)

She moves, sees the table set, the breakfast sizzling on the stove;
in a vase a few wild flowers. Something outside the door catches
her eye. She looks and sees the mop standing in the empty pail
among the weeds. Now she turns to him. She is moved by his need
for her. She hurries toward him at the stove.

                         ROSLYN
Here, let me cook!

                         GAY
Just sit down, it's all done.

He dishes out eggs for both of them, sits opposite her. She stares at
him. He starts eating.

                         ROSLYN
You always do this?

                         GAY
          (Denying)
Uh-uh. First time for me.

                         ROSLYN
Really and truly?

Gay nods; his having gone out of himself is enough. She starts eating.

                         ROSLYN
Oooo! It's delicious!

She eats ravenously. He watches with enjoyment.

                        GAY
You really go all out in everything, don't you. Even the way you
eat. I like that. Women generally pick.

In reply she smiles and almost nods. She returns to eating. Their
mutual satisfaction in the food is important; we dwell on it for a
moment. With a full mouth . . .

                        ROSLYN
The air makes you hungry, doesn't it!

He laughs softly. Now he is sipping his coffee. He lights a
cigarette, always trying to sound her. She eats like one who has
starved. Now she stops for a breath.

                        ROSLYN
I love to eat!
              (Happily she looks around at the room)
I'd never know it was the same house. It even smells different!

Suddenly she goes around the table and kisses his cheek.

                        ROSLYN
You like me, huh.

He draws her down to his lap, kisses her on the mouth, holds her with
his head buried in her. She pats his neck, but we see an uneasiness
on her face mixed with her happiness. He relaxes his hold. She gets
up, walks to the doorway, looks out at the endless hills, the horizon.

                        ROSLYN
I can see what you mean -- there is something here. It feels like a
new start . . . maybe it's because it's so bare.
              (Slight pause)
Birds must be brave, y'know? -- to live alone. And when it gets dark?
Whereas they're so small, y'know?
              (She smiles to him from the doorway)
You think I'm crazy?

                        GAY
            (Denying)
Uh-uh. I'm glad to see you like it here.

                        ROSLYN
Don't most women?

                        GAY
It never bothered me if they didn't.

                        ROSLYN
You're a kind man.

                        GAY
I ain't kiddin' you.

She respects his seriousness, and turns back to look out again. For
a moment we see her from his viewpoint, golden in the sunlight.
We see the mixture of yearning and mystification in his eyes as he
sips his coffee and smokes.

                        GAY
You seen a lot, haven't you?

                        ROSLYN
Yes.

                        GAY
So've I. I never see anybody like you, though.

                        ROSLYN
Why?

                        GAY
I don't know -- you got respect for a man.

                        ROSLYN
            (She turns to him in the doorway)
Don't most women?

                        GAY
Uh-uh. You the first woman hasn't told me her husband wasn't much
of a man.

                        ROSLYN
And what do you say?

GAY

Nothin' much. Cowboy's supposed to be dumb, y'know. They come out
here from all the states -- all kinds -- stenographers, social
register women with chauffeurs and maids, college teachers, all
kinds. And they find a cowboy, and if they think he's stupid
enough, they'll say and do all the things they didn't dare in New
York and Chicago and St. Louis. And it's pitiful.

ROSLYN

Why is it pitiful?

GAY

Because they don't amount to nothin'. Try to remember them and all
that comes to mind is . . . a hairbrush and a suitcase. They got
no respect for themselves, y'know? Or for anybody else. You have.
And I appreciate it. I ain't kiddin' you either.

ROSLYN

    (Slight pause)
Thanks. I mean thanks for not laughing at me.

    (HE looks at her mystified)

ROSLYN (Cont'd)

People do, you know. I don't know why.

GAY

I could guess why.

ROSLYN

Why?

GAY

Well . . . people are mostly kiddin' -- even when they ain't kiddin'.
But you -- even when you're kiddin' you ain't kiddin'. What you got
to do is put it on a little bit, and you could go places. It's only
a game, y'know -- and you takin' it like it's serious. People always
laugh at that.

ROSLYN

Is it a game to you?

GAY

Well, I don't mix much -- and when I do, I just let 'em talk. I mean
I'm friendly, but I ain't <u>with</u> them.
    (He gets up)
Let's go outside -- sun is warm by now.

He helps her to hop down to the ground, and he takes her hand and
they walk through the weeds, reflecting. They come to the lumber
pile and sit on it.

                    GAY
Y'know, Roslyn, I don't think I've known a woman I'd grieve about if
she left. I've always enjoyed sayin' goodbye. But there's somethin'
about you -- I don't know what -- I'd be lonesome. For a long time.

                    ROSLYN
I'm glad.
          (She kisses his cheek)
Where do you usually live out here?

                    GAY
I got a sleepin' bag in my truck. I stay over Guido's house, sometimes.
I don't need much.

                    ROSLYN
You ever see your children?

                    GAY
Couple times a year. They come to the rodeos when they know I'm
gonna be in them. I'm a pretty good roper, y'know.

                    ROSLYN
My mother had a son by her first husband, but I never met him.
And you know? --
          (Laughs)
I feel lonesome for him sometimes.

                    GAY
My daughter's about your size now.
          (He sighs)
Time sure flies.
          (With a quickened urgency)
. . . I hope you stay a good long time. Will ya?

                    ROSLYN
          (Sensing his tightening grasp on her)
I don't know. I . . .
          (Her eye falls on something in the
          grass)
Say! Could we use that for a step?

Gay walks over and picks up a cinder block.

                              GAY
Just might at that.

He goes the few yards to the front door and sets the block under it.

                              GAY
There now!

                              ROSLYN
Let me try it!

She hurries and runs up the step into the house, then turns and
hops down.

                              ROSLYN
It's perfect!   I can come in and I can go out!

Suddenly, her simple enthusiasm moves him, and he laughs and lifts
her, cradling her in his arms.

                              GAY
Sometimes, you're like a little baby girl!

She laughs, his feeling warming her.

                              ROSLYN
You're a dear man!

She kisses his neck as he walks up the step, carrying her into the
house, both of them laughing with joy.   Dissolve.

We open on a vast shot of Pyramid Lake, an endless water surrounded by
abrupt lava-like hills, bare of vegetation or sign of human interference,
the sky cloudless, featureless.   Now, panning we discover Roslyn's
car parked at the shore, and beside it, Gay, sitting on a blanket,
drying his arms and chest with a towel.   He is looking toward the water.

We shoot the water and out of it Roslyn surfaces, laughing.   She
stands now, rising out of the water, glistening in the sun, breathing
deeply, looking at the almost astounded admiration in Gay's face.

                          GAY
              (Of her beauty)
I just never saw anything like it!

She bursts out laughing as he comes onto the beach, bends and kisses
his head.

                         ROSLYN
Let's run! I love to run!

                          GAY
Lemme catch my breath!'

She dashes away, trotting along the beach. We hold on him for a moment;
he almost shakes his head with wonder. His dog is sitting beside
him, watching her too.

We truck with her as she runs. Now she throws out her arms as though
embracing an invisible world, and then as she is slowing, Gay runs
into the shot and devours her lips, and she laughs. And now they
stroll along the shore, back toward the car, catching their breaths.

They come to the blanket. She sprawls onto it, still wet. She looks
up at him, smiling in knowledge of his need for her. He slowly
comes down beside her. Lays his head in the pit of her arm.
Silence.

                         ROSLYN
              (Softly, her face to the sky)
There's no sound at all!

He doesn't move. She turns her head.

We shoot the mute, barren hills along the opposite shore, the bare
lake.

                         ROSLYN
In Chicago, everybody's busy.
              (Pause)
Those hills are funny -- you keep waiting for them to do something.
              (She laughs)
I hope Guido isn't mad -- I mean he doesn't come around.

GAY
(He sits up now)
He's probably just sleepin'.

ROSLYN
For two weeks?!

GAY
That's what he mostly does -- sleep and read comic books.   Why would
he be mad?

ROSLYN
Well, it's his house.   And I think he kind of liked me.

GAY
Women don't mean much to Guido.

ROSLYN
Really?   Why?

GAY
I don't know.   He never got over that wife dyin'.   That's what he
says, anyway.

ROSLYN
I don't know.   You can never tell about people.   I've known men
. . . so-called happily married, y'know?   And the night before their
wedding they were calling me up.   I mean <u>calling me up</u>.

GAY
Well . . . I could understand that.

ROSLYN
But what were they getting married for?

GAY
(Looks at her for a moment -- a
little incredulously)
You think there's got to be a reason for everything, don't you?

ROSLYN
I don't know.   Maybe I do.

GAY
Let me tell you something.   I never heard a complaint out of my wife.
Come home one night, find her in a car with a fella.   Turned out to
be one of my real old friends.   Cousin of mine, matter of fact.

                         ROSLYN
Oh, poor Gay!

                          GAY
Nobody can figure that out. And I've give up tryin'.

                         ROSLYN
Then what do you do?

                          GAY
Only thing you <u>can</u> do -- roll with it. 'Cause there's nothin' you
can change, Honey.

                         ROSLYN
          (From out of her own vision)
But what if it's so terrible you have to change it?

                          GAY
Then you get out. Like you got out.

                         ROSLYN
But when you get out enough times, Gay, it isn't enough. I mean
there's got to be more to it than just getting out all the time.
Although . . . I used to go to restaurants, y'know? -- and I danced
in places -- you ever see the husbands and wives sitting there? --
not talking to each other, looking around? -- I mean <u>looking</u>.

                          GAY
I guess you believe in true love, don't you?

                         ROSLYN
I don't know . . . I never saw it, but . . . what good is it if nobody
really cares? You know what I mean? -- I mean, I'm not <u>curious</u> any
more. And once you're not curious, what is there to go on? You know
what I mean? It's kind of sad, and boring.

                          GAY
I'll swear to that.
          (He sits up, facing the lake)
I tell you something. I never told it to anybody.

                         ROSLYN
I won't tell! . . . Gee, it's nice to talk to you, Gay!
          (She sits up beside him)

                          GAY
It's a funny thing. I've hated every woman I ever been with.
Afterwards.

                              GAY (Cont.)
                   (He turns to her, a little shy grin)
And I'm known for just the opposite. Now that's a funny thing,
ain't it?

                              ROSLYN
Why is that?

                              GAY
I don't know! That's why you keep surprisin' me. I can't get
enough of you, and I think I never will. . . . And I don't know
just what to do about it.

                              ROSLYN
Why must you do something?

                              GAY
                   (For the first time he appears afraid
                   and humorless)
'Cause I can't stand the idea of losing you.
                   (Pause)
What would I have to do for you to marry me?

                              ROSLYN
Oh, Gay . ... you wouldn't want to marry anybody! But I'm glad you
feel that way.
                   (She laughs, kisses him)
You'll get tired of me!

She gets up suddenly with a stone in her hand and now she winds up
and throws it high into the water. It falls with a little splash.
She looks around across the long borders of the lake. Suddenly she
yells . . .

                              ROSLYN
Hello!!
                   (She turns back to him where he sits)
You want to do something? Let's yell!

                              GAY
                   (With a strained laugh)
What for!

                              ROSLYN
I don't know, I just thought of it!
                   (She rushes to him and pulls him to
                   his feet)

                          ROSLYN (Cont.)
Come on, it'll relax you! Nobody can hear us! In the whole world!
Come on, one, two, three . . !

She yells, and he, abashed, joins her but not with full voice.

                          ROSLYN
Louder! Come on, Gay, let go!

Once more they both yell. He joins now with fuller voice. And he
laughs with her. And they yell again across the empty lake, and we
come in close on their faces, calling into the emptiness. Dissolve.

We open on a new view of Guido's house. Some simple but rather
dramatic changes have changed its atmosphere. The weeds have been
scythed, creating a nearly lawn-like surrounding. Gay's truck and
her car are neatly parked together on the concrete garage slab beside
the house. Laundry is hanging from a line. Flowers have been
planted in a bed near the doorway. The pile of weathered clapboards
is still where it was, but near it are two outdoor chairs waiting for
people to sit and enjoy the view, and a beach umbrella shades them.
The outside walls of the house still are only partially sheathed,
the remainder showing the black composition board panels. It is as
though the house, too, were trying to locate itself, trying to complete
its function.

Now, panning over the scene, we discover a vegetable garden near
the house. Gay is hoeing. The plants are still immature. He is
sweating in the hot morning sun.

Roslyn appears in the doorway with a pitcher. She observes him with
a happy expression, and calls.

                          ROSLYN
Want some lemonade?

He turns, and starts to answer when they both hear an engine in the
sky and turn.

We shoot Guido's plane as it starts a dive, its wing dents flashing
in the sun, its worn tires visible.

We shoot Gay, calling to her in the doorway.

                                   GAY
          (Excitedly)
That's Guido!

She, too, is happy to see the plane. They both wave, and the plane
now swoops down. The cockpit door is folded down on the side of the
fuselage, revealing Guido to his boot tops. He is goggled, and as he
sweeps over their heads he waves. Behind him, also goggled, sits
another person -- also waving. The plane climbs just over the roof
of the house and away.

Roslyn comes over to Gay with the lemonade pitcher. Gay is still
staring into the sky at the vanishing plane, the hoe in his hand.

                                 ROSLYN
Who was that with him?

                                   GAY
Hush!
          (He listens)
He might be landing out back.

                                 ROSLYN
          (Listens)
I can't hear anything.

                    (HE listens a moment, then takes
                    the pitcher)

What does he -- just fly around?

                                   GAY
          (Drinks)
Boy, that's good.
          (He hands her the pitcher)
He might be goin' after mustangs.

                                 ROSLYN   *
Oh. What's mustangs?

                                   GAY
Wild horses. There's some left up in the mountains about eighty
miles back. We go after them now and then.

                                 ROSLYN
          (In her stillness)
What do you mean?

                         GAY
We round them up and sell 'em in town. I been thinkin' of going
down to see Guido about it one of these days. I guess he got the
same idea himself. Let me finish this and we go see him tonight.
Sit down, keep me company.

She sits on a stone nearby, watches him as he proceeds down the row,
hoeing.

                       ROSLYN
Who owns the mustangs?

                         GAY
Nobody; they're up there wild. Nothin' but chickenfeed horses, not
good for much. Ever see that canned dogfood?

                       ROSLYN
Oh!

                         GAY
Lotta that is wild horse. . . . Well now . . . what have we here!

He has come upon a nibbled lettuce. Now on further inspection he
sees several more eaten away to the stem. She has got up and is
standing with him, looking at the destroyed plants.

Gay looks around into the bushes which surround the garden.

                       ROSLYN
What is it?

                         GAY
It's plain old rabbit, and I'm gonna get him!

He drops his hoe and starts toward his truck beside the house,
calling, "Margaret! Come here now!"

The dog appears around a corner, alert and eager. Gay goes to his
truck and takes a shotgun out from behind the seat, and a handful
of shells. He is loading the gun when Roslyn comes into the shot
with the lemonade pitcher. She is trying to appear smiling, but
her tension is clear.

                       ROSLYN
Maybe they won't eat any more.

                              GAY
              (Busy with his gun, eager for the kill)
No, ma'm; once they zeroed in on that garden it's them or us --
there won't be a thing left by the end of the week.

He starts past her with his gun. She touches his arm. She is trying
to suppress her anxiety.

                            ROSLYN
Couldn't we wait another day and see? -- I can't stand to kill
anything, Gay.

                              GAY
                (Still unaware . . .)
Honey, it's only a rabbit.

                            ROSLYN
But it's alive, and . . . it doesn't know it's not supposed to eat our
garden. I mean . . . it doesn't know any better, does it?

                              GAY
Now you just go in the house and let me . . .

                            ROSLYN
                (Gripping his arm)
Please, Gay! I know how hard you worked . . .

                              GAY
Damn right I worked hard!
                (Pointing angrily at the garden)
I never done that in my life for anybody! And I didn't do it for
some bug-eyed rabbit!

He takes off toward the garden, the eager dog at his heel. She tries
to turn back to the house, but she is driven to follow him. A little
breathless now, with the lemonade still clinking in her hand . . .

                            ROSLYN
Gay, please listen . . !

                              GAY
                (Turning on her now, his eyes full
                of anger)
You go in the house now and stop bein' silly!

                            ROSLYN
                (Affronted)
I am not silly!

(HE starts off again, and SHE calls)

You have no respect for me!

(HE turns, astounded, and furious.
SHE pleads)

Gay, I don't care about the lettuce!

                    GAY
Well, I care about it! How about some respect for me?

They are both turned toward a sound from behind the house. Gay walks
a few steps toward one corner when, from a trail that climbs the hill
behind the house, Guido appears, helping Isabelle along. She is no
longer wearing a sling but her arm is still bandaged.

                    ROSLYN
          (With great relief and joy)
Isabelle! Guido, how are you!

Roslyn rushes to her friend and embraces her.

                    ISABELLE
Oh, dear girl!

Gay walks into the shot; he is also happy at this visit.

                    GAY
          (To Guido)
I thought I saw a passenger.
          (Shaking hands with GUIDO)
How you been, fella? We never heard you land!

                    GUIDO
She stopped by my house for directions to get here . . .

                    ISABELLE
And he socked me into that horrible airplane!
          (To Roslyn)
My, you look thrivin'!

                    GUIDO
          (He has been glancing at the place,
          and now walks to get a better vantage)
What's been goin' on here? Am I in the right place?

Roslyn is extraordinarily attentive to him, with great sympathy.
And Guido, despite the conventionality of his remarks, is being moved
by what he sees.

                    ROSLYN
Did you see the vegetable garden?
          (She turns to Gay)
Gay did it! Took him a whole week just to get the soil turned over!

                    GAY
          (He walks up beside her and now that
          her feeling for him has returned, he
          puts an arm around her waist, and with
          wry pride . . .)
Mowed the grass and put in them flowers, too. Even got your windows
unstuck, and your fireplace don't smoke any more.

                    GUIDO
          (He turns from Gay to Roslyn. There
          is a subtle resentment toward both
          of them, but at the same time a self-
          pity which makes Roslyn guilty)
Roslyn, you must be a magician. The only thing this boy ever did for
a woman was to get out the icecubes.

          (THEY all laugh)

                    ROSLYN
          (Pointing to the outdoor furniture)
We got chairs! Come, sit down!

                    GAY
          (Taking GUIDO's arm)
Let's show him the inside! Wait'll you see this, Guido! I've moved
that furniture so many times, I'm gettin' calluses on my back.

He and Guido move together toward the doorway. Roslyn and Isabelle
follow behind, but we separate them by a close shot.

                    ISABELLE
Darling, you look so lovely! -- you found yourself, haven't you!?

                    ROSLYN
Well, I . . .
          (To dispel her hesitation, she hugs
          ISABELLE)
I'm so glad you came! Look! -- we have a step now!

She helps Isabelle into the house -- Isabelle giving a marveling look
at the flower bed beside the step as she mounts up.

                         ROSLYN
Watch your arm -- how is it?

They are entering the living room and we shoot them from within.

                         ISABELLE
It's still weak as a bird's wing, but . . .

              (She breaks off, looking around the
              room. GAY and GUIDO are standing,
              looking. GAY is quite proud)

Well I never in my life . . .

A silence. They look around the room. Indian blankets cover the
formerly bare studs; wild flowers brighten the tables and window
sills; the furniture is rearranged, cleaned; the newly curtained
windows are no longer smeared with dust and cobwebs. There is a
feeling here of a shelter.

                         ISABELLE
Well! Huh! My! -- it's magical.
              (Tears flow into her eyes. She looks
              at Roslyn, then she addresses Gay)
I just hope you know that you have finally come in contact with a
real woman!
              (She suddenly throws her arms around
              ROSLYN)
Oh, my darling girl!

                         ROSLYN
Come, see the bedroom! Come, Guido!

She pulls them both to the bedroom . . .

                         ROSLYN
I hope you don't mind we changed things around . . .

Gay, with an excitement previously unknown to him, goes in the opposite
direction to the refrigerator, takes out cubes.

The three -- Roslyn, Guido, Isabelle -- enter the bedroom. It too is transformed, repainted, brightly curtained, a carpet on the floor, a few botanical pictures on the walls, a dressing table, a bright spread on the bed.

Guido -- on whom we concentrate -- looks about and his eyes fall on the place above the bed where formerly hung the picture of himself and his dead wife. A print of Western landscape hangs there now. Roslyn sees the direction of his gaze.

                    ROSLYN
Oh! -- I put your picture in the living room!

                    GUIDO
Uh-huh . . . Put in a closet too!

                    ROSLYN
Oh yeah, Gay did it!

She swings the door of the closet open to show him. Inside the door half a dozen photos of her are tacked up. They are girlie photos for the doorway of a second-class nightclub, herself in net tights, on her back, etc. . . . She only realizes now -- partly by the flush on his face as he sees the photos, that she has shown them to him.

                    ROSLYN
Oh, they're stupid, don't look at them!

          (She closes the door. HE looks at
          her half embarrassed for her, half
          perplexed)

Gay put them up for a joke! Come! Let's have a lot of drinks!

                    GUIDO
          (He turns to Roslyn)
Can you make her out?

                    ISABELLE
All I know is, this was the dreariest-lookin' house till she got into it.

                    GUIDO
I tell you the truth, I look at her sometimes I don't know whether to laugh or cry.

                    ISABELLE
              (Directly at him)
You ain't laughin', boy.

They emerge into the living room where Gay is coming toward them
with two drinks. In the background, Roslyn in the kitchen is spreading
crackers around a piece of cheese on a platter.

                    GUIDO
              (With envy, at least)
Man, what'd you ever do to deserve this? You sure got it made this
time.

                    ROSLYN
              (Calling to them from the kitchen area)
Sit down, everybody! I got wonderful cheese!
              (With a great joy)
It's so nice to have company!

They are dispersing to the couch and chairs, but she rushes to
Guido, who is about to sit on the couch.

                    ROSLYN
No! Sit in the big chair.
              (Leading him -- HE embarrassed -- to
              the most imposing chair in the room)
This must have been your chair, wasn't it?

                    GUIDO
Matter of fact it was -- I did all my studying in this chair. --
When I was still ambitious.

              (He sits -- but in a certain way.
              SHE rushes back to the kitchen area)

                    ROSLYN
Maybe you'll get ambitious again, you can't tell! I'll get you some
cheese!

                    GAY
              (Sprawling on the couch)
You been flyin' much since I saw you?

                    GUIDO
I took a fast look this morning -- up back in the mountains . . .

                          GAY
Spot anything up there?

                          GUIDO
Well . . .

Roslyn intervenes, offering Guido the cheese and crackers.

                          GUIDO
Thanks, Roslyn.

                          ROSLYN
          (As she goes on to serve Isabelle,
          she points to the photograph of
          Guido and his wife on a table)
I put your picture there -- is that all right?

                          GUIDO
You don't have to keep it out, Roslyn -- I wouldn't mind if you put
it away.

                          ROSLYN
          (Serving Gay)
Why?!   It's part of the house, Guido.   Y'know?
          (She sets the cheese platter down and
          sits beside Gay on the couch, taking
          a drink from the table where he sat
          it for her.   Now THEY are settled)
I mean it's still your house.

                          GUIDO
You must've had a real family, Roslyn -- didn't you?

                          ROSLYN
Oh, no!   I never had anybody -- we never lived in the same place more
than a couple months.   I just . . . I don't know, I just make it how
I think it should be.   I mean in my imagination . . . Here, Isabelle
-- rest your arm on this!

She leaps up with a cushion from the couch and sets it under Isabelle's
bandaged arm.

                          ISABELLE
Oh, don't bother with me, dear!

                          ROSLYN
Why?   Might as well be comfortable!

She goes back to the couch, sits beside Gay, as . . .

                    GUIDO
I'm going to tell you something, Roslyn.
          (With a strained, self-deprecating
          grin)
I hope you don't mind, Gay -- because I love this girl, and you
might as well know it.

                    GAY
          (Putting a proprietary arm around
          ROSLYN's shoulders)
Well you'd be out of your head if you didn't.

                    GUIDO
          (To Roslyn -- he is under a driving
          strain, and THEY are all uncomfortably
          aware of it)
I spent four years in the war; bombed nearly every city in Europe.
And every time I came back to base, I started to design this house.

                    ROSLYN
Really.

                    GUIDO
I changed it a hundred times. And then I got home, married, and I
built it. And with all that planning I could never get it to look
like my idea of it. . . . And now it almost does.

                    ROSLYN
Well you didn't have much time, Guido. If she'd . . . lived,
y'know? -- maybe you'd . . .

                    GUIDO
That's what I've always told myself. But here you are, a stranger
out of nowhere -- you just walk in, and it all lights up. And I'm
sure you know why, too.

                    ROSLYN
          (Her voice faint, in the face of his
          great feeling)
Why?

                    GUIDO
          (With a simplicity which is not
          belied by the seeming pedantry of
          his sentence)
Because you have the gift of life, Roslyn. You really want to live,
don't you?

                              ROSLYN
Well . . . doesn't everybody?

                              GUIDO
                    (With a glance at the picture)
No, I think most of us . . . are just looking for a place to hide and
watch it all go by.

                              ISABELLE
Amen!

                              GUIDO
                    (Raising his glass)
Here's to your life -- I hope it goes on forever!

                              ROSLYN
                    (Raising her glass)
And yours. And yours, Isabelle!
                    (With the faintest sense of
                      afterthought)
. . . And yours, Gay!

We must notice the slightest flicker in Gay, an awareness that he has
been placed slightly to one side. They drink.

                              ROSLYN
Gay did all the work, you know!

                              GAY
                    (With a certain condescension toward
                      her)
Yeah, and the rabbits are really enjoyin' it too! What'd you spot up
back? -- anything?

                              GUIDO
                    (We must note Guido's awareness, now,
                      of conflict between them)
There's a small herd. About fifteen horses, I'd say.

                              ISABELLE
                    (To Roslyn)
I will never understand cowboys! They're all crazy about animals and
they think nothin' of grinding up those poor wild horses for dog food.

                              GAY
What else they good for, Isabelle?

ISABELLE

No more than what I'm good for, but I'd sure hate to be canned.

(THEY laugh)

I will admit, though, I've had myself some real swell times, mustangin'
up there.

GAY
(Laughing suggestively)
I bet you have!

ISABELLE

Oh, I was young once -- miserable as I appear right now. I've been
up there with fellas that took out two thousand horses in three days.

GAY

I've took as many as three thousand in one day.

ROSLYN
(Her fascinated eyes trying to place
him now)
You did, Gay?

ISABELLE

Honey, I couldn't get the vision of it out of my mind for weeks.
Hour after hour, just pourin' those beautiful horses out of the
mountains . . . But it's better than three rodeos. Oh, they're real
mean when they get up there!

ROSLYN
(To Guido)
But would you make anything out of just fifteen?

GUIDO

Not too much. I guess it's just somethin' you like to do, or you
don't. I do.

GAY

There's always the chance we might come on a hundred all of a sudden.
That'd be some real money.

GUIDO

Not likely any more, Gay; we've got them pretty well cleaned out.
(Laughs)
Don't try to make it sound too sensible, boy.

                              GAY
Hell, I don't care how it sounds, I just want to get my two hands on
a rope again, that's all I want.

                             GUIDO
All right . . . if you're hot on it. Whyn't you come along, Roslyn? --
you watch this man in action you'll really see something. He's about
the best roper I think ever lived.

                              GAY
            (With a quickening of comradeship)
You watch him work that plane, too. You'll never see flyin' like that
in your life. This man's a bird!
            (To Guido)
We'll have to pick up another fella.

                             GUIDO
I was going to say -- remember that kid from California? Buckin'
horse rider you were in the rodeo with last year? I see him in town
last night . . . if he's still there.

                              GAY
Oh! he's a good boy. What say we get hold of him?
            (Gets up)
I'll meet you in town. Better not let him get away.

                             GUIDO
Good enough.
            (He gets up)
Be a lot of fun, Roslyn, think about it.

                            ROSLYN
            (Rising. Trying to down her sense
            of incomprehension)
I guess I don't understand why you do it.

                             GUIDO
            (He grins at her)
Well, maybe if you come along you can explain it to us. Gay, whyn't
you pick me up at the house?
            (To Isabelle)
How are you for flyin' back to my place?

                            ISABELLE
I'd love it, but I'm too old to die.

                            ROSLYN
Sure, you come with us!

                         GUIDO
See you later!
            (At the door, his eye falls on the
            photo of himself and his wife; then
            he glances at the room, then to Roslyn)
Well, wherever she is she knows what I had in mind now. Come on,
Gay, spin that propellor for me, will ya?

Guido goes out the door, and Gay, following, turns to Roslyn in the
doorway. We must feel an uneasiness under his smile.

                         GAY
Whyn't you get into a dress, Honey? Maybe we'll have a couple drinks
in town.

                         ROSLYN
Okay!

                         GAY
            (He draws her to him)
Now that's the way to be -- you smile like the sun comin' up. . . . Be
right back.

He goes out and joins Guido and both of them walk across the grass.
Roslyn -- and we -- watch them as they go with the energy peculiar
to men excited by a mission. She calls from the doorway.

                         ROSLYN
Be careful, Guido! Flying, I mean!

Guido turns without halting and waves, and with Gay disappears around
the corner of the house. She turns to Isabelle.

                         ROSLYN
Poor Guido! Now that she's dead he knows just how to live with her.

                         ISABELLE
That's always the way, darling.

                         ROSLYN
But why?! I mean, why can't we ever live _now_?

We dissolve on the intense questioning look on her face.

We open inside Roslyn's car on an empty highway; Gay driving, Roslyn in the center, Isabelle at the window. They are all chuckling.

                         GAY
Isabelle, they oughta put you on the television.

                       ROSLYN
          (As though they had discussed this
          earlier)
Why don't you stay with us? We could have some fun!

                      ISABELLE
No, I'll pick up my car at Guido's and get on home . . .
          (A little shyly)
. . . Tell you the truth, Honey, my husband popped up.

                       ROSLYN
Where!

                      ISABELLE
I got him in your old room.

                       ROSLYN
Well that's wonderful, Iz! . . . Will he . . . stay?

                      ISABELLE
Few days more. They're on vacation.

                       ROSLYN
Oh. His wife too.

                      ISABELLE
          (She is quite nervous, but humorous
          too)
Oh sure. Clara -- you remember my talkin' about Clara. She was my
best friend . . . and she's sweeter than ever.

The mystery of it is in Roslyn's eyes now.

                         GAY
She sure must be to make you so glad to see her.

                      ISABELLE
Oh, Charles could never've stayed married to me!

                       ROSLYN
But why, Iz!

ISABELLE
(She starts to chuckle)
I even lost the vacuum cleaner once!

(Gay laughs, but Roslyn is smiling
with a certain painfulness)

They <u>still</u> haven't found it! -- He said such a sweet thing to me last night. "Isabelle," he said, "I always knew how to find my way home in the dark when we were married -- I just followed the smell of something burning!"

Gay bursts out laughing; Isabelle laughs until she sees the pained smile on Roslyn's face -- and then tears show in Isabelle's face as she suddenly pulls Roslyn to her and kisses her.

ISABELLE
Darlin', why do you worry so about people?!

We dissolve.

We open on a glass-enclosed phone booth on the sidewalk of a very small Nevada town. It is outside a bar. Perce Howland is inside it with the phone to his ear. He is in his late twenties, looks like he has slept in his clothes. There is a seeking quality in his face, a powerful naivete which is itself a force.

He opens the door of the booth for some air, and his eye follows a car whose engine we hear drawing up. A great glad smile opens on his face.

PERCE
Gay Langland! Why you old buzzard you!

We shoot Gay getting out of the car and coming toward him -- Roslyn and Guido are getting out behind him. He and Perce shake hands.

GAY
You callin' up your mama again?!

PERCE
Tryin' to, but they keep puttin' me into Wyoming! Hey, Pilot, how you doin'!

Perce's eye falls on Roslyn.

GAY

This is Roslyn, Perce.
          (To Roslyn)
Perce Howland, Roslyn.

ROSLYN and PERCE

Hi.

Perce cannot help eyeing her as one of Gay's divorcees.

GAY

Like to talk to you, Perce; we . . .

PERCE
          (Alerted by a voice in the phone)
'Scuse me, Gay! Hello, Ma? Perce, Ma.

Roslyn, Gay, and Guido move away to the car at the curb. Gay takes
out a knife, cleans his nails. Guido, who now is dressed in good
slacks and a sport shirt and black-and-white shoes, puts one foot
on the bumper and re-ties his laces, brushes dust off the shoes.
Roslyn's glances are darting to Perce, as . . .

PERCE
          (Tenderly)
Perce, Ma. I'm okay. No, I'm in Nevada now -- I was in Colorado.
Won another first prize, Ma. Hundred dollars. Yeah, real good
rodeo -- I was gonna send you a birthday present but I had to buy some
boots. . . . No, Ma, I haven't been in no hospital, I only bought
some boots. Married! What I want to get married for? -- I just
bought some boots, that's all, Ma!
          (Deeply affected, he tries to laugh)
Whyn't you try believin' me, Mom, make everybody feel better.
          (She is obviously berating him)
Okay . . . okay, Ma . . . yeah, okay.
          (Trying to bring back brightness)
That good about first prize, though? They give me a silver buckle for
my belt, too.
          (Holds up the buckle toward the phone)
Got a buckin' horse on it and my name written out underneath.
          (Now, moved)
I knew you'd be; first thing I thought was how proud you'd be. No,
I don't show a mark on me -- I haven't broke anything since I told
you. I swear! Maybe I'll call you Christmas! Okay, operator!
No, Ma, I can't come home -- now please don't ask me that again.
Say hello to Frieda and Uncle George and Victoria . . .

                              PERCE (Cont.)
                    (His expression becomes stiffer)
          Well, tell him thanks and . . .
                    (Almost curtly)
          <u>Okay</u>, tell him I said hello! Bye now! I . . . Hello? Hello!
                    (He is cut off, but . . .)
          God bless you too.

He has been opening and closing the door for air throughout the call.
At the end it is open. His somber look disappears as he steps out on
the sidewalk.

Perce comes out of the booth onto the sidewalk, greatly relieved.

                              GAY
          Seems to me every time I run into you you're telephoning your Mama.

                              PERCE
          Well, she been kind of touchy since my old man died.
                    (Suddenly)
          <u>Look</u> out!

Without warning Perce suddenly yanks Gay's shirt out of his pants.
In what is obviously an old game, Gay then grabs Perce's wrist,
tries an arm lock but has to turn his back to do it. Perce snatches
Gay's wallet out of his back pocket and yanks his arm free and
stands away, holding up the wallet triumphantly.

                              PERCE
          Every time!

                              GAY
          Just didn't want to break your arm, boy.

                              PERCE
                    (Tossing the wallet back to Gay)
          Poor old Gay, can't hold his pay!

With which he laughs and wraps his arm around Gay's neck and they
return to where Guido and Roslyn are standing.

                              PERCE
                    (To Roslyn)
          I've had the best times with these two scoundrels! You wouldn't be
          goin' down to the rodeo, would you?

                              GUIDO
Why?   You entered?

                              PERCE
I aim to if I can get me a ride down there. . . . And if I can raise
ten bucks for the entrance fee. . . . And if I can get a loan of a
buckin' horse when I get down there.
                    (He laughs)
I'm real equipped!

                              GAY
How'd you like to do some mustangin' with us?   We need a third man.

                              PERCE
                    (Surprised)
Why, Pilot, you still flyin' that five-dollar airplane?

                              GUIDO
Lot safer than a buckin' horse.

                              PERCE
Lot higher, too, comin' down!

                              ROSLYN
                    (To Guido)
Your plane that old?

                              GAY
Now don't start worryin' about him, Honey.
                    (To Perce and Guido)
'Cause if she starts worrying, she can worry.

                              ROSLYN
                    (Laughs)
Well I just asked!

                              PERCE
                    (He is drawn toward her intensity --
                    turns to Gay)
You got a right to if you ever see that B-6 and seven-eighths he
flies.   I didn't know they still had mustangs around here.

                              GAY
Up back in the mountains about eighty-five miles.   It's a good two
days' work if you're interested.   Lot of fun, Perce, you'll like it.

                              PERCE
                    (He thinks, glances at Roslyn)
How many you figure to take out?

                              GUIDO
I spotted fifteen this morning.

                               GAY
                    (Quickly)
Well there might be more though.

                              PERCE
Is that all? Fifteen? What're you gonna get outa that?

                               GAY
Well . . . fifteen's fifteen. Six cents a pound, comes to somethin'.
You're with us, okay?

                              PERCE
Well wait a minute now, Gay . . .
          (Embarrassed at opposing Gay)
I . . . I've broke mustangs up home, but takin' them for meat . . .
          (He laughs, not knowing why)
Like if there was a thousand or somethin' it'd make some sense. But
just to go up there and take fifteen horses . . . I mean the idea
of it, y'know? I don't know why, but it just kinda hits me sideways,
that's all.

As his sensitivity to it is revealed, we concentrate on Roslyn's
face -- she is moved by him, happy he is there. There is no pause . . .

                               GAY
Doin' it for twenty years, Perce -- tell you what. We'll drive you
down to the rodeo; put up the ten for the entrance fee, and I'll
get a loan of some good stock for you down there. You come along
with us tomorrow morning and get us some mustang.

                              PERCE
                    (Slight pause)
And you buy a bottle of good whiskey right in there so I'm primed
up for that rodeo!

                               GAY
Just wait right there!
          (He starts into the bar putting his
          hand in his pocket)

                              PERCE
I ain't waitin' anywhere!

Gay having turned to go into the bar, Perce tackles him from behind, lifts him on his shoulder and runs into the bar with him as Roslyn and Guido laugh.

We open inside Roslyn's car. It is traveling through a new kind of territory. Here there is not even sage, only a sterile white alkali waste. It is midday.

Gay is at the wheel, Roslyn beside him; Guido and Perce in the rear seat. As we open Guido has a whiskey bottle tilted to his lips. They are all a little high. Guido passes the bottle to Roslyn over her shoulder, and she silently drinks, then hands it over to Gay, who takes a short one and hands it back. Guido never takes his brooding eyes from Roslyn. She makes a half-turn in her seat and gives the bottle to Perce, who drinks, and holds the bottle on his knee, staring out at the white waste going by.

Their eyes are narrowed against the harsh light. They have been driving a long time. Now Gay overtakes a horse van trailer hitched to a new car, and as we pass it Perce leans out his window and waves at the Stetson-hatted cowboy driver.

                         PERCE
I hope you get me a good horse, Gay. I'm primed today, gonna get me a first prize.

                         ROSLYN
              (Turns in her seat to him)
I hope you do! -- You mean a horse that's not too wild, huh?

                         PERCE
Oh, no -- I like to show what I can do. I want somethin' I can fight, that's what I want.

                         ROSLYN
              (She sees into him)
But isn't the idea to stay on longer than anybody?

                         PERCE
Well, you want to show what you can do, though. I've broke this arm twice in the same place. You don't do that fakin' a fall, y'know. I don't fake anything. Some of these riders'll drop off and lay there like they're stone dead. Just putting on a show, y'know. I don't fake it, do I, Gay?

                         GAY
That's right. You're just a natural-born damn fool.

                    ROSLYN
Why! That's wonderful . . . to be that way, I mean.
          (To Perce)
I know what you mean. I used to dance in places . . . and everybody
said I was crazy. I mean I really tried, you know? Whereas people
don't know the difference.

                    GUIDO
          (He has been looking at her feverishly)
What kind of dancing you do?

                    ROSLYN
          (With embarrassment)
Oh . . . just what they call interpretive dancing. Nightclubs.
You know.

She starts to turn forward, then turns back.

                    ROSLYN
I was good, though. . . . I could've been!

Again she starts to turn forward, then turns back to Perce.

                    ROSLYN
I'm glad you don't fake it, Perce!

                    GUIDO
          (With a suddenness)
Why? What's the difference?

                    ROSLYN
I don't know . . . The real thing is always better, isn't it?

                    GUIDO
          (With an over-meaning. A resentment
          too)
But would you know it if you saw the real thing?

We shoot Gay glancing up at the mirror at Guido behind him.

                    ROSLYN
          (She receives his challenge)
Oh, you know it, Guido. Be surprised.
          (Then suddenly, to make up for even
          this conflict with him she grabs the
          bottle from Perce)

                    ROSLYN (Cont.)
Here, have a drink, Guido! Buck up, come on, have a good time!

Guido is forced to smile and Perce erupts. Guido drinks.

                    PERCE
Gay, I want this girl to go along mustangin' tomorrow, you hear?!

          (He holds onto ROSLYN's arm, she laughs)

'Cause I'd get awful tired lookin' at your ugly face for two whole
days up there!

                    GAY
          (Into the mirror)
She can't even bear to see a rabbit shot.

                    ROSLYN
          (With a sudden resolve)
I'd like to come along! Let me? I mean . . . it's happening, and
if a thing is happening a person ought to be able to stand it! Let
me come with you, Gay? I promise, I won't say a word!

                    GAY
Oh, that'd be the day!
          (Nodding ahead)
Here we come!

They all look ahead, and we shoot the first sight of the town -- a
giant borax plant covered with white dust. Just visible beyond it is
the single street of the town. We are approaching the place along
a wide curve of highway. Now we see the main street -- a mob has
filled it.

Back in the car.

                    PERCE
          (With great, and sudden excitement)
Hey! -- look at that crowd! Man! -- this is gonna be a real go!

The car is now slowing to nudge its way into the packed street.
Perce sees somebody he knows and sticks his head out the window.

                    PERCE
There's old Rube! Hey, Rube! Whatcha say!

"Rube" waves back.

                          PERCE
Hey, there's old Bernie! Watcha say, Bernie!

Bernie waves back.

                          PERCE
                 (To Gay)
Hey, they got some real riders here today! You get me a good horse
now, will ya?

                          GAY
                 (He glances at Perce, whose face is
                 now between him and Roslyn)
Just come out in one piece, now, 'cause you gotta go mustangin'
tomorrow.

Roslyn is looking at Perce's face a few inches from her eyes -- she
sees the pure lust for glory in him -- and we see the new emotion
flowing from her toward him -- a kind of pity, a personal involvement
in his coming trial.

Perce jerks away to call out the window.

                          PERCE
There's Franklin! Hey, Franklin-boy!

Now we cut to view of the town and the crowd through which the car
is crawling.

The entire town consists of a block-long row of bars, one jammed
next to the other, their neon lights on in daylight. The side of
the street opposite the bars is simply a double railroad track where
a line of freights is now parked.

From the barfronts to the railroad track, down the whole length of
the town, the street is jammed with cars, trucks, horse vans and a mob
of people moving in and out of the nearly stalled traffic.

There are cowboys in working clothes, and many in the tight shirts
and jeans they saw in movies. There are many kids, dressed like their
elders. There are farmers in overalls, women in Sunday best. Here
is a cowboy trying to back a horse out of a little trailer-van right
into the stream of traffic; three girls not yet sixteen walking in front
of a gang of cowboys who are making them; a mother holding onto her

teen-age daughter's wrist as she pushes through the crowd. Here are
two deputies, 45's hanging from their hips, bouncing a Cadillac up
and down to unhook its bumper from that of a battered pickup truck
behind it. In the pickup is a gang of kids with a farmer driving.
In the Cadillac, its convertible top down, are three betting types
and a show-girl, all bouncing up and down and striving to retain
their dignity.

TRUCKING SHOT: MAIN STREET. AFTERNOON.

Now the camera moves above the people and the cars. We hear a
cacophony of jazz -- each bar's jukebox is pouring its music into
the street, one number changing to another as we pass the screened
doorways. Now there is an enormously loud voice from a nearby
public address system, announcing something we can't make out, and
then a crowd roaring as in a stadium -- the rodeo arena is in
action but we cannot see it yet.

We come upon an Indian standing perfectly still while the crowd pours
around him. He is staring off at something -- or at nothing -- a
bundle of clothes under his arm.

Before the bars are parked cars, their bumpers only a yard or two
from the barfronts. We move toward one car. In its front seat
behind the steering wheel sits Gay's dog, Margaret, all alone.

We move past this -- Roslyn's car to the bar toward which it is
pointed. The jazz coming out of this bar is deafening. As we
approach the screen door a sweet little old lady appears on the street,
carrying a collection can which she endlessly shakes. She wears a
lacey hat and a polka-dot dress and she is sweating. She opens the
screen door and enters the bar and we follow her inside.

MEDIUM SHOT: THE BAR. INTERIOR.

There is a bar perhaps fifty feet long and just about as many people
in the place as we could get in. The Old Lady pushes up to a cowboy
and his girl who are drinking at the bar and shakes the can under
the cowboy's face.

                    OLD LADY
Church Ladies' Auxiliary, Tom.

                    COWBOY
Sure.
          (He drops a coin in the collection
          can)

                              OLD LADY
                    (To the Cowboy's Girl, shaking the
                    can)
How about you, sinner?

                              GIRL
                    (Laughs)
Oh, Ma! I got no money!

                              OLD LADY
                    (To Another Man, nearby)
Come on, Frank. Church Ladies' Auxiliary.

                              FRANK
You just got me in the bar next door.

                              OLD LADY
Well, that'll larn you to stay put. Come on.

He groans and puts in money. A shout goes up. The Old Lady turns
toward the noise.

MEDIUM SHOT: THE BACKS OF A CROWD OF MEN, A FEW GIRLS, FORMING A
CIRCLE NEAR THE BAR.

Old Lady enters the shot, pushing through into the clear.

MEDIUM SHOT: OVER THE HEADS OF THE CROWD, INTO THE CENTER OF THE
CIRCLE.

Roslyn is hitting a little white ball attached by a rubber band to a
ping-pong paddle. Near her is an amazed, goggle-eyed little boy who
owns the paddle, and Perce, who has a drink in one hand and a lot of
money in the other. Roslyn also has a drink in her free hand.

                              PERCE
Forty-two, forty-three, forty-four . . . (and on)

Now a young cowboy steps up to Perce and hands him a bill.

                              FIRST COWBOY
Ten bucks she don't do seventy!

                              PERCE
                    (He nods, takes the money, without
                    losing his count)
Fifty-four, fifty-five, (etc.)

A Second Cowboy suddenly steps out and pats Roslyn low on the back.

                              SECOND COWBOY
Go it, Roz!

We instantly shoot Gay's face -- he is in the clear at the bar, and
he has seen the Second Cowboy feeling Roslyn. Guido, standing
beside Gay, looks and sees that Gay is getting irritated. Gay now
scans the faces in the crowd.

We shoot the crowd -- the men eyeing Roslyn's body.

We shoot Gay: he sees Guido's expression as he watches Roz -- and
it has the same near-lewdness of some of the crowd. A new shout
goes up, and Gay turns to . . .

We shoot Roslyn and Perce in the clearing. Now she is hitting the
ball on the bounce, and taking a drink at the same time. Perce is
continuing his count at her side. Perce is absorbed, young, somehow
at one with Roslyn as he urges her on with his counting.

Around them betting is going on in the crowd. And we concentrate
on the Second Cowboy who is now inflamed by Roslyn; he is only a
few feet behind her and she is backing toward him.

The Old Lady steps up close to Roslyn, calling into her ear as she
shakes the collection can.

                              OLD LADY
Play for the Lord! Steady, Sinner!

                              ROSLYN
          (Unnerved)
Please!

                              OLD LADY
          (To Perce, demanding the money in
          his hand)
Help the good work, boy, do it while the spirit's in ya.

                              PERCE
Seventy-one, seventy-two, SHUT UP, four, SEVENTY-FIVE, (and on)

A shout goes up at this new victory. Roslyn is now a foot from the
Second Cowboy with her back to him, and he grabs her from behind and
starts to kiss her. Gay is on him and is about to hit him when he
is pulled away by others. Guido appears next to Gay and draws on

his arm, grabbing Roslyn with his other hand, and he pulls both of them
toward the door. Perce is close behind and they emerge into the
mobbed street.

Roslyn turns Gay to her; she is moved by his suddenly evident
protective passion which she feels great gratitude for. (In the
background Perce is counting the money, Guido looking on)

                    ROSLYN
I'm sorry, Gay, I didn't mean to do it that long! But thanks for
helping me!
          (She clasps his face)
I embarrass you?

He takes her arm and walks in between two parked cars. The threat
of losing her in the moments earlier, the lust of others for her,
has wiped out his reserve.

                    GAY
I'd marry you.

                    ROSLYN
          (With a sad and joyous mixture)
Oh, no, Gay, you don't have to! But thanks for saying that!

                    GAY
I'm not just sayin' anything. I'd get a divorce tomorrow. I'm a
resident, I could get it in a day.

Perce bursts into the scene, Guido behind him. They are squeezed
in between cars.

                    PERCE
Hundred and forty-five dollars! Ain't she great, Gay? She is the
greatest yet!

With which Perce throws an arm around her as he puts the money in her
hand. Instantly the Old Lady appears under Perce's arm, shaking the
can under Roslyn's face, her eyes avid for the money.

                    OLD LADY
          (To Roslyn)
Sinner! I can tell you want to make a big donation! You got it in
your eyes. Some do, some don't -- you got the fear of the Lord in

                              OLD LADY (Cont.)
the middle of your pretty eyes! You're lookin' for the light,
Sinner, I know you and I love you for your life of pain and sin!
Give it to the one that understands, the only one that loves you in
your lonely desert!

At first amused, then drawn-and-repelled, then . . . half frightened
and yet somehow contacted by this woman's mad desire to bless her,
she starts to hand the Old Lady the whole wad of money. But Gay
intercepts.

                                GAY
She ain't sinned that much.
                    (Hands the OLD LADY one bill)
Here's ten . . .
                    (Gives her another)
And here's ten more to settle for the twenty.

                              OLD LADY
Lord be praised! We're gonna buy a fence around the graveyard,
keep these cowboys from pasturing their horses on the graves.
Sweetheart, you've gone and helped our dead to rest in peace!
Go reborn!

She ducks out of sight and instantly a cowboy appears in the shot.

                              COWBOY
You Perce Howland, ain't you?

                              PERCE
That's me.

                              COWBOY
                    (Indicating across the street)
You better get on your horse!

                              PERCE
                    (To the others)
Hey, come on! You watch me now, Roslyn!
                    (To Gay)
Can I kiss her for good luck?

                                GAY
                    (Grinning)
Once.

Perce kisses her. When their lips part -- they both seem surprised.
Perce turns with a glance at Gay -- turning from his own emotion
so suddenly displayed, and goes into the crowd. Gay starts after
him . . . Roslyn stops him.

>   ROSLYN
>   (Half to reassure Gay)
> Take care of him, huh? -- I mean he's like a little boy!

Gay, despite his resistance to her feeling for Perce, hugs her
quickly and follows Perce into the crowd.

CLOSE SHOT: RODEO ARENA. THE GATE OF A CHUTE OPENING.

Rider on a bucking horse charges out. Beyond him we see makeshift
bleachers and the crowd. It is a small-town, home-made arena.

MEDIUM SHOT: THE HORSE AND RIDER IN THE ARENA.

He is staying on.

MEDIUM SHOT: THE TIMING JUDGE.

With a stop-watch in his hand he is glancing from the rider back to
his watch.

MEDIUM SHOT: HORSE AND RIDER.

The rider is still on.

MEDIUM SHOT: THE INDIAN.

He stands just inside the barrier which protects the audience, his
bundle under his arm, watching impassively, a swath of blue sky behind
and above his head.

MEDIUM SHOT: THE BLEACHERS.

Roslyn and Guido are sitting together. She is avidly watching.
Guido is interested, but that's all. He turns now to look at her
profile. His heated eyes rove her face, her neck and body. She is
absorbed in the spectacle. Quickly she turns to him.

>   ROSLYN
> How does he ever get off?

As she says this, the crowd roars suddenly, and people around them half-stand in their seats. Alarm shows in her face as she turns to the Arena.

                    GUIDO
          (Nodding toward the arena)
That's how.

MEDIUM SHOT: THE RIDER, SCOTTING TO HIS FEET AND RUNNING FROM THE HORSE'S FLYING HOOVES.

MEDIUM SHOT: ROSLYN AND GUIDO.

                    ROSLYN
          (Startled)
Gee, I didn't know it was so dangerous!

                    GUIDO
          (As though declaring his determination
           toward her)
Same as everything else worth doing.

She looks at him with surprise.

MEDIUM SHOT: THE OUT-RIDER COMING ALONGSIDE THE BUCKING HORSE AND UNDOING ITS BUCKING STRAP.

MEDIUM SHOT: ROSLYN AND GUIDO. THE STANDS.

                    ROSLYN
What'd he just take off?

                    GUIDO
Oh, that's the bucking strap. It's got nails to dig into the horse's belly and makes him buck.

                    ROSLYN
Well that's not fair!

He starts to laugh, but her intensity stops him.

                    ROSLYN
Do _you_ think that's fair? Drill his belly with nails?

                    GUIDO
You couldn't have a rodeo otherwise.

                    ROSLYN
Well then you shouldn't have a rodeo!

The crowd suddenly roars and stands, and she and Guido rise, but he
is staring at her with deep puzzlement as she turns toward the
arena . . .

MEDIUM SHOT: A CHUTE. PERCE AND GAY.

They are straddling a closed chute, their legs slung over the top,
watching the bucking horse rider in the arena.

                    PERCE
That's a good horse. Hope I get one.

                    GAY
          (His eyes roving the stands)
I hope you're sober.

                    PERCE
          (Following Gay's eyes)
Hell, I've won prizes where I couldn't remember the name of the town.
          (He sees Roslyn in the stands, waves)
There she is!

          (Now GAY waves to her)

LONG SHOT: ROSLYN AND GUIDO IN STANDS.

She and Guido wave back. She waves with energy, encouragingly.

MEDIUM SHOT: PERCE AND GAY ON SHUTE.

                    PERCE
          (Both of them looking at her in the
          distance. -- With a barely repressed
          inner excitement)
You sure got a good sport there, boy. -- What does she, just float
around?

                    GAY
          (Looks at Perce not wanting to admit
          his feeling for her, not to appear
          naive)
Seems that way, don't she?

                              PERCE
She's hard to tell about.   I don't know.
              (Looks off into the stands at her)
Although you gotta respect her, don't you?

                              GAY
Sure do. . . . Listen now . . . don't encourage her to go up with us
tomorrow.   She won't like mustangin'.

                              PERCE
First time I heard you care what a woman liked or didn't like.

                              GAY
              (Looking off at stands)
Well . . . I do.

                              PERCE
              (With an attempt at a laugh)
I wouldn't try to move in on you, Gay -- unless you wouldn't mind.

                              GAY
              (Looks at him with a grin -- and
              somehow unwillingly)
Boy -- I'd mind.

They both laugh to destroy the tension, and this unwitting avowal of
their conflict brings them closer, and Gay slaps Perce on the back
with a warmth, as a horse is led into the chute at their feet.

                              GAY
              (Wryly, but somehow wanting to reach
              out to Perce, despite their conflict)
I'm supposed to take care of boy, boy, so watch it now.

Perce glances toward the stands with pleasure at this news.

                              PERCE
Well, here I go!

He descends from the fence onto the horse with Gay lending a hand, and
he looks up at Gay.

                              PERCE
My address is Black River . . .

He is cut off by the public address system.

                    PUBLIC ADDRESS SYSTEM
On a bucking horse, PERCE HOWLAND out of Black River, Wyoming!

                         PERCE
          (On the restive horse)
California, not Wyoming!

A cowboy pulls the bucking belt tight.   The horse kicks the chute
planks.

                         GAY
You ready boy!?

                         PERCE
Go!   Go!

                         GAY
          (Calling down to the waiting attendant
          outside the chute gate)
Open up!

The gate opens, the horse charges out.   The crowd roars.

LONG SHOT: PERCE IS HOLDING ON AS THE HORSE BUCKS UNDER HIM, HIGH
AND WILD.

MEDIUM SHOT: ROSLYN AND GUIDO.

                         GUIDO
          (Calling)
Go it, boy!

Roslyn is looking on, torn between the hope of Perce's victory and
terror -- she holds her hands to her ears as she watches.

MEDIUM SHOT: TIMING JUDGE WITH HIS STOPWATCH IN HIS HAND.

CLOSE SHOT: CHUTE FENCE.   GAY'S FACE.

He is watching tensely from the chute fence, then turns to look
quickly at ROSLYN IN THE STANDS.

CLOSE SHOT: BLEACHERS.   ROSLYN'S FACE.

She is watching with tears in her eyes.

CLOSE SHOT: PERCE'S FACE.

His teeth are bared with the tension of his fight as he is flung up
and down, the sky over his head.

CLOSE SHOT: THE BLEACHERS. THE INDIAN.

He is watching impassively at the foot of the bleachers.

CLOSE SHOT: BLEACHERS. ROSLYN AND GUIDO.

Now she shouts as though to rescue Perce.

> ROSLYN
Perce! Perce!

She turns, as though for help to Guido, but, as he roots for Perce,
he has a look of near-rage on his face, a flow of animal joy that
disconcerts her, and more alone than before with her terror, she
turns back to the field.

CLOSE SHOT: CHUTE FENCE. GAY.

As a sudden roar goes up from the crowd, Gay raises up on the fence
with a look of what almost seems like joy on his face, but his rising
movement is to help . . .

MEDIUM SHOT: PERCE ON THE HORSE.

He is being thrown. He lands on his face and lies still.

CLOSE SHOT: STOPWATCH IN JUDGE'S HAND, THE SECOND HAND BEING HALTED.

MEDIUM SHOT: GAY. JUMPING ONTO THE FIELD FROM THE FENCE, HE RUNS
TOWARD PERCE.

MEDIUM SHOT: GUIDO.

Pushing down the bleacher rows to the field, Roslyn standing in her
bench behind him.

CLOSE SHOT: ROSLYN'S FACE.

She is stretching to see over the crowd, staring and weeping, blank
horror on her face. Now she starts down the bleachers toward the field.

MEDIUM SHOT: THE FIELD. GAY.

He is arriving over the inert Perce. He turns him over. Guido
comes into the shot, lifts Perce's head, feeling his neck.

CLOSE SHOT: PERCE OPENS HIS EYES.

His face is bloody, covered with dirt.

                         PERCE
California.

                         GUIDO
Move your head, Perce.

                         PERCE
              (PERCE, dazed, sits up. He speaks
              to the air)
Who? You all right, Pa?

                         GUIDO
Let's get him over to the ambulance.

They try to lift him, but he pushes their hands away, struggling to
his feet, saying:

                         PERCE
Who? Who said . . . ?

He staggers about into the arriving Roslyn. She is very frightened
and weeping. She tries to brush the dirt off his face.

                         ROSLYN
Get a doctor! Where's the doctor!

                         PERCE
              (Beginning to focus)
Who took my hat!

Gay goes and gets his hat from the ground as he is moved along by
Roslyn and Guido. He resists them, looking over his shoulder for his
hat.

                         PERCE
Wait now, I want my hat!

                           GAY
Here's your hat.

                           PERCE
                (Putting it on and resisting them
                distrustfully, but moving along)
Wait now!

They are passing through a gate in the arena fence into an area of
parked cars. An ambulance in the background in a clearing.

                           ROSLYN
                (Supporting him, and holding onto
                his flailing arms)
Where's the doctor?

                           PERCE
Where's my hat, Pa?

                           GAY
You got it on, Perce.

Perce suddenly pulls away and yells at Roslyn . . .

                           PERCE
Lemme go, Frieda!

                           GAY
Take it easy, boy, she ain't your sister.

Gay comes up to him, holding out his hand to calm him. Perce is
staring, perplexed, at Roslyn. She is feeling a terror.

Gay again takes hold of his arm.

                           GAY
You're just a little dizzy, Perce. Come on now.

Perce moves with Roslyn holding his arm, Gay helping. He stares,
perplexed, at Gay. They arrive at the ambulance. An attendant is
waiting. But he is not in white. He wears an ordinary shirt and
pants. His hands are hairy.

                           ATTENDANT
Let's take a look, now.

The attendant holds Perce's face.

                    ROSLYN
Let him sit down!

She sits him on the edge of the ambulance floor, the door being open.

                    ROSLYN
      (Distrustfully)
Are you a doctor?

                    PERCE
      (He starts to rise)
I don't want a doctor.

                    ATTENDANT
      (Pressing him back)
Sit down, boy. I'm no doctor. I'll just clean you up a little.

The attendant reaches into the ambulance for something.

                    ROSLYN
      (With a growing feeling of helplessness)
Well, isn't there a doctor?

                    ATTENDANT
      (Reappearing with a bottle of alcohol
      and a swab)
Not for thirty miles, ma'm. Now hold still, boy.

The attendant swabs the dirt off Perce's face. Perce involuntarily
grimaces.

                    PERCE
My nose!

                    ATTENDANT
Yeah, that looks busted, might be.

                    ROSLYN
      (Urgently, with a jagged edge of anger)
Gay, come on, let's take him to a doctor.

                    PERCE
I ain't havin' a doctor!

                              ROSLYN
Gay, don't stand there!

Gay bends and looks closely at Perce's face as the attendant swabs
it; then he straightens up.

                              GAY
              (To Roslyn, resentment flaring in his
              face at her)
He ain't bad hurt.

                              ROSLYN
              (Now openly furious at Gay)
How do you know? Let's take him!

She reaches down to lift Perce.

                              ROSLYN
Come with me, I'll take you in my car!

                              GAY
              (He forcefully, but not too covertly,
              takes her from Perce)
Now don't start runnin' things, Roslyn!

                              ROSLYN
              (With an over-meaning -- into his eyes)
He's your friend, isn't he?! I don't understand anything . . !

A loud yelp of pain from Perce turns them to him -- the attendant
is pressing an adhesive tape across the bridge of his nose. Perce
delicately touches his nose as Gay bends down to him where he sits
on the edge of the ambulance floor.

                              GAY
You all right, ain't you Perce?

Attendant presses a band-aid across the bridge of Perce's nose.

Perce exhales a breath of pain, then feels his nose.

                              GAY
Perce, you all right?

He blinks, looks up at them, still dazed.

                    PERCE
Did I win?

                    GAY
Almost, boy. You done good, though.

                    PERCE
That was a good tough horse. Wasn't it?

                    GAY
Oh, that was a killer. You done good.

Perce tries to stand, but falls forward onto his hands and knees.
Roslyn quickly bends to lift him up.

                    GAY
Leave him alone, Roz, he'll get up.

Gay separates her from Perce who remains for a moment on all fours,
catching his breath. In horror, in a sea of helpless non-understanding,
she looks down at him. Now he raises himself with great difficulty to
his feet. Guido hands him his hat which has again fallen off. The
public address system erupts, incomprehensibly.

                    PERCE
          (Referring to the public address
          announcement)
'That me?

                    GAY
Not yet. You still got a coupla minutes.

                    ROSLYN
What for!

                    GAY
He's got a bull to ride. Come on Perce, walk yourself around a little
bit.

Gay, putting Perce's arm over his shoulder, walks down an aisle of
parked cars with him. Perce is not sure-footed yet, but is getting
steadier. They walk slowly, in the sea of cars.

                         ROSLYN
               (To Guido, who is standing near)
          Guido, he's not going in there again?!

                         GUIDO
               (With a certain celebration of life's
               facts)
          I guess he wants to ride that bull!

                         ROSLYN
          But . . . !

          Frustrated, she runs to Gay and Perce and stands before them speechless
          in fury and horror. They halt, momentarily.

                         GAY
          Just let him walk it off, Roz, come on now.

          Gay presses her aside and with Perce continues walking down the aisle
          of cars. She has to squeeze in beside them, sometimes forced behind
          them by an obstructing fender.

                         ROSLYN
          What are you doing it for, Perce? Here, whyn'cha take what we won in
          the bar!

          Struggling with her purse to get money out, she tries to keep up with
          them.

                         ROSLYN
          You helped me win it, Perce, come on, take it. Look, it's over a
          hundred dollars. You don't have to go back in there!

          She is holding the money over his shoulder from behind him. He halts,
          turns. She presses up to him. He is staring at her. She feels
          encouraged now. She gently touches his cheek, smiling pleadingly.

                         PERCE
               (His face brightening)
          After I'm done, let's go get us some good whiskey, huh?

          Gay laughs with a certain pride -- as though this proved the foolishness
          of her concern. And Guido smiles.

                              ROSLYN
Let's do it now. Come on. Please!

                              PERCE
You're a good sport, Roslyn. I like you to watch me now. I'm
pretty good ridin' bulls.

                              ROSLYN
But why're you doing it?

                              PERCE
Why -- I put in for it, Roslyn. I'm entered.

The public address system erupts again, incomprehensibly.

                              PERCE
Get me up there, Gay, I'm just warmin' up!

They start for the door in the fence leading into the arena. She
hurries along with them. Guido is following, still smiling at her
concern. He is progressively drunker.

                              ROSLYN
Gay, please!

But they go on through the doorway into the arena. Perce turns to
her over his shoulder.

                              PERCE
I like ya to watch me, Roslyn! Don't you be scared now!

They disappear into the arena doorway. She turns to Guido beside her,
as though for help. She sees he is blandly accepting the situation.
"I told you so" is on his face. She turns quickly, scanning the world
for help.

LONG SHOT: FROM HER VIEWPOINT THE CAMERA SHOOTS ALL THE PARKED CARS.

No human being is in sight -- only row after row of cars.

MEDIUM SHOT: SHE TURNS TO GUIDO.

                              ROSLYN
          (She is weeping)
You just don't care! -- I'm sorry I pitied you!

Instantly from the arena comes back the roar of the crowd, mixed with the babble of the public address system. She runs at top speed toward the doorway into the arena. Guido runs after her, alarmed, with a sudden sense of great loss.

                    GUIDO
Roslyn!

CLOSE SHOT: BRAHMA BULL.

The face of an immense, white Brahma bull.

MEDIUM SHOT: PASSAGEWAY. THE BULL.

Its handlers are leading it through a passageway toward a chute.

MEDIUM SHOT: GAY HELPING PERCE TO CLIMB UP THE OUTSIDE OF THE CHUTE WALL.

They mount the wall and look down into the chute and then up the passageway leading into it and see . . .

MEDIUM SHOT: A NEW VIEW -- THE BULL AND HANDLERS FROM ABOVE, AS THEY ENTER THE CHUTE.

A man is looping the bucking belt around the bull's hind quarters, but letting it hang loose for the moment.

CLOSE SHOT: GAY AND PERCE ON THE CHUTE WALL.

Perce is wide-eyed with fear and calculation. He is blinking hard to clear his head and softly working a wad of tobacco in his cheek. Gay turns to him from the bull which is now directly under them. In Gay's eyes is both a look of pride in Perce and a brutality.

                    GAY
You okay, boy? You want it?

                    PERCE
          (He hesitates, looking down at the
          bull; he has the excitement of one
          already injured)
Hell, yes.

He instantly makes to descend and straddle the bull.

ROSLYN'S VOICE

Perce!

He looks up and Gay does. Gay smiles pridefully, almost tauntingly
at . . .

MEDIUM SHOT: FROM THEIR VIEWPOINT. ROSLYN ABOVE THEM IN THE STANDS.

She is a few yards away. She is holding the money. She looks
pleadingly.

ROSLYN

Gay, don't let him! Perce, here's your prize! Why . . . ?

She holds out the money toward him. Now Guido, no longer smiling,
appears beside her, having caught up with her. She is cut off by the
public address system.

PUBLIC ADDRESS SYSTEM

Now, folks, who do you think is back with us! We still got some real
men in the West! On a Brahma bull, again, out of Black Hills,
Colorado, PERCE HOWLAND!

The crowd roars. Roslyn is struck dumb by the inexorable march of
it all. She looks down, calling defeatedly:

ROSLYN

Gay!

MEDIUM SHOT: GAY AND PERCE ON CHUTE WALL.

Gay helps as Perce descends and straddles the bull. Mounted, he turns
up to Roslyn.

PERCE

You watch me now, sport!

A handler yanks the bucking belt up tight. The bull shoots its head up,
the gate opens, and Perce goes charging out into the arena.

LONG SHOT: THE BULL BUCKING PERCE.

CLOSE SHOT: THE BULL'S HOOVES POUNDING THE EARTH.

CLOSE SHOT: PERCE.

Holding on as he heaves and twists upward against the sky, almost
bending in half.

SHOTS OF THE CROWD'S LUST.

CLOSE SHOT: PERCE FLUNG VIOLENTLY ABOUT ON THE BULL'S BACK.

MEDIUM SHOT: ROSLYN AND GUIDO, IN THE BLEACHERS.

Horror is growing on her. Guido, tensely watching, is not cheering
now, but turns to her as though to comfort her. As he does so, she
turns from the arena and hurries off, past spectators. Guido
starts after her, when the spectators around them suddenly stand up
with a roar.

CLOSE SHOT: ROSLYN IN CROWD.

She turns her head to look at the field, stretching to see -- and
shock bursts onto her face.

CLOSE SHOT: PERCE LYING STILL IN THE DIRT.

MEDIUM SHOT: GAY LEAPING OFF CHUTE WALL ONTO THE FIELD AND RUNNING.

MEDIUM SHOT: THE JUDGE, STOPWATCH IN HIS HAND, LOOKING DOWN AT
THE FIELD WITH ALARM. THE CROWD IS QUIET.

MEDIUM SHOT: THE BRAHMA BULL IN ARENA.

Bare-backed now, he is lunging and kicking as the mounted out-rider
tries to corner him and keep him away from Perce's inert body.

CLOSE SHOT: THE OUT-RIDER'S ALARMED FACE.

LONG SHOT: THE CROWD, STANDING, WATCHING IN SILENCE.

                                                    DISSOLVE:

LONG SHOT: MAIN STREET OF THE TOWN. TWILIGHT.

The bar fronts. The jazz cacophony coming from each bar. Cars
parked tight, up to the screen doors of the bars. Traffic, thinner
now, is moving along the street. People leaving and entering bars.
The armed troopers, in pairs, standing in the neon glare.

MEDIUM SHOT: ROSLYN IN THE CAR. TWILIGHT.

Through the side window she is seen in the front seat, stroking the
dog's head in her lap. She is staring ahead; her face, tired with
having wept, reflects the red and blue neons blinking on and off.
She is still breathing deeply in the aftermath of a sobbing spell.
Gay appears at the window beyond her. He puts his head in. He has a
wry expression on his face, knowing she is displeased with him; and
amused at her displeasure . . .

                         GAY
Come on, we're gonna have some drinks.

Roslyn turns to him blankly. He opens the door, and sits
beside her in the front seat.

                         ROSLYN
Is he still unconscious?

                         GAY
Probably, but it ain't noticeable.

He turns around in the seat. She follows his gaze through the
rear window.

LONG SHOT: PERCE. THROUGH THE REAR WINDOW. TWILIGHT.

Perce is heatedly arguing with the Rodeo Judge behind the car.
Perce's head is enormously wrapped in yards of white bandage. Guido
is standing between him and the Judge, blinking sleepily. We can't
hear their words.

MEDIUM SHOT: CAR INTERIOR. ROSLYN AND GAY.

                         GAY
          (She is still watching Perce)
He got up to argue with the judge about who won the bullride. You
still mad at me?

She turns to Gay, her feelings in turmoil.

                         ROSLYN
          (She speaks into his eyes)
Do I mean anything to you, Gay? -- It could have been anybody,
couldn't it?

                              GAY
I'm half out of my mind for you, don't you know that?
              (He grips her face, almost angrily)
Why don't you know that!

                            ROSLYN
              (Her heart gladdening)
It's just sometimes . . . nobody seems to really care about anything,
or anybody . . . in particular, I mean. A particular person. You
know? I mean . . . like we're all . . . going to stand there and
watch the other die. You know?

                              GAY
What're you talkin' about! I went in for him with a wild bull
runnin' loose!

                            ROSLYN
Yes! Oh, Gay -- you are a sweet man! Let me go to the mustangs
with you tomorrow!

                              GAY
I don't think you'd like it, Honey, I . . .

                            ROSLYN
No, I want to go! I'm going.
              (With a resolution)
I don't want to be different than anybody else. I mean, it's
happening, and if a thing is happening . . . It's just that I've
seen some things in my life, Gay, that . . .

Perce sticks his head into the car. The tape is still on his nose,
the bandage like a turban on his head. He is slightly high from the
shock. Guido sticks his head in on the other side of the car.

                            PERCE
Hey, Roslyn! -- Did you see me?

                            ROSLYN
              (Wiping the tears from her eyes and
              smiling)
Oh, you were wonderful, Perce! Whyn'cha get in and we'll take you
back to . . .

                            PERCE
Oh, no, we got to have some fun now!

                              GAY
Sure, come on!

                              ROSLYN
                    (She hesitates, then . . .)
          Okay! -- How do you feel?

                              PERCE
          Like a bull kicked me!

          Guido opens the door for her as Gay gets out on Perce's side of the
          car.

          CLOSE SHOT: GUIDO AND ROSLYN.

          As she emerges from the car she quietly asks Guido . . .

                              ROSLYN
          Is he really all right?

                              GUIDO
          In two weeks he won't remember this -- or you either. Why don't you
          give your sympathy where it's appreciated?

                              ROSLYN
                    (Pointedly, but with a warm laugh)
          Where's that?

          She walks past him; he follows. They meet Gay and Perce in front of
          the car.

                              PERCE
                    (He opens the screen door of the
                    bar for her)
          In we go!

          Gay has her arm as her escort; Perce is on her other side, his arm
          wavering over her back but not touching her: He is recognizing Gay's
          proprietory rights. Guido walks behind them. They enter the bar.

          MEDIUM SHOT: BAR INTERIOR. GAY, GUIDO, PERCE, ROSLYN.

          As they press through the crowd, she calls through the racket into
          Perce's ear.

                              ROSLYN
          Why don't you let me take you to a doctor?

                              PERCE
I ain't bad hurt! If you are bad hurt, doctor can't help you, and
if you ain't you don't need a doctor.

They spread out around a table and take seats. There is a feverish
intensity in Perce's speech and in his eyes. As they sit, he calls
over to the bartender.

                              PERCE
Hey, whiskey! For eight people!

He gets into his chair.

                              PERCE
Boy, I feel funny!
          (He laughs)
That man give me some kind of injection? Whooo! I see the prettiest
stars, Roslyn.

He reaches for her hand and holds it. Gay, whose arm is over the back
of Roslyn's chair, grins uncomfortably. Roslyn pats Perce's hand
and then removes her own. Perce does not notice this, and again takes
her hand. All this occurs as he continues talking without a break.

                         PERCE (continuing)
I never see stars before. You ever see stars, Gay? Damn bull had
the whole milky way in that hoof!

Gay laughs. Guido smiles. Roslyn is torn between concern for his
condition and a desire to celebrate her relief that he is alive.

                              PERCE
          (Goes right on)
Say, was that you cryin' in the ambulance? Was that her, Gay?

                              GAY
Sure was.

                              PERCE
          (He fervently shakes her hand)
Well, I want to thank you, Roslyn!

A waiter puts two glasses of whiskey before each of them.

                              PERCE
Now!
              (Raising two glasses, one in each
              hand)
Here's to my buddy, old elderly Gay!

                              ROSLYN
              (As she clinks glasses with him)
Gay's not old!

                              PERCE
And here's to old, elderly pilot! And his five-dollar elderly
airplane!

They all have glasses raised.

                              PERCE
And my friend, Roslyn! We're all buddies, ain't we Gay?

                              GAY
              (Grinning)
That's right.

                              PERCE
Then what're you gettin' mad at me for, buddy!

He swallows his drinks. The jukebox explodes with "Charlie My Boy."
The others drink. Suddenly Perce reaches over and lightly slaps Gay's
cheeks with both his hands.

                              PERCE
Get a smile on, Gay! -- I ain't dead yet!

Gay, straining to ignore the underlying taunt he senses here, grasps
Perce's wrists to get his face free. Perce suddenly gets up and with
a whoop gets a headlock on Gay. Gay stands, lifting Perce off the
floor over his back -- and now Gay is laughing as the tension is
released in a quick wrestling contest which lasts only a moment and
ends with . . .

CLOSE SHOT: GAY AND PERCE.

                              PERCE
              (Intimately; with great need)
Just lemme dance with her, will ya? Just a dance?

                        GAY
            (Liberally)
Sure! Roslyn, whyn't you dance with Perce?

                        ROSLYN
Okay!

She gets up and Perce walks the few feet to the dance area with her.
We remain at the table with Gay and Guido, who is getting more and
more morose. Gay sits.

                        GAY
            (With a more open intensity)
I'd like you to tell her not to come tomorrow. Guido? I want you to
back me up. Tell her there's rattlers up there.
            (He drinks his second drink)
Hear?

                        GUIDO
            (He is staring at her off screen)
She'll be there, Gay.

Gay looks at him with suspicion, then turns to . . .

CLOSE SHOT: ROSLYN AND PERCE DANCING.

                        PERCE
My father had this exact same record. This is old-fashioned music.
Know how he used to dance?

                        ROSLYN
How?

He goes into a flat-footed, hicky step. She falls into it with him.
They laugh. People around them watch as he clomps about with her.
Suddenly he looks into her laughing face . . .

                        PERCE
You're ready for anything, ain't you? You're a real good sport!

He draws her warmly into his arms, and dances seriously for a moment.
But he is unsteady and she is trying unobtrusively to help him stay
on his feet.

PERCE

Whoo! I still got two stars left in my head.
              (Directly to her eyes)
Don't tell Gay, but I hope you're comin' with us tomorrow.

ROSLYN

I am!

PERCE
              (The news brightens his face)
I want to tell you something . . . Come on -- let's see the world!

They have danced up to a doorway and he pulls her through it. They
emerge behind the saloon. The moonlit desert stretches out beyond
them but close by are trash cans, empty liquor cartons, and a
glistening mound of empty bottles. Still holding onto her hand he
looks up at the moon, then around at her, and suddenly he is shy,
as though he had already gone beyond a certain mark with her.

PERCE
We'll go right in -- I just like to get my head to stop spinnin'.

ROSLYN
That's all right -- sit down, why don't you?

He turns about and faces her.

PERCE
How come you got so much trust in your eyes?

ROSLYN
              (As though she feels otherwise)
Do I?

PERCE
You . . . Don't laugh at a fella.

ROSLYN
Why would a girl laugh at you?

He winces in pain and holding his head, sits on the ground, she
coming down beside him to prevent him from toppling over. He peers
at her face as though through darkness.

ROSLYN
Let me take you to a doctor!

                              PERCE
Old Gay. He's a great fella. I learned a lot from Gay. About
horses and about women.

                              ROSLYN
What about women?

                              PERCE
              (Shrugs)
He says I do wrong -- I'm all the time tryin' to save them.

                              ROSLYN
From what?

                              PERCE
Just seems to me they waste women out here. Everywhere. Just grind
'em up. I guess you know about that, don't you?

                              ROSLYN
Yes.

                              PERCE
You got a face . . . pleases me. . . . What're you floatin' around
out here for?
              (SHE doesn't reply, not knowing if
              he is criticizing or sympathizing)
You got feelin's. I can see that.

                              ROSLYN
Doesn't everybody?

                              PERCE
Nobody ever cried for me before. Not since I left home. No stranger.

He rolls over and lays his head on her lap.

                              PERCE
Your face . . . just pleases me! Let me stay here, just a minute.

                              ROSLYN
Sure! It's okay.
              (She presses his knee so that he
              stretches his legs out)
There!

                              PERCE
You . . . belong to Gay, don't you?

                          ROSLYN
                  (With a certain tension)
        I don't know where I belong.

                          PERCE
        Me neither.
                  (He reaches up, touches her face)
        Roslyn?

                          ROSLYN
        Yes.

                          PERCE
        I'm a little dizzy but I know what I'm sayin'. I don't know why, but
        I like to tell you something. . . . I know a lot of people but I
        can't . . . tell 'em anything, you know?

                          ROSLYN
        Oh, I know! You can tell me.

                          PERCE
                  (Now, his body relaxes)
        What're you supposed to do, when . . ?
                  (He breaks off, starts again)
        See . . . I have a good home. I mean I'm not like Gay or Guido. I
        never floated around. Till last year. My father . . . he got shot,
        see . . .

                          ROSLYN
        Oh, my!

                          PERCE
        It was an accident. Some hunters. Didn't see him through the trees.
        And . . . my mother . . .
                  (With a tortured, questing look)
        Wasn't three months, she got married, see? -- That's okay, but . . .
        See, I'm the oldest, and I told her, I says, "You better get a paper
        from this fella, or he's gonna have the whole ranch in his pocket,
        see?" 'Cause I was supposed to get it, see. And sure enough, he
        come to me and offer me wages -- on my own father's place!

                          ROSLYN
        What does she say?

                          PERCE
        That's what I can't figure out. She . . . changed, y'know? She always
        was so . . . dignified, walked like a saint when he was alive. And
        all of a sudden -- she don't hear me, any more. I mean . . .

                         PERCE (Cont.)
         (A new tack)
I took off. But I've seen the big towns now, and the crowds, and
I've won first prize lots of times. But -- it don't go anywhere.
         (With an increasing agitation of
           quest)
I mean . . . there ain't nothin' I can grab at. It's like those
stars there -- you see 'em, but . . . you can't touch 'em. It's
short arms in a tall place. . . . You know what I mean?

Quite suddenly, she kisses him.

                         PERCE
         (Surprised)
You . . . like me?

                         ROSLYN
I wish . . . I could help you! But I can't reach it either!

He starts to raise himself to kiss her, and his face is suddenly
pain-wracked, and he grips his head . . .

                         PERCE
         (Almost crying out)
Damn that bull!

The back door suddenly swings open throwing the raw light of the saloon
on them. Gay comes out, walking unsteadily, sees them with some
surprise on the ground.

                         ROSLYN
He's sick, Gay!

                         GAY
Why, he's doin' pretty good for a sick man!

He comes over and pulls both of them to their feet.

                         GAY
Come on now, I want you to meet my kids!

                         ROSLYN
Your kids here!

                              GAY
They come for the rodeo! I ain't seen them in a year. You oughta see
the welcome they give me, Roslyn! Nearly knocked me over.

He pulls Perce along. They go through the door, Gay in effect embracing
both of them.

                              GAY
                    (To Roslyn)
She's gonna be nineteen! She got so pretty! -- just happen to be here
for the rodeo, the both of them! That great?

                            ROSLYN
                    (Her pity for him redoubled)
Oh, that's wonderful! I'm so glad for you, Gay!

They go into the bar.

                                                        CUT TO:

MEDIUM SHOT: BAR. GAY, PERCE, ROSLYN AND GUIDO.

Gay, now drawing Roslyn by the hand, and she holding onto Perce's
hand, come up to the crowded bar where Guido is standing in a drunken
swirl of his own. The air is muddy with smoke and jazz. Perce is
blinking hard, trying to see. Roslyn is watching him even as she
attends to Gay. Gay reaches Guido first.

                              GAY
Where are they?

                             GUIDO
Where are who?

                              GAY
My kids! I told them I'd be back in a minute! You heard me tell
them!

                             GUIDO
Went out there.

Guido points to the door to the street, then looks appraisingly at
Roslyn and Perce. Gay looks hurt and angered, then pushes through
to the door and goes out.

MEDIUM SHOT: STREET OUTSIDE BAR. GAY.

He comes out into the street. He looks about at the parked cars and
the moving groups of people and the armed deputies . . . and yells.

                              GAY
Gaylord! Gaylord?

Now Roslyn comes out of the bar, helping Perce. Guido is with them
carrying a bottle. Their attention is instantly on Gay -- excepting
for Perce who immediately lays his cheek on the car fender.

                              GAY
Rose-May! Gaylord! Gaylorrrrd?

Guido comes up beside Gay. Roslyn remains, holding onto Perce who
threatens to slide off the fender, but her anxious attention is on
Gay.

                             GUIDO
Gaylord! Here's your father!

People are beginning to congest around them, some seriously curious,
some giggling, some drunk . . . Roslyn remains with Perce just behind
Gay and Guido, watching Gay, tears threatening her eyes.

                              GAY
                 (He never stops calling)
Gaylord, where you gone to! I told you I was comin' right back.
You come here now!

A woman, middle-aged, dressed like a farmer's wife, comes up to Gay.

                             WOMAN
Don't you worry, Mister, you'll probably find them home.

Gay looks at her -- at the security emanating from her sympathetic
smile. He turns and climbs up onto the hood of the car; he is very
drunk, and shaken. He looks over the crowded street from this new
elevation. Just below him Roslyn and Guido are looking up into his
face. Drunks mill around below, the bar lights blink crazily behind
him, the armed deputies look on from the doorways, and the jazz
ceremony is flying around his ears like lightning.

We shoot him from below, his hat askew, his eyes perplexed and his need
blazing on his face. He roars out . . .

                              GAY
Gaylord!   I know you hear me!

We shoot the by now large crowd around the car, the faces of alien
strangers.

                              GAY
                    (He bangs his fist on the roof of
                    the car)
I know you hear me!   Rose-May -- you come out now!

He suddenly slips, falls on the car hood, and tumbles on top of Perce
and both end piled on the ground.   The crowd roars with laughter.
Roslyn quickly lifts up his head and kisses him, weeping.   He stares
dumbly at her, as . . .

                              ROSLYN
I'm sure they're looking for you, Gay!   They must've thought you'd
left!

But he knows they have left.   And she hugs his head and rocks him.

                              ROSLYN
Oh, poor Gay, poor Gay!

Dissolve.

We open inside the car.   It is speeding on the dark highway.   Guido is
driving, the dog asleep beside him.   In the back seat Roslyn sits, one
arm around the unconscious Perce, whose legs hang out a window, the
other arm around Gay, asleep against her breast.   Her eyes are closed.

Suddenly the car bumps up and down, and Guido is trying to bring it
back on the highway.

From outside we shoot the car as it is swerving back onto the highway.
A figure rises from the roadside, brushes himself off, picks up his
bundle, and walks impassively on.   It is the Indian.

Inside the car, the ride smooth again, Roslyn has opened her eyes.
She is drunk and exhausted, a feeling of powerlessness is on her.
Guido has a vague look of joy on his face as he drives.   This dialogue
starts as the bumping of the car gives way to smooth driving on the
highway again.

                              ROSLYN
                  (Helplessly, as in a dream)
       Aren't you going too fast? Please, huh?

                              GUIDO
                  (Glazed)
       Don't worry, kid, I never kill anybody I know.

       We shoot the speedometer climbing toward eighty.

                              ROSLYN
       A fellow smashed up my best girlfriend. All they found was her
       gloves. Please, Guido. She was beautiful, with black hair . . .

                              GUIDO
       Say hello to me, Roslyn.

                              ROSLYN
       . . . Hello, Guido. Please, huh?

                              GUIDO
       We're all blind bombardiers, Roslyn -- we kill people we never even
       saw. I bombed nine cities. I sure must've broken a lot of dishes
       but I never saw them. Think of all the puppy dogs must've gone up,
       and mail carriers, eyeglasses . . . Boy! Y'know, droppin' a bomb is
       like tellin' a lie -- makes everything go quiet. Pretty soon you
       don't hear anything, don't see anything. Not even your wife. --
       The difference is that I <u>see</u> you. How do you do that to people?
       You're the first one I ever really <u>saw</u>.

                              ROSLYN
       Please, Guido, don't kill us . . .

                              GUIDO
       How do you get to know somebody, kid? I can't make a landing.
       And I can't get up to God, either. Help me. I never said help me
       in my life. I don't <u>know</u> anybody. How do I land, Honey? Will you
       give me a little time? Say yes. At least say hello Guido.

                              ROSLYN
                  (Terrified)
       Yes. Hello Guido.

       We shoot the speedometer. From over ninety it begins to descend.
       We shoot Guido.

                         GUIDO
Hello, Roslyn.

Dissolve.

LONG SHOT: EXTERIOR. NIGHT. THE CAR.

This is a different section of road running along the foot of the
hillside. The headlights weave back and forth across the white
line. Now the car comes to a halt. It remains still for a moment,
as though, within, the driver is getting his bearings. Now it
turns sharply left and climbs up a trail.

LONG SHOT: EXTERIOR: NIGHT. ROSLYN'S HOUSE.

Gradually her house is being illuminated by oncoming headlights.
Now the car comes into camera view and halts a few yards from the
house, facing it. Lights remain on, illuminating the unfinished
outside wall and the lumber and building materials lying around
on the ground. Now the motor is shut off.

CLOSE SHOT: FROM THE RIGHT WINDOW GUIDO IS SEEN AT THE WHEEL.

He is very drunk. The dog is asleep beside him. Guido opens the
door and lumbers out of the car. He opens the rear door and blearily
looks in.

CLOSE SHOT: ROSLYN.

She is sleeping, sitting upright. Perce is asleep on her lap, his
feet out the window; Gay is still on the floor.

CLOSE SHOT: GUIDO'S FACE.

It is full of longing and sorrow for himself. He looks down at
Perce, then at Gay, and as though they were unbearably interfering,
he steps back from the car and walks into the darkness.

MEDIUM SHOT: GAY, PERCE AND ROSLYN, IN BACK SEAT.

Loud hammer blows are heard. Roslyn opens her eyes; Gay sits up.

                         GAY
Okay, I'll drive, I'll drive.

                         ROSLYN
              (Still looking through the windshield
               for the source of the sound)
We're here, Gay.

GAY
(Looking dumbly around)
Where?

She sees something in the headlights through the windshield. She
carefully slides out from under Perce's head.

MEDIUM LONG SHOT: SHE WALKS UNSTEADILY FROM THE CAR TOWARD THE
HOUSE.

CLOSE SHOT: HER FACE.

As she walks into the headlight beams, first curious, then incredulous
at what she sees. Now she stands still; the hammer-blows are a few
feet away. A kind of awe shows on her face as she looks upward.

MEDIUM LONG SHOT: FROM ROSLYN'S VIEWPOINT.

Guido is drunkenly hammering nails into a sheathing board, attaching
it to the unfinished wall of the house. It is on crooked, but he
gives it a final pat of satisfaction, then goes to the lumber pile
and takes off another board, nearly falling with that, and goes and lays
it up against the wall, trying to butt it up against the previously
nailed board.

CLOSE SHOT: GUIDO'S FACE.

He hammers. As in a dream, the kind of pleasure and pain that comes
of being freed of earthly logic, yet being driven toward some always
receding center. Roslyn comes up to him. She is about to weep,
it seems.

ROSLYN
Oh, I'm sorry Guido. Guido? I'm so sorry.

He continues, dumbly hammering.

ROSLYN
Won't you hit your hand, it's so dark? It's dark, Guido, look how
dark it is!

He hammers on. She almost turns, spreading her arms and looking
skyward.

ROSLYN
Look, it's all dark!

A sob breaks from her.

                    ROSLYN
Please stop! -- How can I help you? -- I can't do anything right
myself!

                    GAY'S VOICE
               (Nearby. He calls angrily:)
What the hell you stompin' the flowers for?!

Roslyn turns quickly.

MEDIUM LONG SHOT: GUIDO CONTINUES TO HAMMER WHILE ROSLYN TURNS TO
GAY WHO COMES UP TO GUIDO AND SWINGS HIM AROUND BY THE SHOULDER AND
BENDS TO THE GROUND.

                    GAY
You busted all the damn' heliotropes!

Gay is on his hands and knees now, trying to stand up the fallen
flowers. Guido is looking down dumbly, the hammer in his hand.

                    GAY
Look at that! Look at that now!

He holds up a torn stem.

                    GAY
What in hell good is that now!

                    ROSLYN
He was trying to fix the house!

                    GAY
               (Rising unsteadily to his feet,
                menacingly)
What call he got to fix the house!

                    ROSLYN
               (Trying to restrain him as HE
                stumbles to his feet)
Don't! Don't, Gay! Please! He . . . He's just trying to say hello!
It's no crime to say hello!

                    PERCE'S VOICE
               (Offscreen, crying out)
Who's doin' that!

They turn to look.

MEDIUM SHOT FROM THEIR VIEWPOINT: PERCE.

He is staggering into the headlight beams, trying to free his head
and arms from yards of unraveling bandage flowing off his head.
He is fighting it off as one would a clinging spider-web, turning
around and around to find its source.

> PERCE

Who's doin' that!

Roslyn hurries toward him.

> ROSLYN

Don't! Don't take it off!

She reaches him and tries to unwind his arms.

> PERCE

Get it off. What's on me!

> ROSLYN

You need it. Stop tangling it. It's your bandage.

> PERCE
> (Perturbed, he stops struggling and
> looks now at the bandage, as though
> for the first time)

What for a bandage?

Roslyn is starting to laugh despite her concern.

CLOSE SHOT: GUIDO AND GAY, LOOKING ON. GUIDO IS QUIETLY, BUT DEEPLY
LAUGHING, GLASSY-EYED. GAY IS BEGINNING TO FEEL THE LAUGHTER'S
INFECTIOUSNESS.

MEDIUM SHOT: ROZ AND PERCE, GUIDO AND GAY IN THE BACKGROUND.

> ROSLYN
> (Feeling an hysteria of laughing
> coming on)

For your head!

PERCE

My . . . ?

He breaks off as he raises his hands and feels the bandage wrapped
around his head.

PERCE

I have this on all night?

He looks angrily at Guido and Gay, who are roaring now, and to them
he says:

PERCE

Who tied this on me!

He is trying to pull it off his head.

ROSLYN

The ambulance did it. Don't take it off.

PERCE
(Unwinding and unwinding the bandage)
You leave me at a disadvantage all night? Who put it on! Gay,
you . . .

He lunges toward Gay and trips on a board, and the whole pile of
lumber begins to topple with a great crash.

Guido and Gay fall about, dying with hysteria.

Roslyn is between laughter and tears, while extricating Perce from the
lumber.

ROSLYN
Get him up. Gay, come here! Guido! Carry him. Please. He can't
help himself!

The men come to help her, and still laughing crazily they lift Perce
and almost carry him to the door of the house. Now she goes inside
ahead of them.

                         PERCE
Who put it on? -- Leave me at a disadvantage all night?

As they get him through the door of the house:

                         PERCE
Where's this? Let me alone. Where is this place!

The lights of the living room come on. Gay and Guido sprawl on
furniture, catching their breath.

                         ROSLYN
This is my house. . . . Or Guido's.
          (Laughs)
Well it's a house, anyway!

Perce glances dizzily around the living room, says:

                         PERCE
Oh.

He collapses on the floor; Gay and Guido erupt once more in laughter.
She catches Perce as he falls, letting his head down easily.

                         ROSLYN
Get me a pillow.

No one replies, so she turns and sees

MEDIUM SHOT: FROM HER VIEWPOINT, GAY ON COUCH.

He is sprawled out. He opens his eyes, looking up at her, the broken
flower on his chest under a relaxing hand.

                         GAY
Sure wish you'd met Gaylord. Looks just like me -- only young.
          (With a look of reproach at her)
Like I was, young.

He breaks off, closing his eyes.

MEDIUM SHOT: GUIDO ON FLOOR.

He is asleep, breathing hard, the hammer in his hand resting on his thigh. He is propped up against a chair-leg. Roslyn comes and lays him down on a cushion. The hammer slips onto the floor with a thump; she takes it out of his hand. Now she goes to Gay, covers him with an Indian blanket from across the back of the couch. She takes the flower gently from him. She looks over at Perce on the floor and goes to a nearby daybed, pulls the blanket off, and covers Perce. The contact of the blanket puts him in motion; he immediately starts to sit up.

                    PERCE
          (Resentfully)
No, Ma, don't, don't.

He turns his face away from her hand in a dream of pain.

                    ROSLYN
Oh, you poor baby boy.

She stands, a little unsteadily, goes and turns off the light, and finding herself at the door to the outside, walks out of the house.

LONG SHOT: THE CAR WITH THE LIGHTS ON, FROM HER VIEWPOINT.

She walks unsteadily to the car, reaches in and pushes the switch. The lights go off.

CLOSE SHOT: ROSLYN EMERGING FROM THE CAR.

Straightening up, she finds the flower in her hand. She looks up at the sky.

LONG SHOT: THE MOON, RACING ACROSS THE STARRY SKY.

CLOSE SHOT: ROSLYN'S FACE.

She is looking at the moon, tired, her eyes far-seeing, absorbed in wonder.

                    ROSLYN
Hello!

She raises her hand, as though to draw down attention from the sky, then softly . . .

                    ROSLYN
Help!

LONG SHOT: THE MOON.

Clouds racing over the stars. Now, gradually the stars grow dimmer.
The sky turns a paler blue, gradually turning pink. The CAMERA
tilts down now, across the heavens to a new, much more grand horizon.
An immense sage-dotted desert with towering mountains in the far
distance.

ANOTHER SHOT:

The sun is high, an eagle swoops and picks a rabbit off the desert,
and takes off again.

ANOTHER SHOT:

Afternoon. A rattler, emerging from rocks, a rabbit hopping away
from it. The CAMERA pans, past the rattler over the vast expanse,
until in the distance a cloud of dust is seen moving across the
desert.

MEDIUM SHOT: GAY'S TRUCK.

The dust cloud is following it -- an old but still serviceable
truck with a flat bed behind the cab. On the bed, lashed to the
back of the cab, is a drum of gasoline, with a hand-cranking pump
protruding from its top. It is bumping along over the sage and
here and there over whitened skeletons of cattle.

As the truck passes us, Perce spits out the window.

MEDIUM SHOT: CAB INTERIOR.

Gay is driving. Roslyn, beside him, has the dog in her lap, its
muzzle on her shoulder. Perce is just drawing his head in from
the right window. The sun narrows their eyes. They bump along
facing the desert before them.

MEDIUM SHOT: CAB INTERIOR. GAY, ROSLYN, PERCE

Gay is driving, Roslyn in the middle, Perce beside her. The dog
is on her lap, its muzzle on her shoulder. She turns from the
windshield, looks at Gay, then at Perce whose nose is still bandaged.
She suddenly remembers, and reaches down to the floor, takes up a
bag of apples, gives one to each man. They eat thankfully. She
looks on with satisfaction. To Gay . . .

                    ROSLYN
Not bad having a woman along, is it?

                          GAY
Nothin' I like better . . . if they behave.

Pause. She looks ahead, the smile going from her face.

                         ROSLYN
I won't bother you! I just didn't understand, yesterday . . .
               (Now with almost a laugh, but the
               tension puffs her eyes)
I mean a person can't change things, y'know? -- if they're happening?
I promise not to be a pest again!

Gay and Perce laugh. The truck suddenly mounts a little rise and
ahead they see the massive face of the mountains a distance away.
The reality of the hunt darts into her and her eyes widen, her
voice faltering.

                         ROSLYN
Is that where they are? -- up there?

                          GAY
               (Nods)
Honey, now you goin' to see what livin' is.

                         ROSLYN
         (Trying, despite a sense of imminence)
Okay!

Suddenly Guido's plane zooms down over the roof of the cab and they
see it flying straight ahead of them a few feet off the ground toward
the mountains, its wings wiggling a greeting. They laugh in surprise.
And Gay speeds up the truck now -- and his face and Perce's gain
excitement, the knitting-together of action as . . .

Dissolve.

We open on a wide shot of the mountains; it is the end of twilight,
when the purple light is turning blue. Incredible masses of stars
are coming out. The mountains, secretive and massive, wait. At
their foot the campfire shimmers -- the only moving thing in the
world.

Now, closer, we see the four around the fire. Nearby stands the
truck, and a little further away the lashed plane, both flickered by
moon and firelight like intruding monsters resting before an onslaught.

We open from a distance sufficient to muffle the dialogue, so that
we are aware now that we are close enough in to hear distinctly,
that we have come upon a hiatus in the talk. Guido is sipping
coffee, unable to keep his eyes from Roslyn across the fire from
him. She is putting away the last of the dried dishes into the
tote box. Gay is idly going through the dog's fur for fleas, and
Perce is carefully knotting a broken shoelace. Gay now glances
at Guido.

                         GAY
Well, if that's the end of the story, I vote we hit the sack.

                        ROSLYN
Let's talk a while! -- It's so beautiful here! ---
          (To Guido)
Is your father still alive?

                        GUIDO
No, he died down there in Brazil.   That's a story too.   They're
supposed to have eaten him.

                         GAY
Who!

                        GUIDO
The natives down there.   The last clinic he had was someplace up the
Mazon.   And they turned on him.

                        ROSLYN
Gee.

                        PERCE
What made him wander around down there like that, you suppose Pilot?

                        GUIDO
I don't think he'd be able to tell you that himself, Perce.   I
suppose the same thing that makes anybody do anything.

                        ROSLYN
What's that?

                        GUIDO
Oh . . .
          (Directly to her, but with a certain
          diffidence, as though he must hold
          down his full feeling)
. . . Loneliness.   And tryin' to break out of it.   Some people go to
play golf, some people turn on the television -- some go out to save
humanity.

                    GUIDO (Cont.)
          (Glancing toward the stars)
It's like there was a big turbine somewhere out there, and we're all
tryin' to get hooked into the wires somehow, and feel that warm
juice goin' through. . . . But you know that better than I do.

                    ROSLYN
          (Surprised)
Me?

                    GUIDO
You don't know it. You got it. That's even better.

We shoot Gay's growing alertness to Guido's pursuit of her.

                    ROSLYN
Got what?

                    GUIDO
That big connection. I never saw anybody was hooked into it the
way you are. What happens to anybody, it happens to you. That's
a blessing.

                    ROSLYN
          (From an expression of dead
          earnestness she suddenly laughs)
People tell me I'm just nervous!

                    GUIDO
Oh, sure, they have to find some way to laugh at it. But . . . some
won't laugh. A few.

                    GAY
          (He suddenly claps his hands to get
          the dust off, and rising to his feet . . .)
Well, I don't know about you educated people, but us ignorant folks
gotta go to sleep!

As Roslyn starts to get up her eyes fall on the dog. It is huddled
on the ground, visibly shivering, an odd attention in its eyes, its
head watchfully set between its paws.

                    ROSLYN
Gay?

He turns to her.

                                    ROSLYN
Why is the dog shivering?

                                     GAY
                    (He looks at the dog)
Oh, she'll do that up here.
                    (He glances toward the mountains)
She gets a whiff of those horses, I guess. They must be close by,
Guido . . .

Roslyn has gone to stroke the dog. Suddenly it bares its teeth and
nearly snaps her hand. She leaps away, terrified. Gay is instantly
furious.

                                     GAY
Hey, you damn fool! Come here!

The dog crawls to him on her belly.

                                    ROSLYN
Oh don't hurt her, she didn't mean it! -- The horses ever kick her
or something?

                                    GUIDO
                    (He is pitched high; daring)
It's not the horses she's afraid of.

They all look at Guido.

                                    GUIDO
It's us.

                                     GAY
                    (He is angered in a wider sense)
What're you talkin' about now, Guido? I never mistreated this dog.

                                    GUIDO
Just common sense, Gay. She's been up here enough times to know what
we're gonna do. We're goin' to kill animals, and she's an animal.
How's she know she's not next? They're not as stupid as people, y'know.

                                     GAY
                    (Smiles and glances to Roslyn as
                    though to force her attention on
                    his meaning)
This is big news to me, Guido -- I never heard you feel so much pain
about animals.

                              GUIDO
Well, I wouldn't exactly call it pain, it . . .

                              GAY
I don't guess you would,
          (With a glance at Roslyn)
seein's how you helped me take better'n four thousand horses out of
these hills. . . . And seein's how I never heard you mention a word
about animals till tonight.

                              GUIDO
I'm not complainin', Gay.

                              GAY
Glad to hear it -- I just didn't want this girl to get the wrong
idea, y'know?
          (He unrolls a bedroll near the fire)
Here now, Roslyn, you can keep yourself nice and warm by the fire.

He smiles at her, then starts unrolling his own roll -- Perce and
Guido are unrolling theirs nearby.

We shoot Roslyn staring down at the quivering dog. Then she looks
up and we shoot the dark, secret mountains looming up beyond the
fire. Now she looks at Gay who is smoothing out his bedroll.

                              ROSLYN
          (Her voice tight and nervous)
Maybe I could sleep on the truck, okay? Just in case something comes
creeping around?

                              GAY
Suit yourself. Just thought it'd be warmer near the fire.

He picks up her bedroll and starts past her to the truck.

We shoot Perce absorbing the situation . . . and Guido.

                              ROSLYN
Gay?
          (HE halts)
Maybe tomorrow . . .
          (Involuntarily her stomach is
          shaking. She is struggling against a
          flood of fear)
I could stay back here while you go. Would you mind?
          (Brightly)
I could have dinner ready when you get back!

                          GAY
Now look, Honey, it ain't gonna be as bad as all that up there.

                          ROSLYN
I know, but I just . . . suddenly I don't think I could stand it.

                          GAY
And what you gonna do if a snake shows up here tomorrow and you're
all alone?

                          GUIDO
          (Reasonably)
I could fly her home in the morning before we start work.
I'd be back in twenty minutes.

Gay turns to Guido, his jaw hardening. Then he turns to Roslyn.

                          GAY
You want to do that?

                          ROSLYN
          (Tears are in her eyes -- trying
          to placate him)
It's just that they're alive, you know? And if a thing is alive,
I . . . . Gay, I'm not criticizing you, but I . . .

                          GAY
          (He is furious, but restrains it)
Suit yourself, Honey, Guido be happy to fly you back.

                          ROSLYN
          (She almost stutters at being unable
          to communicate to him. She
          raises a hand wanly . . . and to all . . .)
Well . . . goodnight.

                       GUIDO and PERCE
'Night!

Gay walks ahead of her carrying the bedroll to the truck. He spreads
it out. She climbs up on the truck bed watching him. His face is
puffed with resentment. The bedroll prepared, he turns to her. They
are out of the others' hearing.

                          GAY
'Night now.

                    ROSLYN
          (She grasps his sleeve as HE starts
          to turn)
Please don't be mad at me.
          (HE is silent)
You see? -- I told you -- I can't get along with people. Now you
know.

Suddenly, almost harshly, he pulls her to him and kisses her.

                    GAY
You gonna come along with me tomorrow. And when I'm finished, you're
gonna tell em, "Gay, I want to stay with you the rest of my life."

                    ROSLYN
Gay, you don't understand. I . . .

                    GAY
Honey, I understand a lot more than I look like. You can't live lest
you kill -- that goes for the shoeleather on your feet to the steak
in your belly right now. You might have bought it in the store, but
you're made of what you killed, or somebody killed for you. It's been
that way since the first day of the world,
          (He glances offscreen to Guido)
and no lie is gonna change it.
          (He pats her)
You get some sleep now. . . .
          (He smiles)
I'll show you what livin' is, tomorrow.

He goes from her and we with him. Arriving at the diminishing fire,
he finds Guido and Perce with eyes closed in their bedrolls. He
takes off his shoes, slips into his bedroll. The dog comes and
lies down beside him.

                    GAY
Shame on you, you damn fool. . . . Everybody's showin' off!

He turns on his side, and closes his eyes.

The Camera now moves in close until the whole screen is filled with
the alert eyes of the dog, the firelight flickering on them. We
must feel the instinct, the sense of coming death -- the communication
between these eyes and the still unseen animals that are soon to die.

We move to Perce, over his back and around to his face. His eyes are
now open, he stares at what he has seen and heard. Slowly he turns
his head toward . . .

The truck. We cut to it now. Roslyn is in her sleeping bag, seemingly
asleep. Close in, we see her opening her eyes. She is confused,
struggling to understand her feelings. She turns her head now,
looking off toward . . .

The dark, immovable mountains beyond whose crests the animals graze.

Back to her, to her eyes. Suddenly she starts.

Perce has appeared beside the truck -- shielded by it from possible
sight of Gay and Guido at the fire.

                    PERCE
          (Whispering)
I just wanted to tell you . . . I've been up and down this world and
it nearly killed me couple a times, and you the first one ever cried
for me. That's the only thing there is, and don't let anybody tell
you you're wrong.

                    ROSLYN
I don't know . . . anything.

                    PERCE
          (He at first timorously, then with
          conviction, cups her face in his hand)
I know.
          (He looks deeply into her eyes.
          Suddenly he kisses her hand)
'Night, now.

He looks offscreen as though for Gay, then back to her.

                    PERCE
I love you . . . Roslyn.

He goes out of sight. She turns in the opposite direction -- toward
the fire. She sees him making his way back to his bedroll, getting
into it. On her face is the intensified question of the validity of
her feelings.

We cut to Gay. He opens his eyes, sees Perce getting into his bedroll. Guido is snoring. Gay stares, the dog open-eyed beside him. On these two pairs of eyes . . .

Dissolve.

We open on a long shot of the mountain ridges from the vantage of the camp location. The first rays of dawn are brightening the sky.

The Camera descends on the camp now, and discovers great, business-like activity. Perce is on the truck bed cranking gas from the drum into the plane. Guido is on top of the wing holding the hose and peering into the tank.

Gay is walking over to a kind of mound, partially covered with drift sand. He reaches down, grasps something and pulls -- a tarpaulin is peeled off revealing a dozen truck tires.

On the wing Guido raises his hand, peering into the tank, and calls . . .

                    GUIDO
Okay, hold it!

Gay calls to them from the pile of tires.

                    GAY
Let's go, Perce, gimme a hand here!

Perce hops off the truck, gets in and backs it to the tires. Guido clambers down off the wing, reaches into the open-sided cockpit and draws out a shotgun pistol which he proceeds to load from a box of shells.

Now we discover Roslyn, who is rolling up the bedrolls and tying them. She happens to look and see the pistol in Guido's hand, hesitates, then returns to her job. The dog comes up to her. She smiles down at the animal, then with some initial fear, reaches out and pats it. Happily she calls to Gay . . .

                    ROSLYN
She's not snapping any more, Gay!

Gay is just heaving a truck tire onto the bed of the truck with Perce's help. He turns to her, smiles.

                              GAY
Things generally look a little different in the morning!

                              GUIDO
                    (Calling from the plane)
I guess I'm ready, Gay!

Guido is drawing out of the plane a shredded air force jacket whose
lambswool lining is visible through the outside leather. He and Gay
go to each wingtip and unlash the plane. Perce goes to the tail,
unlashes it. Roslyn comes near and watches now. Perce now comes
alongside her and watches. Gay walks back to the cockpit with Guido.

                              GAY
How you want her?

Guido looks up at the sky, holding a palm up to feel the breeze.
He points.

                              GUIDO
That way.

Gay goes to the tail, lifts it and swings the plane to face the
direction of take-off. Then he walks along the plane to the propellor
and waits. Guido is about to get into the cockpit.

Roslyn, as though to relieve the weirdly changed atmosphere, calls
rather gaily to Guido.

                              ROSLYN
Boy, that's some jacket! Little breezy, isn't it?

                              GUIDO
Went on a lot of missions in this thing. Wouldn't take a hundred
dollars for it . . . bullet proof.

They chuckle as he climbs in, sits. And to Roslyn . . .

                              GUIDO
Glad you decided to stay with us. Probably never see this again in
history, y'know.

                              ROSLYN
Take care, now!

Guido registers his thanks for her solicitude.

                    GUIDO
          (To Gay)
Okay, boy, turn your partner and doe-see-doe!

Gay glances behind him to see if there is any obstruction to his
back-step, reaches up, pulls the prop, steps back.

                    GUIDO
And again. With feeling now!

They laugh. Gay once more turns the prop.

                    GUIDO
          (Throwing the ignition switch)
Contact now! -- and let us pray.

Gay with special care grasps the prop, pulls down. The engine
huffs and dies.

                    GUIDO
That's that damn car gas for ya -- okay, let's try her again.

Gay pulls the prop. The engine smokes, huffs, and with a sudden
resolution, clatters up to a roar. Guido straps himself in, lays
the pistol on his lap, pulls down his goggles, and with a wave to
them, guns the engine. The plane moves away from them, gains speed
and takes the air. Now it wheels in air and comes back, roaring
over their heads and away toward the mountains. They turn with it.

We fasten on the three faces squinting against the prop blast. Gay
is the first to move -- he looks for an instant at Perce and Roslyn.
They feel his glance and both turn to him -- a tinge of guilt is
on both of them. Gay smiles.

                    GAY
Here we go.

He turns toward the truck and starts to walk, they behind him. We
cut to . . .

A shot, from the plane, of the mountain wall. It is quickly approaching, bare rock.

Inside the plane. Guido lifts his goggles. He looks up at the clear blue sky. His lips moves as though in prayer. He lowers his goggles, looks down.

LONG SHOT: FROM PLANE. THE MOUNTAINS.

The barrier face of the mountains suddenly passes under the plane. Music strikes a mixed mood of the pastoral and a new weird quality. Now the sharp interior walls and steep valleys show, uninhabited, half in shadow, with patches of grass here and there. A hidden secret world is opened.

LONG SHOT: THE PLANE IN VALLEYS.

The plane is flying just above the crests of the mountains, turning with the valleys.

CLOSE SHOT: PLANE INTERIOR.

Guido is looking down through the open-sided cockpit. Suddenly his head moves sharply.

LONG SHOT: HORSES FROM PLANE VIEWPOINT.

Suddenly, a herd of six horses -- five and a colt -- are seen in sunlight far below, grazing close to the upthrust wall of a valley.

CLOSE SHOT: PLANE INTERIOR.

Guido instantly pulls the stick back; the plane climbs sharply. Now he banks and turns. Now he checks his instruments, and reaches under the seat and takes out the pistol which he holds in his right hand. Now, after checking below with a glance, he presses the stick forward and abruptly dives.

LONG SHOT: HORSES FROM PLANE.

The herd is coming in to the Camera, fast. Now it starts to move in a gallop along the wall of the valley.

LONG SHOT: PLANE DIVING ON THE HORSES.

The plane is zooming in over the horses, its wingtips only yards from the valley walls; the horses are galloping ahead of it.

CLOSE SHOT: PLANE INTERIOR.

Guido pulls the stick back and the plane noses upward; he points the pistol down as he passes over the herd, and fires.

LONG SHOT: HORSES FROM PLANE.

With the shot the horses surge ahead even faster, and as we climb away from them,

DISSOLVE TO:

CLOSE SHOT: INTERIOR OF TRUCK CAB: GAY, ROSLYN, PERCE, DOG.

They are bumping along over the sage. The dog is on the floor now with its muzzle on the seat between Gay and Roslyn. They are sitting differently now than earlier -- there is a certain half-conscious fear of touching one another. Perce has his arms folded across his chest; Roslyn's hands are in her lap. Now Gay takes one hand off the wheel and lays it on her knee.

                    GAY
          (Happily)
How you doin'?

                    ROSLYN
Okay.

Perce glances at his hand on her knee. She does not see his glance, but, in effect, makes Gay remove his hand by reaching to the dog's head and patting it.

                    ROSLYN
She's starting to shiver again.

                    GAY
She'll get over it. Just let her be now.

We sense that he feels a vague rebuff.

LONG SHOT: TRUCK MOVING INTO LAKEBED.

The truck bumps along on the sage desert, but now it crosses a border where the sage and soil abruptly end and a prehistoric lakebed begins. It is entirely bare, glaringly white, and hard as concrete. Now the truck halts. It is close to a little hummock bordering the lakebed.

MEDIUM SHOT: TRUCK.

Perce emerges as the engine is turned off. He looks around as
Roslyn comes down out of the cab. Gay is emerging from the other side
of the truck, and walks around to them where they stand scanning the
lakebed. The silence is absolute. There is no wind.

                         ROSLYN
It's . . . like a dream!

LONG SHOT: LAKEBED.

Set between mountain ranges the lakebed stretches about twenty-five
miles wide and as long as the eye can see. Not a blade of grass or
stone mars its absolutely flat surface from which heatwaves rise.

MEDIUM SHOT: THE THREE.

They are scanning the lakebed.

                         PERCE
I seen a picture of the moon once. Looked like this.

                         ROSLYN
Where are the horses?

                         GAY
         (Pointing)
He'll be drivin' them out through that pass.

She and Perce look.

LONG SHOT: THE PASS.

It is perhaps a mile away, an opening in the mountain face.

MEDIUM SHOT: THE THREE.

                         ROSLYN
Does anybody own this land?

                         GAY
I don't know. Government, probably. Just call it God's country.
Perce? -- let's get that drum off.

Gay goes to the truck and hops onto the bed and proceeds to unlash the gasoline drum. Perce stands on the ground and helps Jimmy the drum to the edge of the truck. Now Gay hops down and both men let it down to the ground and roll it off to one side, away from the truck. Roslyn watches for a moment, then goes to the cab and leans in.

CLOSE SHOT: THE DOG.

Over her shoulder, we see the dog quivering on the floor of the cab. She reaches toward it.

MEDIUM SHOT: GAY AND PERCE.

Gay goes to one of the tires and draws a rope from inside it and experimentally circles it over his head and throws it.

Perce, seeing him occupied, walks over to the cab and looks in from the side opposite to that of Roslyn.

CLOSE SHOT: ROSLYN AND DOG.

Over Perce's shoulder we see Roslyn pressing her face against the dog's. Then she reaches up to the rear-view mirror, and turns it to look at herself and sees Perce and smiles.

> ROSLYN
> (Almost a whisper)

Thanks . . . for telling me that last night. I always think I'm wrong, you know?

CLOSE SHOT: PERCE'S FACE, ROSLYN'S VIEWPOINT.

He is looking at her longingly, and deeply troubled.

> PERCE
> (In a hushed voice)

I'd be careful what I said to Gay. For a while out here.

Gay's face appears beside Perce's.

> GAY

Lemme get the glasses.

Perce steps aside. Gay moves into the truck doorway, hardly looking at Roslyn who now fixes her hair in the rear-view mirror. Gay reaches

behind the seat and draws out a large binocular case. He looks at
her now, grinning, a hurt in his eyes. Then he takes the binoculars
out of the case.

MEDIUM SHOT: THE THREE.

From the rear of the truck we see Gay and Perce on one side, and
Roslyn coming toward us on the other side. Gay is putting the glasses
to his eyes, Perce watching him. He holds the glasses up to his eyes
for a long moment, looking toward the pass.

CLOSE SHOT: ROSLYN'S FACE.

A beginning of real fright is in her eyes. She is looking at . . .

CLOSE SHOT: PERCE, WITH GAY IN THE SHOT LOOKING THROUGH GLASSES.

Perce glances at her from Gay, and winks encouragement, but without
smiling.

MEDIUM SHOT: THE THREE.

                         ROSLYN
               (Forcing a bright tone)
See anything?

                         GAY
               (Putting the glasses on a tire on
               the truck-bed)
Not yet.   Climb up, make yourself comfortable.   He'll be a while
yet.

Gay comes over and gives her a boost. She mounts the truckbed.
He climbs up, and sits inside a pile of two tires, his legs hanging
over the edge at the knees, his armpits supporting his trunk.

                         GAY
Go ahead.   It's comfortable.

She does as he did; Perce mounts onto the truck.

                         ROSLYN
It is comfortable!   Try it, Perce.

Perce does the same. The three sit in silence as Gay again raises
the glasses and looks through them.

                        PERCE
I hear something.

                        GAY
            (Putting down the glasses)
What?

                        PERCE
Tick, tick, tick, tick, tick.

                        GAY
It's my watch.

                        ROSLYN
Boy, it's quiet here!
            (She tries to laugh)

                        GAY
            (Exhaling, relaxing in the tire)
Ayah!

He leans his head back, closing his eyes. Perce and Roslyn are, in
effect, joined by a viewpoint toward Gay, a consciousness which
feeds dangerously upon itself. They look at one another, forced, as
it were, to betray themselves or to keep their eyes on neutral
objects. Now with his eyes still closed Gay smiles. Roslyn and
Perce look at him. Now he begins to chuckle, opening his eyes and
shaking his head.

                        GAY
Guido sure tickles me sometimes. He really put on a show for you
last night. I thought for a minute there he'd bust out cryin'
for the poor mustangs.

                        ROSLYN
You can't tell, Gay. Maybe he always felt bad about them, but he
never said anything. People do a lot of things they don't want to.

                        GAY
            (He turns with a certain arch look
            to Perce)
You joinin' the mourners' brigade too?

                        PERCE
            (Caught between Gay's view and Roslyn,
            he looks off into the distance)
Well . . . long as I'm here I'll do what I said I'd do.

Gay's face loses its humor, and he turns toward the distance. After
a moment, he turns to Roslyn . . .

                              GAY
They're nothin' but misfit horses -- you know that don't you?
They're too small for ridin', and all they do is eat out good
grassland. Cow outfits shoot them on sight and let 'em rot.
                    (SHE doesn't answer, not wanting
                     to rile him. HE turns to Perce)
Perce? You know that, don't you?

                             PERCE
Yeah, I know.

                              GAY
Well? -- why don't you say so?

He picks up the glasses and looks at the pass. He puts down the
glasses. There is not a sound in the world. He lights a cigarette.

                              GAY
Human nature's a funny thing -- man'll drop a bomb, kill a hundred
thousand people, he's a hero. Same man kills a horse -- all hell
breaks loose. Or you take these pet-lovers -- raise a stink about
the mustangs and go right out to the store and buy a can of horse
meat for little Fido. . . . You understand that, Perce?

                             PERCE
I guess the right hand don't want to know what the left hand is doin'.

                              GAY
Yeah -- but some man's gotta be the left hand, don't he?

He looks at Roslyn -- he is somehow riding a wave of inner assurance
that takes a taunting tone; he reaches over and shakes her knee.

                              GAY
You lookin' real good today, Honey!

She can't help but smile to him.

                              GAY
What you say -- when we get through here we go into Reno, and dance,
and have us a time, huh?

                            ROSLYN
Okay!

                         GAY
Maybe you can get yourself a girl, Perce.

                         PERCE
            (Preoccupied)
I hear something.

Gay listens. He raises the glasses, sees nothing, puts them down.

                         GAY
What?

                         PERCE
Engine, sounds like.

They listen.

                         GAY
Where?

                         PERCE
            (Indicating with an open hand the
            general direction of the pass)
Out that way.

                         GAY
            (Listens)
Too soon. He wouldn't be in the pass yet.

                         ROSLYN
Wait.
            (She listens)
I hear it.

                         GAY
            (He listens. Now a certain pique is
            noticeable in him because he can't
            hear it)
You don't hear nothin'; I ain't that old. Just your blood pumpin'
in your head, is all.

                         ROSLYN
Ssh.

            (GAY watches her. PERCE is also
            tensed to listen)

                         GAY
I always had the best ears of anybody, so don't tell me you . . .

                        PERCE
            (Suddenly pointing, and screwing up
            out of the tire to sit on its rim)
Isn't that him?

The three look off; Roslyn and Gay trying to locate a point in the
sky far away. They too wriggle out of the tires and sit on the rims.

                       ROSLYN
I see it! There! look, Gay!

Almost insulted he scans the sky -- then unwillingly raises the
glasses.

LONG SHOT: THROUGH BINOCULARS.

The mountain pass is brought up close; and flying out of it is the
plane, tiny even in the glasses.

MEDIUM SHOT: THE THREE.

                         GAY
            (He puts down the glasses. He blinks
            his eyes hard. He is angered)
He never worked this fast before. I . . . I'd've seen him but I
didn't expect him so soon.

                        PERCE
            (To assuage Gay)
I could see him glinting in the sun. It was the glint. That's **why**.

Now, very distantly, an explosion is heard.

                       ROSLYN
What's that?

                         GAY
He fired.

She watches the pass with growing apprehension and fascination.
Perce glances at her in concern, then back to the pass. They are all
perspiring now in the warming sun.

                              GAY
I've ..at here waitin' two-three hours before he come out. That's
why I didn't see him.
                    (Now, however, glances at Perce, and
                    as though he can afford the compliment)
You got good eyes, though, boy.

Gay raises the glasses again. Silence. All three watch.

                              GAY
There they come. One . . . two . . . three . . . four . . . five . . .
six. I guess he'll go back for the others now.

                              PERCE
Give me a look, heh?

Gay gives him the binoculars. Perce looks.

                              GAY
See the others yet?

                              PERCE
No. There's . . . six. And a colt.

CLOSE SHOT: ROSLYN'S FACE.

There is a deepening of tension; almost a wincing.

                              GAY'S VOICE
You sure?

                              PERCE'S VOICE
Ya. It's a little colt.

CLOSE SHOT: PERCE'S FACE IN PROFILE, WITH BINOCULARS RAISED.

                              PERCE
It's a spring colt.

He lowers the glasses, faces into camera.

                              PERCE
                    (With finality; not quite accusing,
                    but nevertheless with an inference
                    of question as to what will be done

                              PERCE (Cont.)
              with it)
It's a colt, Gay.

MEDIUM SHOT: THE THREE.

Gay, concerned, but with barely a look at Perce, takes the glasses.
Perce turns to watch the pass again. Roslyn turns and watches
Gay's profile for a moment. Now, Gay lowers the glasses, faces her
fully. He will not be condemned.

                              GAY
Want a look?

He gives her the glasses. She hesitates, but then tensely raises
them to her eyes.

LONG SHOT: THROUGH BINOCULARS. HORSES AND PLANE.

The herd is galloping in file; the colt bringing up the rear with its
nose nearly touching its mare's tail. Now the plane dives down on
them and they lift their heads and gallop faster. The screen image
shakes -- as though the hands holding the binoculars had lost their
steadiness. Then the image flows out crazily as the lenses are
being lowered.

MEDIUM SHOT: THE THREE.

Roslyn is lowering the glasses, a high tension in her eyes.

                              GAY
              (He will bull it through with her until
              she moves to him)
See them clear?

Roslyn nods, and hands him back the glasses. Gay stands, glancing
down at her with a smile that has in it a certain gratification. He
raises the glasses again. She quickly wipes her fingers over her
eyes. Another shot is heard. She opens her eyes to look. Perce
and Gay are fixed on the distant spectacle. She gets to her feet
and hops down off the truck. Perce looks to her.

                              ROSLYN
              (Faintly)
. . . Maybe it's cooler in the truck.

She walks to the cab and climbs in. Gay and Perce remain on the
truck bed, sitting again on the edges of the tires. Perce seems
affected by her emotion. Gay, with a glance, notes this.

                            GAY
Take it slow, boy, take it slow. I'll take care of her.

A pause. Perce wants very much to go down to Roslyn. Gay holds him
with his authority. Now Perce turns to Gay . . .

                           PERCE
I thought you said there was fifteen. There's only six.

                            GAY
Probably lost a few. That'll happen.

                           PERCE
Don't make much sense for six, does it?

                            GAY
Six is six. Better'n wages, ain't it?
          (PERCE doesn't answer)
I said it's better than wages, ain't it?

                           PERCE
          (With damaged conviction)
I guess anything's better'n wages.

                            GAY
          (After a moment)
Perce? We've just about cleaned 'em out up here, but if you're
interested in some real money, there's a place about a hundred
miles northeast -- Thighbone Mountain. I never bothered up there
'cause it's awful tough to get 'em out. Gotta get 'em on horseback
up there. But there's five hundred on Thighbone Mountain. Maybe
more.
          (PERCE is silent, staring at the pass)
That'd be _real_ money -- you could buy yourself some good stock,
maybe even a little van -- hit those rodeos in style.

                           PERCE
          (Deeply troubled)
I don't know, Gay -- tell you the truth, I don't even know about
rodeos any more.

                            GAY
I'm beginnin' to smell wages all over you, boy.

                              PERCE
I don't know, Gay -- I've seen it all and there's nothin' to it,
there's nothin' to any of it. I sure wish my old man hadn't of
died. You never saw a prettier ranch.

                              GAY
Fella, when you get through wishin', all there is, is doin' a man's
work. And there ain't much of that left in this country. Everything
else is wages. I'd sooner be dead in the hot place.

Suddenly they are bolted upright by a ferocious snarling of the dog
and Roslyn's screaming. Both of them leap off the truck bed as Roslyn
jumps out of the cab, going backwards. Gay rushes to the cab and
sees the dog on the seat, its teeth bared, snarling.

                              GAY
What're you botherin' that dog for!

                              ROSLYN
She was shaking so I . . .

                              GAY
              (To the dog)
Get down here!

The dog, tail between its legs, slides down to the ground. Gay
reaches in behind the seat, takes out a length of cord, ties it to
the dog's collar, and leashes the dog to the bumper. The dog crawls
under the truck in the shade, and lies down. Gay now goes to Roslyn
who is quivering; he starts to put his arm around her . . . Roslyn
halts and looks up into his face.

                              ROSLYN
              (As though he must immediately do
              something for the dog)
She's scared to death, Gay!

                              GAY
              (Almost an outburst)
Well, that's what she's supposed to be, I guess! Sometimes we're
scared, sometimes we're glad . . . that's life, ain't it? You can't
change that . . .

A shot is heard, very close now -- it turns him toward the sky, and he
immediately starts toward the truck, walking sideways as he talks to

her behind him . . . Perce is in the background turning toward the
source of the shot.

                         GAY
Just roll with it, Honey, and see how you make out!

He gets to the truck and immediately reaches in behind the seat
and draws out two iron spikes and a short-handled sledgehammer.
Now he turns for an instant and looks toward.

The plane is just completing a dive -- much closer now. The horses
are now clearly visible. They are galloping straight toward the
bare white lakebed but they are still on the sage-dotted desert.

Back to Gay -- he turns quickly and walks past Perce who is staring
at Roslyn now. She, in turn, is looking toward the horses.

                         GAY
Give us a hand here, Perce.

Perce follows Gay who hands him a spike which Perce props up as Gay
drives it into the ground, ties a rope to it, and then pacing off
several yards, does the same with the second spike and ties a rope
to that.

Now Gay leaves Perce and walks to the truck, tosses the hammer in
behind the cab, and for an instant halts to look at . . .

Roslyn. She is wide-eyed, staring at the horses.

Gay, with businesslike pace, unleashes the dog, walks it to one
of the spikes and ties her.

Now Gay comes and puts an arm around Perce's shoulders, and in
effect makes Perce walk with him away from where Roslyn is standing.
Gay is calm-faced, but his eyes are quick and they are hurt. We
truck with their stroll.

                         GAY
Maybe we better make that a farewell party for you tonight. Okay?

                        PERCE
Gay, you're the one man in the world I never wanted any trouble
with. You the best friend I think I ever had. But you can't treat
her like she . . . She's got feelin's, Gay . . .

                              GAY
                    (He smiles)
Boy, you're savin' women again. But this one don't need savin',
hear? I'm takin' a little trouble with this one, straighten her out
a little bit -- 'cause this is the one I'm gonna keep.

From offscreen, Roslyn calls.

                              ROSLYN
Gay?
                    (GAY and PERCE turn and start back to
                    her. SHE is pointing toward the horses
                    and is very excited, full of hope)
They won't go any further! See? They want to go back!

From their viewpoint we shoot the horses and the plane. They have
reached the border of the white lakebed and have broken file, scattering
right and left in order to remain on the familiar sage desert,
frightened of crossing over onto the strange, superheated air of the
lakebed.

Gay and Perce have come up beside Roslyn now, all looking toward
the horses.

                              ROSLYN
                    (She turns to Gay and suddenly grasps
                    his shirt, pleadingly)
They want to go home! Please, Gay . . !

Gay looks past her, and she turns . . .

We shoot the plane diving down on the horses within a yard of their
heads -- and now they break out onto the lakebed, re-forming their
grouping as earlier, and the plane now flies above the lakebed itself
and is not climbing for another dive.

Back to the three and the truck . . . Gay takes Roslyn's arm and walks
her quickly to the truck cab, but she resists entering. They stop.

                              GAY
If it's happening, you said you want to see it. Well, here's your
chance to give it a good look.

He heists her into the cab, slams the door, quickly puts his head
in, turns her face to him and kisses her lips.

                          GAY
We're gonna have a big time tonight!

With great joy he steps away and leaps up onto the truck bed.
Perce is still on the ground, indecisively standing there.

                          GAY
Git up here, Perce, let's see what you can do now!

Perce feels the force of Gay's command, and also sees what is
evidently Gay's victory -- for Roslyn is sitting motionless in the cab
and is not obstructing. He leaps aboard the truck bed.

We shoot the plane now -- it is just touching down on the lakebed and
is taxiing toward the truck. The horses are now trotting only, but
far away.

Back to the truck -- Gay hands Perce the end of a webbing strap whose
other end is buckled to the post at Gay's corner. Perce passes the
strap across his back and buckles the end to the post at his corner,
so that both men are held, if rather precariously, to the cab and cannot
fall backward. Gay now turns to the pile of tires behind him and
takes out a coil of rope from the top tire. This Perce does too from
the pile behind him. Both men heft their ropes, grasping them just
behind the nooses, limbering them, adjusting them.. . .

MEDIUM SHOT: FROM MEN'S VIEWPOINT. THE PLANE AND GUIDO

The plane taxis up fast and the motor stops as it comes between the
two spikes driven into the ground. Guido jumps out of the cockpit and
runs to one spike, then the other, lashing the ropes to the plane
struts. The dog, leashed to one of the spikes, snarls at him but he
brushes her off and lashes the rope. With his goggles on his forehead,
his face puffed with preoccupation, he trots over to the cab and jumps
in.

CLOSE SHOT: CAB INTERIOR: GUIDO AND ROSLYN.

Without a glance at Roslyn, he turns the key, starts the engine, puts
the truck in gear, and roars off at top speed across the lakebed.
He is peering ahead through the windshield.

                          GUIDO
Grab hold now, we're gonna do a lot of fast turning.

Roslyn holds onto the dashboard, excitement pumping into her face.
The faded air force insignia on his shoulder is next to her face.

LONG SHOT: THROUGH THE WINDSHIELD.   THE HORSES ON LAKEBED.

Through the windshield the open lakebed spreads before us.   A mile
off two black dots are seen, rapidly enlarging.   Now their forms become
clear; two horses standing, watching the oncoming truck, their ears
stiffly raised in curiosity.

CLOSE SHOT: CAB INTERIOR.   ROSLYN AND GUIDO.

She looks from the horses to Guido.   His goggles are still on his
forehead; a look of calculation, of action, of zeal is coming into
his face.   She is feeling the first heat of terror, and turns to
look forward, her hands grasping the dashboard.

LONG SHOT: THE HORSES.

The same two horses, a hundred yards off now and rapidly coming into
the camera.   Their rib cages are expanding and contracting, their
nostrils spread.   Now one of them turns and gallops, then the other,
both keeping close together.

LONG SHOT: TWO HORSES, SEEN THROUGH WINDSHIELD, INCLUDING GUIDO
AND ROSLYN IN CAB.

From behind their heads the Camera shoots, taking in the hood of the
truck, Guido driving, and Roslyn beside him.   He steers right up to
the flying rear hooves of the horses.   Now they wheel, and Guido turns
sharply with them -- the truck sways dangerously -- and he works brake
and gas pedal simultaneously.   Now the horses straighten, and in doing
so they separate from one another by a foot or two and Guido presses
the truck into this space which quickly widens, and he speeds even
faster and now there is one horse on each side of the truck, running
abreast of the cab windows.

Roslyn, her eyes fascinated and frightened, looks at the horse
running only a yard to one side of her.

CLOSE SHOT: THE HORSE, FROM ROSLYN'S VIEWPOINT.

It is a medium-size stallion, glistening with sweat.   We can hear the
roaring wheeze of its breathing, and the strangely gentle tacking of its
unshod hooves on the hard lakebed.   It is stretching its body to the
utmost.

CLOSE SHOT: STALLION'S HEAD.

The eyes are blind with terror.

CLOSE SHOT: ROSLYN'S EYES.

She is staring with rising horror at its eyes.

CLOSE SHOT: STALLION'S HEAD.

From behind, a noose falls over the stallion's ears and
hangs there. It won't fall over his head.

CLOSE SHOT: PERCE ATOP TRUCK.

He is trying to whip his rope to make its noose fall over the
stallion's ears.

CLOSE SHOT: GUIDO.

He calls past Roslyn to Perce, whom he can't see. He almost seems
angry.

                    GUIDO
Go on, get him! Throw again, Perce!

At this instant we see the other horse beyond Guido's head as a
noose falls cleanly over its head and down over its neck. Guido
calls out the window on his side -- the left:

                    GUIDO
Attaboy, Gay!

MEDIUM SHOT: GAY AND PERCE ON TRUCK BED.

Seen from the front, Gay and Perce are squinting against the wind,
which wips their hat-brims and their shirts. Gay, having just lasso'd
his horse, is now letting go of the rope; his horse is veering off
to the left, away from the truck. It pulls out the rope to its
limit, then suddenly yanks the heavy truck tire off the top of the
pile behind him.

The horse is left behind by the truck; as it feels the pull of the
rope it rears in air and comes to a halt.

Now Perce, who has looped up his rope, is circling it over his head,
and throws it. The noose falls over the horse's head (this horse --
the stallion, is on the truck's right, on Perce's side). Perce's
horse veers right, away from the truck and pulls a tire off from behind
Perce.

GAY
(Shouting with joy)
That's the way!

Perce returns an excited look. Gay stretches and claps him on the shoulder, laughing. They are suddenly joined.

LONG SHOT: FROM CAB INTERIOR: GUIDO AND ROSLYN.

The Camera shoots past Guido, who is steering sharply to reverse the truck's direction; Roslyn is looking out the window at the horse just lasso'd by Perce.

LONG SHOT: PERCE'S HORSE PAST ROSLYN'S FACE.

Over her shoulder, shooting through her window, we see in the middle distance the stallion being forced to a halt by the dragging tire. The truck is slowing as it nears the stallion, which now has turned with lowered head to face the tire. Now it rises up in the air, its forefeet flailing at the air. Suddenly the truck speeds up again, changing direction. Roslyn turns to Guido.

ROSLYN
They'll choke, won't they?

GUIDO
We're comin' back in a minute!

LONG SHOT: THROUGH WINDSHIELD: THREE DISTANT HORSES ON LAKEBED.

We are moving fast toward three rapidly enlarging specks; their forms quickly emerge; they turn and run. Now a fourth, that of the colt, emerges from the screening body of the mare. The colt runs with its nose nearly in the mare's long, full tail.

MEDIUM SHOT: PERCE AND GAY ATOP THE TRUCK: SEEN FROM FRONT

Both men are twirling their lassoes over their heads, their bodies leaning outward over the truck's sides. The sound of clattering hooves grows louder and louder.

CLOSE SHOT: GAY'S FACE.

He is living.

CLOSE SHOT: PERCE'S FACE.

A look of confusion, sympathy, rising in his eyes as he twirls his noose.

MEDIUM SHOT: PERCE'S VIEWPOINT OF MARE AND COLT RUNNING.

Perce is now above and a length behind the big mare and her colt. He is readying his noose, getting set. Suddenly Roslyn's head sticks out of the window of the cab, looking up at him pleadingly. She is almost within arm's length of the colt, which is galloping beside her.

CLOSE SHOT: PERCE'S FACE.

He has seen her, the fright and pain in her face.

CLOSE SHOT: GAY'S FACE.

> GAY
>
> Get that horse!

Now Gay throws his noose at the horse on his side.

MEDIUM SHOT: PERCE ON TRUCK.

With a sudden surge of resolution Perce throws his rope. It lands over the mare's head and she veers to the right, the colt veering with her.

LONG SHOT: ROSLYN IN FOREGROUND SEEING LASSO'D MARE AND COLT.

Past Roslyn's cheek, shooting through the right window, we see the mare being halted by the dragging tire and the colt running almost rib to rib with her.

LONG SHOT: THE TRUCK.

We see the truck swerving to follow the one remaining horse which it quickly overtakes. Gay throws and lasso's this horse which pulls a tire off the truck and is coming to a halt, bucking and flinging its heavily maned neck against the tightening pressure of the remorseless noose. Now the truck turns back and slows as it approaches the mare and colt, and finally halts. A door of the truck opens and Roslyn hops out. Gay and Perce come down off the truck bed. Roslyn does not emerge.

MEDIUM SHOT: GAY, GUIDO, PERCE, WITH MARE AND COLT. TRUCK IN BACKGROUND.

The three men come over to the mare. She circles to keep them in
front of her, and the colt keeps nuzzling up against her. The mare
is a full-sized horse, covered with sweat, her rib cage barreling out
and in, her legs slim and quivering, her nostrils distended. Her
eyes are terrorized. The men halt a few yards from her.

MEDIUM SHOT: ROSLYN IN CAB FROM PERCE'S VIEWPOINT.

She is facing the windshield, not able to look at the mare. It is
unknown whether her oddly deadened expression means anger, acceptance
or fear.

MEDIUM SHOT: THE THREE MEN AND MARE AND COLT. TRUCK IN BACKGROUND.

                        PERCE
She's too big for a mustang, ain't she? I bet she's branded.

                        GAY
I don't see any brand.

                        GUIDO
Get your ropes, Gay.

Gay turns and goes to the truck and opens the door. Roslyn turns
to him, but slowly, as though her soul were elsewhere.

CLOSER SHOT: GAY AND ROSLYN. TRUCK INTERIOR.

She merely stares at him, blankly. He hardly pauses; reaches in
behind the back of the seat and takes out two coiled ropes. Gay
glances again at her as he turns away -- His face shows a mystification.
He walks toward the mare.

CLOSE SHOT: PERCE'S FACE.

He is perplexed by her evident attitude.

MEDIUM SHOT: THE THREE MEN AND MARE AND COLT: TRUCK IN BACKGROUND.

Facing the mare, Gay is twirling his rope over his head; Guido
stands beside him, a second rope in his hands. Gay throws. The
noose falls open just behind the forefeet of the mare. Now Guido
walks toward her; now he counts. The mare backs.

CLOSE SHOT: MARE'S FEET STEPPING INTO NOOSE.

She has stepped into the noose which quickly is pulled, binding her
two forefeet together.

MEDIUM SHOT: THE MEN AND MARE AND COLT.

Gay stands holding his rope taut. Now Guido throws his rope; and
the noose falls behind the mare's hind hooves. Gay makes a sudden
movement and a shout, and she backs, and Guido pulls his rope and
binds her hind feet together. Now both men are on the same side of
the horse. They jerk their ropes. The mare's feet are pulled from
under her and she falls to the ground on her side. The colt dances
away and comes back, standing close to her. She lies there gasping
for breath. The men approach her. She raises up her head menacingly.
Gay hurries to the tire and pulls it so her head is held flat
to the earth.

                    GAY
          (To Perce)
Hold this down, boy.

Perce comes and sits on the tire.

MEDIUM SHOT: ROSLYN IN TRUCK FROM PERCE'S VIEWPOINT.

She is turning to look at the mare -- an inward stare of incomprehension
on her face.

MEDIUM SHOT: GAY AND GUIDO WITH MARE AND COLT.

Guido is slipping the noose along the mare's neck until it reaches
just under her jaws.

                    GAY
She's an old one.

                    GUIDO
Probably.

                    GAY
Take a look. I want to tell Roslyn.

Guido parts her lips and looks into her mouth.

                    GUIDO
About fifteen, sixteen.

                    GAY
If she's a day.

Perce comes over and the two men stand up. Gay unbinds the mare's
hooves and they all step away. The horse clambers to her feet.
She inspects her colt, which presses against her. The men return
to the truck. Roslyn's door is still open.

                         GAY
She's fifteen years old if she's a day, Roslyn.

Roslyn looks past him at the mare. She does not speak.

                         GAY
She's not a real mustang. Probably ran off sometime and went wild
up there. She's old, though, Roslyn, wouldn't last another winter.

Guido has gotten behind the wheel beside her. Gay turns from her
and climbs up on the truck. Perce stands looking at the mare.
Gay calls down to him:

                         GAY
Let's go, Perce!

Perce turns toward the truck, glancing at . . .

MEDIUM SHOT: ROSLYN FROM PERCE'S POINT OF VIEW.

She is still staring at the mare. She does not look at Perce.

MEDIUM SHOT: PERCE.

He swings up onto the truck. The truck moves off.

LONG SHOT: TRUCK MOVING OFF, MARE AND COLT IN FOREGROUND.

The mare, with the colt nuzzling her, stares after the vanishing
truck. The breeze blows her long tail and her mane. She is still
breathing with difficulty. The terror is still in her eyes.

CLOSE SHOT: CAB INTERIOR: GUIDO AND ROSLYN.

The inwardness of her look remains. Guido, driving, glances at her,
and defensively . . .

                         GUIDO
We'll shift the nooses on all of them now, so they won't suffocate
themselves.

She turns to him, eyes wide, as though facing a wonder, an astonishment
too great to utter. Her strangeness unhingeing his composure because
he is uncertain whether she is in the act of learning something new,
or condemning him beyond belief. He clings to the first idea for a
moment . . .

                    GUIDO
. . . What I tried to tell you last night is that . . . I think I
understand what you're after. You want to shake hands with life, you
want to put your arms around it all, don't you? Well, that's what
I want, too.

Her stare, incredulous now, remains fixed on him. She should seem
as though her whole history were alive in her, seeking voice. Her
silence remains.

                    GUIDO
I wish we could talk someplace. Seriously, I mean. There's something
about you I feel I· could . . .

She suddenly claps her hands over her ears. Alarm flares in his
face . . . but he has to drive, and we cut as he is glancing back
and forth from her to the forward direction.

We shoot Perce and Gay sitting side by side on the tail of the truck.

                    GAY
That mare was a lucky break -- she's good and heavy, she'll bring a
lot.

A curious expression is on Perce's face -- if possible, we must relate
it to the intense aura previously seen on Roslyn's face; an
incommunicable vision that is larger than consciousness, wider than
what is seen. He turns to Gay with this look . . .

                    PERCE
Gay, I didn't know there'd be only six. It's kind of crazy for only
six.

                    GAY
          (We must see that he notes an oddness.
          He almost laughs, but not with humor)
It sure sounds crazy, to look at you.

                    PERCE
I mean it, Gay, there's hardly beer money in it . . .

                              GAY
You gettin' to sound like Guido last night ---
          (He laughs now, reaches over and
          pats Perce)
Now stop flappin' your wings -- you gonna take off.

                              PERCE
          (The force of the ordinary, known world
          which Gay's clear eyes represent draws
          him back, and now faltering again . . .)
It's just when you think of it, y'know? -- it kinda . . .

                              GAY
Well think yourself back down, Perce -- all they are is a bunch of
half-dead motheaten old mustangs, same as you've seen a hundred
times before. Don't you go nutty on me now.

The truck is slowing to a halt and Gay hops off, and with a rope in
his hand starts for a horse near which they have stopped. This
becomes . . .

MONTAGE: They rope another horse and trip it over. The impression
of the horses' hooves being tied, the horses being tripped, the
nooses being slipped up their necks; meantime a purplish hue is
staining the light. Quick shots of Gay, all business, as he throws
a rope; of Guido jerking a rope to trip a horse; of Perce looking
at Roslyn and trying to help with the work at the same time. Until,
finally.

MEDIUM SHOT: THE THREE MEN APPROACHING THE STALLION; TRUCK IN.
BACKGROUND.

This one is different. As soon as the men approach, the stallion's
rear feet fly up at them. He bares his teeth. He rears, and then
runs at them and scatters them. Roslyn, as though from a dream,
comes out of the truck and watches the horse. Perce happens to be
close to her at this moment. Gay throws a rope behind the stallion's
forefeet.

MEDIUM SHOT: PERCE AND ROSLYN.

                              ROSLYN
This the stallion?

                              PERCE
Ya.

                              ROSLYN
Those were his mares.

                              PERCE
Probably.

                              ROSLYN
The colt . . . was his.

A dreadful, nearly insane look of pain on her face stops his reply.

MEDIUM SHOT: STALLION'S FOREFEET ROPED.

The stallion has walked into the noose and Gay pulls his forefeet
together and holds the rope taut. Guido throws a noose behind
his hindfeet. The stallion pulls furiously on the neck-noose,
even dragging the tire a few feet.

                              GAY
Get that tire, Perce, dammit!

With a start Perce automatically obeys, runs and sits on the tire.

CLOSE SHOT: ROSLYN'S FACE.

She speaks in a normal tone, which Gay couldn't possibly hear now.
But she is not talking to herself.

                              ROSLYN
Gay? Why are you killing him?

MEDIUM SHOT: GAY AND THE OTHERS WITH STALLION.

Gay is struggling to hold the rope taut which holds the stallion's
forefeet. Now Guido pulls up on the noose around the hindfeet.
Bound, the stallion stands with pinioned feet and sways but does
not fall.

Suddenly Roslyn laughs. Separated from the context, she would seem
to be free of pain, and with her laughter she runs on light feet to
a point between Gay and the horse.

Gay sees her laughing face and even in his tension his expression
relaxes happily, in surprise.

                              ROSLYN
Let's make it a game!

                              GAY
Just stand aside, honey . . .

He reaches to move her but she dances out of reach and laughs, a torture in her eyes.

                    ROSLYN
You won -- you won, Gay!

She leaps to the rope and tries to pull it from Gay.

                    ROSLYN
Come on, Gay, you won -- now let him go! -- it's not fair!

                    GAY
Let go that rope!

                    ROSLYN
          (Starting to weep, but holding onto
          the rope)
Oh, Gay, darling . . .

                    GAY
          (Yanks the rope, and she is flung back
          out of his way; and angrily to Guido . . .)
Pull him!

Both he and Guido yank hard on their ropes to trip the stallion. The stallion keeps on his feet.

                    GAY
One, two, go!

They pull together. The stallion's forefeet are pulled back and he comes down on his knees and his nose thuds against the lakebed staining its whiteness with blood from his nostrils. He remains with his hind hooves on the ground, however, swaying but still upright, in part supported by his nose on the ground, as though he were doing an obeisance. His ribs are heaving, and little clouds of dust blow up from around his nostrils on the clay. Guido again pulls on the rear legs. The stallion remains upright, his every muscle tensed against his fall. Perce has been struggling to keep the tire from slipping under him with each pull of the stallion's neck. What was a technique has now become a personal conflict.

                    GAY
          (Angrily; implying Guido is not
          fully trying)
Trip the damn horse, Guido! Come on now -- one, two, go!

Just as he says "go!" Roslyn runs at him, pounding his back with her fists.

                              ROSLYN
Stop it! That's not fair!

                              GAY
              (Trying to fend her off and still
              hold his rope taut)
Get off me! Roslyn!

He suddenly lets one hand go and swings it around, facing her, and hits her across the neck and sends her flying back. Perce jumps up yelling:

                              PERCE
Hey!

Then rushes to stand between Roslyn who is raising herself off the ground, and Gay.

                              GAY
Git on that tire, Perce! Don't say anything to me, just get on that tire and hold this horse!

                              PERCE
Don't have to hit her, Gay.

                              GAY
You get on that tire. We'll settle this in a minute.

Perce goes back to the tire and sits, holding it down.

                              GUIDO
              (Still holding his rope taut)
Let's take it easy, Gay.

                              GAY
              (Exploding at Guido)
Who _you_ tellin' to take it easy?!

He walks to Guido, keeping his rope taut, and hands it to him.

                              GAY
Hold onto that tight now.

Guido holds both ropes. Gay, his hands free now, faces the stallion.
He walks up to the stallion approaching it from the side. He lays
both hands against the stallion's neck. From behind him . . .

                            ROSLYN
You liar!

The power of her contempt turns them all to her in surprise.

                            ROSLYN
All of you!
          (Clenching her fists she screams into
          their faces)
Liars!

Unnerved, Gay starts toward her from the stallion. Afraid, she calls
at him . . .

                            ROSLYN
I don't care what you do to me, you're a liar! -- teaching me "how
to live"! -- what a laugh! -- all you want is to kill everything!
You don't fool me any more! -- None of you! Nobody in this world
will ever fool me!!

Furious, Gay steels himself and turns back to the stallion, and
pushes hard on its neck. It sways on hobbled feet, sucking in the
air, blood trickling from its nostrils.

                            ROSLYN
Man! Big man!
          (To all)
Why don't you kill yourselves and be happy!

The horse topples onto its side. A great sob escapes her at the
sight. Gay kneebends, and taking care to keep his hands clear of
the stallion's teeth, he loosens the noose and slides it up the neck
under its jaws. Now he stands and faces her. She is sobbing, looking
directly at him.

                            ROSLYN
"Roll with it," heh?
          (She points into his face)
You roll with it. You, with your "God's country," -- roll with it.
But find somebody else to do it with. There's a million of them!

                         ROSLYN (Cont.)
But you're not going to kill me; none of you, nobody is big
enough to kill me! I hate you!

                            GAY
We've had it now, Roslyn.

                          ROSLYN
Oh you sure have -- all I could give, you had. And a couple others
before you, Gay Langland, and now you can sneer like they sneer,
but I'll tell you a secret -- I'll never be ashamed of myself again.
Because none of you ever got near me -- I am alive! -- and you never
got near it, Gay. I pity you -- you missed it all. You're three,
dear, sweet, dead men.

Desperately striving to keep her dignity in the face of Gay's clear
hatred and contempt, she walks past the three of them and gets into
the truck.

In silence, driven deep into himself, Gay now breaks the motionless
after-moment, and going toward Guido . . .

                            GAY
Let's reckon it up.
          (Turns)
Perce?

Perce hesitates, then joins Gay and Guido alongside the truck bed.
Roslyn remains in the truck, her body visibly shaken with
suppressed sobbing. The three do not look at her, but we see her in
the background. Now, all their voices are very dry.

                            GAY
What you reckon, Guido?

In Guido's eyes the emptiness is like a lake. He is coiling a rope.
After a moment . . .

                           GUIDO
Well, . . that mare might be six hundred pounds.

                            GAY
That brown's about four hundred, I'd say.

                           GUIDO
Just about, ya.

                            GAY
                (Nodding toward the stallion)
    Must be five hundred on him anyway.

                           GUIDO
    A little lighter, I'd say. Call it nineteen hundred, two thousand
    pounds altogether.

                            GAY
    How's that come out now?

                           GUIDO
                (Looks up in the air, figuring)
    Well, six cents a pound -- that's . . .
                (He figures with silent moving lips)

    In the momentary silence the stallion paws the ground. Perce
    looks toward it. Now from the cab we hear her sobs fully pouring
    out of her. Gay and Guido keep their eyes on each other against
    these sounds.

                           GUIDO
    Be about hundred and ten, hundred and twenty dollars.

                            GAY
    Okay, how you want to cut it?

                           GUIDO
                (As though he had lost a certain interest)
    Anyway you like . . . I'll take fifty for myself and the plane.

                            GAY
    Okay. I guess I oughta have about forty for the truck and me.
    That'd give you twenty-five, Perce -- that all right?
                (PERCE, staring at the stallion,
                seems not to have heard)
    Perce?

                           PERCE
    . . . You fellas take it -- I just . . . went along for the ride anyway.

    Perce turns at once and mounts the truck and lies down on it; Gay is
    affronted by this total absence of interest, and by Perce's evident
    allegiance to Roslyn's mood. Perce has his hands clasped under his
    head, his face toward the sky, his eyes remote. Guido goes around

the front of the truck to get into the driver's seat. Roslyn is
still in the cab.

                        GAY
I'll drive, Guido.

                        GUIDO
          (Halts in front of the truck)
Oh. Okay.

Guido starts back to the rear of the truck. Gay comes around to
get into the driver's seat. Roslyn, without a word, starts to get
out. Gay reaches across the seat and grasps her arm.

                        GAY
Where you going?

                        ROSLYN
I'll sit on the back . . . I don't want to ride with you.

                        GAY
          (He pulls her into the seat with
          great force)
You damn well goin' to ride with me. Close the door.

He keeps his grip on her arm. She pulls the door shut. He lets go
of her arm and, shutting his door with his left hand, turns the key
with his right, starts the engine, shifts gears, and she suddenly
opens her door as the truck starts to move and jumps out. He slams
on the brake, leaps out, runs around the front of the truck. She
is running aimlessly across the lakebed, he after her.

Perce, as though sensing Gay's violence, jumps off the truck and
Guido after him.

Just as Gay catches up with her and seems about to hit her, Perce
reaches them. Perce pushes Gay in the chest to part him from
Roslyn. Gay starts back for Perce with his fist raised. Guido
arrives and butts his whole body up against Gay whom he holds
back. Gay turns on Guido who shouts crazily into his face . . .

                        GUIDO
She's crazy!

The emergent conviction in Guido's manner stops Gay. Roslyn quickly
looks at him, and Perce. Now Guido, out of his life, turns to

Roslyn, a bitter curl on his mouth. He is almost shivering -- as
though this were coming out as a surprise to him too.

GUIDO

They're all crazy. You try not to believe it because you need them;
she's crazy. You struggle, you plan, you build, but it's never
enough, it's never a deal; because we gave them the spurs and
they're going to use them. I got the marks, I know this racket.
They don't even know what they're doing themselves. They're crazy.
        (Directly to her, as above)
It comes from being asked too much and being told too little; I
know this racket. I just forgot what I knew for a little while.

He goes to Gay and puts his arm over his shoulder, a buddy, with
a warm grin.

GUIDO

Let's go, boy -- forget it, before somebody gets hurt and never
knows why.

Gay, not so much opposing him but, so to speak, including Guido's
vision with his own, does not move along with Guido.

GAY

        (To Roslyn)
Let's get aboard now.

She doesn't move at first, so Gay walks to the truck, Guido just
behind him. Guido hops onto the truck bed. Gay turns at the cab
door, waiting for her to get into the truck. Perce is near her,
watching her every nuance. With her eyes on the ground she walks
toward the truck. But when she arrives there . . . Perce behind
her . . . she starts to climb onto the truck bed. Gay reaches
and takes her arm to draw her into the cab. She strikes out to
free her arm . . .

ROSLYN

No!
        (She looks at him)
No.

GAY

        (He is beyond anger. His need is
        overt. He grips her by both arms
        and moves her to the cab)
You damn well goin' to ride with me.

He forces her into the cab, swings her knees around, and slams the
door. Then he walks around the front of the cab and gets in beside
her. He starts the engine. Perce starts to board the truck bed,
but halfway on he drops back to the ground. The truck starts
moving and he runs to the cab and walking alongside . . .

                              PERCE
Gay? Just hold it a minute, will ya?

Gay stops the truck. Perce is on Roslyn's side of the cab, talking
past her face.

                              PERCE
Roslyn? You won all that money in the bar -- maybe Gay'll sell you
the horses.
                    (SHE quickly looks up at him, his
                    feeling reaching into her)
How about that, Gay?

                              GAY
I wouldn't want to leave you here, Perce, get on the truck.

Gay abruptly starts the truck moving. Perce leaps aboard as the
bed passes before him. Alone with Guido . . .

                              GUIDO
You'd better not fool with <u>him</u>, boy. This is none of your business.

                              PERCE
I never "fooled" with anybody, Pilot. And I've had all kinds of
people tell me what my business was and it never did seem to do any
good.

We quickly dissolve on the tension between them.

We open on a shot of Guido on top of the plane wing, holding the
gas hose and peering into the tank, while Gay is pumping gas from
the drum which is now on the truck bed again. In the background
stand the mare and colt. Roslyn is in the cab and Perce has his head
almost inside -- they are evidently talking it over quietly. We
have hardly opened the shot when Perce draws away from the window
and walks up to Gay on the truck bed. Perce has his thumbs in his
pockets; he knows he is holding a lighted match near powder.

                              PERCE
She says she wants to buy them, Gay.

Gay, making to ignore him, goes on pumping the gas. Guido glances
warily at Gay's stoney face.

                    PERCE
What's the difference she pays you or the dealer pays you?

                    GUIDO
          (On the wing)
Okay, hold it!

Guido comes down off the wing with the hose, and goes with it to
Gay, who coils it around the drum.

                    GUIDO
I got room for one if anybody wants to fly back.

Gay hops down off the truck, wiping his hands, his sense of humiliation
mounting in his silence.

                    GUIDO
Whyn't <u>you</u> come along with me, Perce?

                    PERCE
I believe I'll go back the way I came.
          (To Gay)
How about it, Gay? -- you'll get your same money.

                    GAY
That's right, Perce -- the same money she stuck in front of your face
yesterday so you wouldn't go back in after that bull. But I seem to
recall you went back in there anyway, didn't you?

A confusion shows in Perce's face.

                    PERCE
I . . . I guess maybe that didn't have any more sense than this does,
Gay . . . seein' I nearly got myself killed, for nothin'.

                    GAY
Oh, not for nothin', Perce -- you were a man then . . .
          (The insult registers on Perce's
          face)
and that's the only way a real man goes. -- For nothin', for what
they just don't have the numbers to count. I wouldn't take a
thousand dollars a head for these particular animals. Nobody's

                              GAY (Cont.)
cuttin' loose what I took the trouble to tie.   Come on, Guido, I'll
get you started.

He walks past Guido and past Roslyn in the cab and goes to the plane.
Guido follows, pauses before her.

                              GUIDO
                    (Quietly, with fear for the next
                    moments)
I think you'd better come with me.

                              ROSLYN
                    (Between pity and despair)
Who are you?   Do you know?

Guido, as though stabbed, walks on, gets into the cockpit.   Gay is
already gripping the propellor.

We cut to Perce who comes to the cab and sticks his head in.   There
is a holding-of-breath quality in him now.

                              PERCE
You want me to, I'll cut 'em loose.

She looks past him and we shoot the mare and the colt beyond . . . The
colt has faded itself underneath the mare whose long tail is blowing
in the breeze.   The light is falling fast.

We shoot her face, absorbed in the sight of the animals.

                              ROSLYN
Look -- already they're so peaceful!   How easy everything agrees to
die . . !   I guess it's no more stupid than everything else I ever
saw.

Off-screen we hear the plane engine turning over, and it sputters out.

                              PERCE
Tell me what you want, I'll do it.
                    (He quickly turns her face to him)
I never saw the sense in this anyway, but I didn't have nerve enough
to say so.

                                ROSLYN
                (Hopelessly)
No, don't, don't fight about it. I never knew whether or not to
pass something by . . whereas I always stopped, y'know; and it always
ends like this, where I'm the one they hate, and I'm the one they
laugh at. They must be right, Perce -- like you said yourself --
there's just nothing to anything.
                (She looks past him at the mare and
                colt)
. . . How peaceful they are! -- maybe even dying isn't real.

The plane engine suddenly roars up.

They turn and see Gay coming toward the truck. The plane is moving
away across the lakebed, taking off. Gay is coming in at a stride,
his mind made up. Perce comes around to the front of the truck to
intercept him.

                                PERCE
Gay? I . . .

Gay walks right past him, opens the cab door. Perce comes at a
quickened pace around to the other door and opens it as the engine
starts and the gears grind angrily. Now Gay spits out his words.

                                GAY
I'm comin' back in the dealer's truck to pick up these animals --
you want to help me you get your share. Get on the back.

Perce suddenly reaches in and pulls out the ignition key, which
stops the engine, but Gay knocks it out of his hand and holds it.
Roslyn sits terrified between them.

                                PERCE
She's offerin' you your money. You don't take it, it's nothin' but
butcherin' horses. And if that's a man, then I don't want to be one.

                                GAY
                (He puts the key into the lock,
                . starts the engine)
What she's lookin' to buy ain't horses, and it ain't for sale and
never will be.
                (To Roslyn directly, with a hurt grin)
I'm gonna teach you that . . . startin' right now.

He suddenly, desperately, pulls her to him and kisses her. Now Perce
pulls at his hand, and when he lets her go she starts to weep in
fright.

> GAY
> Boy, hop on back there and don't give me any more trouble, 'cause
> I ain't old enough to take it.

Gay reaches across and grips the door handle to close it. Surprisingly,
Perce steps away, Gay slams the door. But Perce turns and starts at
a trot toward the mare.

> GAY
> Where you goin'?

Roslyn looks off toward Perce, astonished, frightened.

CLOSE SHOT: GAY'S FACE.

A sudden realization strikes him. Horror and anger show.

> GAY
> Perce!

MEDIUM SHOT: GAY AND ROSLYN AND TRUCK.

Gay comes at a half-trot around the front of the truck. He pauses
not far from Roslyn, who now turns to look at his angering and
astounded face. He starts off at run.

MEDIUM SHOT: PERCE.

He is now breaking into a run. He glances behind now and whatever
there was of a dazed expression is gone; he shows determination now
and even anger. As he runs he reaches into his pocket and draws out
a clasp pocket knife and opens the biggest blade.

MEDIUM SHOT: ROSLYN RUNNING.

She has gotten out and is just started away from the truck to follow
them, terrified.

MEDIUM SHOT: GAY RUNNING.

> GAY
> Perce, you can't do that!

MEDIUM SHOT: MARE AND COLT AND PERCE.

Perce reaches the tire and falls on it and saws at the rope.   In
the background, coming up fast, Gay is running and yelling.   The
mare is restively dancing about, the colt scrambling to its feet.

CLOSE SHOT: KNIFE AND ROPE.

The rope is nearly cut.

MEDIUM SHOT: GAY AND PERCE.

Gay, on the run, leaps onto Perce's back and pulls at his arm, to
free the rope from it . . . and the rope flies out, cut.   Roslyn
reaches them and starts to try to pull Gay off Perce.   Gay sees
the mare starting to trot away.   He jumps up and runs toward it,
trying to grab the rope which is trailing behind from her neck.
The colt may interfere with his running.   He lunges now for the
rope and falls, and gets up and runs on after the mare which, now
that the colt is beside her, picks up speed.

Perce grabs Roslyn's hand and starts her running with him back
toward the truck.   He lets go of her and runs at his top speed, she
following behind.   She turns as she runs and sees . . .

LONG SHOT: GAY AND MARE AND COLT.

Gay is slowing to a halt as the mare and the colt gallop away.   He
turns and . . .

CLOSE SHOT: GAY'S FACE.

Fury bursts into his panting face at what he sees . . .

MEDIUM SHOT: TRUCK WITH ROSLYN GETTING IN.

The truck is already starting to move.   Roslyn jumps in, as frightened
of being left with Gay as of joining Perce.

CLOSE SHOT: CAB INTERIOR.   PERCE AND ROSLYN.

He is speeding the truck away.   He switches on the headlights; it is
dusk.   With growing pity and terror she looks out the window and
sees . . .

MEDIUM LONG SHOT: GAY ON LAKEBED.

He is roaring at them as they pass, waving his fists and starting
to run after the truck.

CLOSE SHOT: ROSLYN'S FACE.

A wave of guilt passes onto her face. In her uncertainty she turns
to Perce. He is like one inspired by rebellion, a wild determination
on his face. Glancing at her he reaches over and draws her closer
to him -- a gesture like Gay's earlier.

MEDIUM SHOT: PERCE AND ROSLYN, CAB INTERIOR.

He suddenly swerves the wheel, jamming on the brakes. She looks out
ahead and sees . . .

MEDIUM SHOT: MARE AND COLT CROSSING TRUCK.

He has swerved to avoid the mare and colt. They are running in a
madness now, hearing the truck. The mare's tail flies straight out
as she rapidly gallops away at an angle from the truck, the colt
right behind her.

MEDIUM SHOT: PERCE AND ROSLYN.

She turns from watching the disappearing mare and colt, and cries
out . . .

                    ROSLYN
Oh, Perce! I don't know!

He glances at her surprised, perplexed, drives on.

MEDIUM SHOT: STALLION.

The stallion is watching what we can hear -- the oncoming sound of the
truck. He lowers his head. The truck enters the shot, stops short.
Perce jumps out, runs to the tire. The stallion rears. Perce sits
on the tire to hold it still as he saws at the rope. Roslyn runs
out of the cab, glancing guiltily toward the camera for a sign of Gay.
Suddenly the rope parts. The stallion, free, kicks up his rear legs
and starts to rush them. Perce pulls her out of the way and yells
wordlessly to scare off the stallion. Before the reality of the freed
stallion Roslyn feels her first conviction.

                    ROSLYN
          (In an ecstasy and terror)
Go! Go home! Go home!

Perce runs toward the stallion which turns and gallops away.
Breathless, they watch him for a moment, then run to the truck.
Roslyn gets into the cab. Perce halts for a moment, seeing . . .

LONG SHOT: TWO HORSES.

They are distant, but clearly seen. They are still tied to tires.
We hear the sound of the truck taking off, the whine of the transmission.

QUICK DISSOLVE TO:

LONG SHOT: DISTANT HEADLIGHTS.   GAY IN FOREGROUND.

He is running tiredly toward the headlights which are impossibly distant
but have come to a halt out there.

CLOSE SHOT: GAY'S FACE.

He is insane with fury and frustration. His breath is wheezing out
of his lungs like the horses' before. Now he turns his head at a
sound and halts. It is nearly dark. The moon is shining. We now
hear galloping. It stops quickly. Gay listens to the silence. A
horse is out there, he knows, but where? Now a hoof beat is heard,
a trotting, now a galloping come in fast.

MEDIUM SHOT: GAY AND STALLION.

He sees the stallion coming out of the darkness, gets himself set --
but he is exhausted and unsteady. The stallion is running directly
toward him. Gay sidesteps, the stallion passes him, and he heels
into the clay. The stallion drags him but slows, then turns. Gay
keeps the rope taut, and dodges and dances to keep himself always in
front of the animal which is now facing him, rearing in fury. Gay
is fighting to hold him as though to let him go were to lose his very
existence. He is laughing in exhaustion. Now the horse charges at
him, flailing its forefeet close to his head, and he dodges, and
again the charge. The hoofs fly and Gay goes down on his face,
sprawled on the clay lakebed. The horse gallops away. Gay does not
move.

CLOSE SHOT: GAY'S FACE.

He is breathing into the clay. Blood is flowing out of his nose.
Little spouts of white dust puff up under the breath spurting from
his nostrils. His eyes are shut; the skin on one upturned palm is
rubbed raw and bloody by the rope.

We hold on him. The sound of the truck is heard. It increases. Gay's form is illuminated by the headlights which quickly become bright, and the sound of the truck stopping, its breakes squealing, is heard.

Roslyn comes out of the truck and quickly goes to him. She bends over him, turns him on his back as Perce arrives beside her. She sees his face and tears come to her eyes. She sweeps his head into her arms, crying . . .

                    ROSLYN
Gay! Oh, Gay!

Now she looks at his face, frantically tries to wipe it clean of dirt and blood . . . and he opens his eyes. She is weeping, watching for the meaning of his look as gradually his eyes see and the daze moves aside. And he sees her. Expression flows into his face, the eyes take life. And she sees the fathomless hurt, the depth of despair looking at her.

We shoot Perce from the ground level. He turns his face away.

She is sobbing, and now she strives to raise Gay. Perce bends to him and starts to lift him to his feet, but Gay brushes him away and Roslyn, too, with the same gesture, and falls back helplessly on the earth. Now he turns on his side, raises up on his elbow, then pitches forward, and rests for a moment on his hands and knees, his head hanging between his shoulders. She is sobbing over him, not daring to speak.

With a gigantic effort, Gay stands. Both of them want to help him, for he sways dangerously, but they dare not. He faces around to the truck and walks toward it. They follow like a cortege in the moonlight, she weeping into her hands, Perce face to face with an odd disaster he cannot grasp excepting that something very large has been knocked askew.

Gay arrives at the open door of the truck, raises the tonnage of his body and gets himself onto the edge of the seat. They come up near the door and halt. The only sound in the world is their winded breathing and Roslyn's sobs. Gay is facing out of the truck for he cannot yet turn himself in, and is staring out between the two of them, sucking air.

Roslyn raises her eyes to him. The pity and guilt on her face strike Perce, and he suddenly feels like an intruder. She dares now to slowly reach out, and when Gay does not react, she gently lays her hand on his wrist. He still makes no move to dismiss her, and she closes her grip on his arm. Suddenly she falls to her knees before him and kisses his hand many times.

                              ROSLYN
Oh, Gay. Gay! I swear . . . I never meant to harm you!

Slowly he lowers his eyes to her, a look as old as his life.

                              GAY
Should've listened to me. Kept tryin' to tell you.
          (Like a farewell)
Tryin' and tryin'.

                              ROSLYN
Tell me. Tell me! Teach me! I don't know anything!

Perce moves away into the darkness.

                              GAY
Can't nothin' live, unless somethin' dies.

                              ROSLYN
          (As much to reject the guilt as to
          deny his disaster)
Why? Don't say that, Gay!

                              GAY
I ain't sayin' it. That's the way it's made.

                              ROSLYN
          (With a cry)
I didn't kill you, Gay! You told me yourself it was finished here.
I didn't clean them out, you did. You couldn't have lived on them
any more . . . _even_ if you'd never seen me!

We see that his eyes concede, however unwillingly, and the bitterness
in them alters a little as he must look out at what he knows.

                              ROSLYN
What were you going to do? Die when there were no more left to
take?
          (She lovingly touches his face)
Oh, Gay -- I know how you loved it here. To know you always had
them, waiting to feed you, keeping you free, how you are -- and
still be a friend to everything? There must be. I see it. I
believe it. I know it . . . Don't lose me, Gay!

He pulls her to him, but he has not risen enough within to kiss her;
he buries his face in her neck, his loss and his gain forcing a kind
of moan from him. She separates enough to hold his face and kiss his
lips, and looking at him . . .

                              ROSLYN
How brave you are! I know!

Now, as though he once again felt his dignity, and more -- a thankful
throwing-in of his lot with her, he kisses her. They separate, and
there is a great wonder in his eyes. She lets him gently back into
the seat, and pulls his legs up into the truck. With his head
thrown back he never takes his eyes off her, seeing her like a new
thing. She closes the door and goes alongside the truck to come
around the other side.

She comes on Perce, seeing him standing with his back to her a few
yards beyond the headlight beams. She hesitates for an instant,
then goes up behind him.

                              ROSLYN
Perce?

He turns to her. His eyes are filled with tears. We sense she must
steel herself a little against a flood of pity for him.

                              ROSLYN
Would you drive us home?

He is hurt, and his hurt holds him an instant. But he walks ahead
of her and holds the door open for her to enter, and stands there,
waiting, out of his native gentility, for her to enter.

                              ROSLYN
Thank you, Perce.

She gets in. He gets in beside her and starts the engine. Gay
leans forward to see Perce past Roslyn.

                              GAY
We gotta pick up the dog.

                              PERCE
                   (Without turning to him)
Okay.

He lets in the clutch and the truck moves along.

                    GAY
Perce?

                    PERCE
Ya?

                    GAY
It's a long way before we hit the highway. You see that great big
star, off on the left there?

                    PERCE
Yeah.

                    GAY
Just stay on that. It'll take us right home.

Perce turns the wheel, staring ahead at the star. Gay rests back in
the seat, and leans his head on Roslyn's shoulder. She takes up
his hand and holds it.

We shoot the three of them watching that star, their heads turned
with the turning of the car until they are all facing straight
ahead in its path.

We shoot the star through the windshield, and now, never losing it,
we move through the windshield. The truck comes into the shot,
the headlight beams going away into the darkness, moving off out
of sight with the sound of the engine as the camera imperceptibly
tilts up until it is filled entirely with stars and absolute silence.

                    THE END

Charade

1963—A Stanley Donen Production;
released by Universal Pictures
Director   Stanley Donen
Script   Peter Stone
Source   Story, "The Unsuspecting Wife," by
Peter Stone and Marc Behm
Stars   Cary Grant, Audrey Hepburn, Walter Matthau,
James Coburn

Charade was preordained to be successful at the box office (as, indeed, it was) the moment that Cary Grant and Audrey Hepburn agreed to star in it; for separately each was, in 1963, among the last of the old-time stars, capable, by name on the marquee of a theater alone—never mind what it's *about*—of luring the elusive mass audience like a huge candle flame. Together they needed not so much a script as a vehicle, something to keep them busy doing things for about ninety minutes. The young screenwriter Peter Stone carefully tailored his script to fit them, the demands of their "public images," and the expectations of their public. In that sense *Charade* is an old-fashioned film, a throwback to the days when stars were many and all scripts were written for them. In another sense, the mixed quality of its story—part suspense tale, part love story, part parody—it is quite contemporary.

Stanley Donen, the director, had previously done both musicals and comedies, his credits beginning with *On the Town* (1950) and including such films as *Singing in the Rain, Seven Brides for Seven Brothers, Funny Face,* and *The Pajama Game.*

Predictably the critics greeted it with mixed feelings. Philip Hartung in *Commonweal* handled the problem by simply stating that the whole plot structure is entirely secondary. "The film holds you mainly for the ornaments in the charade," he wrote. Bosley Crowther, ever a staunch foe of cinematic violence, and especially with Christmas coming on, wrote in the *New York Times* (December 5): "I tell you, this lighthearted picture is full of gruesome violence." But he added that it was, nonetheless, "fast-moving, urbane entertainment in the comedy-mystery vein." He noted the originality of Stone's handling of the material in a script "packed with sudden twists, shocking gags, eccentric arrangements and occasionally bright and brittle lines." And, finally, he attempted to identify and classify the quality of Donen's direction, calling it a "style that is somewhere between the screwball comedy of the 1930s and that of Hitchcock on a 'North By Northwest' course." Following that lead, Brendan Gill criticized it for its attempts "to shock us into conventional *rigor Hitchcockis*"; and he complained that the plot "has as many loose ends as a Maypole," and that the dialogue is replete with "classic nineteenth-century lines. . . ." But, reasonably tossing judgment aside, Gill asked, "Who would bother to criticize these trifles when Cary Grant and Audrey Hepburn are the stars of the picture and Paris is its setting?"

Stanley Kauffmann, to himself as true as Polonius advised Laertes to be, found Audrey Hepburn "inescapably appealing," but found fault with the contrived plot. And he belatedly (*The New Republic*, December 21) brought up the Hitchcock analogy—"With *Charade* the director Stanley Donen makes a bid for the comedy-mystery laurels of Hitchcock but matches only a leaf or two from both the master's wreath and book."

Pauline Kael proceeded to say that *Charade* (in *I Lost It At The Movies*), "although no more than a charming confectionary trifle, was, I think, probably the best American film of last year—as artificial and enjoyable in its way as *The Big Sleep*." Later, coupling it with *The Manchurian Candidate,* she attributed to both films "a freshness and spirit that makes them unlike the films of any other country."

Perhaps the last word comes from *Movies on T.V.* (1968), where *Charade* is given three and one-half stars and briskly described as "a lightweight affair, but the stars and the stylish direction by Stanley Donen keep it alive."

The Script   The final shooting script of *Charade* is dated on the title page "1 October 1962." But individual notations on pages show that even then, with the script "locked in" and copyrighted, there were revisions and changes made on eleven more dates, up through 23 January 1963. After that there were a number of penciled-in deletions and revisions, which are indicated in this printed version. The script of *Charade* is conventionally organized, using the standard format of numbered master scenes. It is a longish script with some 486 master scenes. Some sections are, as the reader will see, broken down into small and exact camera shots. Others depend on description of action within a numbered master scene—action which would require a large number of camera setups and angles. Note that in scene 90 there is a parenthetical, full-paragraph description of "the orange game," explaining the game in some detail. It is also noteworthy that there is, for a contemporary script, a good deal more dialogue than is usual, perhaps because both Audrey Hepburn and Cary Grant had long since demonstrated the ability to read lines quickly and clearly, adding a dimension of verbal play not often found in contemporary films.

Credits   Producer, Stanley Donen; Director, Stanley Donen; Screenplay, Peter Stone and Marc Behm; Art Direction, Jean D'Eaubonne; Music, Henry Mancini; Photography, Charles Lang, Jr.; Editor, James Clark.

Cast		
	Peter Joshua:	Cary Grant
	Reggie:	Audrey Hepburn
	Bartholomew:	Walter Matthau
	Tex:	James Coburn
	Scobie:	George Kennedy
	Gideon:	Ned Glass
	Grandpierre:	Jacques Marin
	Félix:	Paul Bonifas
	Sylvie:	Dominique Minot
	Jean-Louis:	Thomas Chelimsky

CHARADE

FADE IN (BEFORE TITLES)

1.   EXT. FRENCH COUNTRYSIDE -- DUSK
      Silence -- complete silence for the urbanite, though the
      oncoming darkness is punctuated with the sounds of farm
      country -- a few birds, a distant rumble of thunder from
      some heavy clouds on the horizon, a dog's barking.

      CAMERA PANS the green, squared-off flatland, lit only by
      a fine sunset in its final throes. Then, gradually,
      starting from nothing, a rumble is heard, quickly growing
      louder and louder until the sound of a train can be
      recognized.

      CAMERA PANS quickly, discovering the railroad line atop a
      man-made rise of land, and the speeding passenger train is
      upon us, flashing by with a roar.

      Then, as if from nowhere, the figure of a man hits the
      embankment and rolls crazily down to the bottom into the
      thick underbrush. * * * alongside the tracks.

2.   CLOSE SHOT -- BODY
      It lies in the bushes, still, unmoving -- dead. CAMERA
      PANS AWAY to the quiet peaceful countryside as the sound
      of the train fades off until there is silence once more.

      TITLE MUSIC begins with a crash.

                        (MAIN TITLES)

3.)
4.)   DELETED
5.)

6.   FADE IN
      EXT. MEGEVE -- DAY
      A handsome and elegant hotel perched on the mountain-side
      overlooking the French resort town. A large, open sun
      deck -- tables, gaily coloured parasols, sun bathers.

---

1.   [growing]

One of the latter is REGINA LAMPERT, a lovely young girl.
She is, besides taking in the sun, involved in her favorite
activity -- eating.

Then -- a dark, ominous shape intrudes in the f.g. FOCUS
CHANGES to bring into sharp relief a revolver -- shining,
black and ugly in the sunlight.

REGGIE, unaware of her danger, continues to eat.

The finger tightens around the trigger and finally the
gun shoots -- a stream of water arcs, with unerring aim,
straight into REGGIE's face.

7. ANOTHER ANGLE
Including JEAN-LOUIS, a French boy of six or so. REGGIE
looks at him sternly.

> JEAN-LOUIS (in for trouble)
> Oh, la.

> REGGIE
> Don't tell me you didn't know it was loaded.
> (calling) Sylvie!

8. WIDER ANGLE
SYLVIE GAUDET, French, attractive, blonde, in her early
thirties, comes from the railing of the sun deck to join
REGGIE and JEAN-LOUIS.

> REGGIE
> Isn't there something constructive he can
> do -- like start an avalanche?

> SYLVIE (to JEAN-LOUIS)
> Va jouer, mon ange.

JEAN-LOUIS scampers off, content to have gotten off so
lightly. SYLVIE notices REGGIE's lunch which consists of
cold chicken, potato salad, rolls and butter, wine and
coffee.

> SYLVIE
> When you start to eat like this something
> is the matter.

No answer from REGGIE. SYLVIE begins reading a magazine
as REGGIE continues eating.

                        REGGIE
          Sylvie -- I'm getting a divorce.

                        SYLVIE
          Ça alors! From Charles?

                        REGGIE
          He's the only husband I've got. I tried
          to make it work, I really have -- but --

                        SYLVIE
          But what?

                        REGGIE
          I don't know how to explain it. I'm just
          too miserable.

     REGGIE picks up a chicken leg and starts off. SYLVIE
     regards the devastated table before following.

                        SYLVIE
          It is infuriating that your unhappiness
          does not turn to fat!

8A.   INT. SWIMMING POOL -- DAY
       A magnificent indoor, glass-enclosed pool, the vista of
       snow-covered mountains seen through the ceiling-high
       windows beyond. REGGIE and SYLVIE are passing through,
       their conversation continuing.

                        SYLVIE
          But why do you want a divorce?

                        REGGIE * * *
          Because I don't love him.

                        SYLVIE
          But that is no reason to get a divorce!

8B.   EXT. HOTEL TERRACE -- DAY
       An open balcony running around two sides of the pool,
       sun-worshippers lying in deck-chairs. REGGIE and SYLVIE
       appear, their conversation continuing.

8A.   [(sitting)]

                         SYLVIE
          With a rich husband and this year's
          clothes you will not find it difficult
          to make some new friends.

                         REGGIE (sitting)
          I admit I moved to Paris because I was
          tired of American Provincial, but that
          doesn't mean I'm ready for French Traditional.
          I loathe the idea of a divorce, Sylvie,
          but -- if only Charles had been honest
          with me -- that's all I ask of anybody
          -- the simple truth. But with him,
          everything is secrecy and lies. He's
          hiding something -- something frightening
          -- something terrible -- and evil.

     She stops as she is aware of a weird figure hovering over
     her. She wheels, terrified.

9.   CLOSE SHOT -- PERUVIAN SNOW-MASK
     A strange, grotesque knitted mask that completely covers
     the face except for eyes, nose and mouth. The eyes inside
     this particular mask stare down at REGGIE.

                         MAN
                    Does this belong to you?

     CAMERA PANS down to include JEAN-LOUIS, his hand held
     firmly by the man in the mask.

10. WIDER ANGLE
     Including REGGIE, MAN, SYLVIE and JEAN-LOUIS. REGGIE is
     too terrified to answer. Realizing this, the man, PETER
     JOSHUA, takes off the snow-mask to reveal a handsome,
     tanned face.

                         PETER
               Oh, forgive me. (indicating JEAN-LOUIS)
               Is this yours?

                         REGGIE (indicating SYLVIE)
               It's hers. Where'd you find him, robbing
          a bank?

                         PETER
          He was throwing snowballs at Baron
          Rothschild. (a pause) We don't know
          each other, do we?

                         REGGIE
          Why, do you think we're going to?

                         PETER
          I don't know -- how would I know?

                         REGGIE
          I'm afraid I already know a great many
          people. Until one of them dies I couldn't
          possibly meet anyone else.

                         PETER (smiling)
          Yes, of course. But you will let me know
          if anyone goes on the critical list
          (he starts off).

                         REGGIE
          Quitter.

                         PETER (turning)
          How's that?

                         REGGIE * * *
          You give up awfully easily, don't you?

Eyeing one, then the other, SYLVIE sizes up the situation
and rises.

                         SYLVIE
          Viens, Jean-Louis -- let us make a walk.
          I have never seen a Rothschild before.

SYLVIE and JEAN-LOUIS start off, but not before the boy
squirts PETER with his pistol.

                         PETER (drying)
          Clever fellow -- almost missed me.

                         REGGIE
          I'm afraid you're blocking my view.

                         PETER (moving)
          Sorry. Which view would you like?

---

10.   [(joining him)]

                    REGGIE
The one you're blocking. This is the last
chance I have -- I'm flying back to Paris
this afternoon. What's your name?

                    PETER
Peter Joshua.

                    REGGIE
I'm Regina Lampert.

                    PETER
Is there a Mr. Lampert?

                    REGGIE
Yes.

                    PETER
Good for you.

                    REGGIE
No, it isn't. I'm getting a divorce.

                    PETER
Please, not on my account.

                    REGGIE
No, you see, I don't really love him.

                    PETER
Well, you're honest, anyway.

                    REGGIE
Yes, I am -- I'm compulsive about it --
dishonesty infuriates me. Like when you go
into a drugstore.

                    PETER
I'm not sure I --

                    REGGIE
Well, you go in and you ask for some
toothpaste -- the small size -- and the man brings
you the large size. You tell him you wanted
the small size but he says the large size <u>is</u>
the small size. I always thought the large
size was the largest size, but he says that
the family size, the economy size and the

                    REGGIE (Cont.)
giant size are all larger than the large size
-- that the large size is the smallest size
there is.

                    PETER
Oh. I guess.

                    REGGIE
Is there a Mrs. Joshua?

                    PETER
Yes, but we're divorced.

                    REGGIE
That wasn't a proposal -- I was just curious.

                    PETER
Is your husband with you?

                    REGGIE
Oh, Charles is hardly ever with me. First it
was separate rooms -- now we're trying it
with cities. What do people call you -- Pete?

                    PETER
Mr. Joshua. (turning to go) Well, I've
enjoyed talking to you.

                    REGGIE
Now you're angry.

                    PETER
No, I'm not -- I've got some packing to do. I'm
also going back to Paris today.

                    REGGIE
Oh. Well, wasn't it Shakespeare who said:
"When strangers do meet they should * * * erelong
see one another again"?

                    PETER
Shakespeare never said that.

                    REGGIE
How do you know?

                    PETER
It's terrible -- you just made it up.

                    REGGIE
          Well, the idea's right, anyway. Are you
          going to call me?

                    PETER
          Are you in the book?

                    REGGIE
          Charles is.

                    PETER
          Is there only one Charles Lampert?

10A.   DELETED

10B.   CLOSE SHOT -- REGGIE
        Her face clouding.

                    REGGIE
          Lord, I hope so.

11.   EXT. AVENUE FOCH -- LAMPERT APARTMENT HOUSE -- DAY
        The Arc de Triomphe at the far end of the Avenue. CAMERA
        PANS to pick up a TAXI as it pulls up before the handsome
        building. Inside are REGGIE, SYLVIE and JEAN-LOUIS.

12.   MED. SHOT -- TAXI -- LAMPERT APARTMENT HOUSE
        As REGGIE climbs out and the DRIVER begins unloading her
        suitcases.

                    REGGIE
          Goodbye, Sylvie, and thanks. (She turns
          toward the house).

        JEAN-LOUIS sticks his head out of the taxi window.

                    JEAN-LOUIS
          When you get your divorce will you be
          going back to America?

13.   MED. SHOT -- THE TAXI
        REGGIE looks at SYLVIE, surprised.

                    SYLVIE
          He knows everything.

                    REGGIE (to JEAN-LOUIS)
          Don't you want me to stay?

                              JEAN-LOUIS
             Yes, of course -- but if you went back and
             wrote me a letter --

                              REGGIE
             -- you could have the stamps. I'll get
             you some here, okay?

                              JEAN-LOUIS
             Okay.

REGGIE walks toward the house with the DRIVER, who carries
her cases. She presses the button that electrically opens
the front door.

14.   DELETED

15.   INT. APARTMENT LANDING -- DAY
       As the elevator rises REGGIE gets out, followed by the
       driver. He puts down the bags in front of the apartment
       door.

                              REGGIE (handing him a tip)
             Merci.

The driver leaves. She goes to the door and presses the
minuterie, the button that turns on the time-light, and the
lights come on. Then she rings the doorbell. There is no
answer. She rings again. Still nothing. Sighing, she
digs out her key and starts to fit it into the lock. At
this moment the minuterie expires, plunging the scene into
darkness.

                              REGGIE'S VOICE
             Wonderful.

She finds the button and the light goes on again. She
inserts the key and turns it.

16.   INT. LAMPERT APARTMENT -- ENTRANCE HALL -- DAY
       CLOSE SHOT -- DOOR as it opens and REGGIE steps into the
       CLOSE SHOT.

She stops, her expression changing.

17.   REVERSE SHOT
       From REGGIE's p.o.v. as CAMERA PANS the entrance hall. It
       is bare -- no furniture, no rug, no pictures, no nothing.

18.   MED. SHOT -- REGGIE
      She stares for a moment, then goes back out into the
      landing.

19.   INT. APARTMENT LANDING -- DAY
      As REGGIE steps back outside. She looks at the nameplate
      beside the door.

20.   INSERT NAMEPLATE
      It reads "MR. AND MRS. CHARLES LAMPERT."

21.   INT. APARTMENT LANDING -- DAY
      REGGIE looks at the plate in disbelief, then turns and
      hurries back into the apartment.

22.   INT. LAMPERT APARTMENT -- DAY
      As REGGIE hurries into the entrance hall.

                     REGGIE
              Honorine -- !

No answer.

Now, CAMERA FOLLOWING, she goes into the Salon. It is
also empty -- stripped bare. There are squares of the wall's
original color where paintings used to hang, the hooks still
in the wall.

She rushes now, going into the bedroom, CAMERA FOLLOWING
crazily, lurching and careening behind her. The bedroom,
too, is empty. She goes to the built-in wardrobe closets
and throws open all the doors. Only some hangers remain.
She pulls open the drawers -- nothing!

                     REGGIE
              Charles -- !

She turns, and running now, goes through another door to
the library, CAMERA FOLLOWING. The rows of shelves are
as empty as the rest of the apartment. She begins to turn
in a circle, looking for something, anything. In a panic
she turns and runs out, colliding suddenly with a MAN whom
she (and we) have not noticed until the moment of impact.
REGGIE screams.

23.   CLOSE SHOT -- INSPECTOR GRANDPIERRE
      A heavy-set man of no particular age with tobacco-colored
      hair, and thick glasses.

                    GRANDPIERRE
          Madame Charles Lampert?

24.   WIDER ANGLE
      Including REGGIE, in a state of near-shock.

                    REGGIE
          Yes.

                    GRANDPIERRE
          * * * I am Inspector Edouard Grandpierre
          of the Police Judiciaire. Would you be
          so kind as to come with me, please?

25.   INT. MORGUE -- DAY
      We see a large metal drawer being opened and an all-too-
      familiar shape outlined under a damp sheet of muslin.

26.   ANOTHER ANGLE -- OVERHEAD
      Looking straight down at the tops of REGGIE's, GRANDPIERRE's
      and an ATTENDANT's head and smack into the open drawer.
      GRANDPIERRE lifts a corner of the sheet at the bottom and
      reveals a bare foot with a ticket tied to its big toe.
      He stoops to read it. Satisfied, he recovers the foot,
      then moves to the other end to uncover the head. As the
      sheet starts to lift:

27.   REVERSE SHOT
      REGGIE as she looks down into the CAMERA. She closes her
      eyes for a moment, then looks again.

                    GRANDPIERRE'S VOICE (o.s.)
          Well, Madame -- ?

      She nods.

      She nods again. GRANDPIERRE moves into the SHOT.

                    GRANDPIERRE
          You loved him?

                    REGGIE
          I'm very cold.

_____

24.   [How do you do?]

GRANDPIERRE nods as he turns to the unseen ATTENDANT.
CAMERA suddenly moves as the 'drawer' is slid back into
the wall. BLACKNESS comes with a loud clang and continues
while the echo dies.

28.   INT. GRANDPIERRE'S OFFICE -- DAY
CLOSE SHOT -- DESK DRAWER (FROM ABOVE) as it is pulled open.
A photograph of Charles Lampert lies face up in the drawer.
A hand reaches in and pulls it out.

29.   WIDER ANGLE
Including GRANDPIERRE sitting behind his desk, and REGGIE,
sitting across from him. The office is as bare as most
policemen's offices. GRANDPIERRE studies the photo.

                    GRANDPIERRE
          We discovered your husband's body lying next
          to the tracks of the Paris-Bordeaux railroad
          line. He was dressed only in his pajamas.
          Do you know of any reason why he might have
          wished to leave France?

                    REGGIE
          Leave?

                    GRANDPIERRE
          Your husband possessed a ticket of passage
          on the 'Maranguape.' It sailed from Bordeaux
          for Maracaibo this morning at seven.

                    REGGIE (a pause)
          I'm very confused.

She starts to rummage through her bag. GRANDPIERRE shoves
a package of French cigarettes across the desk to her. But
she pulls a package of nuts out of her bag. She begins
separating the shells with her thumb nail and eating the
nuts, depositing the shells in the ashtray. GRANDPIERRE
watches this for an instant.

                    GRANDPIERRE
          He was American?

                    REGGIE
          Swiss.

                    GRANDPIERRE
          Oh. Swiss. His profession?

                        REGGIE
          He didn't have one.

                        GRANDPIERRE
          He was a wealthy man?

                        REGGIE
          I don't know. I suppose so.

                        GRANDPIERRE
          About how wealthy would you say?

                        REGGIE
          I don't know.

                        GRANDPIERRE
          Where did he keep his money?

                        REGGIE
          I don't know.

                        GRANDPIERRE
          Besides yourself, who is his nearest relation?

                        REGGIE
          I don't know.

                        GRANDPIERRE (exploding)
          C'est absurde, Madame. To-tale-ment absurde!

                        REGGIE (embarrassed)
          I know. (pause) I'm sorry.

GRANDPIERRE sighs, puts down his pencil and pushes a button
on the desk. He removes a cigar from his desk and inserts
it into his mouth.

                        GRANDPIERRE
          Is it all right?

                        REGGIE
          I wish you wouldn't.

He rips the cigar out of his mouth and slams it back into
the drawer, closing it fiercely. A UNIFORMED POLICEMAN
sticks his head in the door.

                        GRANDPIERRE
          Les effets de Lampert.

GRANDPIERRE (Cont.)
The POLICEMAN leaves and closes the door.

> On Wednesday last your husband sold the entire
> contents of the apartment at public auction.
> Furniture, clothing, kitchenware -- everything.
> The gallery, in complying with his wishes, paid
> him in cash. One million two hundred and fifty
> thousand New Francs. In dollars, a quarter
> of a million. The authorities in Bordeaux
> have searched his compartment on the train.
> They have searched it thoroughly. They did
> <u>not</u> find $250,000, Madame.

He opens the desk drawer, puts the cigar back in his mouth
and lights a match by scratching it against the glass desk-top
before he remembers REGGIE's request. He puts it back in
the drawer again. The door opens and the POLICEMAN enters
again, this time carrying a wicker basket which he deposits
on GRANDPIERRE's desk, and leaves. GRANDPIERRE peers into
the basket.

> GRANDPIERRE
> These few things are all that was found in the
> train compartment. There was no other baggage.
> Your husband must have been in a <u>great</u> hurry.

He begins to take them out, placing them on the desk,
identifying each item as he does.

> One wallet containing three thousand francs --
> one agenda -- (pausing, he opens the notebook) --
> his last notation was made yesterday -- Thursday --
> (reading) "Five p.m. -- Jardin des Champs-Elysées"
> (looking up) Why there?

> REGGIE
> I don't know. Perhaps he met somebody.

> GRANDPIERRE (drily)
> Obviously. (returning to the items in the
> basket) One ticket of passage to South America
> -- one letter, stamped but unsealed, addressed
> to you --

> REGGIE (lighting up)
> A letter? May I see it?

GRANDPIERRE hands her the letter and watches her closely as she reads it.

>   REGGIE (reading)
> "My dear Regina: I hope you are enjoying your
> holiday. Megeve can be so lovely this time of
> year. The days pass very slowly and I hope to
> see you soon. As always, Charles. P.S. Your
> dentist called yesterday. Your appointment has
> been changed." (she looks up, puzzled) Not
> very much, is it?

>   GRANDPIERRE
> We took the liberty of calling your dentist --
> we thought, perhaps, we would learn something.

>   REGGIE
> Did you?

>   GRANDPIERRE
> Yes. Your appointment <u>has</u> been changed. (he
> smiles at his little joke, then returns to the
> basket). One key to your apartment -- one comb --
> one fountain pen -- one toothbrush -- one tin of
> tooth powder (he looks up) -- that is all.

He slides a sheet of paper and pen across to her, then starts to put the things back into the basket while he speaks:

>   If you will sign this list you may take the
> things with you.

>   REGGIE (sighing)
> Is that all? Can I go now?

>   GRANDPIERRE
> One more question. Is this your husband's
> passport?

He reaches into the desk drawer and pulls out a passport which he hands to her.

30.   INSERT -- PASSPORT
The cover indicates that it is Swiss. REGGIE's hand opens it to a picture of a man -- the man we saw in GRANDPIERRE's photo. Under it is the name: "CHARLES LAMPERT."

31.   MED. SHOT -- REGGIE AND GRANDPIERRE

                        REGGIE
            Of course it is.

                        GRANDPIERRE
            And this?

He hands her another passport.

32.   INSERT -- SECOND PASSPORT
        The cover is American. When it is opened, we see the
        identical picture, but the name under it reads: "CHARLES
        VOSS."

33.   MED. SHOT -- REGGIE AND GRANDPIERRE

                        REGGIE
            I don't understand.

                        GRANDPIERRE
            And this? And this?

He hands her, one at a time, two more passports.

34.   INSERT -- THIRD AND FOURTH PASSPORTS.
        One is Italian which, when opened, shows the same photo
        with the name "CARLO FABRI." The other is Venezuelan, the
        same photo, and the name "CARLOS MORENO."

35.   MED. SHOT -- REGGIE and GRANDPIERRE

                        GRANDPIERRE
            Have you nothing to say, Madame?

REGGIE looks down at the four passports, then back to
GRANDPIERRE.

                        REGGIE (hopefully)
            It's all right if you want to smoke your
            cigar now.

36.   INT. LAMPERT APARTMENT -- DUSK
        The house is empty as before. Now it is silent, the late
        afternoon light coming from outside. REGGIE stands by a
        window. A canvas airline bag rests on the floor nearby.

        Suddenly there is the noise of a DOOR OPENING.

37.   CLOSER SHOT -- REGGIE
       As her head turns, in alarm, toward the noise. There is a
       moment of silence, then FOOTSTEPS are heard, coming closer.

38.   ANOTHER ANGLE
       As PETER enters.

                         REGGIE (surprised)
                   What are you doing here?

                         PETER
                   I phoned but nobody answered. I wanted to
                   tell you how sorry I am -- and to find out
                   if there was anything I could do.

                         REGGIE
                   How did you find out?

                         PETER
                   It's in all the afternoon papers. I'm very
                   sorry.

                         REGGIE
                   Thank you.

       A silence.

                         PETER
                   I rang the bell but I don't think it's
                   working.

                         REGGIE
                   Yes it is -- I heard it this morning.

       He looks around for the light switch, then goes to it and
       flicks it on -- nothing happens. He flicks it a few more
       times.

                         REGGIE
                   They must have turned off the electricity.

       She shakes her head. PETER looks around.

                         PETER
                   Where did everything go?

                         REGGIE
                   Charles sold it all -- at auction.

                    PETER
Do you know what you're going to do?

                    REGGIE
Try and get my old job back at UNESCO, I
suppose.

                    PETER
Doing what?

                    REGGIE
I'm a simultaneous translator -- like Sylvie,
only she's English to French -- I'm French
to English. That's what I did before I married
Charles. The police probably think I killed
him.

                    PETER
Instant divorce you mean?

                    REGGIE
Something like that. But I'm sorry it
ended like this -- tossed off a train like a
sack of third-class mail.

                    PETER (taking her hand)
Come on. You can't stay here.

                    REGGIE
I don't know where to go.

                    PETER
We'll find you a hotel.

                    REGGIE
Not too expensive -- I'm not a lady of
leisure anymore.

                    PETER
Something modest but clean -- and near enough
to UNESCO so you can take a cab when it rains
-- okay?

She nods. He picks up the airlines bag and they start out.
REGGIE stops at the door and looks back.

                    REGGIE
I loved this room -- but Charles never
saw it -- only what was in it. All those

                              REGGIE (Cont.)
                    exquisite things -- * * * (Looking around)   I
                    think I prefer it like this.

38A.   INT. FUNERAL CHAPEL -- DAY
        CLOSE SHOT of a phonograph. A hand appears, starts the
        record on it spinning, then places the arm at the beginning.
        An instant later ORGAN MUSIC starts with a roar.

39.   INT. FUNERAL CHAPEL -- DAY
        CLOSE SHOT of the coffin. It rests on a low platform, with
        a bouquet or two of flowers near the head, the lid open.
        Inside, the face made up to look lifelike (but failing),
        lie the remnants of Charles Lampert.

40.   CLOSE SHOT -- GRANDPIERRE
        The INSPECTOR sits quietly, eyes downcast, staring at his
        hands in a prayer-like attitude. CAMERA PULLS BACK,
        revealing row after row of empty wooden bench-like seats in
        the large, dimly lit, high-ceilinged room. Finally, in the
        first row, REGGIE and SYLVIE are discovered. Besides
        GRANDPIERRE, they are the only ones present. REGGIE turns
        around to look at the empty room. They speak in whispers.

                              REGGIE
                    It's not exactly what I'd call a large
                    turn-out.

                              SYLVIE
                    Didn't Charles have any friends?

                              REGGIE
                    Don't ask me -- I'm only the widow.
                    (indicating GRANDPIERRE) If Charles
                    had died in bed we wouldn't even have
                    him.

                              SYLVIE
                    At least he knows how to behave at
                    funerals.

41.   CLOSE SHOT -- GRANDPIERRE
        His eyes still lowered. CAMERA PANS DOWN to feature his
        hands -- he is methodically trimming his nails with a
        small clipper.

---

38.   [he didn't love me—he collected me.]

42.   TWO SHOT -- SYLVIE AND REGGIE

                         SYLVIE
                Have you no idea who could have
                done it?

                         REGGIE
                Until two days ago all I really knew
                about Charles was his name -- now it turns
                out I didn't even know that.

         The front DOOR of the Chapel is heard opening and a shaft
         of daylight streams in. The WOMEN turn.

43.   MED. SHOT -- CHAPEL DOOR
         The short, heavy-set figure of a MAN is outlined against
         the bright outdoor light. He stands for a moment, then
         closes the door after him. LEOPOLD GIDEON, short-sighted,
         bald, in his middle forties, glances around nervously,
         like a barnyard bird. Then he walks down one of the side
         aisles of the Chapel.

44.   CLOSE SHOT -- GRANDPIERRE
         As he watches GIDEON.

45.   CLOSE SHOT -- REGGIE
         As she watches him.

46.   MED. SHOT -- THE BIER
         GIDEON arrives at the coffin. He stops, looks down at
         LAMPERT's body for a moment. Then, suddenly, in rapid
         succession, he sneezes six times. He takes a small bottle
         from his pocket, shakes a pill from it and swallows it dry.
         He turns and walks back up the aisle, looking for a place
         to sit. He comes face to face with GRANDPIERRE, stops,
         turns to sit somewhere else.

47.   TWO SHOT -- REGGIE AND SYLVIE

                         SYLVIE
                Do you know him?

                         REGGIE
                I've never seen him before.

                         SYLVIE
                He must have known Charles pretty well.

                              REGGIE
              How can you tell?

                              SYLVIE
              He's allergic to him.

SYLVIE turns and glances at GIDEON. Again, the sound of
the DOOR opening interrupts them. They turn to look.

48.   MED. SHOT -- CHAPEL DOOR
      Again the figure of a MAN is outlined in silhouette against
      the outside brightness. When he closes the door we can see
      "TEX" PENTHOLLOW, a slim, rangy man with sandy-colored hair,
      a weatherbeaten face, washed-out blue eyes -- also in his
      forties. He wears a velvet-corduroy suit, string tie and a
      bright yellow flower in his lapel. A bulldurham tag hangs
      from his outside breast pocket, dangling from its string.
      He starts down the aisle toward the bier, CAMERA LEADING
      him, and we notice his unsteady gait. He turns to look at
      the others present.

49.   TRAVELLING SHOT -- TEX'S P.O.V.
      MOVING down the aisle. GRANDPIERRE's face, then GIDEON's,
      then REGGIE's and SYLVIE's -- all staring at CAMERA.

50.   MED. SHOT -- THE BIER
      As TEX arrives. He stands staring at LAMPERT's body,
      swaying on his feet until he reaches out and grabs the
      side of the coffin to steady himself. Then he takes the
      flower from his lapel and throws it into the open box.

51.   CLOSE SHOT -- TEX

                              TEX (heavy Texas accent)
              Ariva durchy, Charlie.

52.   WIDER ANGLE
      As TEX turns away from the coffin and approaches REGGIE and
      SYLVIE, addressing the latter -- after having first reached
      for his hat which he discovers he isn't wearing.

                              TEX
              Miz Lampert, m'am . . .

SYLVIE points to REGGIE. Unruffled, TEX starts over,
addressing REGGIE this time.

                              TEX
              Miz Lampert, m'am . . .

                          REGGIE
          Yes?

                          REX
          Charlie had no call handling it this-a-way.
          He sure didn't. No siree.

                          REGGIE
          I don't understa--

     But TEX has nodded his head and moved off to find a seat.
     When he spots GIDEON, the two men stare at each other.
     Finally, TEX chooses a seat away from him and sits.

53. MED. SHOT -- CHAPEL DOOR
     It flies open, this time with a bang, and the large MAN
     who appears almost fills the frame.

54. CLOSER SHOT -- TEX
     As the loud noise awakens him with a snort, mid-snore.

55. MED. SHOT -- THE DOOR
     Closing the door, we see HERMAN SCOBIE, a heavy-weight --
     tall and wide, but not fat -- with black hair combed straight
     back and heavy bushy eyebrows of a matching color, which
     meet over his nose and join up. About the same age as the
     first two men, SCOBIE is dressed in a battered raincoat, his
     hands thrust deep in the pockets. He marches down the aisle,
     looking straight ahead, CAMERA PANNING with him. He stops
     before the coffin and stares into it.

56. CLOSE SHOT -- SCOBIE
     As he stares down into the coffin, his tongue trying to
     dislodge a bit of food caught in his teeth. He stares hard
     at the body, squinting his eyes. Then he removes one hand
     from his pocket, removes a pin from the inside of his lapel,
     picks his teeth with it, then slowly lets the hand down,
     into the coffin.

57. CLOSE SHOT -- SCOBIE'S HAND
     The pin held between thumb and forefinger, he jabs it slowly
     but positively deep into the back of one of the dead man's
     hands. There is no reaction.

58. CLOSE SHOT -- SCOBIE
     He watches the dead man carefully, still squinting. Then
     finally satisfied, he returns the pin to his lapel and walks
     back up the aisle and out of the door, slamming it after him.

59.   CLOSE SHOT -- REGGIE
        Having watched SCOBIE exit. Suddenly a hand falls on her
        shoulder. She jumps in alarm and utters a little cry of
        fright.

60.   ANOTHER ANGLE
        Featuring a funeral ATTENDANT, a cadaverous type (aren't
        they all) with a black cut-away coat and an over-solicitous,
        unctuous manner. He is eternally bent at the waist, in a
        sort of half bow. He offers REGGIE a letter which she takes.

                        REGGIE
                Merci, Monsieur.

                        ATTENDANT
                Pas du tout, madame, pardon -- pardon -- pardon.

        He backs off and is gone. REGGIE looks at the letter, back
        and front, then starts to open it.

                        SYLVIE
                Who is it from?

                        REGGIE
                The American Embassy.

        She pulls out the letter and starts to read it.

61.   INSERT -- THE LETTER
        It bears the Great Seal as a letterhead and the typed
        message reads:

                "Dear Mrs. Lampert:
                Please drop by my office tomorrow
                at noon-thirty. I am anxious to
                discuss the matter of your late
                husband's death.
                                Sincerely,
                (signed)   H. Bartholomew."

62.   TWO SHOT -- REGGIE AND SYLVIE
        SYLVIE has been reading over REGGIE's shoulder.

                        SYLVIE
                What is that about?

                        REGGIE
                I don't know. But if this is a sample of
                American diplomacy I'm buying a fallout shelter.

63. EXT. AMERICAN EMBASSY -- ESTABLISHING -- DAY
     The fine old building in the Rue Gabriel.

64.- DELETED
68.

69. INT. EMBASSY CORRIDOR -- DAY
     As REGGIE leaves the elevator two young DIPLOMATIC TYPES
     step in, immersed in conversation.

                    1ST DIPLOMATIC TYPE
          I bluffed the Old Man out of the last pot --
          with a pair of deuces.

                    2ND DIPLOMATIC TYPE
          What's so depressing about that?

                    1ST DIPLOMATIC TYPE
          If I can do it, what are the Russians
          doing to him?

     The elevator door closes on them. REGGIE reacts to this and
     starts down the hall, finally stopping at the door.

70. MED. SHOT -- DOOR
     It is marked "307-A H. BARTHOLOMEW." REGGIE checks the
     letter, then opens the door.

71. INT. BARTHOLOMEW'S OUTER OFFICE -- DAY
     The office is empty, the typewriter on the secretary's desk
     is covered with its plastic shroud. REGGIE enters, looks
     for somebody, notices that the door to the private office is
     slightly ajar.

                    REGGIE (tentatively)
          Hello -- ? (There is no answer) Hello.

                    BARTHOLOMEW'S VOICE (o.s.)
          (from the private office) Is there anything
          wrong, Miss Tompkins?

                    REGGIE
          Uh -- Miss Tompkins isn't here.

     BARTHOLOMEW comes to the door and looks in. He is a pale
     grey-haired man who looks, on first examination, older than
     his forty-odd years. Sickly would be the word that describes
     him best -- pallid, consumptive-looking. He wears heavy
     tortoise-framed glasses which fall down his nose and cause
     him to push them back in place every so often with a quick
     automatic motion.

                          BARTHOLOMEW
          I'm sorry -- my secretary must have gone
          to lunch. You are -- ?

                          REGGIE
          Mrs. Lampert -- Mrs. Charles Lampert.

                 BARTHOLOMEW (looking at his watch)
          Come in, Mrs. Lampert. You're quite late.

He motions for her to enter, standing aside to let her do
so.

72.   INT. BARTHOLOMEW'S PRIVATE OFFICE -- DAY
      A small cubicle -- there is a silver-framed photo of three
      kids on the desk. BARTHOLOMEW indicates a chair, then
      goes behind his desk and sits. A can of lighter fluid
      stands open on the desk and a crumpled hankie beside it.

                          BARTHOLOMEW
          Excuse me for a moment, Mrs. Lampert --
          it's a stubborn little devil.

He works at a stain on his necktie with lighter fluid and
hankie.

          Dry-cleaningwise, things are all fouled
          up. I had a really good man - an excellent
          man on the Rue Ponthieu, but H.Q. asked us to
          use the plant here in the building -- to ease the
          gold outflow.

                          REGGIE
          Mr. Bartholomew -- are you sure you know
          who I am?

                    BARTHOLOMEW (looking up)
          Charles Lampert's widow -- yes? (going back
          to the tie) Last time I sent out a tie
          only the spot came back.

He looks up at her, laughs silently, then goes back to his
tie.

          Voilà! As they say.

He puts away the lighter fluid in a desk drawer, smells
the hankie, passes on it, then sticks it in his pocket.

He opens another drawer and pulls out various * * * sandwiches
wrapped in waxpaper, a salt and peper shaker, a tube of
mustard, a bottle of red wine and two Dixie cups.

> BARTHOLOMEW
> Have some, please. I've got . . . (checking)
> . . . liverwurst -- liverwurst -- chicken and --
> liverwurst.

> REGGIE
> No thanks.

He uncorks the wine, fills a cup and begins eating.

> BARTHOLOMEW
> Do you know what C.I.A. is, Mrs. Lampert?

> REGGIE
> I don't suppose it's an airline, is it?

> BARTHOLOMEW
> Central Intelligence Agency -- C.I.A.

> REGGIE (surprised)
> You mean spies and things like that?

> BARTHOLOMEW
> Only we call them agents.

> REGGIE
> We? You mean you're -- ?

> BARTHOLOMEW
> Someone has to do it, Mrs. Lampert --

> REGGIE
> I'm sorry, it's just that I didn't think that
> you people were supposed to admit --

> BARTHOLOMEW
> I'm not an agent, Mrs. Lampert -- I'm an administrator
> -- a desk jockey -- trying to run a bureau
> of overworked men with under-allocated funds.
> Congress seems to think that all a spy needs --

72.   [things]

                    REGGIE
Agent.

                    BARTHOLOMEW
Yes -- that all he needs is a code book and a
cyanide pill and he's in business.

                    REGGIE
What's all this got to do with me, Mr. Bartholomew?

                    BARTHOLOMEW (his mouth full)
Your husband was wanted by the U.S. Government.

                    REGGIE (a pause)
May I have a sandwich, please?

He hands her a sandwich and fills a wine-cup for her.

                    BARTHOLOMEW
To be more specific, he was wanted by this agency.

                    REGGIE (eating)
So that was it.

                    BARTHOLOMEW
Yes. We knew him, of course, by his real
name.

                    REGGIE (almost choking)
His -- real -- ?

                    BARTHOLOMEW
Voss -- Charles Voss. All right, Mrs. Voss --
(taking a photo from his desk) -- I'd like you
to look at this photograph, please -- by the
way, you saw this one, didn't you? (indicating
the kids on the desk) Scott, Cathy and Ham, Jr.

                    REGGIE
Very sweet.

                    BARTHOLOMEW
Aren't they? Now look at this one, Mrs. Voss, and --

                    REGGIE
Stop calling me that! Lampert's the name on
the marriage license.

> BARTHOLOMEW
> Yes -- and tell me if you recognize anyone.
> Just a moment. Have a good look.

He reaches back into the drawer and pulls out a glass which
he gives her.

73.   CLOSE SHOT   PHOTO
FOUR MEN, all in army uniform, sitting behind a table. The
glass is held over the first, magnifying the face.

74.   CLOSER SHOT   PHOTO
It's a photo of a young CHARLES LAMPERT.

> REGGIE'S VOICE (o.s.)
> It's Charles!

> BARTHOLOMEW'S VOICE (o.s.)
> Very good.

> REGGIE'S VOICE (o.s.)
> He looks so young -- when was this taken?

> BARTHOLOMEW'S VOICE (o.s.)
> 1944. The next face, please.

The glass and CAMERA move to the next man -- a young TEX.

> REGGIE'S VOICE (o.s.)
> It's the man who came to the funeral
> yesterday -- I'm sure of it -- a tall
> man in a corduroy suit and string tie.

> BARTHOLOMEW'S VOICE (o.s.)
> Does the name Tex Penthollow mean
> anything to you?

> REGGIE'S VOICE (o.s.)
> No.

> BARTHOLOMEW'S VOICE (o.s.)
> Next, please.

The glass and CAMERA move to the third face -- a young GIDEON.

> REGGIE'S VOICE (o.s.)
> Yes -- and he was there, too -- a little
> fatter now -- and less hair -- but it's
> the same one.

                    BARTHOLOMEW'S VOICE (o.s.)
          Do you know <u>him</u>, Mrs. Vo -- Mrs. Lampert?
          Leopold W. Gideon?

                    REGGIE'S VOICE (o.s.)
          No.

                    BARTHOLOMEW'S VOICE (o.s.)
          The last one, please.

The glass and CAMERA move to the fourth face -- a young
SCOBIE.

                    REGGIE'S VOICE (o.s.)
          That's a face you don't forget -- he
          was there too --

                    BARTHOLOMEW'S VOICE (o.s.)
          Herman Scobie. And you've never seen
          him before, either?

                    REGGIE'S VOICE (o.s.)
          No, thank heaven.

75.   MED. SHOT -- REGGIE AND BARTHOLOMEW

                    BARTHOLOMEW (a pause, regarding her)
          Mrs. Lampert, I'm afraid you're in a great
          deal of danger.

                    REGGIE
          Danger? Why should <u>I</u> be in any danger?

                    BARTHOLOMEW
          You're Charles Voss's wife -- now that he's
          dead you're their only lead.

                    REGGIE
          Mr. Bartholomew -- if you're trying to
          frighten me you're doing a really first-
          rate job. (she takes another sandwich).

                    BARTHOLOMEW
          Please, do what we ask, Mrs. Lampert --
          it's your only chance.

                    REGGIE (eating)
          Gladly, only I don't know what you want!
          You haven't told me.

                    BARTHOLOMEW
Oh, haven't I? The money -- Mrs. Lampert --
the money. The $250,000 Charles Voss
received from the auction. Those three
men want it, too -- they want it very badly.

                    REGGIE
But it's Charles' money, not theirs.

                    BARTHOLOMEW (laughing)
Oh, Mrs. Lampert! I'd love to see you
try and convince them of that! (drying
his eyes) Oh, dear.

                    REGGIE
Then whose is it? His or theirs?

                    BARTHOLOMEW
Ours.

                    REGGIE (she looks at him
for a moment). Oh, I see.

                    BARTHOLOMEW
And I'm afraid we want it back.

                    REGGIE
But I don't have it.

                    BARTHOLOMEW
That's impossible. You're the only one
who <u>could</u> have it.

                    REGGIE
I'm sorry it's impossible. It's the truth.

BARTHOLOMEW is silent for a moment, thinking.

                    BARTHOLOMEW
I believe you.

                    REGGIE
Thanks very much.

                    BARTHOLOMEW
Oh, you've got the money all right --
you just don't <u>know</u> you've got it.

                    REGGIE
Mr. Bartholomew -- if I had a quarter
of a million dollars, believe me, I'd
know * * * it.

                    BARTHOLOMEW
Nevertheless, Mrs. Lampert -- you've got it.

                    REGGIE
You mean it's just lying around someplace --
all that cash?

                    BARTHOLOMEW
Or a safe-deposit key, a certified check,
a baggage claim -- you look, Mrs. Lampert --
I'm quite sure you'll find it.

                    REGGIE
But --

                    BARTHOLOMEW
Look for it, Mrs. Lampert -- look just as hard
and as fast as you can. You may not have a
great deal of time. Those men know you have
it just as surely as we do. You won't be safe
until the money's in our hands. Is that clear?

REGGIE nods. He writes something on a pad of paper and
tears it off, handing it to her.

                    BARTHOLOMEW
Here's where you're to call me -- day or night.
It's a direct line to both my office and apartment.
Don't lose it, Mrs. Lampert -- and please
don't tell anyone about coming to see me. It
could prove fatal for them as well as yourself.

                    REGGIE
Wait a minute -- you think those three
men killed Charles, don't you?

                    BARTHOLOMEW
We've no proof, of course, but we
rather think so, yes.

---

75.   [about]

                    REGGIE
    Well, there you are! Charles had the
    money with him -- so whoever killed him
    has it -- they have it!

BARTHOLOMEW shakes his head.

                    REGGIE
    Why not?

                BARTHOLOMEW (grimly)
    Because they're still here.

                    REGGIE
    Oh.

                    BARTHOLOMEW
    Like I said, Mrs. Lampert -- I'm afraid
    you're in a great deal of danger.
    Remember what happened to Charles.

REGGIE takes the last sandwich and begins eating furiously.

76. DELETED

77. EXT. ESPLANADE DES CHAMPS-ELYSÉES -- DAY
     MED. SHOT -- GUIGNOL. One of the French Punch and Judy
     shows set up on certain days in the small park alongside
     the broad avenue between the Rond Point and the Place de
     la Concorde. At the moment, Judy, as always, is beating
     Punch with a bat. The sound of CHILDREN laughing and
     screaming can be heard.

78. VARIOUS CLOSE SHOTS -- THE CHILDREN
     Sitting on small benches lined up to face the stage. Their
     attention is fixed on the show, their belief totally
     suspended by the play as only children's can be -- laughing
     at the slapstick, booing the villain, frightened by the
     perils.

79. MED. SHOT -- REGGIE
     Sitting on the last bench, next to some CHILDREN. They are
     laughing but she isn't -- she just watches, her attention
     caught up but her face void of emotion. The bench is too
     low for her, forcing her knees up almost under her chin.

     After a moment, PETER comes up behind her and, stepping over
     the benches, sits beside her. She doesn't seem to notice.

(Throughout the following scene the CHILDREN and the
ACTORS can be heard in the b.g.)

> PETER
> Reggie -- ?

She turns and looks at him for a moment.

> REGGIE (vaguely)
> Hallo, Peter.

> PETER
> You telephoned me to meet you. I've
> been standing on the corner back
> there -- waiting for you.

> REGGIE
> I'm sorry -- I heard the children laughing.

A ROAR from the CHILDREN. REGGIE and PETER turn toward
the stage.

79A.   MED. SHOT -- GUIGNOL
       PUNCH and JUDY are arguing loudly.

80.   TWO SHOT -- REGGIE AND PETER

> PETER
> What's going on?

> REGGIE
> Don't you understand French?

> PETER
> I'm still having trouble with English.

> REGGIE
> The man and the woman are married --

81.   CLOSE SHOT -- GUIGNOL STAGE
       PUNCH and JUDY are batting each other on the head.

> PETER'S VOICE (o.s.)
> Yes, I can see that -- they're batting
> each other over the head with clubs.

Finally, JUDY knocks PUNCH out of sight and a PUPPET
wearing a three-cornered hat appears.

PETER'S VOICE (o.s.)

Who's that with the hat?

82. MED. SHOT -- GRANDPIERRE
Wearing a hat, he stands off in the background, watching.

REGGIE'S VOICE (o.s.)

That's the policeman - he wants to
arrest Judy for killing Punch.

83. CLOSE SHOT -- GUIGNOL STAGE
JUDY and the POLICEMAN are batting one another.

PETER'S VOICE (o.s.)

What's she saying now?

REGGIE'S VOICE (o.s.)

That she's innocent -- she didn't do it.

PETER'S VOICE (o.s.)

She did it all right -- take it from me.

REGGIE'S VOICE (o.s.)

I believe her.

PUNCH's head appears on the other side of the stage, says
something, then ducks out.

PETER'S VOICE (o.s.)

Who was that?

REGGIE'S VOICE (o.s.)

Punch, of course.

84. TWO SHOT -- REGGIE AND PETER

PETER

Of course? I thought he was dead.

REGGIE

He's only pretending, to teach her a lesson --
only -- (her face clouding) -- only he is dead,
Peter -- I saw him -- he's not pretending. Somebody
threw him off a train. What am I going to do?
Charles was mixed up in something terrible.

PETER

I wish you'd let me help you. Whatever it is,

                        PETER (Cont.)
              it doesn't sound like the sort of thing that
              a woman can handle all by herself.

85.   CLOSE SHOT -- GUIGNOL STAGE
      JUDY has gotten the upper hand and is now batting the
      POLICEMAN's brains out.

86.   CLOSE SHOT -- GRANDPIERRE as he winces

87.   TWO SHOT -- REGGIE AND PETER

                        PETER
              Have you got a mirror? (she nods)
              Give it to me.

      She hands it to him and he holds it in front of her face.

                        PETER
              Right there, between your eyes -- see?
              Worry lines. You're much too young and
              too pretty to have anything like that.
              How about making me vice-president in
              charge of cheering you up?

                        REGGIE (jumping at the suggestion)
              Starting tonight?

                            * * *

88.   INT. NIGHTCLUB -- NIGHT
      MED. SHOT -- EMCEE. He stands on the dance floor in front
      of a five-piece Latin dance band, a spotlight on him,
      wearing his professional smile as he speaks into a mike.

                        EMCEE
              Bonsoir mesdames et messieurs, good evening
              ladies and gentlemen, guten Abend, meine
              Damen und Herren -- ce soir, comme tous les
              soirs, l'attraction ici, au Black Sheep
              Club, c'est vous! Venez, mesdames et
              messieurs, step right up, ladies and gentlemen,

---

                            [PETER
87.   Well.
                            REGGIE
              Dinner, fun and games?]

                    EMCEE (Cont.)
        kommen Sie her, meine Damen en Herren,
        avanti, signore e signori -- avanti!

89.   MED. SHOT -- REGGIE AND PETER
      At their table. REGGIE is dressed in a lovely Givenchy dress.

                    PETER
        What was all that?

                    REGGIE
        Fun and games. Evidently we're the
        floorshow.

                    PETER
        You mean you and me?

                    REGGIE
        No, everyone. Come on -- avanti, avanti!

      She rises and pulls him along.

90.   WIDE ANGLE
      Including the dance floor as most of the patrons go to it,
      laughing self-consciously and looking around.

                    EMCEE
        Écoutez bien - les règles sont tres simples
        - the rules are very easy - deux équipes --
        two teams -- each with one orange -- une orange --
        eine apfelsine -- un' arrancia -- held under
        the chin, like so -- (does it) -- comme ça --
        and passed to the player behind you -- sans
        vous servir de vos mains -- using nothing but the
        chin -- no hands -- and keeping the orange at
        all costs from touching the floor. Commencez,
        Mesdames et Messieurs -- begin, ladies and
        gentlemen -- signore e signori, comminciate!

      The EMCEE now circulates, forming teams, telling the
      patrons to line up, making sure there is a woman next to
      every man. REGGIE and PETER are the second couple in
      their line.

      Then the EMCEE picks up a basket of oranges and places one
      under the chin, held securely against the chest, of each
      man at the head of the line. Blowing a whistle, a signal
      for the game to begin and the band to play, the men turn

to the women behind them and attempt to transfer the
oranges from under their chins to under the chins of the
women -- without using their hands.

(This maneuver can only be accomplished by embracing one's
partner passionately and firmly pressing the orange against
the partner's throat until he or she can grip it tightly
enough with the chin to turn and offer it to the person
next in line, where the process begins anew. However, the
slightest miscalculation, which can be brought about by
any number of human frailties -- haste, modesty, inhibition
or lack of co-ordination -- will surely result in losing
control of the orange so that it either falls to the floor
[where it can only be picked up by the chin] or it starts
to roll and slide from its proper place to some other,
less proper, spot on the human anatomy, forcing the man or
woman to retrieve it -- again, with the chin only. This
latter is an activity which can prove extremely satisfying
to old friends, or even new friends who wish to become
old friends, but can only be a torment for total strangers
and/or the English).

91. VARIOUS SHOTS -- ORANGE GAME
     Some of the couples in various states of confusion,
     entanglement and intimacy -- all of them, naturally,
     hilarious.

92. TWO SHOTS -- PETER AND GIRL
     It is his turn to take the orange from a very short, but
     quite shapely young girl in a strapless dress (held up by
     an abundance of cantilever). PETER 'takes' when he sees
     the twin obstacles which might -- and probably will --
     encumber the game but increase his worldly experience.
     The contest begins: because of her stature he is forced
     to move in low, making the ordinary embrace needed for
     success difficult, if not impossible. Then, inexorably, the
     orange starts to slip down the GIRL's front. Manfully he
     goes after it.

93. CLOSE SHOT -- REGGIE
     She is enjoying it thoroughly.

94. TWO SHOT -- PETER AND GIRL
     Bending her over backwards, in a sort of frontal half-nelson,
     PETER makes a last valiant effort and, voilà, grips the
     orange under his chin -- amid much cheering and congratulations
     from members of his TEAM.
     Now he turns to REGGIE and they face one another for a moment.

                    PETER
          En garde.

                    REGGIE
          Lay on, Macduff.

They go at it, working their bodies together to make it all
possible. Then, for a moment, the game and the onlookers
seem less important than their proximity. But, alas, they
are too good despite themselves and the transfer is
accomplished -- again with appreciative cheers from the TEAM.

REGGIE, with the orange now tucked firmly under her chin,
turns to the next team-member in line and is locked in an
embrace before she realizes her partner is LEOPOLD GIDEON,
the short, fat, balding man seen at the funeral and later
in BARTHOLOMEW's photo.

REGGIE starts to draw back but GIDEON holds her tightly.
Putting his chin around the orange he is able to speak
quietly in REGGIE's ear.

95.   CLOSE TWO SHOT -- REGGIE AND GIDEON
        Her eyes show her fright as he whispers:

                    GIDEON
          Mrs. Lampert --

                    REGGIE
          What do you want?

                    GIDEON
          Didn't Charles tell you, Mrs. Lampert?

                    REGGIE
          Tell me what?

                    GIDEON
          It doesn't belong to you, Mrs. Lampert
          -- you do know that, don't you?

                    REGGIE
          I don't know anything.

                    GIDEON
          Mrs. Lampert, any morning now you could
          wake up dead.

                    REGGIE
          Leave me alone -- !

                    GIDEON
          Dead, Mrs. Lampert -- like last week's news --
          like Charles, Mrs. Lampert --

                    REGGIE (shouting)
          Stop it!

96.   CLOSE SHOT -- REGGIE'S AND GIDEON'S FEET
      As REGGIE hauls off and kicks GIDEON full in the shin.

97.   CLOSE SHOT -- GIDEON
      He stiffens as the pain registers. Instead of shouting he
      merely closes his eyes.

98.   WIDER ANGLE
      Including REGGIE and GIDEON and PETER standing by, as well
      as some spectators. PETER comes quickly forward.

                    PETER
          Reggie -- what's the trouble?

      REGGIE realizes that GIDEON no longer offers any resistance.
      She steps back, leaving GIDEON holding the orange, foolishly,
      under his chin, his eyes still closed. REGGIE stares at him
      for a moment.

                    REGGIE
          He -- he was stepping on my foot.

99.   CLOSE SHOT -- GIDEON
      Slowly, his eyes open and tears stream from them, rolling
      down his cheeks. He speaks while holding the orange.

                    GIDEON
          Forgive me -- it was quite unintentional,
          I'm sure.

100. WIDER ANGLE
      GIDEON turns to the woman behind him and the game resumes.

                    REGGIE (starting off)
          Wait for me -- I won't be long.

      She goes off toward the rear of the club and starts down a
      flight of stairs.

101.   CLOSE SHOT -- PETER
       Watching her go, a concerned look on his face.

102.   INT. NIGHTCLUB LOUNGE -- NIGHT
       A small, dimly lit area with a door to the combination
       men's-women's room and a 'phone cabin with a solid door.
       The music and shouting from upstairs float down. REGGIE
       comes down the stairs and goes to the 'phone, flicking on
       the light and closing the door after her.

103.   INT. PHONE BOOTH -- NIGHT
       REGGIE takes a jeton ('phone token) from her bag and drops
       it in the slot. Then she takes out a slip of paper (the
       one given her by BARTHOLOMEW) and dials the number written
       on it. She listens to it ring, then evidently he answers.

                         REGGIE (into 'phone)
                 Mr. Bartholomew -- it's me, Reggie Lampert --
                 listen Mr. Bartholomew, I've seen one of
                 the (she stops) Mr. Bartholomew? Can you
                 hear me?

       She realizes she has not pushed the button which takes her
       coin and allows the party at the other end to hear her
       voice.

                         REGGIE
                 Hello -- Mr. Bartholomew -- it's me --
                 Regina Lam . . .

       Suddenly the door of the booth opens and REGGIE wheels to
       look, slamming down the receiver as she does.

104.   REVERSE SHOT -- 'PHONE BOOTH -- NIGHT
       TEX PENTHOLLOW, the second man from the funeral (and photo),
       the man in the corduroy suit and string tie, stands in the
       doorway, his face calm, a hand-rolled but unlit cigarette
       in his mouth. He has put one foot against the side of the
       door so she can't leave. REGGIE stares at him, terrified.

                         TEX
                 Howdy, Miz Lampert.

                         REGGIE
                 Wha-- what do you want?

       TEX takes a book of matches from his pocket.

                              TEX
              You know what I want, Miz Lampert . . .

                              REGGIE
              No -- no, I don't.

                              TEX
              C'mon now -- sure you do. An' you'd better
              give it to me, Miz Lampert -- cuz I ain't
              foolin'. No sireebob!

He strikes a match and lights his cigarette, holding the
burning match in his hand afterward.

                              REGGIE
              I don't know what --

TEX, without a word, throws the still-lit match into the
booth, onto REGGIE's lap. She beats it out frantically.

                              REGGIE
              What are you doing?

TEX lights another match and throws it into her lap. She
beats this one out too.

                              REGGIE
              Stop that!

                              TEX
              Don't make too much noise, Miz Lampert --

He lights another match and reaches out toward her hair with
it. She shrinks back.

                              TEX
              It could get a whole lot worse.

Then he throws it into her lap. As he continues to speak he
punctuates each phrase or so with another lit match. REGGIE
is too busy beating them out to do anything else.

                              TEX
              It belongs to me, Miz Lampert -- an' if you
              don't give it to me your life ain't * * *
              gonna be worth the paper it's printed on.
              You savvy what I'm sayin', Miz Lampert?

>   REGGIE (desperate)
>   Please stop -- please!

>   TEX
>   You think on it real careful-like, Miz Lampert
>   -- y'hear?

105.   CLOSE SHOT -- REGGIE
         As she frantically beats out the matches, her eyes on her
         work.

>   REGGIE
>   You're insane, absolutely insane!

She looks up, then blinks her eyes.

106.   INT. 'PHONE BOOTH OVER REGGIE'S SHOULDER
         There is no one there. REGGIE rises and steps out of the
         booth.

107.   INT. NIGHTCLUB LOUNGE -- NIGHT
         As REGGIE looks around. There is no one there.

107A.   INT. PHONE BOOTH
         As REGGIE returns, sits and starts to put another jeton into
         the slot. She notices her hand is shaking. She reaches back
         into her bag, removes a piece of candy, puts it into her mouth
         and leans her head back against the wall, closing her eyes.
         Suddenly the door opens and REGGIE shrieks -- but this time
         it is PETER.

>   PETER
>   What are you doing in here?

>   REGGIE (a sigh of relief)
>   Having a nervous breakdown.

108.   INT. HOTEL LOBBY -- NIGHT
         REGGIE and PETER enter the deserted lobby.

>   PETER
>   You haven't said a word since we left the
>   club -- what happened back there?

>   REGGIE
>   I -- I'm not sure if I'm supposed to tell you
>   or not.

                         PETER
            I don't think I follow you.

                         REGGIE
            He said if I told anybody it could prove
            fatal for them as well as me.

                         PETER
            Who said?

                         REGGIE
            That's what I'm not supposed to say.

                         PETER
            Stop this nonsense! If you're in some sort
            of trouble I want to know about it.

                         REGGIE
            Stop bullying me. Everybody's bullying me.

                         PETER
            I wasn't --

                         REGGIE
            Yes, you were -- you called it nonsense. Being
            murdered in cold blood isn't nonsense. Wait
            until it happens to you sometime.

She goes to the desk, followed by PETER, where the NIGHT
CLERK greets them sleepily.

                         NIGHT CLERK
            Bonsoir.

                         REGGIE
            Bonsoir. Quarante-deux, s'il vous plait.

The NIGHT CLERK gets the key off a hook and hands it to
REGGIE.

                         NIGHT CLERK
            Bonne nuit.

                         REGGIE (to PETER)
            Would you mind seeing me to the door?

                         PETER
            Of course not.

They go to the elevator where he opens the door for her.

109.   INT. ELEVATOR -- NIGHT
As REGGIE and PETER enter the small cage. It is somewhat
cramped, forcing them to stand close together.

                         REGGIE
            This is quite a place for making friends,
            isn't it?

He presses the button and the elevator starts to rise.

                         PETER
            You said this afternoon that your husband was
            mixed up in something.

                         REGGIE (busy examining the cleft
                                 in his chin)
            How do you shave in there?

                         PETER
            What was it?

                         REGGIE
            What was what?

                         PETER
            What your husband was mixed up in.

                         REGGIE
            Look, I know it's asking you to stretch your
            imagination, but can't you pretend for a
            moment that I'm a woman and that you're a --

                         PETER
            Don't you know I could already be arrested
            for transporting a minor above the first floor?

The elevator stops.

                         PETER
            We're here.'

                         REGGIE
            Where?

                         PETER
            On the street where you live.

                         REGGIE
            How about once more around the park?

He reaches across her and opens the door.

> PETER
> Out.

110.   INT. HOTEL CORRIDOR THIRD LANDING -- NIGHT
As REGGIE leaves the elevator, followed by PETER. They
walk to her door. There is a moment of silence as she
looks at him.

> REGGIE (imitating PETER)
> Him: 'Do you mind if I come in for a nightcap,
> Reggie?' Her: 'Well -- it _is_ awfully late.'
> Him: 'Just one, all right?' Her: 'Promise
> you'll behave yourself.' Him: 'Sorry, baby,
> I never make promises I can't keep.'

> PETER
> How would you like a spanking?

> REGGIE
> How would you like a punch in the nose?
> Stop treating me like a child.

> PETER
> * * * Then stop acting like one. If you're
> really in some kind of trouble, I'd like
> to hear about it. Otherwise, it's late, I'm
> tired and I'm going home to bed.

> REGGIE
> Do you know what's wrong with you?

> PETER
> What?

> REGGIE
> Nothing. Good night.

> PETER (smiling)
> Good night.

He turns and leaves. She smiles slightly, then turns and
puts the key into the door and opens it.

111.   INT. REGGIE'S ROOM -- NIGHT
Featuring the door. REGGIE enters, then stops abruptly,
the doorknob still in her hand.

112.   ANOTHER ANGLE
        The room has been torn apart. And standing in the center
        is HERMAN SCOBIE, the large man in the battered raincoat.
        He starts slowly advancing toward REGGIE.

                        SCOBIE
            Where is it, lady -- where've you got it?

113.   CLOSE SHOT -- REGGIE
                        REGGIE (terrified)
            I don't know -- I don't know! I don't --

        She stops as she sees something.

114.   CLOSE SHOT -- SCOBIE'S HAND
        Instead of a human hand there is a twin-pronged metal one.

115.   WIDER ANGLE
        SCOBIE sees where REGGIE is staring; looks down at it
        himself, then lunges at her, raising the hand to strike.

                        SCOBIE
            I want it -- give it to me -- it's mine!

        The hand is starting to come down. REGGIE, moving quickly,
        turns and flies out.

                        REGGIE (screaming)
            Peter -- ! Peter -- !

116.   INT. HOTEL CORRIDOR THIRD LANDING -- NIGHT
        As REGGIE runs out; slamming the door after her, the metal
        hand crashes against the wooden panel inside the door and
        splinters through it, visible on this side now. Petrified
        with fear, REGGIE can only stare dumbly at the protruding
        claw.

117.   ANOTHER ANGLE
        As PETER comes running up to her. He sees the metal hand.

                        REGGIE
            A man -- he tried to kill me!

        Pushing her aside, PETER takes hold of the key (still in
        the outside lock) and turns it slowly and quietly. Then,
        using all his weight, he slams the door open as far as it
        will go, making sure to hold it that way as he steps in.

118.   INT. REGGIE'S ROOM -- NIGHT
        Inside, PETER pulls back the door and slugs the startled
        SCOBIE full on the jaw. His head bangs back against the
        wall but he manages to raise a foot and push PETER violently
        away, sending him sprawling back, toppling across the bed
        and over, head first, onto the floor on the other side,
        where he disappears. Hurrying, SCOBIE puts his foot against
        the door and pushes it away, ripping his metal hand free.
        He then rushes to the open window and climbs out.

119.   INT. HOTEL CORRIDOR THIRD LANDING -- NIGHT
        REGGIE waits anxiously. When she hears nothing, she
        gingerly looks into the room.

120.   INT. REGGIE'S ROOM -- NIGHT
                            REGGIE (entering cautiously)
                Peter -- ? (alarmed) Peter! Where are you?

121.   ANOTHER ANGLE
        Showing the disarranged room, empty of people. Then, slowly
        PETER's hand appears from behind the bed, shaking groggily.
        REGGIE rushes to him and helps him sit on the bed.

                            REGGIE
                Peter -- are you all right?

                            PETER
                I think I sprained my pride. (He looks around)
                Where'd he go?

                            REGGIE
                Out of the window, I guess -- I didn't see him.

        PETER goes, unsteady on his feet, to the window and looks
        out. He then turns back.

                            PETER
                Lock the door and the window -- and don't
                let anyone in except me. I'll be back in
                a minute.

                            REGGIE
                Be careful, Peter.

                            PETER (one leg over the sill)
                You took the words right out of my mouth.
        He climbs out.

122.   EXT. HOTEL WINDOW THIRD FLOOR -- NIGHT
        Outside the window to REGGIE's room is a small, false
        balcony, consisting mostly of railing, with barely enough
        room between it and the building's facade for a man to
        stand. PETER appears and looks down over the railing.

123.   EXT. HOTEL SIDEWALK (FROM ABOVE) -- NIGHT
        SHOOTING STRAIGHT DOWN; there is no one on the street and
        it is too far to jump.

124.   MED. SHOT -- PETER -- BALCONY
        He now looks around. REGGIE's is the last such balcony
        on one side, but there are two or three on the other.
        PETER climbs over the railing and, holding on to it with
        one hand, reaches for the railing on the next balcony.

125.   CLOSE SHOT -- PETER'S HAND
        As it stretches for the railing; it is several inches
        short of touching it.

126.   MED. SHOT -- PETER
        As he straightens up and prepares to jump.

127.   EXT. HOTEL FACADE -- NIGHT
        From the GROUND. PETER; high above, jumps to the next
        balcony.

128.   MED. SHOT -- PETER
        As he climbs over the railing of the second balcony. He
        sees a light coming through the window and looks in.

                        WOMAN'S VOICE (o.s.)
                Oh!

        PETER leaves the window quickly, climbing over the railing
        on his way to the next balcony. As he does the following
        exchange is heard (in British English).

                        MAN'S VOICE (o.s.)
                What is it now, Pamela?

                        WOMAN'S VOICE (o.s.)
                It happened again, Henry -- another strange
                man peered in the window at me and then went
                away.

                        MAN'S VOICE (o.s.)
                Bad luck, Pamela.

129. EXT. HOTEL FACADE -- NIGHT
      From the GROUND as PETER jumps to the next balcony.

130. MED. SHOT -- PETER
      As he climbs over the rail onto the third balcony. There
      is a light coming from this window, too. PETER looks in.

131. MED. SHOT -- WINDOW -- OVER PETER'S SHOULDER
      Inside the room are GIDEON, TEX, and SCOBIE in the midst of
      a heated discussion.

                         GIDEON
           That was a dumb move, Herman -- a dumb move.

                         TEX
           And then some. If you'd only told us you
           was goin' to her room we could've kept 'em
           busy --

132. INT. GIDEON'S HOTEL ROOM -- NIGHT

                         TEX
           -- but sneakin' in there on your own that-a-way,
           why, man, you was <u>bound</u> to get yore tokus
           kicked. I mean, what'd you think he'd do -- walk
           up 'n' shake you by that hand of yores?

                         PETER'S VOICE (o.s.)
           That's right, Herman -- you didn't leave me
           much choice.
      They all turn toward the window.

133. WIDER ANGLE
      As PETER climbs in through the window and joins them.

                         PETER (to SCOBIE)
           I didn't hurt you, did I?

      SCOBIE shakes his head and turns away.

                         GIDEON (eagerly)
           Never mind that -- did you get the money?

                         PETER
           How could I with the three Marx Brothers
           breathing down my neck? You said you'd
           let me handle it alone -- ! The girl trusts
           me. If she's got it I'll find out about
           it. But you've got to leave me alone.

                    SCOBIE (to GIDEON and TEX)
We took all the chances -- it belongs to
us, not him!

                    TEX
Don't be un-neighborly-like, Herman --
don't forget he done us a li'l ol' favor.

                    SCOBIE
Yeah? What's that?

                    TEX
He took care of Charlie for us.

                    GIDEON (to PETER)
We appreciate it, really we do.

                    SCOBIE
But who asked him? Three shares are
enough -- I'd say he's out!

                    PETER
A third of nothing is nothing, Herman.
Make up your minds -- she's waiting for me.

                    GIDEON (thoughtfully)
I don't see how another twenty-four hours
could hurt.

                    TEX
Shoot no, not after all these years.

                    SCOBIE
Then he gets it out of your share, not mine!
Not <u>mine</u>!

SCOBIE turns and storms out of the door, slamming it.
GIDEON begins sneezing, takes a bottle of pills from his
pocket and swallows two white tablets.

                    GIDEON
I suggest you get about your business --
nothing soothes Herman like success.

                    TEX (chuckling)
That's right -- it's like ticklin' a
alligator's belly.

                         PETER
          Who's got the room next to hers?

                         TEX
          Me. How come?

                         PETER
          Get another one, will you? I'm going to
          need it.

     PETER starts for the door.

                         TEX
          If you find the money -- you won't forget
          t' tell us about it, will you, fella?

                         PETER (turning at the door)
          Don't worry.

                         TEX
          Oh, I ain't worryin -- but see this pudgy
          little fella here? (indicating GIDEON)
          He worries -- an' he's even meaner'n I am.

134. INT. REGGIE'S ROOM -- NIGHT
      As she waits anxiously, smoking a cigarette. There is a
      KNOCK at the door.

                         REGGIE
          Who is it?

                         PETER'S VOICE (o.s.)
          It's me. Peter.

     REGGIE unlocks the door and opens it. PETER enters and
     she closes the door again --

                         PETER
          There was no trace of him. All right, Reggie
          -- suppose you tell me what this is all about.

                         REGGIE
          There are three men -- he's one of them --
          they think I have something that belongs
          to them.

                         PETER
          What?

                    REGGIE
          A quarter of a million dollars.

PETER is silent for a moment.

                    PETER
          Go on.

                    REGGIE
          That's all.

                    PETER
          No, it isn't -- where's the money?

                    REGGIE
          I don't know. Those men killed Charles
          to get it. But he must not have had it
          with him on the train.

                    PETER
          So they think he left it with you.

                    REGGIE
          But he didn't! I've looked everywhere
          (tears welling) -- and if I don't find it --
          (wailing) -- those men are going to kill me.

She falls in his arms to be comforted.

                    PETER
          No, they won't -- I won't let them.

                    REGGIE (sobbing)
          Please help me, Peter -- you're the only
          one I can trust.

                    PETER
          Of course I'll help -- I told you I would,
          didn't I? Come on now --

He takes out his handkerchief and dries her eyes.

                    REGGIE
          I'm so hungry I could faint. (trying to smile)
          I've -- I've gotten your suit all wet.

                    PETER
* * * That's all right -- it's drip-dry.

                    REGGIE
Peter -- you've got to promise me something.
Promise you'll never lie the way Charles
did. Why do people have to tell lies?

                    PETER
Usually it's because they want something --
and they're afraid the truth won't get it
for them.

                    REGGIE
Do you tell lies?

A pause. The phone rings. REGGIE answers it.

                    REGGIE (into the phone)
          Hello?

135.   INT. OUTDOOR 'PHONE BOOTH -- NIGHT
        SCOBIE holds the receiver in his metal hand.

                    SCOBIE
          Mrs. Lampert? -- it's me -- the man who was
          in your room a few minutes ago --

136.   INT. REGGIE'S ROOM -- NIGHT

                    REGGIE (on the phone)
          What do you want?

                    PETER (whispering)
          Who is it?

                    REGGIE (covering the receiver)
          The man you had the fight with.

137.   INT. PHONE BOOTH -- NIGHT

                    SCOBIE (on the phone)
          Is Dyle with you?

138.   INT. REGGIE'S ROOM -- NIGHT

---

134.   [So what]

CLOSE SHOT -- REGGIE

                    REGGIE
          Who?

139.   INT. PHONE BOOTH -- NIGHT

                    SCOBIE (on the phone)
          The man who hit me, lady -- Dyle -- that's
          his name. What's wrong -- is he still there?

140.   INT. REGGIE'S ROOM -- NIGHT
       REGGIE's back is turned to PETER so he can't see her face.
       He watches her.

                    REGGIE (on the phone)
          Yes -- that's right.

                    PETER
          What is it, Reggie -- what's he saying?

       She shakes her head.

141.   INT. PHONE BOOTH -- NIGHT

                    SCOBIE (on the phone)
          Don't trust him -- don't tell him anything.
          He's after the money.

       He hangs up.

142.   INT. REGGIE'S ROOM -- NIGHT
       Slowly, REGGIE lowers the 'phone from her ear and hangs it
       up. She hesitates a moment.

                    PETER
          What'd he say?

                    REGGIE
          He -- he said if I didn't give the money
          he'd kill me.

                    PETER
          I wouldn't take that too seriously.

                    REGGIE (a pause)
          I believe what he said.

                        PETER
        They're only trying to scare you, that's
        all.

                        REGGIE
        How do you know what they're doing?

                        PETER
        I don't -- but as long as they think you
        have the money, or know where it is, or have
        it without knowing where it is, or don't even
        know you have it --

                        REGGIE
        What are you talking about?

                        PETER
        You mustn't let what he said bother you.
        It was only words.

                        REGGIE (softly)
        Words can hurt very much.

                        PETER (a pause)
        Go to sleep -- I'll see you in the morning.

                        REGGIE
        Don't put yourself out.

                        PETER
        Hey -- I'm on your side. Remember that.

                        REGGIE
        Yes. I'll remember. Good night.

                        PETER
        Good night.

He starts out, pausing by the door and examining the hole
SCOBIE made in it.

                        PETER
        But if you'll take my advice -- (smiling) --
        you'll undress in the closet. Oh, and if
        you need me, just bang on the wall. I'll
        be next door.

143.   INT. HOTEL CORRIDOR -- THIRD LANDING -- NIGHT
       As PETER (now called DYLE) leaves REGGIE's room and closes
       the door. He pauses for a moment, listening, hears nothing,
       then bends down and starts pulling at a loose thread in one
       of his socks. As usual, the thread unravels -- and unravels --
       and unravels some more until it seems that the entire sock
       has come unknit. Now, taking the long thread, he bends
       down near the door and, taking his tie-pin, attaches one
       end of the thread to the bottom of REGGIE's door. He then
       runs the thread along the floor to his door (next door) and
       works it underneath.

144.   INT. DYLE'S ROOM -- NIGHT
       As DYLE enters, the thread in his hand. He goes to a nearby
       table where he attaches the thread to the heavy room key,
       which he then balances on the extreme edge of the table.

145.   INT. REGGIE'S ROOM -- NIGHT
       REGGIE is on the phone.

                         REGGIE (excited)
                 -- But I _am_ calm, Mr. Bartholomew -- what I
                 called to tell you was there's someone else --
                 someone who wasn't in that photograph you
                 showed me. He says his name is Peter Joshua --
                 but it isn't -- it's Dyle. (a pause) Mr.
                 Bartholomew? -- are you still there?

146.   INT. BARTHOLOMEW'S APARTMENT -- NIGHT
       BARTHOLOMEW on the phone. He is silent for a moment, his
       face troubled.

                         BARTHOLOMEW
                 I don't know who this Mr. Dyle is, but it's
                 just possible we were wrong about who killed
                 your husband.

147.   INT. REGGIE'S ROOM -- NIGHT

                         REGGIE (on the phone)
                 You mean _he_ might have -- Mr. Bartholomew,
                 I'm catching the next plane out of here --
                 I'm not going to sit here and wait for
                 someone to make chopped liver out of _me_!

148.-
150.   DELETED

151.   INT. BARTHOLOMEW'S APARTMENT -- NIGHT

                         BARTHOLOMEW (on the phone)
                Where are you now -- can you meet me?
                Do you know Les Halles?

152.   INT. REGGIE'S ROOM -- NIGHT

                         REGGIE (on the phone)
                Yes, where? (a pause) -- in fifteen
                minutes. I'll be there.

153.   DELETED

154.   INT. REGGIE'S ROOM -- NIGHT
        REGGIE hangs up the phone, picks up her bag, checks her hair
        in the mirror, then starts for the door. She stops as she
        notices the connecting door leading to the room next door,
        DYLE's room. She goes to it, silently slips out the key and
        bends to peer through the keyhole.

155.   INT. DYLE'S ROOM -- NIGHT (THROUGH KEYHOLE)
        DYLE is removing his coat. Before he lays it over a chair,
        he takes a gun from the inside pocket, checks it, and tucks
        it into his belt.

156.   INT. REGGIE'S ROOM -- NIGHT
        REGGIE reacts in surprise and fright, jumps quickly away
        from the door. She hurries to the door leading to the hall
        and reaches for the knob.

157.   INT. DYLE'S ROOM -- NIGHT
        CLOSE SHOT -- ROOM KEY. The thread attached to it is pulled
        (by the action of REGGIE's door opening) and the key falls
        to the floor with a clatter.

158.   WIDE ANGLE
        Including DYLE, as he reacts, his head wheeling to look
        at the key. Snatching his coat, he runs for the door.

159.   INT. HOTEL CORRIDOR -- THIRD LANDING -- NIGHT
        As REGGIE sneaks past DYLE's door. When she has passed, the
        door opens and DYLE appears. REGGIE takes off on the run,
        turning the corner and starting down the stairs.

                         DYLE
                Reggie -- !

        He starts after her.

160. INT. HOTEL LOBBY -- NIGHT
It is deserted, except for the sleeping NIGHT PORTER; as
REGGIE comes running down the stairs.

                    DYLE'S VOICE (o.s.)
          Reggie . . . !

She turns, looking back towards the sound of his voice, but
does not slacken her speed. She runs out the front door.

161. EXT. HOTEL ENTRANCE -- NIGHT
As REGGIE runs out. She looks up the street, sees a TAXI
and hails it.

                    REGGIE
          Taxi -- !

It pulls over to the curb. Looking once more over her shoulder
she takes a bill out of her pocket, opens the cab door, slams
it loudly without getting in and hands the bill to the
driver.

                    REGGIE
          N'importe où - vite! Allez-y!

She jumps back into the shadows of a nearby doorway as the
TAXI pulls away. At the same time DYLE runs out of the
hotel. Another TAXI is coming down the street. DYLE
hails it frantically.

                    DYLE
          Taxi -- ! Taxi -- !

It pulls up and DYLE opens the door.

                    DYLE (pointing)
          Follow that taxi.

                    DRIVER
          Comment?

                    DYLE
          Taxi! Follow!

                    DRIVER
          Je ne comprends rien.

Desperately, DYLE reaches into his coat pocket and pulls out
a small dictionary and begins flipping through the pages.

162.   CLOSE SHOT -- REGGIE
       In the shadows. She lifts her eyes in annoyance.

163.   MED. SHOT -- TAXI

                       DYLE (finding the word)
            Suivre -- el taxi!

                       DRIVER
            Ah! Oui, Monsieur.

164.   ANOTHER ANGLE
       REGGIE comes out of the shadows, looks after DYLE's taxi,
       then hails another one which pulls up.

                       REGGIE (to DRIVER)
            Aux Halles -- vite!

165.-
167.   DELETED

168.   EXT. LES HALLES -- NIGHT
       REGGIE and BARTHOLOMEW walking. The Central Market is
       teeming with activity -- trucks creeping around other
       trucks, cases of fruit and vegetables stacked on every
       inch of sidewalk, WORKERS of all types milling around,
       unloading trucks and stacking crates, little electric carts
       scooting in and out -- and nearby, one of the huge, high-roofed
       sheds where the butchers work.

169.   TWO SHOT -- REGGIE AND BARTHOLOMEW
       CAMERA LEADING them as they walk.

                       BARTHOLOMEW (looking around)
            Incredible, isn't it? Zola called it 'le
            ventre de Paris' -- the womb of Paris, the belly.

       She takes a banana from a nearby stall.

                       REGGIE (peeling it)
            What did you want to see me about, Mr.
            Bartholomew?

                       BARTHOLOMEW (leaves a coin on the crate)
            Were you followed?

                       REGGIE
            Yes, but I lost him. I really did it quite
            brilliantly. I'm beginning to think women

                    REGGIE (Cont.)
make the best spies.

                    BARTHOLOMEW
Agents.

                    REGGIE
He has a gun, Mr. Bartholomew -- I saw it.

                    BARTHOLOMEW
Who?

                    REGGIE
Dyle, or whatever his name is.

                    BARTHOLOMEW
What does your Mr. Dyle look like, Mrs.
Lampert?

                    REGGIE
He's hardly my Mr. Dyle.

                    BARTHOLOMEW
Describe him.

                    REGGIE
Well -- he's tall -- over six feet -- rather
thin -- in good physical shape, I'd say --
dark eyes -- quite handsome, really.

                    BARTHOLOMEW (shaking his head)
No.

                    REGGIE
No, what?

                    BARTHOLOMEW
That's not Carson Dyle.

                    REGGIE (stopping)
Carson?

                    BARTHOLOMEW
There's only one Dyle connected with this
affair, Mrs. Lampert -- that's Carson.

                    REGGIE
You mean you've known about him all along?
Why didn't you tell me?

BARTHOLOMEW looks at her for a moment, then glances around;
his attention is drawn inside the doorway.

> BARTHOLOMEW
> It's enough to make you a vegetarian,
> isn't it?

170. INT. LES HALLES BUTCHERS' SHED -- NIGHT
Almost as far as the eye can see, row upon row of beef sides,
hung on hooks.

171. TWO SHOT -- REGGIE AND BARTHOLOMEW (TRAVELLING)
As REGGIE looks at the hanging beef.

> REGGIE
> It's just lucky I'm not hanging next to
> those things right now.

She shudders, throws away her banana and turns back to
BARTHOLOMEW.

> REGGIE
> Mr. Bartholomew -- why didn't you tell me
> you knew about Dyle?

> BARTHOLOMEW
> I didn't see any point. Dyle's dead.

> REGGIE
> Dead? Mr. Bartholomew, -- maybe you'd
> better tell me what this thing's all about.

* * *

172.)
)
  to)   DELETED
)
209.)

---

171.   [BARTHOLOMEW (a pause)
              Why not? Let's go someplace where we can
              sit down.

They start off.]

210.   INT. LES HALLES BISTRO -- NIGHT
         Lined up at a zinc bar are several Butchers, their white
         smocks stained with blood. * * * REGGIE AND BARTHOLOMEW
         * * * sit at the table.

                              * * *

                         BARTHOLOMEW
              I suppose you're old enough to have heard
              of World War Two?

                           REGGIE
              Barely, yes.

                         BARTHOLOMEW
              In 1944, five members of the O.S.S. -- the
              military espionage unit -- were ordered
              behind the German lines for the purpose of
              delivering $250,000 in gold to the French
              Underground. The five men --

         A WAITER arrives

                           WAITER
              Vous désirez?

                         REGGIE (smiling)
              They always do that.

                         BARTHOLOMEW (to the WAITER)
              Café.

                           REGGIE
              Gratinée, choucroute garnie, salade de
              pommes -- et un ballon de rouge.

---

210.   [REGGIE and BARTHOLOMEW enter, passing the bar on their
         way to a corner table.

                         BUTCHERS (to REGGIE)
                    Bonsoir, Mademoiselle—
                    Salut, poupée—
                    Etc.]

         [install themselves]

                           [REGGIE
                    I'm listening, Mr. Bartholomew.]

                    BARTHOLOMEW
          Mrs. Lampert, I really hadn't planned on
          spending the entire night here.

                    REGGIE
          Can I at least keep the onion soup?

BARTHOLOMEW shrugs.

                    REGGIE (to the waiter)
          La soupe tout simplement.

The WAITER nods and goes.

                    REGGIE (anxiously)
          Go on, please -- five men -- $250,000
          -- the French Underground --

                    BARTHOLOMEW
          Yes. The five men. They were, of course,
          your husband, Charles, the three men who
          showed up at his funeral yesterday, and
          Carson Dyle. But something went wrong and
          they were unable to locate their contact.
          It must have been at that point that they
          decided to steal the money.

                    REGGIE
          Steal it how?

                    BARTHOLOMEW
          By burying it, and then reporting that the
          Germans had captured it. All they had to
          do was come back after the war, dig it up
          and split it five ways -- a quarter of a
          million with no questions asked.

                    REGGIE (fascinated)
          May I have a cigarette, please?

BARTHOLOMEW pulls out a package and she takes one, looks at
it and rips off the filter tip. He winces.

                    REGGIE
          I hate these things -- it's like drinking
          coffee through a veil.

She puts the other end in her mouth, then picks up the matches
and lights it.

>   BARTHOLOMEW
>   Everything went smoothly enough until after
>   the gold was buried -- then, before they
>   could get out, they were ambushed by a
>   German patrol. A machine gun separated
>   Scobie from his right hand -- and caught
>   Carson Dyle full in the stomach.

REGGIE takes another cigarette from his pack, rips off the
filter (he winces again) and puts it into her mouth.

>   BARTHOLOMEW
>   What's wrong with that one?

He points to the cigarette she just lit, still practically
brand-new in the ashtray.

>   REGGIE
>   Oh. Nothing, I guess. What happened then?

She hands over the newer one to BARTHOLOMEW, who sadly
examines its mutilated end while REGGIE returns to the first
cigarette.

>   BARTHOLOMEW
>   Have you any idea what these cost over here?

>   REGGIE
>   Please go on, Mr. Bartholomew -- what
>   happened then?

>   BARTHOLOMEW
>   Scobie was able to travel, but Carson Dyle
>   was clearly dying, so they --

The WAITER returns with the coffee and onion soup.

>   WAITER
>   La soupe, c'est pour qui?

>   REGGIE
>   Pour moi. Go on, Mr. Bartholomew.

The WAITER puts down the cup and bowl and leaves.

>   BARTHOLOMEW
>   Carson was dying so they were forced to
>   leave him. They finally got back to the
>   base, made their report and waited for the

                    BARTHOLOMEW (Cont.)
war to end. Only Charles couldn't wait
quite as long as the others. He beat them
back to the gold, took everything for himself
and disappeared. It's taken Gideon, Tex
and Scobie all this time to catch up with
him again.

                    REGGIE
But if they stole all that money -- why can't
you arrest them?

                    BARTHOLOMEW
We know what happened from the bits and
pieces we've been able to paste together --
but we still have no proof.

                    REGGIE
But what has all this got to do with the
C.I.O.?

                    BARTHOLOMEW
C.I.A., Mrs. Lampert. We're an extension of
the wartime O.S.S. It was our money and we
want it back.

                    REGGIE
I'm sorry, Mr. Bartholomew, but nothing you've
told me has changed my mind. I still intend
leaving Paris -- tonight.

                    BARTHOLOMEW
I wouldn't advise that, Mrs. Lampert. You'd
better consider what happened to your husband
when he tried to leave. Those men won't be
very far away -- no matter where you go. In
fact, I don't even see any point in your
changing hotels. Please help us, Mrs. Lampert.
Your government is counting on you.

                    REGGIE
Well, if I'm going to die, I might as well
do it for my country.

                    BARTHOLOMEW
That's the spirit.

                    REGGIE
Oh, stop it. What do you want me to do?

                    BARTHOLOMEW
        We're anxious to know who this man is -- the
        one calling himself Dyle.

                    REGGIE
        Maybe he really is Dyle. He could still be
        alive.

                    BARTHOLOMEW
        No, Mrs. Lampert.

                    REGGIE
        But no one actually saw him die.

                    BARTHOLOMEW
        No, Mrs. Lampert. His death is registered
        with the War Department in Washington.

                    REGGIE
        Oh. Then who's this one?

                    BARTHOLOMEW
        I don't know -- but I think you'd better find
        out, don't you?

                    REGGIE
        Me? Why me?

                    BARTHOLOMEW
        You're in an ideal position -- he trusts you.
        (grinning) Besides, you said yourself, women
        make the best spies.

                * * * REGGIE (resigned)
        Agents.

211.   EXT. HOTEL (PLACE ST. ANDRÉ DES ARTS) -- LATE AFTERNOON
        DYLE leaves the hotel and turns into the Place. A moment
        later, REGGIE comes cautiously from the hotel. As she
        watches DYLE, a SANDWICH-MAN advertising a driving school
        passes the hotel. REGGIE falls in behind him, his tall
        placard hiding her from view.

212.   EXT. PLACE ST. ANDRÉ DES ARTS -- LATE AFTERNOON
        First comes DYLE, passing a sidewalk cafe on the corner, then
        the SANDWICH-MAN and REGGIE. The SANDWICH-MAN turns off,
        leaving REGGIE out in the open. A moment later, DYLE
        passes a GIRL painting a canvas, her easel set up in the

middle of the sidewalk. He stops when he has passed her and
turns to look at her work. REGGIE, not knowing what to do,
and afraid she will be seen by DYLE, who is now looking her
way, spins and sits at the sidewalk cafe's nearest table, her
back to DYLE. It is already occupied by a middle-aged
TOURIST.

213.   TWO SHOT -- REGGIE AND TOURIST
        The TOURIST, complete with camera, beret and guide book,
        looks up from his coffee, surprised. He stares at REGGIE and
        she stares back. Finally, not knowing what else to do, she
        smiles, then takes a portion of his brioche and eats it.
        He smiles back emptily, not knowing what to make of her.
        REGGIE turns to look at DYLE.

214.   MED. SHOT -- DYLE
        He has made his judgment of the painting and now moves on.

215.   TWO SHOT -- REGGIE AND TOURIST
        The TOURIST has finally found the courage to speak. As
        he opens his mouth to make a sound, REGGIE, her eyes on
        DYLE, rises quickly from the table and goes, leaving a very
        confused TOURIST with his mouth open. He blinks, then
        leaves some money on the table and starts after her.

216.   EXT. PLACE ST. ANDRÉ DES ARTS -- LATE AFTERNOON
        REGGIE following DYLE. As she passes the GIRL painting,
        she cannot resist turning to see the work.

217.   CLOSE SHOT -- PAINTING
        An abstract jumble, nothing recognizable.

217A.   CLOSE SHOT -- REGGIE
        As she looks from the painting to reality.

217B.   EXT. PLACE ST. ANDRÉ DES ARTS -- LATE AFTERNOON
        As the scene really looks.

218.   MED. SHOT -- REGGIE
        She shrugs, continues after DYLE. Now we see that the
        tourist, in turn, is following her.

                        TOURIST (calling)
                Fraulein --

REGGIE doesn't stop.

                        TOURIST
                Fraulein --

                        REGGIE (turning but continuing)
                  What are you doing, following me? Stop it --
                  we're going to look like a parade.

            She continues after DYLE.   The TOURIST hesitates, then
            continues after her.

218A.   MED. SHOT -- DYLE
        He goes to the curb and starts to step off, attempting to
        cross the Rue Danton, but finds the light against him. He
        turns back in REGGIE'S direction.

218B.   MED. SHOT -- REGGIE
        Realizing she has to do something before DYLE spots her, she
        turns and takes the TOURIST's arm and starts walking with
        him back toward the cafe.

                        REGGIE (smiling and rattling on)
                  How are you? When did you arrive in town?
                  Are you enjoying Paris? It's lovely, isn't
                  it? So many wonderful things to see and do,
                  it makes one's head spin to think of it.

            She looks back over her shoulder and sees that DYLE is now
            crossing the Rue Danton, heading for the platform of a bus
            now stopped at the curb.

                        TOURIST (smiling)
                  Fraulein --

            REGGIE pulls away from him.

                        REGGIE
                  If you don't stop following me I'll call
                  the police.

            She leaves him standing there, more confused than ever, as
            she starts after DYLE again.

            DYLE has hopped on the back of the bus as it pulls away.

            REGGIE hurries across the street, hailing a taxi.

                        REGGIE
                  Taxi -- !

219.   INT. AMERICAN EXPRESS -- LATE AFTERNOON
        DYLE enters. CAMERA PANNING with him to the head of a
        stairway leading downstairs, a sign indicating that it leads

to the "MAIL ROOM & TELEPHONES." CAMERA PANS back to the door as REGGIE enters.

220.   DELETED

221.   INT. AMERICAN EXPRESS MAIL ROOM -- LATE AFTERNOON
DYLE walks to one of several windows. A sign over it reading:
"A - D."

222.   MED. SHOT -- STAIRS
REGGIE comes down the stairs. Suddenly she stops.

223.   MED. SHOT -- DYLE
CAMERA ZOOMS in to sign on "D."

224.   CLOSE SHOT -- REGGIE
A confused look on her face.

225.   MED. SHOT -- DYLE
As his turn comes, he addresses the CLERK.

                    DYLE
        Dyle, please . . . D - Y - L - E.

                    CLERK
        Yes, Mr. Dyle. I remember.

226.   CLOSE SHOT -- REGGIE
Watching.

227.   MED. SHOT -- MAIL WINDOW
The CLERK takes out a bundle of letters and quickly sorts
through it.

                    CLERK
        I'm sorry, Mr. Dyle -- nothing today.

                    DYLE
        Thanks -- see you soon.

He turns and heads out, starting up the stairs where REGGIE
was but is no longer. As he reaches the fourth or fifth
step, a VOICE is heard over the loudspeaker.

                    VOICE (o.s.)
        Mr. Dyle, please -- you're wanted on the
        telephone -- Mr. Dyle. Cabin 4.

DYLE stops in his tracks, pondering what to do.

                    VOICE (o.s.)
          Mr. Dyle. Cabin 4 please.

He stops and comes down the stairs, going to the back of
the room and into the cabin marked "4."

                    DYLE (picking up phone)
          Yes?

CAMERA DOLLIES across an empty cabin to discover REGGIE in
the third one, on the phone.

228.   INT. REGGIE'S CABIN   INT. DYLE'S CABIN
        REGGIE on the phone.   DYLE on the phone.

               REGGIE   DYLE (surprised)
        Good morning, Mr. Dyle   Reggie?

        It's the only name I've got,   No cat and mouse -- you've
        How about you?   got me. What do you want
                                         to know?

        Why you lied to me.   I had to -- for all I knew
                                         you could have been in on
                                         the whole thing.

        Well, you know now, so
        please tell me who you are.

                                         But you know my name --
                                         it's Dyle.

        Carson Dyle is dead.   Yes, he is. He was my
                                         brother.

        Your --   The Army thinks he was killed
                                         in action by the Germans, but
                                         I think they did it -- Tex,
                                         Gideon and Scobie -- and your
                                         husband -- because he wouldn't
                                         go along with their scheme to
                                         steal the gold. I think he
                                         threatened to turn them in
                                         and they killed him. I'm
                                         trying to prove it. They
                                         think I'm working with them.
                                         But I'm not, and that's the
                                         truth. I'm on your side,
                                         Reggie -- please believe that.

                         REGGIE
         How can I? You lied to me -- the way
         Charles did -- and after promising you
         wouldn't. I want to believe you, Peter
         * * * . . . oh, but I can't call you that
         anymore, can I? It will take me a while
         to get used to your new name -- which
         I don't even know yet. What is it?
         (pause) Aren't you going to tell me?
         (pause) Hello -- ?

She opens the door of the cabin and starts out.

229.   MED. SHOT -- PHONE CABINS
        As REGGIE steps out of her cabin and starts looking in the
        others. They are all occupied except one and she looks
        inside it.

230.   CLOSE SHOT -- EMPTY CABIN
        The receiver hangs by its cord, swinging back and forth.

231.   MED. SHOT -- REGGIE
        As she looks at it, confused.

232.   INT. AMERICAN EXPRESS -- DAY
        DYLE and SCOBIE stand together, waiting for the elevator,
        SCOBIE clearly holding a gun in the pocket of his raincoat.

                         SCOBIE (quietly)
         If you do anything funny, or try to talk
         to anyone, I'll kill you, Dyle -- here and
         now. Okay?

                         DYLE
         You'll wreck your raincoat.

The self-service elevator doors open, one or two PASSENGERS
come out and DYLE and SCOBIE enter. A young GIRL starts in
after them.

                         SCOBIE
         Next car, please.

He reaches out and presses the top button with his metal
hand. The doors close.

233.   DELETED

234.   INT. TOP FLOOR LANDING -- LATE AFTERNOON
As SCOBIE follows DYLE out of the elevator. SCOBIE looks
around -- there is an open door at the end of a short
hall. He and DYLE go to it, CAMERA FOLLOWING. Through the
door, which SCOBIE closes behind them, is a flight of
stairs, leading up to a second door.

                SCOBIE
        Okay -- turn around.

DYLE turns to find SCOBIE'S gun out of the pocket and
pointing at him. SCOBIE now transfers it to his metal
hand and goes to DYLE, where he proceeds to frisk him.
Finding the gun DYLE carries in his inside coat pocket,
SCOBIE removes it. During the following conversation he
will shake open the revolving magazine and let the bullets
fall out onto the floor before handing back the emptied
gun to DYLE. Then he will transfer his own gun back to
his good hand.

                SCOBIE
        Sit down.

Shrugging, DYLE sits on the third step.

                DYLE
        What now?

                SCOBIE
        We wait -- with our mouths shut.

234A.   INT. AMERICAN EXPRESS -- NIGHT
The last EMPLOYEES leave the building as the WATCHMAN
locks the front door after them.

234B.   INT. TOP FLOOR LANDING -- NIGHT
In the semi-darkness, DYLE is still sitting on the third
step, SCOBIE still facing him with a gun.

                DYLE
        How long do you intend -- ?

                SCOBIE
        I said with the mouth shut.

DYLE yawns wide.

                DYLE
        Sorry about that.

                          SCOBIE (listening)
              Okay -- up there.

DYLE gets to his feet and starts up the stairs, followed
by SCOBIE. DYLE stops at the door.

                          DYLE
              Do I knock or something?

                          SCOBIE
              Open it.

DYLE opens the door. The stairs continue up.

                          SCOBIE
              Keep going.

                          DYLE
              The view had better be worth it.

235.   EXT. AMERICAN EXPRESS -- ROOFTOP -- NIGHT
        A spectacular view of the Paris rooftops and the city
        lights beyond. DYLE and SCOBIE come out onto a level
        portion of roof. On the street side, the roof angles
        down abruptly into a steep, slate-covered pitch, broken
        only by two widely separated oval-shaped dormer windows.
        Below these is a rain gutter, then nothing -- for seven
        stories.

                          DYLE
              Very pretty. Now what?

                          SCOBIE
              I'll give you a chance, Dyle -- which is
              more than you'd give me. Where's the money?

                          DYLE
              Is that why you dragged me all the way up
              here -- to ask me that? She has it --
              you know that.

                          SCOBIE
              And I say maybe you both have it! One
              more time, Dyle -- where is it?

                          DYLE
              Supposing I did have it -- which I don't --
              do you really think I'd hand it over?

> SCOBIE (shouting)
> You're out, Dyle -- right now!

SCOBIE aims the gun and starts advancing toward DYLE

> SCOBIE
> Step back.

DYLE turns and looks -- there is nothing behind him but a
sheer drop to the street.

> DYLE
> Back where?

> SCOBIE
> That's the idea.

Moving quickly, DYLE lashes out and hacks SCOBIE's gun hand
with the side of his palm and the gun falls to the roof.
Following through, DYLE punches the large man full in the
jaw, but instead of falling, SCOBIE wraps his arm around
DYLE, holding on tightly until his head clears.

Then, to his amazement, DYLE is lifted into the air and,
unable to break the bear-hold, carried toward the edge of
the roof. Working his arms between their two bodies,
DYLE suddenly flails them out with all his strength and
the hold is broken, but at the price of his coat * * *
and the flesh on his back as SCOBIE's metal claw
rips through both, a wound extending from the center of
DYLE's back to his shoulder.

Both men look around for the gun, spot it simultaneously
and leap for it, both landing short of the mark. Now they
grapple with one another, each trying to break free and
reach the gun.

236. CLOSE SHOT -- THEIR HANDS
Two hands, one real, one metal, inch toward the gun.

237. MED. SHOT -- DYLE AND SCOBIE·
The battle is going to SCOBIE whose weight and strength are
beginning to tire DYLE, who is now on his back, trying to
stop SCOBIE from crawling over him. He has the large man
by both lapels of the raincoat in a last-ditch effort to hold

---

235. [, his shirt]

him. But SCOBIE, his face horribly distorted from the strain, continues to inch forward toward the gun.

Suddenly, DYLE releases his hold. With nothing restraining him, SCOBIE lurches forward, tumbling past the gun, his momentum carrying him onto the sloping part of the roof, where he begins sliding down. SCOBIE beats wildly at the slate with his claw, trying to gouge a grip.

238.   CLOSE SHOT -- SCOBIE'S CLAW
        As it slides across the slate, making a hideous scratching
        sound and causing sparks to fly.

239.   MED. SHOT -- SCOBIE
        As he slides over the edge and disappears.

240.   CLOSE SHOT -- DYLE
        As he watches, hypnotised.

241.   MED. SHOT -- ROOF EDGE
        There appears to be no sign of SCOBIE. Then CAMERA ZOOMS
        IN FOR A TIGHT CLOSE SHOT OF SCOBIE'S metal hand, gripping
        the rain gutter at the very edge.

242.   MED. SHOT -- DYLE
        Having seen the claw, he rises and walks to the very edge of
        the level part of the roof.

                        DYLE (calling)
              Herman!

243.   MED. SHOT -- SCOBIE
        As he hangs, seven stories over the street, by his metal
        hand.

                        SCOBIE
              Yeah?

244.   MED. SHOT -- DYLE
        He finds it hard to believe.

                        DYLE
              How are you doing?

                        SCOBIE'S VOICE (o.s.)
              How do you think?

                        DYLE
              If you get bored, try writing 'Love thy

                              DYLE (Cont.)
               neighbor' a hundred times on the side
               of the building.

          DYLE turns and leaves, going down the stairs.

245.   INT. HOTEL CORRIDOR -- THIRD LANDING -- NIGHT
          The HOTEL MANAGER is busy taping a piece of cardboard over
          the hole ripped in REGGIE'S door by SCOBIE'S metal hand
          the night before. DYLE leaves the elevator and goes to his
          own door. The MANAGER eyes him coldly. DYLE "takes" the
          look.

                              DYLE
               I didn't do it.

                              MANAGER
               The next time madame forgets her key,
               there is another one at the desk.

          DYLE smiles, then enters his room.

246.   INT. DYLE'S ROOM -- NIGHT
          He closes the door and starts to remove his torn coat,
          wincing.

247.   INT. REGGIE'S ROOM -- NIGHT
          REGGIE, smoking on the bed, sits up when she hears DYLE
          moving about in his room. She goes to the connecting door,
          unlocks her side, tries the knob, finds it still bolted
          from his side and knocks.

                              REGGIE
               Is that you?

247A.   INT. DYLE'S ROOM -- NIGHT
          DYLE goes to the door, throws back the bolt and opens the
          door. REGGIE enters.

                              REGGIE
               Didn't anyone ever tell you it's
               impolite to -- (seeing his injured
               back) -- what happened?

                              DYLE
               I met a man with sharp nails.

                              REGGIE
               Scobie?

                         DYLE
          I left him hanging around the American
          Express.

                         REGGIE
          Come on -- I've got something that
          stings like crazy.

She leads him to her room.

247B.   INT. REGGIE'S ROOM -- NIGHT
         As REGGIE and DYLE enter from his room. She leads him to
         the bed.

                         REGGIE
              Take off your shirt and lie down.

As REGGIE goes to the bathroom, DYLE takes off his torn
shirt, revealing a torn and bloody T-shirt. He lies face
downwards on the bed. REGGIE returns, carrying cotton,
gauze, tape, scissors, and disinfectant. She sits next to
him and lifts up his T-shirt to examine the wound.

                         DYLE (wincing)
          Listen -- all I really want is an estimate.

                         REGGIE
          It's not so bad. You may not be able to
          lie on your back for a few days -- but,
          then, you can lie from any position, can't you?

She wets the cotton with disinfectant and begins cleaning
the wound. He winces.

                         REGGIE (hopefully)
              Does it hurt?

                         DYLE
          Haven't you got a bullet I can bite?

She continues working on his back, cleaning it, then bandaging
it while they talk.

                         REGGIE
              Are you really Carson Dyle's brother?

                         DYLE
          Would you like to see my passport?

                    REGGIE
Your passport! What kind of proof is that?

                    DYLE
Would you like to see where I was tattooed?

                    REGGIE
Sure.

                    DYLE
Okay. I'll drive you around there some day.
(his back stinging) Ouch!

                    REGGIE
Ha ha. You could at least tell me what
your first name is these days.

                    DYLE
Alexander.

                    REGGIE
Is there a Mrs. Dyle?

                    DYLE
Yes, but we're divorced.

                    REGGIE
I thought that was Peter Joshua.

                    DYLE (smiling)
I'm no easier to live with than he was.

                    REGGIE (finishing the bandage)
There -- you're a new man.

As they continue talking, he rises from the bed and goes
into his own room. REGGIE remains on the bed, watching
him through the open door as he puts on a fresh T-shirt
and shirt.

                    DYLE
I'm sorry I couldn't tell you the truth,
but I had to find out your part in all this.

                    REGGIE
Alex -- how can you tell if someone is
lying or not?

                    DYLE
You can't.

                    REGGIE
There must be some way.

                    DYLE
There's an old riddle about two tribes
of Indians -- the Whitefeet always tell
the truth and the Blackfeet always lie.
So one day you meet an Indian, you ask
him if he's a truthful Whitefoot or a
lying Blackfoot. He tells you he's a
truthful Whitefoot, but which one is he?

                    REGGIE (thinking)
Why couldn't you just look at his feet?

                    DYLE
Because he's wearing moccasins.

                    REGGIE
Oh. Well, then he's a truthful Whitefoot,
of course.

                    DYLE
Why not a lying Blackfoot?

                    REGGIE (confused)
Which one are you?

                    DYLE (entering, smiling)
Whitefoot, of course.

                    REGGIE
Come here.

He goes to the bed.

                    REGGIE
Sit down.

He sits.

                    REGGIE
I hope it turns out you're a Whitefoot,
Alex -- I could be very happy hanging
around the teepee.

                    DYLE
Reggie -- listen to me --

                    REGGIE
Oh-oh -- here it comes. The fatherly
talk. You forget I'm already a widow.

                    DYLE
So was Juliet -- at fifteen.

                    REGGIE
I'm not fifteen.

                    DYLE
Well, there's your trouble right there --
you're too old for me.

                    REGGIE
Why can't you be serious?

                    DYLE
There, you said it.

                    REGGIE
Said what?

                    DYLE
Serious. When a man gets to be my age
that's the last word he ever wants to hear.
I don't want to be serious -- and I
especially don't want you to be.

                    REGGIE
Okay -- I'll tell you what -- we'll just
sit around all day being frivolous --
how about that?

She starts kissing him on the neck, on the chin, on the cheek.

                    DYLE
Now please, Reggie -- cut it out.

                    REGGIE (pulling back)
Okay.

                    DYLE
What are you doing?

                  REGGIE
Cutting it out.

                  DYLE
Who told you to do that?

                  REGGIE
You did.

                  DYLE
But I'm not through complaining yet.

                  REGGIE
Oh. (She starts kissing him again)

                  DYLE
Now please, Reggie -- cut it out.

                  REGGIE
I think I love you, Alex --

                  DYLE (warning)
Reggie --

She kisses him on the mouth. The phone rings. He tries
to talk as she continues kissing him.

                  DYLE (mumbling)
The phone's ringing --

                  REGGIE
Whoever it is won't give up -- and neither
will I.

The phone continues to ring and she continues to kiss him.
Finally, REGGIE reaches out to the bedstand and takes the
phone off the hook. She brings the receiver up to their
mouths and mumbles into it.

                  REGGIE (on phone)
Sorry -- I was just - uh - nibbling on something.

248.   INT. TEX'S ROOM -- NIGHT
      TEX speaks into the phone.

                  TEX
Miz Lampert, my buddies 'n me, we'd oblige it
mighty highly if you could mosey on across
the hall 'n chew the fat with us for a spell.

249.   INT. REGGIE'S ROOM -- NIGHT
         DYLE is watching her.

                         REGGIE (on the phone)
                 Can you give me one good reason why I should?

250.   INT. TEX'S ROOM -- NIGHT

                         TEX (on the phone)
                 Yes, m'am. A little one -- 'bout seven or eight
                 years old. Th' little tyke keeps callin' you
                 his Aunt Reggie -- ain't that cute?

250A.   INT. REGGIE'S ROOM -- NIGHT
         She covers the phone and turns to DYLE in alarm.

                         REGGIE
                 They've got Jean-Louis!

                         DYLE
                 That sounds like their problem.

                         REGGIE (into the phone)
                 I'll be right there.

250B.   INT. TEX'S ROOM -- NIGHT

                         TEX (on the phone)
                 We'll be waiting' in room forty-seven,
                 Miz Lampert -- so you just wiggle on over.

251.   INT. REGGIE'S ROOM -- NIGHT
         As REGGIE hangs up.

                         REGGIE
                 What day is it?

                         DYLE
                 Tuesday.

                         REGGIE
                 Lord, I forgot all about it -- Sylvie works
                 late Tuesday nights -- she always leaves
                 him with me. They wouldn't do anything to
                 a little boy, would they?

                         DYLE
                 I don't know -- it depends on whether or
                 not they've already eaten.

252.   INT. TEX'S ROOM -- NIGHT
        CLOSE SHOT -- JEAN-LOUIS. He looks around, uncertainly, first
        one way, then the other. CAMERA PULLS BACK to show him sitting
        on SCOBIE's knee, the large man holding him with his good
        hand, the metal one in his pocket. TEX sits next to them while
        GIDEON nervously paces the floor. When GIDEON begins
        sneezing he takes the small bottle of pills from his pocket
        and downs one or two, swallowing some water.

                            SCOBIE
                Hey, Tex -- move the kid to the other knee or
                something, will you? My leg's going to sleep.

        TEX lifts JEAN-LOUIS and puts him down on SCOBIE's other knee.

                            TEX
                Upsy-daisy.

                            JEAN-LOUIS
                Are you a real cowboy?

                            TEX
                Sure am.

                            JEAN-LOUIS
                Then where is your gun?

                            TEX (taking out his gun)
                Right here -- see?

                            GIDEON
                Will you put that thing away!

        A KNOCK at the door. GIDEON goes to open it. REGGIE and
        DYLE enter. She sees JEAN-LOUIS and TEX's gun.

                            REGGIE
                Jean-Louis!

        She snatches him off SCOBIE's lap.

                            TEX
                Howdy, Miz Lampert.

                            SCOBIE (glaring at DYLE)
                Who invited you?

                            DYLE
                Hello, Herman -- it was a happy landing, I see.

                    REGGIE
          I'd better call Sylvie -- she must be frantic.

She starts for the door with JEAN-LOUIS. GIDEON blocks
her way.

                    GIDEON
          I'm afraid that will have to wait, Mrs. Lampert.

                    REGGIE
          But his mother --

                    GIDEON
          She isn't going to be anyone's mother unless
          you answer some questions.

          TEX   SCOBIE
This ain't no game,   We want that money -- now!
Miz Lampert!

                    DYLE (forcefully)
          Be quiet, all of you!

The THREE MEN look at him, surprised by his tone.

                    DYLE
          And stop threatening that boy. * * * He doesn't have
          the money. Mrs. Lampert doesn't * * * either.

                    SCOBIE
          Then who does?

                    DYLE
          I don't know, Herman -- maybe you do.

                    SCOBIE
          Me?

                    DYLE (to TEX)
          Or you -- (to GIDEON) -- or you --

                    GIDEON, TEX & SCOBIE (together)
          That's the most ridiculous -- !
          You gone loco?
          Listen to the man!

---

252.   [Harming him won't get you] [have it.]

                    DYLE
Slowly. Suppose one of you found Charles
here in Paris, followed him, cornered him
on the train, threw him out of the window
and took the money.

                    SCOBIE (after a pause)
That's a crock! If one of us did that he
wouldn't hang around here waiting for the
other two to wise up.

                    DYLE
But he'd have to. If he left he'd be
admitting his guilt -- and the others would
know what happened. Whoever it is has to
wait here, pretending to look for the
money, waiting for the rest of us to give
up and go home. That's when he'll be safe
and not a minute before.

A pause as the THREE MEN look at one another.

                    GIDEON
Up till now we always figured she had the
money -- but you know so much about it,
maybe you've got it.

                    DYLE
Then what am I doing here? You didn't
know anything about me -- I'm the only one
who could have taken it and kept right on
going.

                    SCOBIE
He's just trying to throw us off! They've
got it, I tell you! Why don't we search
their rooms?

                    DYLE (exchanging looks with REGGIE)
It's all right with us --

                    TEX (rising)
What're we wastin' time for? Let's go.

                    DYLE
-- and while we're waiting, we might as well
go through yours.

                    SCOBIE (stopping)
          Not my room!

                    DYLE
          What's wrong, Herman -- have you got something
          to hide? (a pause, then smiling) Then I take
          it there are no objections.

The THREE MEN look at one another unhappily.

                    DYLE
          * * * We'd better exchange keys. Here's mine.

                    SCOBIE
          I'll take that.

He takes DYLE's key and gives DYLE his. GIDEON goes to
REGGIE, takes her key and gives her his own.

                    TEX
          Mine's in the door. Ariva durchy, y'all.

The THREE MEN file out. DYLE and REGGIE exchange looks.

                    DYLE
          Come on -- let's get busy. Who gets your vote?

                    REGGIE
          Scobie -- he's the one who objected.

                    DYLE (handing her the boy)
          He's all yours. I'll do Tex and Gideon.
          Take Jean-Louis with you -- and make sure
          you bolt the door from the inside.

                    REGGIE
          Viens, Jean-Louis -- we're going to have a
          treasure hunt.

                    JEAN-LOUIS (joining them)
          Oh, la! If I find the treasure, will I
          win a prize?

                    REGGIE (to DYLE)
          What should we give him?

---

252.   [You're the ones who brought it up.]

                              DYLE
                    How about $25,000? Or do you think it
                    would spoil him?

          She smiles, takes JEAN-LOUIS' hand and leaves. DYLE turns
          to survey TEX's room.

253.   He goes first to the drawer in the night table -- empty;
          and the bed, looking in it and under it. Then he goes to
          the desk and opens the drawers -- also empty. The bureau
          is next -- he opens all three double drawers and they, too,
          are completely empty. Frowning, he goes to the armoire
          and opens it -- shelves and hanging bar are likewise bare.
          Then, CAMERA PANNING DOWN, he sees the only thing he's
          found so far in the room -- a pair of fine cowboy boots.

254.   INT. REGGIE'S ROOM -- NIGHT
          CLOSE SHOT -- AIRLINES BAG. CAMERA PULLS BACK to include
          GIDEON, staring down at it as it lies on the table in the
          center of the room.

                              GIDEON (eyes on the bag)
                    Tex --

255.   ANOTHER ANGLE
          Including TEX, busy going through the bureau. He looks up,
          then joins GIDEON.

                              TEX
                    What's that?

          GIDEON empties the contents of the bag on the table, then
          starts examining the various items. He opens the wallet.

256.   INSERT - WALLET
          Inside, the initials "C. L." are printed in gold.

                              TEX'S VOICE (o.s.)
                    Charlie's stuff?

                              GIDEON'S VOICE (o.s.)
                    Looks like it.

257.   MED. SHOT -- TEX & GIDEON

                              TEX
                    Mebbe we'd better call Herman.

GIDEON has put the wallet aside and now picks up the letter, removing it from the envelope and reading it.

> GIDEON
> What for? If it's not here, why bother him?

> TEX
> And if it is?

> GIDEON (a pause)
> Why bother him?

A broad grin from TEX. They continue going through the items from the bag.

> TEX
> You sure nuthin's missin'?

> GIDEON
> No. The police have kindly provided us
> with a list.

TEX takes the list, examines it, then folds it and puts it in his pocket. They finish with the items from the bag.

> TEX
> There sure ain't nuthin' here worth no
> quarter of a million.

> GIDEON
> Not unless we're blind.

> TEX (staring at GIDEON)
> You think that mebbe we're fishin' the
> wrong stream?

> GIDEON
> Meaning what?

> TEX
> You don't s'pose one o' us has it, like
> the man said -- I mean, that'd be pretty
> distasteful -- us bein' vet'rens o' the
> same war 'n' all.

> GIDEON (very sincerely)
> You know I'd tell you if I had it.

                         TEX
           Nachurly. Jus' like I'd tell you.

                         GIDEON (imitating)
           Nachurly. And that goes for Herman, too.

                         * * *
                         TEX & GIDEON (together)
           Nachurly!

The two men look at one another, then smile -- then laugh.

258.)
259.)
260.)   DELETED
261.)

262.   INT. SCOBIE'S ROOM -- NIGHT
        REGGIE on the phone, JEAN-LOUIS standing by.

                         REGGIE
           -- He's all right, Sylvie, honestly.
           Just hurry up and get here.

She hangs up and turns to JEAN-LOUIS.

                         REGGIE
           Come on, now -- if you wanted to hide
           something, where would you put it?

                         JEAN-LOUIS (thinking)
           I know. I would bury it in the garden.

                         REGGIE
           Swell -- only this man doesn't have a
           garden.

                         JEAN-LOUIS
           Oh. (afterthought) Neither do I. (Seeing
           something) Voilà!

                         REGGIE
           Voilà what?

---

257.   [GIDEON
           Nachurly!]

> JEAN-LOUIS (pointing)
> Up there! I would put it up there!

REGGIE looks where JEAN-LOUIS is pointing -- to the top
of the high armoire.

> REGGIE
> You know something, cookie? Why not?

Taking one of the straight chairs to the armoire, she
stands on it. Although she is still not high enough to see
anything, by standing on tip-toes she is able to reach with
her hand over the top and grope around blindly.

> REGGIE
> I hope I don't find any little hairy things
> living up there -- wait! There is something!
> If I can just -- yes, I'm getting it -- a case
> of some sort -- it's heavy.

> JEAN-LOUIS (jumping up and down)
> I found it! I found it!

> REGGIE
> If you think you're getting credit for this,
> you're crazy.

> JEAN-LOUIS (ecstatic)
> We won! We won!

REGGIE has finally managed to pull down the case -- a
rectangular black bag about the size and shape of a trombone
case. As she climbs off the chair, JEAN-LOUIS suddenly runs
to the door, unbolts it and runs into the hall, CAMERA
PANNING with him.

263.   INT. HOTEL CORRIDOR - THIRD LANDING - NIGHT
As JEAN-LOUIS runs out into the hall, shouting.

> JEAN-LOUIS
> We found it! We found it!

DYLE is the first one to appear, coming out of GIDEON's room.
TEX has also appeared from REGGIE's room, followed by GIDEON.

> JEAN-LOUIS
> We found it!

The THREE MEN rush by JEAN-LOUIS and squeeze simultaneously
into SCOBIE's room.

264.   INT. SCOBIE's ROOM -- NIGHT
As DYLE, TEX and GIDEON enter, REGGIE is placing the little
straight black chair to its original position. There is no
sign of the black case.

                         DYLE
Reggie -- ? Did you find it?

                         REGGIE
No.

                         GIDEON
What do you mean, no?

                         TEX
The kid said --

                         JEAN-LOUIS (pointing atop the armoire)
Up there! It is up there!

                         REGGIE
No, Jean-Louis.

TEX grabs the chair and moves it to the armoire, climbing
up on it and grabbing the bag.

                         REGGIE
It's nothing, I tell you!

He brings it to the table as DYLE and GIDEON crowd around
him, anxious to see.

265.   CLOSE SHOTS (PANNING)
The ring of faces, one at a time. TEX, his jaw muscles
working feverishly; DYLE, his eyes unblinking, a slight
smile on his lips; GIDEON, his mouth open greedily.

266.   GROUP SHOT
As TEX finally springs the latches and opens the lid.

267.   CLOSE SHOT -- CASE
Inside, neatly packed in velvet fittings, like the parts of
a musical instrument, are various portions of and attachments
for a metal artificial hand.

                          TEX'S VOICE (o.s.)
                Jumpin' frejoles -- it's Herman's spare.

268.   GROUP SHOT -- THE THREE MEN
        As they stare at the case, surprised and just a little
        embarrassed. Slowly TEX lowers the lid. The MEN avoid
        looking at one another.

269.   WIDER ANGLE
        Including REGGIE and JEAN-LOUIS by the door.

                          REGGIE
                Where is he?

        The MEN look at one another.

                          TEX
                Hey, that's right!

                          DYLE (already running)
                He's in my room.

        The THREE MEN hurry past REGGIE and JEAN-LOUIS and out
        of the door.

                          JEAN-LOUIS
                What is the matter?

        But REGGIE doesn't answer. She turns and follows the MEN.

270.   INT. HOTEL CORRIDOR -- THIRD LANDING -- NIGHT
        As DYLE, TEX and GIDEON, followed by REGGIE and JEAN-LOUIS
        cross the hall to DYLE's room. DYLE turns the key which
        is still in the door. He enters, followed by the others.

271.   INT. DYLE's ROOM -- NIGHT
        DYLE, TEX and GIDEON stand in the center of the room,
        looking around. REGGIE and JEAN-LOUIS wait in the open
        doorway. The room looks like a cyclone hit the place,
        but there is no sign of SCOBIE. The sound of running
        water can be heard coming from behind the closed door to
        the bathroom and DYLE is first to notice the water beginning
        to leak out from under the door.

                          DYLE
                Reggie -- you and the boy better wait here.

272.   INT. BATH -- NIGHT
         SCOBIE, still dressed in his raincoat, lies face up, his
         head submerged in the filled tub, the water now pouring
         over the edge. His face is distorted. DYLE's hand appears
         and turns off the water.

273.   DELETED

274.   REVERSE SHOT
         DYLE, TEX and GIDEON staring at CAMERA.

                         TEX
               Now, who'da done a mean thing like that?

                         DYLE (looking carefully at both)
               I'm not quite sure.

                         TEX
               This ain't my room.

                         GIDEON
               Mine, either.

                         DYLE (considering the situation)
               The police aren't going to like this one
               bit.

                         GIDEON (helpful)
               We could dry him off and take him down the
               hall to his own room. (looking at the body)
               He really doesn't look so bad.

                         TEX
               We could put him to bed 'n let one o' them
               fem-de-chambers find him in the mornin'.

         DYLE and GIDEON look at one another.

                         TEX
               Poor ol' Herman -- him 'n good luck always
               was strangers. Maybe now he'll meet up with
               his other hand someplace -- but I sure hope
               it ain't waitin' for him in Heaven.

275.   INT. SCOBIE'S ROOM -- DAY
         CLOSE SHOT -- SCOBIE. The dead man's eyes are open,
         his jaw hanging, his head lying crazily on the pillow.
         CAMERA PULLS BACK to show him lying in bed, dressed in

his pajamas. CAMERA WHIRLS for a TIGHT CLOSE SHOT of a
MAID, her eyes widening as the realization that the man
is dead strikes her. Then she screams.

276.   INT. GRANDPIERRE'S OFFICE -- LATE AFTERNOON
277.   CLOSE SHOT -- GRANDPIERRE. The policeman is apoplectic.

                    GRANDPIERRE
          No! No! No! No!

CAMERA PULLS BACK to include REGGIE, DYLE, TEX and
GIDEON, all sitting silently in the INSPECTOR's office.

                    GRANDPIERRE
          A man drowned in his bed -- impossible! And
          in his pajamas -- the second one in his
          pajamas -- c'est trop bête! Stop lying to me
          -- (tapping the side of his nose) -- this
          nose tells me when you are lying -- it is
          never mistaken, not in twenty-three years
          -- this nose will make me commissaire of
          police. (Tapping his fingers on his desk).
          Mr. Dyle or Mr. Joshua -- which is it?

                    DYLE
          Dyle.

                    GRANDPIERRE
          And yet you registered in Megeve as Mr.
          Joshua. Do you know it is against the
          law to register under an assumed name?

                    DYLE
          No, I didn't.

                    REGGIE
          It's done in America all the time.

* * *

GRANDPIERRE * * * raps for silence on his desk. During the
pause, he looks into each face in turn.

                    GRANDPIERRE
          None of you will be permitted to leave Paris
          -- until this matter is cleared up. Only I
          warn you -- I will be watching. We use the
          guillotine in this country -- I have always
          suspected that the blade coming down causes
          no more than a slight tickling sensation on
          the back of the neck. It is only a guess,
          of course -- I hope none of you ever finds
          out for certain.

278.   DELETED

276./
7.
                    [GRANDPIERRE
          There is a popular misconception that
          Americans are not subject to the laws and
          regulations of other countries. But if any
          of you believe such a thing, let me now
          correct—

During the above speech, DYLE turns to REGGIE, surprised
over her last line. Their exchange goes on during
GRANDPIERRE's lecture.

                    DYLE
          Where is it done in America all the time?

                    REGGIE
          I don't know—you're always hearing stories.

                    DYLE
          Who's been telling you those kind of stories?

                    REGGIE
          Well, I wasn't exactly brought up in an
          isolation booth.

                    DYLE
          Sounds more to me like a poolroom.]

[realizing no one's listening to him,]

279.   EXT. QUAI MONTEBELLO -- LATE AFTERNOON (TRAVELLING) REGGIE
       and DYLE walking along the quai, next to the Seine, CAMERA
       LEADING.

                          REGGIE
               Who do you think did it -- Gideon?

                          DYLE
          Maybe.

                          REGGIE
          Or Tex?

                          DYLE
          Maybe.

                          REGGIE
               You're a big help. Can I have one of those?

       They have passed an ice-cream wagon on the corner of the
       Pont au Double. DYLE shrugs.

                          REGGIE (to the VENDOR)
               Vanille-chocolat.

       During the following, the VENDOR makes a double-decker cone
       and hands it to REGGIE. DYLE pays and they resume their
       walk -- all with no break in the dialogue.

                          REGGIE
               I think Tex did it.

                          DYLE
          Why?

                          REGGIE
               Because I really suspect Gideon -- and it is
               always the person you don't suspect.

                          DYLE (smiling)
               Do women think it's feminine to be so
               illogical -- or can't they help it?

                          REGGIE
               What's so illogical about that?

                          DYLE
               A) It's always the person you don't suspect;

DYLE (Cont.)
B) that means you think it's Tex because you
really suspect Gideon; therefore C) if you
think it's Tex, it has to be someone else --
Gideon.

REGGIE
Oh. I guess they just can't help it.

DYLE
Who?

REGGIE
Women. You know, I can't help feeling rather
sorry for Scobie. (A pause) Wouldn't it be
nice if we were like that?

DYLE (surprised)
What -- like Scobie?

REGGIE
No -- Gene Kelly. Remember the way he danced
down there next to the river in 'American in
Paris' -- without a care in the world? * * *
This is good, want some?

She offers him her cone, thrusting it forward with enough
force to dislodge the ice-cream. It lands right next to
his lapel, over his outside breast pocket.

DYLE (frowning)
I'd love some, thanks.

REGGIE
I'm sorry.

He pulls open the pocket with two sticky fingers and looks
inside, then shakes his head sadly over what he sees. REGGIE
still holds the empty cone, not knowing what to do with it.
Seeing this, he takes it and sticks it into the pocket.

---

279.   [Where did all those violins come from?'

DYLE
From the same place the camera did, I suppose.

REGGIE
I suppose.]

                    DYLE
        No sense messing up the streets.

                         REGGIE
        Alex --

                         DYLE
        Hm?

                         REGGIE
        I'm scared.

                         DYLE
        Don't worry, I'm not going to hit you.

                         REGGIE
        No, about Scobie, I mean. I can't think of
        any reason why he was killed.

They resume walking.

                         DYLE
        Maybe somebody felt that four shares were
        too many --

                         REGGIE
        What makes you think that this somebody
        will be satisfied with three? He wants it
        all, Alex -- that means we're in his way, too.

                         DYLE
        Yes. I know.

                         REGGIE
        First your brother, then Charles, now
        Scobie -- we've got to do something! Any
        minute now we could be assassinated!
        Would you do anything like that?

                         DYLE (surprised)
        What? Assassinate somebody?

                         REGGIE
        No. --

280.   ANOTHER ANGLE
        Including the Cathedral of NOTRE DAME in the background.

                          REGGIE
                -- swing down from there on a rope to save
                the woman you love -- like Charles Laughton * * *
                in 'The Hunchback of Notre Dame'?

281.   INT. HOTEL CORRIDOR -- THIRD LANDING -- LATE AFTERNOON
        As REGGIE and DYLE step from the elevator.

                          REGGIE
                Hurry up and change -- I'm starved.

                          DYLE
                Let me know what you want -- I'll * * *
                pick a suit that matches.

        He goes into his room and she goes into hers.

282.)
283.)
284.)   DELETED
285.)
286.)

287.   INT. REGGIE'S ROOM -- LATE AFTERNOON

        She enters, fixes her hair in the mirror, then goes to the
        door connecting her room with DYLE's. She unlocks it, tries
        to open it, but finds it locked. Disappointed, she knocks.

                          DYLE'S VOICE (o.s.)
                What do you want?

                          REGGIE
                It's the house detective -- why haven't
                you got a girl in there?

288.   INT. DYLE'S ROOM -- LATE AFTERNOON
        He calls to her through the closed door as he empties his
        pockets.

                          DYLE
                Lord, you're a pest.

----

280.   [did]

281.   [try and]

> REGGIE'S VOICE (o.s.)
> Can I come in?

> DYLE
> I'd like to take a bath.

289.   INT. REGGIE'S ROOM -- LATE AFTERNOON

> REGGIE
> Oh, wouldn't it be better ir you did it
> in my room?

> DYLE'S VOICE (o.s.)
> What for?

> REGGIE
> I wouldn't want to use that tub.
> Besides, I don't want to be alone.
> I'm afraid.

290.   INT. DYLE'S ROOM -- LATE AFTERNOON

> DYLE
> I'm only next door -- if anything
> happens, holler.

He sits down to take off his shoes, but is interrupted by
the sound of REGGIE screaming. He races for the connecting
door, pulls back the bolt and rushes in.

291.   DELETED

292.   INT. REGGIE'S ROOM -- LATE AFTERNOON
       As DYLE enters.

> DYLE
> Reggie!

He wheels as the door is slammed and REGGIE, who had been
standing behind it, locks it and pockets the key.

> REGGIE
> Got you.

> DYLE
> Did you ever hear the story of the
> boy who cried wolf?

> REGGIE
> The shower's in there.

He goes to the door leading to the hall and finds that locked as well. She smiles at him.

> DYLE (warning)
> Reggie -- open the door.

> REGGIE
> This is a ludicrous situation. There must be dozens of men dying to use my shower.

> DYLE
> Then I suggest you call one of them.

> REGGIE
> I dare you.

DYLE looks at her, then sits down and starts to remove his shoes.

> REGGIE (has she gone too far?)
> What are you doing?

> DYLE
> Have you ever heard of anyone taking a shower with his shoes on? (to himself)
> What a * * * nut.

Shoes off, DYLE starts for the bathroom, humming.

> DYLE
> I usually sing a medley of old favorites when I bathe -- any requests?

> REGGIE
> Shut the door!

> DYLE
> I don't think I know that one.

Testing the water with his hand, he now steps in fully dressed. REGGIE can't believe her eyes. She goes to the open door for a closer look.

---

292.   [character.]

                    REGGIE
            What on earth are you doing?

293.   INT. BATHROOM -- LATE AFTERNOON
        MED. SHOT -- DYLE. In the shower, making sure his suit gets
        uniformly soaked.

                    DYLE (explaining pleasantly)
                Drip-dry.

He takes the soap and begins washing as if he were washing
himself without the suit.

                    DYLE
                The suit needs it more than I do,
                anyway.

                    REGGIE (fascinated)
                How often do you go through this
                little ritual?

As he takes out his handkerchief and rinses it.

                    DYLE
                Every day. The manufacturer recommends
                it.

                    REGGIE
                I don't believe it.

He opens his coat and reads a label inside.

                    DYLE
                "Wearing this suit during washing will
                help protect its shape."

He flicks a little water in her face, then takes the
nail-brush and scrubs his watch and watch-band. He holds
up his wrist so she can see the watch.

                    DYLE
                Waterproof.

He begins unbuttoning his suit. She turns and leaves,
slamming the door after her.

294./
295.   DELETED

296.   INT. REGGIE'S ROOM -- LATE AFTERNOON
         As REGGIE goes to the armoire to select a dress. The PHONE
         rings and she answers it.

                         REGGIE (into phone)
                  Yes -- ?

297.   INT. BARTHOLOMEW'S APARTMENT -- LATE AFTERNOON
         CLOSE SHOT -- BARTHOLOMEW

                         BARTHOLOMEW (on the phone)
                  Mrs. Lampert? -- Bartholomew. I've spoken
                  to Washington, Mrs. Lampert --

298.   INT. REGGIE'S ROOM -- LATE AFTERNOON

                         REGGIE (on the phone)
                  Go on, Mr. Bartholomew - I'm listening.

299.   INT. BARTHOLOMEW'S APARTMENT -- LATE AFTERNOON

                         BARTHOLOMEW (on the phone)
                  I told them what you said -- about this man
                  being Carson Dyle's brother. I asked them
                  what they knew about him and they told me --
                  you're not going to like this, Mrs. Lampert
                  -- they told me Carson Dyle has no brother.

300.   INT. REGGIE'S ROOM -- LATE AFTERNOON
         CLOSE SHOT -- REGGIE on the phone, looking like the rug
         has been pulled out from under her.

                         REGGIE (pause, quietly)
                  Are you sure there's no mistake?

301.   INT. BARTHOLOMEW'S APARTMENT -- LATE AFTERNOON

                         BARTHOLOMEW (on the phone)
                  None whatsoever. Please, Mrs. Lampert --
                  Be careful.

302.   INT. REGGIE'S ROOM -- LATE AFTERNOON
         REGGIE slowly lowers the phone to its cradle, a worried
         expression on her face. Then the bathroom door opens and
         DYLE appears dressed in a large bath towel. Her back is
         to him.

                    DYLE
         I left * * * my drip-dry dripping --
         is it all right?

She doesn't answer.

         Reggie -- is something wrong?

She shakes her head.

                    DYLE
         You're probably weak from hunger. You've only
         had five meals today. Hurry up and we'll go
         out.

She turns and looks at him.

                    REGGIE
         Do you mind if we go someplace crowded? I --
         I feel like lots of people tonight.

303.   EXT. SEINE - BATEAU MOUCHE -- DUSK
         The large motor launch, moving along the river, gaily
         ablaze with lights.

304.   MED. SHOT -- REGGIE AND DYLE (PROCESS)
         At a table for two by the rail, the city slowly passing in
         the b.g.

                    DYLE
         Reggie -- you haven't spoken a word in
         twenty minutes.

                    REGGIE
         I keep thinking about Charles and Scobie --
         and the one who's going to be next -- me?

                    DYLE
         Nothing's going to happen to you while
         I'm around -- I want you to believe that.

                    REGGIE
         How can I believe it when you don't even know
         who the killer is? I've got that right,
         haven't I? You don't know who did it.

302.   [all of]

                    DYLE
          No -- not yet.

                    REGGIE
          But then if we sit back and wait, the field
          should start narrowing down, shouldn't it?
          Whoever's left alive at the end will pretty
          well have sewn up the nomination, wouldn't
          you say so?

                    DYLE
          Are you trying to say that I might have
          killed Charles and Scobie?

She doesn't answer.

          What do I have to do to satisfy you -- become
          the next victim?

                    REGGIE
          It's a start, anyway.

                    DYLE
          I don't understand you at all -- one minute
          you're chasing me around the shower room and
          the next you're accusing me of murder.

                    REGGIE
          Carson Dyle didn't have a brother.

304A.   WIDER ANGLE

She rises from the table and walks away. DYLE hesitates a
moment, then follows.

                    DYLE
          I can explain if you'll just listen.
          Will you listen?

                    REGGIE (looking at the river)
          I can't very well leave without a pair of
          water wings.

                    DYLE
          Okay. Then get set for the story of my life
          -- not that it would ever make the best-seller
          list.

                    REGGIE
Fiction or non-fiction.

                    DYLE
Why don't you shut up!

                    REGGIE
Well!

                    DYLE
Are you going to listen?

                    REGGIE
Go on.

                    DYLE
After I graduated college I was all set to go
into my father's business. Umbrella frames --
that's what he made. It was a sensible
business, I suppose, but I didn't have the
sense to be interested in anything sensible.

                    REGGIE
I suppose all this is leading somewhere?

                    DYLE
It led me away from umbrella frames, for one
thing. But that left me without any honest
means of support.

                    REGGIE
What do you mean?

                    DYLE
When a man has no profession except the one
he loathes, what's left? I began looking for
people with more money than they'd ever need
-- including some they'd barely miss.

                    REGGIE (astonished)
You mean you're a thief?

                    DYLE
Well, it isn't exactly the term I'd have
chosen, but I suppose it captures the spirit
of the thing.

                    REGGIE (a pause)
I don't believe it.

                    DYLE
Well, I can't really blame you -- not now.

                    REGGIE
But I <u>do</u> believe it - that's what I don't
believe. So it's goodbye Alexander Dyle --
Welcome home Peter Joshua.

                    DYLE
Sorry, the name's Adam Canfield.

                    REGGIE
Adam Canfield. Wonderful. Do you realize
you've had three names in the past two days?
I don't even know who I'm talking to any more.

                    DYLE (now called ADAM)
The man's the same, even if the name isn't.

                    REGGIE
No -- he's not the same. Alexander Dyle was
interested in clearing up his brother's
death. Adam Canfield is a crook. And with
all the advantages you've got -- brains,
charm, education, a handsome face --

                    ADAM
Oh, come on!

                    REGGIE
-- there has to be a darn good reason for
living the way you do. I want to know what
it is.

                    ADAM
It's simple. I like what I do -- I enjoy
doing it. There aren't many men who love
their work as much as I do. Look around
some time.

                    REGGIE
Is there a Mrs. Canfield?

                    ADAM
Yes, but --

                    REGGIE AND ADAM (together)
-- we're divorced.

                        ADAM
             Right. Now go eat your dinner.

304B.   ANOTHER ANGLE

         They walk back to the table, where a WAITER is busy putting
         food on it, mostly on REGGIE's side.

                        REGGIE (miserably)
             I could eat a horse.

                        ADAM (looking at all the food)
             I think that's what you ordered.

                        REGGIE
             Don't you dare to be civil with me! All this
             time you were leading me on --

                        ADAM
             How was I leading you on?

                        REGGIE
             All that marvellous rejection -- you knew I
             couldn't resist it. Now it turns out you
             were only interested in the money.

                        ADAM
             That's right.

                        REGGIE * * * (hur̲t̲)
             Oh!

                        ADAM
             What would you like me to say -- that a
             pretty girl with an outrageous manner means
             more to an old pro like me than a quarter of
             a million dollars?

                        REGGIE
             No -- I guess not.

                        ADAM
             It's a toss-up, I can tell you that.

                        REGGIE
             What?

                         ADAM
              * * * Don't you know I'm having a tough
              time keeping my eyes off you?

REGGIE reacts in surprise.

                         ADAM
              Oh, you should see your face.

                         REGGIE
              What about it?

                         ADAM (taking her hand, nicely)
              * * * It's lovely.
                      - - -

She looks at him with happy amazement, then pushes her plate
away.

                         ADAM
              What's the matter?

                         REGGIE
              I'm not hungry -- isn't it glorious?

The lights go out.

                         REGGIE (alarmed)
              Adam!

                         ADAM
              It's all right - look.

304C.   EXT. SEINE BÂTEAU MOUCHE -- NIGHT
        A searchlight near the boat's bridge has gone on and now
        begins sweeping the river banks. On benches by the water's
        edge, lovers are surprised by the bright light which suddenly
        and without warning discovers them in various attitudes of
        mutual affection. Some are embarrassed, some amused and
        some (the most intimate) damn annoyed. One even shakes his
        fist at the light.

304D.   MED. SHOT -- REGGIE AND ADAM
        Who, like everyone else, leave the table and stand together at
        the rail, watching.

_____

304B.   [I admit that money isn't much in the way of
               company, but it doesn't remind me of my age,
               either. And you do.]

                    REGGIE
You don't look so bad in this light.

                    ADAM
Why do you think I brought you here?

                    REGGIE (indicating the lovers)
I thought maybe you wanted me to see the kind
of work the competition was turning out.

                    ADAM
Pretty good, huh?   I taught them everything
they do.

                    REGGIE
Oh? Did they do that sort of thing way back
in your day?

                    ADAM
How do you think I got here?

She rises on tip-toes and kisses him gently; his only
reaction is to look at her.

                    REGGIE
Aren't you allowed to kiss back?

                    ADAM
No. The doctor said it would be bad for my --
thermostat.

She kisses him again. He responds a little better.

                    ADAM
When you come on, you really come on.

                    REGGIE
Well -- come on.

She starts to kiss him again, but he stops her.

                    REGGIE
I know why you're not taken -- no one can
catch up with you.

                    ADAM
Relax -- you're gaining.

305.)
306.)
307.)   DELETED
308.)

309.   INT. GIDEON'S ROOM -- NIGHT
         MED. SHOT - GIDEON. As he sits bolt upright in bed, startled.
         The room is dark and the phone is ringing. He switches on
         the lamp, looks at the clock (it reads 3:30) and shakes his
         head before picking up the receiver.

                              GIDEON
                   Huh? -- You must be crazy -- it's three-thirty * * *
                   in the morning -- you mean now? -- all right
                   -- I'll be down in a minute.

         He hangs up, swings his feet out of bed and spears his
         slippers, reaching for his robe at the same time. Then he
         shuffles sleepily to the door.

310.   INT. HOTEL CORRIDOR -- THIRD FLOOR LANDING -- NIGHT
         As GIDEON comes out of his room and goes to the elevator.
         The cage is there. He opens the door and enters.

311.   INT. ELEVATOR -- NIGHT
         GIDEON closes the sliding grill and presses a button. The
         cage starts down. GIDEON begins sneezing. Suddenly the
         elevator stops between floors and the lights go out.

                              GIDEON
                   Hey! Turn on the lights!

         Just as suddenly the lights go back on and the elevator
         starts moving down again. Gideon shakes his head and leans
         back, whistling again. The cage comes to his floor and
         starts past it. Seeing this, GIDEON looks confused.

312.   INT. HOTEL LOBBY -- NIGHT
         The NIGHT PORTER is asleep behind the desk. The elevator,
         GIDEON inside, keeps coming down. It passes the lobby level
         and keeps right on going, toward the basement.

                              GIDEON
                   Hey! How do you stop this thing?

         The elevator passes out of sight, still going down. There
         is a silence as the motor stops, and then a series of
         sneezes that ends with a terrifying shriek. The NIGHT PORTER,

rudely awakened, runs to the elevator shaft, his shoes
squeaking horribly. He looks up, sees nothing, then looks
down. He presses the call button and the motor starts.
An instant later the cage appears and stops. The NIGHT
PORTER opens the gate, pulls back the grill and the CAMERA
RUSHES PAST him to pick up GIDEON. His body is sitting on
the floor of the cage, its grotesque sprawling attitude
resembling a puppet's with its strings cut. Except that
GIDEON had no strings to cut -- only a throat. From ear to
ear.

313. INT. HOTEL LOBBY -- NIGHT
      CLOSE SHOT -- GRANDPIERRE. He is now doubly apoplectic.

                    GRANDPIERRE
          Three of them -- all in their pajamas!
          C'est ridicule! What is it, some new
          American fad?

CAMERA PULLS BACK to include REGGIE and ADAM, in their
bathrobes.

                    GRANDPIERRE
          And now your friend -- the one from Texas --
          he has disappeared -- checked out -- pouf!
          into thin air! Where is he?

                    ADAM
          I don't know.

                    GRANDPIERRE
          Madame?

REGGIE shrugs.

                    GRANDPIERRE
          Tell me, Mr. Dyle -- where were you at
          three-thirty?

                    ADAM
          In my room, asleep.

                    GRANDPIERRE
          And you, Mrs. Lampert?

                    REGGIE
          I was, too.

                    GRANDPIERRE
          In Mr. Dyle's room?

                    REGGIE (bitterly)
          No -- * * * in my own room.

                    GRANDPIERRE (pause, lighting cigar)
          It stands to reason you are telling the
          truth -- for why would you invent such a
          ridiculous story?

REGGIE and ADAM exchange looks.

                    GRANDPIERRE
          And if I were you, I would not stay in my
          pajamas. Good night.

GRANDPIERRE turns and leaves. REGGIE and ADAM start down
the hall toward their own rooms.

                    ADAM
          That wraps it up -- Tex has the money.
          Go back to bed -- I'll let you know
          when I've found him.

                    REGGIE
          You're going to look for him -- now?

                    ADAM
          If the police find him first they're
          not very likely to turn over a quarter
          of a million to us, are they?

                    REGGIE
          Adam --

                    ADAM
          There's no time -- I'll call you in the
          morning.

ADAM disappears into his own room.

313A.   INT. ADAM'S (PETER'S) ROOM -- NIGHT
        As ADAM enters, going to the closet to remove his suit.
        The phone rings. He answers it.

---

313.   [here]

<pre>
                         ADAM
                  Yes?

313B.   INT. PHONE BOOTH -- NIGHT
        CLOSE SHOT -- TEX. As he speaks on the phone.
                         TEX
                  Now Dyle, you just listen to me -- my mama
                  didn't raise no stupid children. I know
                  who's got the money 'n I ain't disappearing
                  till I got my share -- 'n' my share's
                  growin' a whole lot bigger ev'ry day.

313BB. INT. ADAM'S (PETER'S) ROOM -- NIGHT
                         ADAM (on the phone)
                  Where are you, ol' buddy?

313C.   INT. PHONE BOOTH -- NIGHT

                         TEX (on the phone)
                  (laughs) I tell you what, fella -- you want
                  t' find me, you jus' turn 'round -- from
                  now on I'll be right behind you. (hangs up)

313CC. INT. ADAM'S ROOM -- NIGHT
        ADAM, before hanging up, reflects on TEX's words, then
        looks behind him. Smiling softly, he hangs up the phone
        and starts for REGGIE's door.

313D.   INT. REGGIE'S ROOM -- NIGHT
        REGGIE slips back into her robe and goes to the connecting
        door.
                         REGGIE
                  What is it?
                         ADAM
                  Open up.

        She undoes the bolt and opens the door. ADAM enters.

                         ADAM
                  I think we were wrong about Tex having the
                  money.
                         REGGIE
                  Why?
                         ADAM
                  I just heard from him -- he's still hungry.
                  That means killing Gideon didn't get it
                  for him -- so he's narrowed it down to us.
                  You've got it.
</pre>

> REGGIE
> I've looked, Adam -- you know I * * * have --

> ADAM
> Where's that airlines bag?

> REGGIE
> Lord, you're stubborn.

> ADAM
> I sure am. Get it.

She goes to the closet and gets the bag.

> ADAM
> Charles must have had the money with him
> on the train, and Tex missed it.

He takes the bag to the bed where he dumps out the contents.

> REGGIE
> But everyone and his Aunt Lillian's been
> through that bag * * * . Somebody would
> have seen it.

> ADAM
> Let's look anyway.

> REGGIE
> Lord, you're stubborn.

> ADAM
> I mean, it's there, Reggie -- if only we could
> see it. We're looking at it right now.

313E.   CLOSE SHOT -- BED WITH CHARLES' BELONGINGS

> ADAM'S VOICE (o.s.)
> Something on that bed is worth a quarter of
> a million dollars.

> REGGIE'S VOICE (o.s.)
> Yes, but what?

313D.   ['ve]

[including me, and I'm in there at least
once a day.]

                        ADAM'S VOICE (o.s.)
          I don't know -- I just don't know.

313F. MED. SHOT -- REGGIE AND ADAM
       As ADAM begins to examine the items one by one.

                        ADAM
          Electric razor -- comb -- steamship ticket --
          fountain pen -- four passports -- toothbrush
          -- wallet -- (he goes through the wallet,
          finds nothing) -- key -- what about that?

                        REGGIE
          To the apartment -- it matches mine
          perfectly.

                        ADAM
          The letter --

He takes it out of the envelope and takes out his glasses
before reading it.

                        REGGIE
          I'll bet you really don't need those.

He hands her the glasses and she looks through them.

                        REGGIE
          You need them. (She hands them back.)

                        ADAM (reading the letter)
          It still doesn't make sense, but it isn't
          worth any quarter of a million, either.
          Have we forgotten anything?

                        REGGIE
          The tooth powder. Wait a minute -- could
          you recognize heroin just by tasting it?

He shakes some powder into his hand and tastes it. REGGIE
watches expectantly.

                        ADAM
          Heroin -- peppermint-flavored heroin.

                        REGGIE
          Well, that's it, I guess -- dead end.

                        ADAM
          Go to bed. You've got to be at work in the
          morning. There's nothing more we can do
          tonight.

                        * * *

                        REGGIE (pause)
          I love you, Adam.

                        ADAM
          Yes, you told me.

                        REGGIE
          No -- last time I said "I love you, <u>Alex</u>."

314.   EXT. UNESCO BUILDING -- ESTABLISHING -- DAY
       The ultra-modern glass and concrete structure behind the
       Ecole Militaire.

315.   INT. UNESCO CONFERENCE ROOM -- DAY
       SEVERAL DELEGATES identified by little plaques in front of
       them listing their respective nations, and their AIDES, sit
       around the large table. They are all wearing earphones.
       The ITALIAN DELEGATE is speaking.

                        [REGGIE
313F.   Oh, really? Can't you think of anything?
                        ADAM
          Hm? What?]
                        [REGGIE
          I could think of something—without even
          thinking.
                        ADAM
          Well, I'm sure you could. Good night,
          Reggie.
                        REGGIE
          Would you mind leaving the door open?
                        ADAM
          If you promise you won't cry wolf.
                        REGGIE
          How can I? No wolves.]

ITALIAN DELEGATE
-- di conseguenza, il Governo Italiano è
decisamente a favore per l'incoraggiamento,
in accordo con le tradizioni etniche rispettive
delle culture basilari dei passi in via di
sviluppo. Per esempio, pregare i Vietnamiti
di aggiungere alle loro risaie ed ai loro campi
di soja tradizionali una raccolta di semola,
non solo sconvolgerebbe le loro secolari
tradizioni ma, oltre tutto, e questo è molto
importante per il Governo che io ho l'onore di
rappresentare disturberebbe l'esportazione
delle derrate farinose italiane in questa parte
del mondo. Signori Delegati vi ringrazio della
vostra attenzione.

316.   INT. REGGIE'S BOOTH -- DAY
REGGIE, wearing her headset, is talking with SYLVIE.

REGGIE
I hope Jean-Louis understands about last
night -- it's just not safe for him to be
around me right now.

SYLVIE
Don't be silly -- he would not do anything.
He is not yet old enough to be interested
in girls. He says collecting stamps is much
more satisfying to a man of his age.

REGGIE (listening to the headset)
Hold it -- Italy just finished. They're
recognizing Great Britain.

SYLVIE
Oh la vache!

SYLVIE jumps up and rushes next door into her booth, shutting
the door after her.

316A.   INT. CONFERENCE ROOM -- DAY
The BRITISH DELEGATE rises to speak, continuing through the
next scene.

BRITISH DELEGATE
Mr. Chairman, fellow delegates -- my distinguished
colleague from Italy. Her Majesty's delegation
has listened with great patience to the Southern
European position on this problem, and while we

find it charmingly stated, we cannot possibly
agree with its content. In 1937, in the British
colonies of Kenya, Uganda and Tanganyika -- and,
if I'm not mistaken, more or less in Somaliland --
a programme of crop rotation was instituted vis-
à-vis arable land which had never before known
the plough, beginning before the soil was able
to know the sort of fatigue now plaguing most
of Western Europe. In 1937, therefore, Her
Majesty's Government -- at that time <u>His</u> Majesty's
Government -- was able properly to assay the
situation. We therefore oppose the resolution.

316B.   INT. REGGIE'S BOOTH -- DAY
The door from the hall opens and ADAM enters.

                    ADAM
Reggie -- I think I've found -- (stopping)
-- are you on?

                    REGGIE
No, it's all right. What's wrong, Adam?

                    ADAM
Nothing's wrong. I think I've found something.
I was snooping around Tex's room and I found
this in the waste basket. I've stuck it back
together.

He hands her a paper.

317.   INSERT -- POLICE RECEIPT
The one GRANDPIERRE gave REGGIE. It has been torn in half
and scotch-taped back together.

                REGGIE'S VOICE (o.s.)
It's the receipt Inspector Grandpierre gave
me -- for Charles' things. I don't see how
that's going to --

318.   MED. SHOT -- REGGIE AND ADAM

                    ADAM
You didn't look. Last night, when we went
through the airlines bag, something was
missing. See -- ? (showing her the list)
"One agenda." It wasn't there.

           REGGIE
You're right. I remember Grandpierre looking
through it. But there was nothing in it -- at
least, nothing the police thought was very
important.

           ADAM
Can you remember anything at all?

           REGGIE
Grandpierre asked me about an appointment
Charles had -- on the day he was killed.

           ADAM
With whom? Where?

           REGGIE
I think it only said where -- but I can't --

           ADAM
Think, Reggie -- you've got to think. It
may be what we're looking for.

           REGGIE
That money's not ours, Adam -- if we keep it,
we'll be breaking the law.

           ADAM
Nonsense. We didn't steal it. There's
no law against stealing stolen money.

           REGGIE
Of course there is!

           ADAM
There is? Well, I can't say I think very
much of a silly law like that. Think, Reggie
-- please think -- what was written in Charles'
notebook?

           REGGIE
Well -- it was a place -- a street corner, I
think. But I don't -- (hearing something
through her earpiece) Hold it. I'm on.

She turns back to the conference, flips a switch and starts
speaking into her headset.

                          REGGIE (translating)
             Mr. Chairman, fellow delegates -- my distinguished
             colleague from Great Britain --

319.   INT. CONFERENCE ROOM -- DAY
        The FRENCH DELEGATE is speaking.

                          FRENCH DELEGATE
             Monsieur le Président, Messieurs les délégués
             -- mon distingué collègue de la Grande
             Bretagne -- le problème vu par mon Gouvernement
             n'est pas aussi simple que nos amis les
             Anglais voudraient nous le faire croire. Mais
             leur pays n'est pas, après tout, un pays
             agricole, n'est-ce-pas? La position française,
             ainsi que nous l'avons soulignée dans
             le rapport numéro trente-neuf bar oblique
             cinquante-deux de la Conférence de l'hémisphère
             occidental qui a eu lieu le 22 mars --

320.   INT. REGGIE'S BOOTH -- DAY
        REGGIE is busy translating.

                          REGGIE
             -- as outlined in report number three-nine-
             stroke-five-two of the Western Hemisphere
             Conference held on March 22 -- (She stops)
             -- no, wait! It was last Thursday, five
             o'clock at the Jardin des Champs-Elysées!
             Adam -- that was it! The garden!

                          ADAM
             It's Thursday today -- and it's almost five --
             come on!

321.   MED. SHOT -- CONFERENCE TABLE
        From REGGIE'S and ADAM'S angle. All the delegates and
        their AIDES suddenly turn, surprised, and look at CAMERA.

322.   REVERSE SHOT -- WINDOW
        From the DELEGATE'S ANGLE. Inside the booth, REGGIE and
        ADAM can be seen heading for the door in a hurry.

323.   MED. SHOT -- CONFERENCE TABLE
        As the DELEGATES look at one another, confused.

324.   EXT. GUIGNOL -- LATE AFTERNOON

325.   TWO SHOT -- REGGIE AND ADAM
        By the locked gate.

                         REGGIE
                Now what?

                         ADAM
                Five o'clock -- Thursday -- the Garden -- it's
                got to be something around here.

                         REGGIE
                But Charles' appointment was last week, not --

                         ADAM
                I know, but it's all we've got left.

                         REGGIE
                Well, you're right there. Ten minutes ago I
                had a job.

                         ADAM
                Stop grousing. If we find that money I'll buy
                you an international conference all your own.
                Now start looking. You take this side and
                I'll poke around over there.

326.   VARIOUS SHOTS -- WHAT THEY SEE
        A quick succession of shots showing:
        1. Children's Merry-go-round
        2. Rond Point des Champs-Elysées with fountains playing
        3. Children's swings
        4. Restaurant Laurent
        5. Balloon salesman

327.   EXT. FOUNTAIN -- LATE AFTERNOON
        ADAM stands by the large fountain, staring off at something
        as REGGIE joins him.

                         REGGIE
                It's hopeless -- I don't even know what we're
                looking for.

                         ADAM
                It's all right -- I don't think Tex does,
                either.

                         REGGIE
                Tex -- you mean he's here, too?

                              ADAM
                  Look.

328.   MED. SHOT -- TEX
        He stands near the merry-go-round, looking at something in
        his hand: Charles' agenda. Now he closes it and moves off,
        disappearing behind a hedge.

329.   TWO SHOT -- REGGIE AND ADAM

                              ADAM
                  I'd better see what he's up to. Stay here --
                  I won't be long.

        ADAM starts off.

                              REGGIE (concerned)
                  Be careful, Adam -- please. He's already
                  killed three men.

330.   DELETED

331.   EXT. RUE GABRIEL -- LATE AFTERNOON
        Between the curb and the Jardin, several temporary wooden
        booths have been set up. They have collected quite a
        CROWD. Into this area comes TEX, followed at a safe
        distance by ADAM. Suddenly TEX stops.

332.)
333.)   DELETED

334.   CLOSE SHOT -- TEX
        As he stares wide-eyed at something.

335.   CLOSE SHOT -- STAMPS
        Neatly displayed on a counter of one of the booths.

336.   CLOSE SHOT -- TEX
        As he wheels to look at another booth.

337.   CLOSE SHOT -- MORE STAMPS
        In another arrangement.

338.   CLOSE SHOT -- TEX
        He turns crazily to look at another booth, then another.

339.   CLOSE SHOT -- EVEN MORE STAMPS
        Various FLASH SHOTS of stamps of all sizes, shapes and colors.

340.   MED. SHOT -- TEX
        As he understands. He turns to rush off and bumps smack
        into ADAM. TEX is startled.

                              TEX
                        Sorry, fella --

        He rushes off past ADAM, who watches him for a moment,
        confused, then turns toward the booth, not yet having seen
        the stamps.

341.   MED. SHOT -- BOOTH
        From ADAM'S angle. There are one or two persons standing
        at the booth. CAMERA ZOOMS in on the display of stamps.

342.   CLOSE SHOT -- ADAM

                              ADAM (amazed)
                        The letter.

        He turns quickly to find TEX.

343.   MED. SHOT -- TEX
        As he hops into the back of a TAXI and it pulls away from
        the curb. ADAM runs toward another TAXI.

                              ADAM
                        Taxi! -- Taxi!

344.   DELETED

345.   INT. HOTEL CORRIDOR -- THIRD LANDING -- LATE AFTERNOON
        As ADAM comes up the stairs and goes to REGGIE'S door.
        Whipping out his gun, he flings open the door.

346.   INT. REGGIE'S ROOM -- LATE AFTERNOON
        From ADAM'S angle. TEX sits in the armchair, staring at
        CAMERA. Next to him is the airlines bag, its contents
        dumped on the floor.

347.   ANOTHER ANGLE
        Including ADAM as he enters, his gun trained on TEX. Without
        speaking he goes to the airlines bag, then stoops down to go
        through the spilled contents, keeping one eye all the time on
        TEX. But he can't find what he's looking for.

                              ADAM (quietly)
                        All right -- where's the letter?

                    TEX (dully)
     The letter? The letter ain't worth nuthin'.

                    ADAM
     You know what I mean -- the envelope with
     the stamps. I want it.

                    TEX (a pause, then beginning to laugh)
     You greenhorn -- you half-witted, thick-skulled,
     hare-brained greenhorn! They wuz both too smart
     for us!

                    ADAM
     What are you talking about?

                    TEX (screaming)
     First her husband, now her -- she hoodwinked
     you! She batted all them big eyes and you
     went 'n fell for it - like a egg from a tall
     chicken! Here! (holding out the envelope)
     You want? Here -- it's yours!

ADAM takes it and looks at it.

348. INSERT ENVELOPE
      The corner containing the stamps is missing, torn off.

349. MED. SHOT -- ADAM AND TEX
      TEX sees the expression on ADAM's face and begins laughing,
      hysterically.

                    TEX
          Look at you! Horn-swoggled by a purty face
          'n all them sweet words! You killed all
          three of 'em for nothin'! You greenhorn!
          You block-headed jackass! You clod -- you
          booby -- you nincompoop -- !

350. EXT. ROND POINT -- LATE AFTERNOON
      REGGIE is looking around for ADAM. She sees something
      across the street. CAMERA SPINS AROUND to discover
      SYLVIE, sitting alone on a bench near the stamp market,
      reading a newspaper.

351. MED. SHOT -- SYLVIE
      As REGGIE approaches her.

                    REGGIE
          Sylvie -- ? What are you doing here?

> SYLVIE (looking up)
> Hello, Reggie -- I am waiting for Jean-Louis.

> REGGIE (looking around)
> What's he up to?

> SYLVIE
> He was so excited -- when he got the stamps
> you gave me this morning. He said he had
> never seen any like them.

> REGGIE
> I'm glad. But what is all this?

> SYLVIE
> The stamp market, of course -- it is here
> every Thursday afternoon. This is where
> Jean-Louis trades his --

> REGGIE (as it dawns)
> Good Lord! The stamps! Where is he?
> Sylvie -- we've got to find him!

> SYLVIE
> What is the matter, chérie?

> REGGIE
> Those stamps -- they're worth a fortune!

> SYLVIE (jumping up)
> What?

> REGGIE
> A fortune! Hurry -- we've got to find him!

They rush off into the market.

352.   TWO SHOT -- REGGIE AND SYLVIE
As they stop among the booths, looking around.

> REGGIE
> I don't see him.

> SYLVIE
> We will separate -- you look over there.

They go off in opposite directions.

353.   MED. SHOT -- REGGIE

As she hurries along a row of stalls, weaving around small
groups of MEN standing together, showing each other stamps.

354.   MED. SHOT -- SYLVIE
Searching in another section of the market.

                    SYLVIE (calling)
      Jean-Louis -- ?

355.   MED. SHOT -- REGGIE
Spotting a BOY, she runs to him and spins him around.

                    REGGIE
      Jean-Louis!

But it isn't.

356.   MED. SHOT -- SYLVIE
Looking everywhere. Suddenly she sees something.

357.   CLOSE SHOT -- GROUP OF MEN -- THEIR LEGS
Only a small boy's elbow and part of his arm show, the
rest hidden by all the legs.

358.   MED. SHOT -- SYLVIE
She recognizes him from these fragments.

                    SYLVIE
      Jean-Louis -- !

She rushes to him, CAMERA PANNING WITH HER. JEAN-LOUIS
stands looking at some stamps. SYLVIE grabs him.

                    SYLVIE
      Jean-Louis -- les timbrés -- où sont-ils?

Smiling, JEAN-LOUIS holds up an enormous sack of assorted
stamps -- hundreds of them.

                    SYLVIE
      Oh, zut! (calling) Reggie -- Reggie -- !

REGGIE runs up and joins them.

                    REGGIE
      Jean-Louis -- thank heavens! Do you
      have -- ! (spotting the sack of stamps)
      What's that?

                    JEAN-LOUIS
          A man traded with me -- all those for only
          four.

                    REGGIE
          Oh, no! What man, Jean-Louis -- where?

JEAN-LOUIS looks in one direction, then in the other,
trying to remember.

                    SYLVIE
          Vite, mon ange -- vite!

                    JEAN-LOUIS (pointing)
          Là bas -- Monsieur Félix.

They all run off down the line of booths. JEAN-LOUIS
stops and points off.

                    JEAN-LOUIS
          Il est là!

359.   MED. SHOT -- STAMP BOOTH
       Closed, deserted, empty.

360.   MED. SHOT -- REGGIE, SYLVIE AND JEAN-LOUIS

                    JEAN-LOUIS
          But he is gone.

                    REGGIE
          I don't blame him. Jean-Louis -- do you
          know where this Monsieur Félix lives?

                    JEAN-LOUIS
          No -- but I will ask.

He goes to the closest booth and shakes the coat sleeve
of the proprietor.

                    JEAN-LOUIS
          Monsieur Théophile -

                    THÉOPHILE
          Oui, jeune homme?

                    JEAN-LOUIS
          Monsieur Félix -- où habite-il?

                    THÉOPHILE
          A Montmartre -- demande à Monsieur August
          au Bar des Artistes -- Place Blanche.

                    JEAN-LOUIS
          Merci, Monsieur Théophile. (returning
          to REGGIE and SYLVIE) He says to ask
          Monsieur Auguste at the --

Before he can finish, SYLVIE, who has heard THÉOPHILE,
has JEAN-LOUIS by the hand, dragging him off at full
speed, REGGIE right alongside.

361.-   DELETED
363.

364.   INT. FÉLIX'S ROOM -- DUSK
        A bare, unkempt little room. FÉLIX, a man in his sixties,
        sits at a table, smoking a pipe. There are stamps and
        albums everywhere. He holds a magnifying glass in his
        hand, busy studying something on the table. There is a
        KNOCK. He looks up. Another KNOCK.

                    FÉLIX
          Entrez.

The door opens and REGGIE, followed by SYLVIE and JEAN-LOUIS,
enters.

                    REGGIE
          Monsieur Félix -- ?

                    FÉLIX (without looking up)
          I was expecting you. You are American too,
          of course.

                    REGGIE (looking at SYLVIE)
          Yes.

                    FÉLIX
          The man who bought them last week was
          American. I did not see him but I heard.
          I knew you would come.

He gestures for REGGIE to come closer. Together with
SYLVIE and JEAN-LOUIS, she goes to the table and looks at
the stamps.

FÉLIX
Look at them, Madame.

365.   INSERT -- STAMPS
Four of them -- a red, a yellow, a blue, and a green, still
attached to the portion of torn envelope.

FÉLIX (o.s.)
Have you ever, in your entire life, seen
anything so beautiful?

366.   MED. SHOT -- REGGIE, FÉLIX, SYLVIE AND JEAN-LOUIS

REGGIE
I'm -- I'm sorry -- I don't know anything
about stamps.

FÉLIX
I know them as one knows his own face, even
though I have never seen them. This yellow
one -- a Swedish four shilling -- called 'De
Gula Fyraskillingen' -- issued in 1854.

REGGIE
How much is it worth?

FÉLIX
The money is unimportant.

REGGIE
I'm afraid it is important.

FÉLIX (shrugging)
In your money, perhaps $65,000.

REGGIE (astonished)
Do you mind if I sit down? (she sits)
What about the blue one?

FÉLIX
It is called 'The Hawaiian Blue' and
there are only seven left. In 1894 the
owner of one was murdered by a rival
collector who was obsessed to own it.

REGGIE
What's its value today?

                    FÉLIX
In human life? In greed? In suffering?

                    REGGIE
In money.

                    FÉLIX
Forty-five thousand.

                    REGGIE (to SYLVIE)
Do you have anything to eat? (To FÉLIX)
And the orange one -- what about the orange
one?

                    FÉLIX
A two-penny Mauritius -- issued in 1856.
Not so rare as the others -- $30,000
perhaps.

                    REGGIE
And the last one?

                    FÉLIX
The best for the last -- le chef-d'oeuvre de
la collection. The masterpiece. It is
the most valuable stamp in the world.
It is called 'The Gazette Guyanne.'

It was printed by hand on colored paper
in 1852 and marked with the initials of
the printer. (looking at it through the
glass) Today it has a value of $100,000.
(a pause) Eh, bien -- I am not a thief.
I knew there was some mistake. Take them.

                    REGGIE (hesitating)
You gave the boy quite a lot of stamps
in return, Monsieur Félix -- are they for
sale now?

                    FÉLIX (looking at the large bag)
Let me see -- there are 350 European, 200
Asian, 175 American, 100 African and
twelve Princess Grace Commemorative -- which
comes to nine francs fifty.

                    REGGIE (fishing money from her purse)
Here's ten.

FÉLIX goes to his wallet for the change.

> REGGIE
> Please keep it.

> FÉLIX
> I am a tradesman, Madame, not a doorman.
> And don't forget these.

He hands her the four stamps and her change.

> REGGIE
> I'm -- I'm sorry.

367.   CLOSE SHOT -- FÉLIX

> FÉLIX (shrugging)
> No. For a few minutes they were mine --
> that is enough.

368.   INT. HOTEL CORRIDOR -- THIRD LANDING -- NIGHT
As REGGIE comes hurrying up the stairs. She goes first to
ADAM'S room and knocks.

> REGGIE
> Adam? Adam, it's me, Reggie -- !

There is no answer. She goes to her own door and, to her
surprise, finds it an inch or two ajar.

369.   INT. REGGIE'S ROOM -- NIGHT
As REGGIE enters. She freezes, having seen something on
the floor.

370.   MED. SHOT -- TEX
His dead body lies on the floor, the wrists of his extended
arms tied to the leg of the bed, his ankles to the steam
radiator. And tied around his head in a plastic, transparent
bag, inside of which the suffocated man's face, the eyes
bulging against the plastic clinging tight to his features,
can be seen all too clearly. REGGIE enters the shot, bending
down to see if he's alive. Then she sees something beside
his hands, near the leg of the bed.

371.   CLOSE SHOT -- CARPET
With his dying effort, TEX has traced a name against the
grain of the maroon carpet -- 'DYLE.'

372.   CLOSE SHOT -- REGGIE
        Astonished and horrified.

                    REGGIE (gasping)
            Dyle --

373.   WIDER ANGLE
        As she gets to her feet and hurries to the phone.

                    REGGIE (on the phone)
            Hello -- Balzac 30-04, s'il vous plait --
            (waiting) -- Mr. Bartholomew! Thank God
            you're there! Tex is dead, Mr. Bartholomew --
            smothered -- and Adam did it -- he killed them
            all!

374.   INT. BARTHOLOMEW'S APARTMENT -- NIGHT
        BARTHOLOMEW, his face lathered for shaving, is on the phone.

                    BARTHOLOMEW
            Just a minute, Mrs. Lampert -- you'd
            better give that to me slowly. Who's
            Adam?

375.   INT. REGGIE'S ROOM -- NIGHT

                    REGGIE (on the phone)
            The one who said he was Dyle's brother --
            of course I'm sure -- Tex wrote the word
            'Dyle' before he died. He's the murderer
            I tell you -- he's the only one left!
            You've got to do something!

376.   INT. BARTHOLOMEW'S APARTMENT -- NIGHT

                    BARTHOLOMEW (on the phone)
            Calm down, Mrs. Lampert -- please. Does
            he have the money?

377.   REGGIE (on the phone)
            No, I do -- it was the stamps on that letter
            Charles had with him on the train. They
            were in plain sight all the time, but no
            one ever bothered looking at the envelope.

378.   INT. BARTHOLOMEW'S APARTMENT -- NIGHT

> BARTHOLOMEW (on the phone)
> The envelope -- imagine that. Mrs. Lampert,
> listen to me -- you're not safe as long as
> you've got these stamps. Go to the Embassy
> right away -- wait, I'd better meet you halfway
> -- it's quicker. Now let's see -- do you
> know the center garden at the Palais Royal?
> -- yes, by the colonnade -- as soon as you can
> get there. Hurry, Mrs. Lampert.

379.   INT. REGGIE'S ROOM -- NIGHT

> REGGIE (on the phone)
> Yes, I'm leaving now -- goodbye.

She hangs up, looks briefly at TEX'S body, shudders, then
hurries to the door.

380.   INT. HOTEL CORRIDOR -- THIRD LANDING -- NIGHT
As REGGIE leaves her room and goes to the elevator. She
presses the button, then notices it is in use. She goes
to the stairs and starts down.

381.   INT. HOTEL STAIRCASE -- NIGHT
Between the landings. The stairs curve around the open
elevator shaft. As REGGIE comes down the stairs, the
cage rises into view. Inside is ADAM. For a moment, she
stops and their eyes meet.

> ADAM
> Reggie -- the stamps -- what've you
> done with -- ?

REGGIE starts running downstairs.

> ADAM
> Where are you going? Wait!

ADAM pushes the emergency stop button and then starts the
cage down.

> ADAM
> Reggie!

382.   INT. HOTEL CORRIDOR -- SECOND LANDING -- NIGHT
As REGGIE comes off the stairs, passes the elevator gate
and starts down toward the lobby, the cage a few feet
behind her.

                         ADAM
                  Reggie -- !

382A.   INT. HOTEL CORRIDOR -- FIRST LANDING -- NIGHT
        As REGGIE continues to run.

383.   INT. HOTEL STAIRWAY -- NIGHT
        Between the first landing and the lobby. REGGIE running,
        the elevator following.

                         ADAM
                  Reggie -- stop!

                            REGGIE
                  Why? So you can kill me too? Tex is
                  dead, I've seen him! He said Dyle did
                  it!

                            ADAM
                  I'm not Dyle -- you know that!

                            REGGIE
                  But Tex didn't -- he still thought -- !

                            ADAM
                  Don't be an idiot!

384.   INT. HOTEL LOBBY -- NIGHT
        REGGIE reaches the lobby first and, without hesitation,
        races toward the front door and out. The confused hotel
        MANAGER behind the desk can only stare in surprise. The
        elevator, ADAM inside, has not yet reached the bottom.

                         ADAM (roaring)
                  Reggie -- ! I want those stamps!

385.   EXT. HOTEL -- NIGHT
        A taxi stands by the curb. REGGIE leaves the hotel and
        runs to it.

                            REGGIE (indicating the direction)
                  Palais Royale -- vite!

        Calmly, the DRIVER points to the little printed sign on
        his windshield reading "ITALIE."

                            DRIVER (pointing the other way)
                  Porte d'Italie, moi.

>   REGGIE
> Mais c'est très vite!   On veut me tuer!
>
>   DRIVER (shaking his head)
>   Italie.

She looks around and sees ADAM come out of the hotel and
straight toward her. She turns and runs off toward the
Place St. Michel.

386.   EXT. PLACE ST. MICHEL -- NIGHT
        As REGGIE comes to the corner. She stops, sees the Métro
        station ("St. Michel") and rushes to it, scampering down
        the stairs. ADAM is behind her.

387.   INT. ST. MICHEL MÉTRO STATION -- NIGHT
        REGGIE comes flying down the stairs and runs past the
        ticket booth, fishing in her bag for her carnet (booklet
        of tickets), casting a quick look behind her. CAMERA PANS
        QUICKLY TO ADAM just coming off the stairs, who runs after
        her.

388.-   DELETED
389.

390.   INT. MÉTRO TICKET GATE -- NIGHT
        REGGIE gets to the gate ahead of ADAM and manages to crowd
        in front of some OTHERS about to pass through. Barely
        stopping, she holds out her ticket to the GUARD to be punched,
        then heads down the platform, still running. ADAM gets to
        the gate but the GUARD stops him as he tries to pass through.

>   GUARD
>   Billet, Monsieur.
>
>   ADAM (breathless)
>   I don't want to go anywhere -- I'm only
>   trying --
>
>   GUARD (pointing off)
>   Billet, Monsieur.

ADAM tries to look past him, to see REGGIE, but gives it up
and goes back toward the ticket booth, on the run.

391.   INT. MÉTRO PASSAGEWAY -- NIGHT (TRAVELLING)
        CAMERA LEADING REGGIE as she runs -- the passageway is
        nearly empty. Her footsteps echo against the tile and
        concrete walls.

392. CLOSE SHOT -- PASSAGEWAY WALL (TRAVELLING)
The jumble of advertising posters as it passes rapidly,
forming a moving band of letters, women, cartoons and
colors.

393. INT. MÉTRO PASSAGEWAY -- NIGHT
REGGIE stops and pauses for a moment at a sign indicating
two different directions, an arrow for each.
                    "DIRECTION:
                    -------Pte D'ORLÉANS
                    Pte DE CLIGNANCOURT-------"

Choosing "Clignancourt," she runs off. CAMERA PANS SHARPLY,
180 degrees, to pick up ADAM rounding the corner in hot
pursuit.

394. INT. MÉTRO PLATFORM -- DAY
REGGIE starts down the platform, looking behind her every
few steps. Suddenly she looks up in surprise -- there,
across the tracks on the opposite platform is ADAM. He
has evidently made the wrong turning back in the passageway.
They stare at each other for a moment. Then the bell rings,
announcing the arrival of a train. ADAM turns, running
back through the exit behind him. Not knowing what to do,
REGGIE looks into the darkness of the tunnel. The approaching
train can be heard.

                    REGGIE (to herself)
          Come on -- <u>please</u> --

She turns to look at the gate -- slowly, the pneumatic door
starts to close. As it does, the train roars into the
station.

394A. INT. MÉTRO PASSAGEWAY -- NIGHT
The gate can be seen slowly closing. ADAM runs to it, tries
to force it back, but cannot. Finally, he jumps up and,
commando style, vaults over it.

395. INT. MÉTRO PLATFORM -- NIGHT
REGGIE is just entering the red center car (the two on either
side are dark green). ADAM runs for the red car and just
manages to make it as the doors slam shut in unison, the
latches falling with a concerted click and the little whistle
blowing to inform the motor-man to depart. The train starts
to move.

396. INT. MÉTRO CAR -- NIGHT
The entire length of the car separates ADAM and REGGIE.

For a moment, their eyes meet, then ADAM starts to weave
his way past the other PASSENGERS, on his way to her.
Suddenly, he is stopped. ADAM turns to see a TRAIN GUARD.

> TRAIN GUARD
> Billet, Monsieur.

ADAM shows him his yellow ticket and starts past him, but
again the TRAIN GUARD stops him.

> TRAIN GUARD
> Vous êtes dans le premier classe, Monsieur.

> ADAM
> What?

> TRAIN GUARD (heavy accent)
> This car is for first class only -- you
> have a second-class ticket.

> ADAM
> But that's what they gave me.

He tries to pull away from the TRAIN GUARD and finds himself
staring into the serious face of a GENDARME.

> GENDARME
> Monsieur -- ?

ADAM looks at the GENDARME, then at REGGIE.

397. INT. "PALAIS-ROYAL" MÉTRO PLATFORM -- NIGHT
As the TRAIN pulls in and comes to a stop.

398. INT. MÉTRO CAR -- NIGHT
The GENDARME opens the door for ADAM and escorts him out.
ADAM turns once more to look at REGGIE as he goes. She
remains on the car.

399. INT. MÉTRO PLATFORM -- NIGHT
The GENDARME gestures for ADAM to enter the green, second-
class car behind the red, first-class one. Reluctantly,
ADAM does.

400. INT. SECOND-CLASS MÉTRO CAR -- NIGHT
As ADAM enters and goes to the door through which he can
see REGGIE in the car ahead. She is gone. Moving quickly,
he returns to the exit door and looks at the platform.

401.   INT. MÉTRO PLATFORM -- NIGHT
        From ADAM'S P.O.V. She is hurrying toward an exit marked
        "SORTIE."

402.   ANOTHER ANGLE
        Featuring ADAM as he hurries from the car. He finds his
        way blocked by FIVE NUNS in large, white butterfly hats.
        It takes him a few precious seconds to work his way around
        them.

403.-
414.   DELETED

415.   INT. MÉTRO SORTIE -- NIGHT
        REGGIE has entered an area leading to the exit. But as she
        reaches the stairway leading up toward the street level, she
        is confronted with an iron grill barring her way. She tries
        to open it, but it is firmly padlocked. A sign hung on it
        reads "FERMÉ LES WEEKENDS." She turns, desperately looking
        for some way out.

416.   INT. MÉTRO PLATFORM -- NIGHT
        ADAM is off the train. He stands on the platform as the
        train doors slam shut, the latches click, the whistle blows
        and the train pulls out. He looks around in all directions,
        looking for some sign of REGGIE. He spots the exit marked
        "SORTIE" (the same one used by REGGIE) and starts toward it.

417.   INT. MÉTRO SORTIE -- NIGHT
        As ADAM enters the deserted area. There is, miraculously, no
        sign of REGGIE. He goes to the locked grill and tries it,
        testing the padlock. CAMERA PANS to a phone booth (solid
        door with a window in the upper half) and we see REGGIE'S hand
        reaching up to dial a number.

418.   INT. PHONE BOOTH -- NIGHT
        REGGIE sits on the floor of the booth, dialing.

                        REGGIE (to herself as she dials)
                Balzac 3 - 0 - 0 - 4.

        She holds the receiver to her ear. The number can be heard
        ringing but no one answers. She hangs up and reaches for
        the phone book, leafing through its pages.

                        REGGIE (whispering)
                Embassies -- embassies --

419.   INT. MÉTRO SORTIE -- NIGHT
         ADAM stands for a minute, looking around, not knowing what
         to do.

420.   INT. PHONE BOOTH -- NIGHT
         REGGIE has finished dialing her number and now pushes the
         button. It clicks loudly.

                              REGGIE
                    Shh. (Into the phone, whispering) American
                    Embassy? Mr. Bartholomew's office, please --
                    Mr. Bartholomew's office --

420A.   INT. EMBASSY SWITCHBOARD -- NIGHT
         An OPERATOR speaking into a headset.

                              OPERATOR
                    Could you speak out, please? I can't quite
                    hear you.

420B.   INT. PHONE BOOTH -- NIGHT

                              REGGIE (on the phone)
                    No, I can't speak any louder -- Hamilton
                    Bartholomew -- B as in -- uh -- Bartholomew --
                    that's right, and the rest as in Bartholomew!

421.   INT. EMBASSY SWITCHBOARD -- NIGHT

                              OPERATOR (On the phone)
                    I'm sorry, but Mr. Bartholomew has left for
                    the day.

422.   INT. PHONE BOOTH -- NIGHT

                              REGGIE (on the phone)
                    But someone's trying to kill me -- you've
                    got to send word to him -- in the center
                    garden of the Palais Royal, by the colonnade
                    -- tell him I'm trapped in a phone
                    booth below him in the Métro station. And
                    my name's Lampert.

423.   INT. EMBASSY SWITCHBOARD -- NIGHT

                              OPERATOR (on the phone)
                    All right, Mrs. Lampert -- I'll see what
                    I can do. Goodbye.

She unplugs the call, plugs in another one and dials
quickly.

> OPERATOR
> Hello, Mr. Bartholomew? -- there was a
> call for you just now, Mr. Bartholomew --
> it sounded quite urgent -- a Mrs. Lampert.

424. INT. BARTHOLOMEW'S STUDY -- NIGHT
It is a man we have never seen before, the physical opposite
of the old BARTHOLOMEW.

> REAL BARTHOLOMEW
> Lampert? I don't know any Mrs. Lampert --
> trapped in a Métro station? Who does she
> think I am, the C.I.A.? All right, you'd
> better call the French police.

425. INT. MÉTRO SORTIE -- NIGHT
MED. SHOT -- PHONE BOOTH. As REGGIE'S head appears, peeking
cautiously over the bottom of the window.

426. REVERSE SHOT
From inside the phone booth. Through the glass ADAM can
be seen, leaving the Sortie area.

427. MED. SHOT -- PHONE BOOTH
Carefully, REGGIE opens the door and comes out. She goes
to the corner and looks around it.

428. INT. MÉTRO PLATFORM -- NIGHT
From REGGIE'S P.O.V. as ADAM walks away from CAMERA, down
the platform. CAMERA PANS TO REGGIE, peeking around the
corner. She looks the opposite way, sees another exit at
the other end of the platform (also marked "SORTIE"). She
looks back once more at ADAM, then makes up her mind and
starts running towards the exit.

429. MED. SHOT -- ADAM
As the bell rings announcing the next train. He turns to
look and sees REGGIE.

> ADAM (calling)
> Reggie -- !

He takes off, running after her.

430. MED. SHOT -- REGGIE
As she runs, ADAM several yards behind her.

ADAM (in b.g. calling)
> Reggie -- wait!

She turns into the exit.

431.   INT. MÉTRO STAIRWAY -- NIGHT
As REGGIE starts up the long, steep flight of stone steps
leading * * * to the street level. ADAM appears behind
her, climbing two at a time and gaining.

ADAM (calling)
> Reggie -- why won't you listen?

REGGIE
> I'm through listening to you!

He is rapidly closing the gap between them. It is clear
that REGGIE is tiring.

ADAM
> But I didn't kill anybody.

REGGIE
> Then who did? You're the only one
> left.

PASSERSBY, descending the stairs, stand aside to let the
two strange Americans pass, watching in wonderment. ADAM
is only a few steps behind now.

ADAM
> Reggie -- please believe me!

REGGIE
No!

As REGGIE wearily gains the top, ADAM lunges for her. He
manages to grab her foot as he falls forward, but all he
winds up with is a shoe which has come loose in his hand.
REGGIE shrieks, then regaining her balance, continues
running, limping in her one shoe. ADAM scrambles to his
feet and starts after her again.

432.   INT. MÉTRO TICKET BOOTH AREA -- NIGHT
As REGGIE, still hobbling, runs through and toward the

---

431.   [up]

stairs, leading to the street. CAMERA PANS TO ADAM, as
he, too, runs through. He is again several yards behind
her.

433. EXT. PLACE PALAIS ROYAL -- NIGHT
As REGGIE comes up the stairs from the Métro. She stops
long enough to kick off her other shoe, then runs across
the street, ignoring the traffic, toward the Rue de Valois
(which forms one side of the Palais Royal). ADAM is
gaining on her again.

434. EXT. PALAIS ROYAL COURTYARD -- COLONNADE -- NIGHT
The smaller court at the Comédie-Française end of the
Palais gardens, separated from the larger garden by a double
peristyle consisting of two twin rows (these separated from
each other by a small marble court) of twenty columns each --
in all, eighty columns. The only person in sight is the
man we have known as BARTHOLOMEW, waiting at the far end
of the columns, looking at his watch impatiently.

Then, from the Rue de Valois side of the Palais, REGGIE
runs into the court. She spots "BARTHOLOMEW" and fishes
in her bag for the stamps as she runs, taking them out and
waving them.

                    REGGIE
        Mr. Bartholomew -- he⁺s chasing me!

ADAM has run into the court and now skids to a stop at the
near end of the colonnade as he spots "BARTHOLOMEW." REGGIE,
still running, is halfway between the two men. "BARTHOLOMEW"
draws his gun but can't get a shot at ADAM, who has ducked in
among the columns.

                    ADAM
        Reggie -- stop! That's Carson Dyle!

This news hits REGGIE hard and she stops, in alarm.

                    REGGIE (breathless)
        Carson -- ?

She looks at "BARTHOLOMEW," then back at ADAM, who has drawn
his own gun.

(NOTE: Both "BARTHOLOMEW" and ADAM are in among the stone
columns at opposite ends of the colonnade, keeping out of
each other's sight. REGGIE stands out in the open, the
stamps in her hand, confused as to which man she should go to).

                    "BARTHOLOMEW" (calmly)
          We all know Carson Dyle is dead, Mrs.
          Lampert.

                    ADAM
          It's Carson Dyle, I tell you!

                    "BARTHOLOMEW"
          You're not going to believe him, Mrs.
          Lampert -- it's too fantastic. He's
          trying to trick you again.

REGGIE looks at one, then the other, not knowing what to
do.

                    ADAM
          Tex recognized him -- that's why he
          said Dyle. If you give him those
          stamps, he'll kill you, too!

REGGIE takes a step toward ADAM.

                    "BARTHOLOMEW"
          Mrs. Lampert -- if I'm who he said, what's
          preventing me from killing you right now?

REGGIE stops, turns back to "BARTHOLOMEW."

                    ADAM
          Because he'd have to come out to get the
          stamps -- he knows he'd never make it!

                    "BARTHOLOMEW"
          What's the matter with you, Mrs. Lampert?
          Are you going to believe every lie he tells
          you? He wants the money for himself --
          that's all he's ever wanted.

                    REGGIE (to ADAM, explaining)
          He's -- with the C.I.A. -- I've seen him at
          the Embassy.

                    ADAM
          Don't be a fool! He's Carson Dyle!

                    "BARTHOLOMEW"
          That's right, Mrs. Lampert -- I'm a dead
          man, look at me.

                        REGGIE
            I don't know who anybody is any more!

                        ADAM
            Reggie -- listen to me!

                        REGGIE
            You lied to me so many times --

                        ADAM (gently)
            Reggie -- trust me once more -- please.

                        REGGIE
            Can I really believe you this time, Adam?

                        ADAM (a pause)
            There's not a reason on earth why you should.

        She looks toward ADAM for a moment, then back to "BARTHOLOMEW",
        then slowly starts toward ADAM.

                        REGGIE
            All right, Adam.

                        "BARTHOLOMEW"
            Stop right now, Mrs. Lampert, or I'll kill
            you.

        REGGIE stops in alarm.

                        ADAM
            It won't get you the stamps, Dyle --
            You'll have to come out to get them,
            and I'm not likely to miss at this range.

                        "BARTHOLOMEW" (now called CARSON)
            Maybe not -- but it takes a lot of bullets to
            kill me. They left me there with five of them
            in my legs and stomach -- they knew I was still
            alive but they left me. I spent ten months
            in a German camp -- with nothing to stop the
            pain and no food -- they were willing to take
            all these chances for the money, but not for
            me. They deserved to die.

435.   MED. SHOT -- ADAM
        During the following, he looks around, looking for some
        way out.

                    REGGIE'S VOICE (o.s.)
            But I didn't have anything to do with --

                    CARSON'S VOICE (o.s.)
            You've got the money. It belongs to me
            now! Please believe me, Mrs. Lampert --
            I'll kill you -- a little more blood won't
            matter.

During this, ADAM has moved out from behind the columns,
creeping cautiously across the open space between the two
colonnades and finally, behind the second.

436.   MED. SHOT -- REGGIE AND CARSON

                    CARSON
            I'll give you five to make up your mind,
            Mrs. Lampert.

She has seen ADAM'S move from her angle, but doesn't know
quite what to do.

                    REGGIE
            Wait, please! I need some time to think!

                    CARSON
            One --

437.   MED. SHOT -- ADAM
As he slowly moves along behind the second colonnade, his
gun ready, trying to get an angle on CARSON.

                    CARSON'S VOICE (o.s.)
            -- two --

Suddenly ADAM stops -- he has caught sight of CARSON through
the columns. But he will have a difficult shot. * * *

                    CARSON'S VOICE (o.s.)
            -- three --

438.   CLOSE SHOT -- CARSON

                    CARSON
            -- four --

---

437.   [between one column of his colonnade and one of CARSON'S.]

CAMERA PANS DOWN to his gun. As his finger tightens on the
trigger and the hammer moves slowly back.

439.   CLOSE SHOT -- REGGIE

                        REGGIE (terrified)
                Adam -- <u>please</u>!

440.   MED. SHOT -- ADAM
        As he aims carefully and fires.

441.   CLOSE SHOT -- COLUMN
        As the bullet creases it.

442.   CLOSE SHOT -- CARSON
        As the deflected bullet rips the shoulder of his coat,
        leaving him unharmed. He wheels.

443.   MED. SHOT -- ADAM
        With CARSON in the b.g., who fires at him. ADAM ducks
        behind the column as the bullet hits it and screams off.
        Quickly, he peers back out and throws another shot.

444.   MED. SHOT -- REGGIE
        Seeing CARSON otherwise occupied, she turns and runs toward
        the open stage door of the Comédie Française behind her.
        (Beside the door is a poster announcing the forthcoming
        schedule of presentations.)

445.   ANOTHER ANGLE
        Including CARSON who, seeing REGGIE running to the door,
        turns and fires at her. But he is too late -- she is
        safely inside. CARSON looks quickly back toward ADAM, then
        takes off after REGGIE.

446.   MED. SHOT -- ADAM
        Over his shoulder we see a broken picture of CARSON running
        toward the theatre door, flashing by the near and far
        columns. ADAM tries to get a shot at him, but can't.
        Finally he runs after him.

447.   INT. COMÉDIE FRANÇAISE -- BACKSTAGE -- NIGHT
        As CARSON enters and slams the door behind him, locking it.

448.   EXT. COMÉDIE FRANÇAISE -- STAGE DOOR -- NIGHT
        ADAM arriving at the door, bangs on it, then looks around,
        frustrated. Several yards away he sees a short stairway
        leading down to a door below the street level. He runs to
        it, tries the door and enters.

449.   INT. COMÉDIE FRANÇAISE -- ORCHESTRA -- NIGHT
        As CARSON enters the auditorium and looks around.

450.   CARSON'S P.O.V.
        As the CAMERA SWEEPS the magnificent old theatre -- boxes,
        seats, stage, but there is no trace of REGGIE.

451.   ANOTHER ANGLE
        As CARSON walks up the aisle checking between the rows of
        seats.

452.   INT. COMÉDIE FRANÇAISE -- TRAPROOM -- NIGHT
        A large room, lit by a single bare bulb, under the stage.
        ADAM appears, moving cautiously, gun ready. He creeps
        along next to the wall, looking around at all the various
        scenic pieces which fill the room.

453.   INT. COMÉDIE FRANÇAISE -- STAGE -- NIGHT
        As CARSON moves carefully across the darkened stage near the
        footlights, looking for REGGIE. At mid-stage, CAMERA PANS
        DOWN to his feet, only a few inches from the prompter's
        box. Inside, huddling down, is a terrified REGGIE, holding
        her breath as she watches him.

454.   ANOTHER ANGLE
        As CARSON moves into the opposite wings, sees the light board
        and throws on all the switches. The stage is bathed in light.
        He returns to the stage.

455.   INT. TRAPROOM -- NIGHT
        ADAM is looking up, having heard the footsteps on the stage
        over his head -- and hearing them now. He looks around
        and sees a narrow, curving staircase leading up. He goes to
        it, and, starting up, finds a door. He tries the knob -- the
        door is locked.

456.   INT. PROMPTER'S BOX -- NIGHT
        REGGIE, cringing back from the bright light, notices the
        doorknob turning. It makes a slight clicking sound.

457.   INT. COMÉDIE FRANÇAISE -- STAGE -- NIGHT
        CARSON, upstage, looking behind a piece of classic scenery,
        hears the doorknob and turns suddenly.

458.   CARSON'S P.O.V.
        We catch a quick glimpse of REGGIE as she ducks down out of
        sight. Too late.

459.   CLOSE SHOT -- CARSON

                     CARSON
         All right, Mrs. Lampert. The game's
         over. Come out of there.

460.   WIDER ANGLE
       REGGIE does not appear.

                     CARSON
         I don't want to kill you, Mrs. Lampert --
         but I will --

461.   INT. TRAPROOM -- NIGHT
       ADAM comes down the stairs from the prompter's box and
       looks up at the ceiling.

462.   MED. SHOT -- CEILING
       It is divided into thirty-six square sections, each numbered
       and lettered -- from 1A to 6F. They are trapdoors.

463.   MED. SHOT -- ADAM
       He looks from the ceiling to a row of levers on one wall.

464.   CLOSE SHOT -- LEVERS
       Thirty-six of them, numbered and lettered to correspond to
       the traps.

465.   INT. COMÉDIE FRANÇAISE -- STAGE -- NIGHT
       As CARSON takes a few steps towards the prompter's box,
       his gun ready.

                     CARSON
         Did you hear me, Mrs. Lampert -- ?

466.   INT. PROMPTER'S BOX -- NIGHT
       REGGIE huddled inside.

467.   INT. TRAPROOM -- NIGHT
       ADAM is listening carefully, trying to figure out where
       CARSON is standing, watching the ceiling.

468.   CLOSE SHOT -- TRAP
       It is marked C-4.

               CARSON'S VOICE (o.s.)
        I won't wait much longer, Mrs. Lampert --

469.   MED. SHOT -- ADAM
       As he turns to the levers and reaches for the one marked
       C-4. He is about to pull it.

470.   INT. COMÉDIE FRANÇAISE -- STAGE -- NIGHT
        CARSON takes a few more steps forward.

471.   INT. TRAPROOM -- NIGHT
        ADAM stops himself from pulling the lever just in time. He
        lets his held breath escape. He looks back at the ceiling.

472.   CLOSE SHOT -- TRAP
        The one marked C-4. As CARSON'S voice is heard, CAMERA
        MOVES to the next trap, marked D-4.

                        CARSON'S VOICE (o.s.)
                I know you're in there, Mrs. Lampert --

473.   MED. SHOT -- ADAM
        He looks at the lever marked D-4. He is perspiring heavily.
        Now he slowly reaches for the lever.

474.   INT. COMÉDIE FRANÇAISE STAGE -- NIGHT
        CARSON is about to move closer to the prompter's box when
        suddenly the stage under him opens and he plummets through
        out of sight. At the same time we hear a SHOT.

475.   CLOSE SHOT -- PROMPTER'S BOX
        As REGGIE slowly peers out.

476.   REGGIE'S P.O.V.
        The empty stage, without being able to see the open trap from
        this low angle.

477.   MED. SHOT -- REGGIE
        As she climbs out of the booth and, seeing the open trap now,
        runs to it, looking down through it.

478.   MED. SHOT -- OPEN TRAP
        FROM ABOVE, over REGGIE'S head. She can see CARSON sprawled
        on the floor below, face down and dead. ADAM stands beside
        the body, looking up at REGGIE and smiling.

479.   ANOTHER ANGLE
        As GRANDPIERRE and his TWO ASSISTANTS, guns drawn, walk onto
        the stage from the wings. They go to the open trap and look
        down at ADAM.

                        GRANDPIERRE
                Mr. Dyle -- you are under arrest for
                the murders of Charles Lampert, Herman
                Scobie, Joseph Penthollow, Leopold Gideon,
                and whoever that is down there.

ADAM is surprised, then shakes his head.

>   ADAM
>   Reggie -- you'd better tell him. He
>   wouldn't dare hit a girl.

480.   EXT. RUE DE RIVOLI -- NIGHT
        As a TAXI rolls by the arcades, CAMERA PANNING with it.

481.   INT. TAXI -- NIGHT (PROCESS)
        REGGIE and ADAM in the rear of the cab. REGGIE has one
        of her feet in her hand, shoe off, rubbing it.

>   REGGIE
>   You didn't have to chase me so hard --

>   ADAM
>   Here, give it to me.

He starts to take the foot but she pulls it back and offers
him the other one.

>   REGGIE
>   That one's done -- start on this one.

He takes the foot and begins rubbing it.

>   REGGIE
>   I'm sorry I thought you were the murderer,
>   Adam -- how did I know that he was as big
>   a liar as you are?

>   ADAM
>   And that's all the gratitude I get for
>   saving your hide.

>   REGGIE
>   The truth, now -- was it my hide -- or the
>   stamps?

>   ADAM
>   What a terrible thing to say. How could
>   you even think that?

>   REGGIE
>   All right, prove it to me -- tell me to go
>   to the Embassy first thing in the morning
>   and turn in those stamps.

ADAM says nothing.

> REGGIE
> I said, tell me to go to the --

> ADAM
> I heard you, I heard you.

> REGGIE
> Then say it.

> ADAM
> Reggie -- listen to me --

> REGGIE
> Never mind -- I'll go by myself.

> ADAM
> What makes you think they're even
> interested? It's only a quarter of
> a million -- it'll cost more than that
> to fix up their bookkeeping. As a
> taxpayer --

482.   EXT. AMERICAN EMBASSY -- MAIN ENTRANCE -- DAY
As REGGIE and ADAM approach the MARINE in full-dress uniform
always on guard at the Embassy.

> REGGIE (to ADAM)
> Who's a taxpayer? Crooks don't pay
> taxes. Excuse me, soldier --

> MARINE
> Marine, m'am.

> REGGIE
> Forgive me. Whom would I see regarding
> the return of stolen Government money?

> MARINE
> You might try the Treasury Department,
> m'am -- Room 216, second floor, Mr.
> Cruikshank.

> REGGIE
> Cruikshank, 216. Thank you, marine.

483.   INT. EMBASSY CORRIDOR -- DAY
Featuring a door marked "216." REGGIE and ADAM appear.

                         ADAM
              Do you mind if I wait out here? The
              sight of all that money being given
              away might make me break out.

484.   INT. EMBASSY TREASURY OFFICE -- DAY
       A SECRETARY sits behind a desk. She looks up as REGGIE
       enters.

                        REGGIE
              Mr. Cruikshank, please -- my name is Lampert.

       The SECRETARY picks up her phone and presses a button.

                       SECRETARY
              Mr. Cruikshank, a Miss --

                        REGGIE
          Mrs.

                       SECRETARY
              -- a Mrs. Lampert to see you -- yes, sir.
              (to REGGIE) Go right in.

       REGGIE goes to the door leading to the private office.

485.   INT. CRUIKSHANK'S OFFICE -- DAY
       Featuring the door as REGGIE enters. She stops suddenly.

486.   ANOTHER ANGLE
       Featuring the desk. Behind it sits ADAM (now CRUIKSHANK).
       REGGIE stares at him, unbelievingly, then looks around,
       confused. By way of explanation he indicates the door to
       the hall.

                    REGGIE (blowing up)
              Well, of all the mean, rotten, contemptible,
              crooked --

                      CRUIKSHANK
              Crooked? I should think you'd be glad to
              find out I wasn't crooked.

                        REGGIE
              You couldn't even be honest about being
              dishonest. Why didn't you say something?

                    CRUIKSHANK
We're not allowed to tell. May I have
the stamps, please?

                    REGGIE (reaching into her bag)
Here -- (hesitating) -- Wait a minute -- how
did Carson Dyle get an office in here,
anyway?

                    CRUIKSHANK
When did you see him -- what time, I mean?

                    REGGIE
Around one.

                    CRUIKSHANK
The lunch hour. He probably worked it out
in advance. He found an office that was
usually left open and just moved in for the
time you were here.

                    REGGIE
Then how do I know this is <u>your</u> office?

                    CRUIKSHANK (picking up the phone)
Mrs. Foster -- send a memo to Bartholomew at
Security recommending that --

                    REGGIE
Bartholomew?

                    CRUIKSHANK (on the phone)
-- recommending that all Embassy offices be
locked during the lunch hour.

                    REGGIE
Starting with his own.

                    CRUIKSHANK (hanging up)
Okay, now -- hand over those stamps.

                    REGGIE
What's your first name today?

                    CRUIKSHANK
Brian.

                         REGGIE
          Brian Cruikshank -- it would serve me right
          if * * * I got stuck with * * * that one.

                         CRUIKSHANK
     Who asked you to get stuck with any of them?

                         REGGIE
          Is there a Mrs. Cruikshank?

                         CRUIKSHANK
          Yes.

                         REGGIE
          But you're -- divorced?

                         CRUIKSHANK
          No.

                         REGGIE (crestfallen)
          Oh.

                         CRUIKSHANK
          My mother -- she lives in Detroit. Come on
          now -- give me those stamps.

                         REGGIE
          Only if you can prove to me that you're
          really Brian Cruikshank.

                         CRUIKSHANK
          How about if next week some time I put it on
          a marriage licence -- that ought to --

                         REGGIE
          Quit stalling -- I want to see some
          identification -- now!

                         CRUIKSHANK
          I wouldn't lie on a thing like that -- I
          could go to jail.

                         REGGIE
          You'd lie about anything.

---

486.   [that's the one]

                    CRUIKSHANK
Well, maybe we'd better forget about it, then.

                    REGGIE
You can't prove it, can you? You're still
trying to -- (the coin drops into the slot) --
<u>marriage license</u>! Did you say -- ?

                    CRUIKSHANK
I didn't say anything. Will you give me
those stamps.

                    REGGIE
You did too say it -- I heard you. ***** * Oh, I
love you, Adam -- I mean Alex -- er, Peter, --
Brian. I hope we have lots of boys -- we can
name them all after you.

                    CRUIKSHANK
Before we start on that, do you mind handing
over the stamps?

                                        FADE OUT

                    <u>THE END</u>

---

486.   [CRUIKSHANK
           You'd better cut down on that eating, too—
           I can tell you that. This job doesn't pay
           very much—and if you don't give me those
           stamps, it won't pay anything at all.]

Appendix

Something of the complexity of modern filmmaking, of the hard and carefully coordinated labor that goes into any production, is suggested by the following two documents.

The first is the initial and closing pages of the final shooting schedule for *The Best Man* (1963). The usual shooting schedule, unless the production is very elaborate, is based on thirty working days. Note that the film is not shot in order of the sequence of scenes. The large number of extras and minor cast numbers needed and the specific days when a location is available and accessible to film equipment are a few factors that help to determine the production sequence as actually drawn up. The problem of the production manager is to arrange the shooting in such a way as to keep costs down efficiently, yet at the same time to permit the director, the principals, and the crew to create the best possible work.

The second item supplements the first. It is a sample from the daily call sheets for Samuel Goldwyn, Jr.'s production of *The Young Lovers* (1963), a low-budget picture with a small cast and limited crew. Note that for the ten numbered scenes only two actors, Peter Fonda and Sharon Hugueny, are involved and only two exterior settings, both on location at the U.C.L.A. campus, which is in Westwood, not far from Hollywood. Yet, including stand-ins, a technical crew of 45 is required, together with 15 vehicles, and a catered lunch for 77. In case of inclement weather, or some other necessity, a cover set—"Schwartz' Classroom"—is indicated. Note that this same studio interior is listed on the advance schedule as the set for the next two working days, September 9 and 10; also given for those two days are the scenes to be shot and their order.

PROD. NO. __914-83__ TITLE __THE BEST MAN (MILLAR/TURMAN PROD)__

DIRECTOR __F SCHAFFNER__ PRODUCER __MILLAR/TURMAN__ ART DIR. __L WHEELER__

PROD BREAKDOWN ASST. __D.MODER__ SCRIPT DATED __8-30-63__

DAYS __30 PLUS__ START DATE __9-16-63__ FINISH DATE __10-25-63__ TYPED __9-3-63__
9 DAYS REHEARSAL

FINAL   SHOOTING SCHEDULE

DATE	SET	PAGES	SEQ	SC'NS	CAST
1st DAY 9-16	STAGE #8 INT. RUSSELL SUITE(D) SCS: 11,12 Meet Alice-Jensen enters. Hockstader appears	5			Russell #1,Alice #7,Jensen #2 Hockstader #3
	TOTAL PAGES	5			
2nd DAY 9-17	LOCATION: AMBASSADOR HOTEL INT. CANTWELL HQTRS(D) SC: 16 Cantwell on TV. He & Don exit. Pickup TV for Sc 15A	3			Cantwell #8, Announcer,Don Cantwell #9, bit photographer, Spastic,announcer #2, 60 extras (attendants,reporters,photographers, men, women, tv crew, guards, 10 Cantwell girls) tv cameras,newsreel camera, tv boom,big sign "Go with Joe" Books,coffee
	INT. KITCHEN(D) SC: 17 Cantwell & Don meet cleaning woman	1 2/8			Cantwell #8,Don #9,cleaning woman bit,3 police etc,4 Russell girls,5 kitchen help

PROD. NO.___914-83___ TITLE_____THE BEST MAN_____

DATE	SET	PAGES	SEQ	SC'NS	CAST
2nd DAY CONT'D	INT. HOTEL LOBBY(D) SC: 43 After lunch 2 ladies thru lobby to elevator	1			Mrs. Gamadge #5, Mabel #10, Sena- tor bit,boys(men 2)bits,5ad libs, extras from int (men,women, elev operator, desk clerk,bell hops) posters, pictures
	TOTAL PAGES	5 2/8			
3rd DAY 9-18	LOCATION: AMBASSADOR HOTEL INT. BAROQUE ROOM(D) SC: 42 Ladies luncheon.Alice & Mabel do best to knife each other	6 2/8			Alice #7,Mabel #10,Mrs.Gamadge #5,Janet #6,Mrs. Claypoole bit #19, Reporters #1 & #3(35),Mrs. Anderson #77, Mrs.Merwin #20, 32 extras(4 bus- boys,photograph- ers,20 women,8 men)drinks
	TOTAL PAGES	6 2/8			
4th & 5th DAYS 9-19 & 9-20	LOCATION: AMBASSADOR HOTEL INT. BALLROOM(N) SCS: 22,23,24,25,26,27,28,28A 28B,29,29A,29B,29C,29D,30,30A 31,31A Dinner party.Hockstader introduces candidates & wives. Celebrity sings.	9 1/8			Russel #1,Jensen #2,Hockstader #3,Tom #4,Mrs. Gamadge #5,Alice #7,Cantwell #8, Don #9,Mabel #10 Claypoole #11, John Merwin #12 Celebrity #1 & #2,Oscar Anderson #13,Mrs.Claypool #19,Mrs.Merwin #20,Chairman #17 Reporter #51, waiter bit, wives at table dignitaries,men,

PROD. NO. 914-83 **TITLE** THE BEST MAN

DATE	SET	PAGES	SEQ	SC'NS	CAST
4th & 5th DAYS CONT'D					women, 3 waiters orchestra, newsmen, photographers
	TOTAL PAGES	9 1/8			
6th & 7th DAYS 9-23 & 9-24	STAGE #8 INT. RUSSELL SUITE(D) SCS: 13,14 Hockstader talks politics with Bill & tells him of his cancer condition. Mrs. Gamadge enters, passes advice to Alice. Bill exits.	9 4/8			Russell #1,Mrs. Russell #7, Hockstader sc 12 #3,Jensen,#2 Mrs. Gamadge sc 14 #5,Janet reporters in hall,man Luggage clothes,bar set-up
	TOTAL PAGES	9 4/8			
8th & 9th DAYS 9-25 & 9-26	STAGE #8 INT. RUSSELL SUITE(D) SCS: 44,44A Russell bathes as Claypoole pledges support. Hockstader enters. Jensen brings in Bascomb who tells about Cantwell's past in army.	8			Russell #1, Claypoole #11, Jensen #2, Hockstader #3, Bascomb #15,aide (sb)1 valet,1 room service
	INT. CANTWELL HOME(FOR TV SET SC) SC: 18C Mother Cantwell interviewed.	2/8			Interviewer,Mrs. Cantwell, T.V. announcer
	INT. SENATE RM(D)(FOR TV SET SC) SC: 18B Cantwell questions Mafia man	4/8			Cantwell,Mafia man,voice over, Extras?
	TOTAL PAGES	8 6/8			
10th DAY 9-27	STAGE #8 INT. RUSSELL SUITE SC: 47 Bascomb finishes story. Jensen says he has arranged meeting.	6			Russell #1, Hockstader #3, Jensen #2, Bascomb #15, Alice #7

PROD. NO. ___914-83___ TITLE _____THE BEST MAN_____

DATE	SET	PAGES	SEQ	SC'NS	CAST
10th DAY CONT'D	As Russell leaves Hockstader has attack, asks for doctor TOTAL PAGES	 6			
11th DAY 9-30	LOCATION: BASEMENT BOMB SHELTER INT. BOMB SHELTER(D) SC: 51 Cantwell reads document, greets Marcus & explains his innocence. Marcus rushes out door into newsmen TOTAL PAGES	5 5/8 5 5/8			Russell #1, Cantwell #8, Bascomb #15, 6 newsmen & photographers
12th DAY 10-1	LOCATION: BASEMENT BOMB SHELTER INT. CORRIDOR OUTSIDE BOMB SC: 52 SHELTER(D) Cantwell poses w/Marcus for photographers	7/8			Cantwell #8, Don #9, Bascomb #15 Jensen #2, photographer bit, reporter bit, 6 reporters & newsmen
27th DAY 10-22	INT. LIMO(PROCESS)(D) SC: 64 Russell 7 Alice riding to arena	1 4/8			Russell #1, Alice #7, driver?, mockup limo, process plates to cover
	INT. LINEN CLOSET(D) sc; 49 Russell & Cantwell meet. Big discussion as Cantwell asks Russell to withdraw from race. 2 exit to hall TOTAL PAGES	4 4/8 6 6/8			Russell #1, Jensen #2, Cantwell #8, Don #9
28th DAY 10-23	LOCATION: AMBASSADOR HOTEL INT. PALM COURT(D) SCS: 1,2 Russell talks to press	5 1/8			Russell #1, Jensen #2, reporters #1,#2, #3,#4,#5, fan, 35 extras (reporters men, women, 1

PROD. NO. 914-83 **TITLE** THE BEST MAN

DATE	SET	PAGES	SEQ	SC'NS	CAST
28th DAY CONT'D					bartender,1 guard,2 waiters) no tv camera
	EXT. PALM COURT(D) SC: 3 Russell tries to call wife on phone. No luck	6/8			Russell #1, Jensen #2,5 reporters,fan, from sc 1, re- porters,man Indian,men, women,elderly lady(SB)6yr old boy(SB)3 Russell girl w.worker, banners,bass drum,mixed but- tons
	TOTAL PAGES	5 7/8			
29th DAY 10-24	LOCATION: AMBASSADOR HOTEL EXT. POOL AREA(D) SCS: 4,5,6,7 Two at pool meet Mrs. Gamadge. They talk, she exits	4 5/8			Russell #1, Jensen #2,Mrs. Gamadge #5,girl bit sc 7,tv in- terviewer sc 7 100 extras (husky woman golfer(SB)men bathers,women bathers,men, women,waiters, tv crew, photogs newsmen,5 Cantwell girls) tv camera tran- sistor radios, private cameras
	INT. HOTEL LOBBY(D) SC: 8 Continuation of pool seq 2 men to elevator	6/8			Mrs. Gamadge, Russell,Jensen, men,women,2 bellhops,from 100 in scs 4-7
	TOTAL PAGES	5 3/8			

PROD. NO. __914-83__ TITLE_____THE BEST MAN_____

DATE	SET	PAGES	SEQ	SC'NS	CAST
30th DAY	LOCATION: AMBASSADOR HOTEL EXT. AMBASSADOR(D) SC: 40 Jensen entering,meets Lazarus	6/8			Jensen,Lazarus, 45 extras(15 picket line (some colored)5 Cantwell girls, man on stilts,2 attendants,men, women,photogs, newsmen,doorman) cars,Jensen's car,Lazarus car
	EXT. AMBASSADOR HELIPORT(D) SC: 58A Cantwell & Aide board copter	1/8			Cantwell #8, Aide bit,men, women,pilot, copter
	EXT. AMBASSADOR SWIM POOL(N) SC: 35 Hockstader asks Claypoole to be VP. Supporter talks to him	7/8			Hockstader #3, Tom #4,Claypoole #11,supporter bit,40 extras (men,women, servers,see colored help)
	TOTAL PAGES	1 6/8			
POST LAST PRODUCTION	INT. COPTER(D) SC: 58B Cantwell on walkie-talkie	3/8			Cantwell,Aide, Pilot,shoot in flight,copter
	TOTAL SCRIPT PAGES	134 7/8			
		★★★★			

TIGERTAIL PROD., INC.

4th day of shooting	CALL SHEET	Prod. No. 5000

PICTURE: "THE YOUNG LOVERS" DIRECTOR: SAMUEL GOLDWYN, JR.

SHOOTING CALL: 8:00 A.M. DATE: FRIDAY, SEPT.6, 1963

SET AND SCENE NO.

EXT. CAMPUS PARKING ENT. (D) U.C.L.A.
Scs. 189, 190

EXT. SMALL PARKING LOT (D) U.C.L.A.
Scs. 214, 215, 216, 217, 218, 219, 220, 221

COVER SET: INT. SCHWARTZ' CLASSROOM

- -

CAST & BITS	CHARACTER & WARDROBE	HAIRDRESSING	MAKEUP	ON SET
PETER FONDA	EDDIE		7:15	8:00
SHARON HUGUENY	PAM	6:00		8:00

STANDINS: THRU GATE

T. CONNERS	MR. FONDA w/car	7:00
1 WOMAN	MISS HUGUENY w/car	7:00

- -

ADVANCE SCHEDULE

MON. 9/9 & TUES.	INT. SCHWARTZ' CLASSROOM (D)	Scs. 68, 69, 70, 71, 72, 73, 74, 75, 76, 77, 78, 79, 80.	STAGE 4
	INT. SCHWARTZ' CLASSROOM (D)	Scs. 262, 263, 264, 265, 266, 267, 268, 269, 270, 271, 272, 273.	STAGE 4
	INT. SCHWARTZ' CLASSROOM (D)	Scs. 103, 104, 105 188C	STAGE 4
	INT. CLASSROOM	Sc. 188D	STAGE 4

CAMERA	TIME:
1 Camera	6:30
1 Cameraman	6:42
1 Operator	6:42
2 Assistants	6:30

TECHNICAL

1 Key & 2nd Grip	6:30
4 Co Grips	6:30
1 Greensman	6:30
1 Laborer	6:30

ELECTRICAL

1 Gaffer & Best Boy	6:30
8 Lamp Opers	6:30
1 Generator	6:30
1 Gen Operator	6:30
1 Booster Lights	6:30

WARDROBE

1 Ward Man	6:30
1 Ward Girl	6:30

MAKEUP

1 Makeup Man	6:00
1 Hairstylist	6:00

SOUND

1 Mixer	6:42
1 Recorder	6:30
1 Mikeman	6:30
1 Cableman	6:30

STILL

1 Still Man	7:00

PROPERTY	TIME:
1 Property Master	6:30
2 Asst Prop Man	6:30
Tarragoo's car	6:30
Eddie's Motorcycle	6:30
Pam's Car	7:00

RESTAURANT

77 Lunches	11:30
1 Gals Coffee Box donuts	7:00

HOSPITAL

1 1st Aid Man	6:30

TRANSPORTATION

1 Standby Car	6:42
1 Car	7:00
1 Car	7:30
1 Bus (41)	6:30
1 Grip Trk	ON LOC
1 Prop Trk	ON LOC
1 Ward Trk	ON LOC
1 Sound Jeep	ON LOC
1 Elec Trk	ON LOC
1 Generator Trk	ON LOC
P.U. trk	ON LOC
1 LU Driver	6:30

Glossary

Above the line expenses (cost)   cost of staff, talent, and story in preparation and production of a motion picture.

Absolute film (also **abstract film**)   a nonrepresentative film whose parts are composed of moving visual patterns.

Abstract music   musical accompaniment to a scene or scenes which aims at more than **crutch music;** based upon correspondence or juxtaposition with the structure and rhythm of the images on the screen.

Abstract set   a nonrepresentational setting without a definite period or locale.

Academy players directory (casting bible)   several volumes listing professional actors available for American film productions; includes photographs.

Accelerated motion (also **fast motion** and **speedup motion**)   by slowing down the camera mechanism during shooting, the resulting projection of action at standard rate (24 frames per second) will appear to be taking place at greater speed; often used for farce or comic effect, also to emphasize mechanistic order; opposite of **slow motion.**

Accent light   a small spotlight focused on a specific detail of a subject; usually placed to one side of the subject or used as backlighting.

Action   anything recorded by the camera in a shot; the command, "Action!" beginning a shot, may be given only by the director.

Action director (also **second unit director**)   a supplementary director for action scenes and scenes without dialogue which do not require the presence of the director.

Action still   a still photograph taken of a scene as it appears in the film, distinguished from other types of still photographs taken during production, such as **art stills, production stills, publicity stills.** See also **Unit still photographer.**

Ad lib extemporaneous dialogue and action not in a prepared script; or working without a script.

Adapt to translate and to change a story, novel, play, or other property for the purpose of making a film.

Aerial shot photograph taken from helicopter, airplane, balloon.

Against the grain (opposite of **on the nose**) any artistic technique in any aspect of the filmmaking process in which one element is used unconventionally, in contrast to audience experience and expectation, to create a sense of conflict, "mixed feelings," and to comment upon the convention violated.

Allusion as in literature, an explicit or implicit reference to another film or films achieved by dialogue, impersonation, music, visual style of shots.

Angle see **Camera angle.**

Animation process by which drawings or objects are photographed so that when shown there will be the illusion of movement.

Answer print (also **first-trial print**) first combined print received from the laboratory and approved as representing the standard for all subsequent prints.

Aperture lens opening admitting light to film; also opening in the camera permitting lens to project images onto the film.

Arc (also **brute**) a large, high-powered carbon light used to illuminate a set for filming.

Arrange to adapt the music created by the *composer* for various voices and instruments.

Art director designs and supervises all sets, exterior and interior, in studio and on location. See also **Production designer.**

Art film used to describe any film, foreign or domestic, ostensibly not intended for large-scale commercial release and distribution.

Art house (or **theater**) a theater specializing in the presentation of art films.

Art still a photograph made of a film actor, not taken from the context of actual filming.

Assemble to begin the editing process by collecting separate shots and arranging them in order.

Assistant cameraman member of camera crew, charged with loading the camera with raw stock and with focusing of lenses.

Assistant director doubles as an assistant to the director and to the unit production manager; generally serves as foreman of the set; specifically charged with handling all bit players and extras, with presence of all players for their shots, notification of all players of their calls, also transportation and set discipline.

Associate producer an immediate assistant to the producer; when the producer is involved in the making of more than one film, he may be charged with the making of one film.

Atmosphere   details of setting, costumes, extras, properties which establish verisimilitude; or aspects of lighting, photography, direction, editing which contribute to convey an emotional mood.

Attitude   the use of **objective** and **subjective** shots by the filmmaker to reveal a meaning or to make a point or statement.

Audience participation shots   any shots in a film in which actors seem to speak to, act, and react to the theater audience or the camera *as camera;* or any scenes or shots in which the audience is explicitly introduced to the process of making the film being seen.

Auteur (French for author)   the filmmaker, in particular, the director, viewed as analogous to the author of a book in the sense that he has authority and control over the creation of the film and responsibility for the finished work, and each work becomes part of his canon; assumes that the director is a responsible artist with a recognizable cinematic manner and style and an artist's concern for specific subjects and areas of experience.

Avant garde   used loosely to describe any films in which form or content or both are experimental.

B & W   abbreviation for black-and-white film.

Back lighting   light directed into the subject and towards the camera from a point behind the subject.

Back projection (also **rear projection**)   projection of a film of an action or setting through a transparent screen, in front of which another action or scene may be filmed. See also **Process shot.**

Background (bg)   that portion of the setting or frame farthest, in real or apparent distance, from the camera.

Background light   light placed on the background to create a visual separation of the subject of a shot from the background.

Background music   music composed and arranged to accompany particular action or dialogue in a film; sometimes prerecorded.

Background players (crowd)   see **Extra.**

Backing   a flat background, which can be a photograph or painting, against which actors are filmed.

Backup schedule   an alternate to the scenes to be shot in regular shooting schedule in the event that, for any reason, the regular schedule cannot be followed.

Balance   when the process of **dubbing** has been completed and the film is a single unit with a single sound track, the editor balances it, equalizing, insofar as possible, the footage in each reel, prior to any preview showing.

Barndoor   a black flap used to block light from shining into the camera lens.

Below the line expenses (cost)   all production expenses involved in filmmaking, including technical facilities, staging and studio costs.

Benshi (Japanese)   live narrator and commentator for silent films.

Big closeup   see **Closeup.**

Bit (player)   an actor with a small speaking part.

Bits (of business)   miscellaneous movements, actions, gestures created by the director and actors for dramatic purposes and for characterization.

Blimp   soundproof camera housing used to eliminate the noise of the camera.

Blocking (also to **block in**)   rehearsal preparation by the director, assistants, actors, and crew in arranging the composition of a scene, with special emphasis on positions, movements, and gesture of the actors; may involve the use of diagrams or sketches or marking the set with chalk lines or tape; also the initial arrangement of lights. See also **Rough in.**

Blowup   an enlargement of a photograph or a particular part of a photograph, or an enlargement of any printed material.

Body makeup woman   a woman charged with all makeup used for female members of the cast, except those specifically reserved for the makeup artist under union regulations.

Bold   a take which has not been printed, has been put aside, and held in reserve for possible use.

Boom   a mobile suspended microphone, held near actors but out of camera range, to record dialogue. See also **Camera boom.**

Bounce light   creation of soft, diffused, general and almost shadowless illumination by reflecting ("bouncing") light off the ceiling.

Breakdown   an estimated budget for the making of a film, derived from analysis of the script, and subdivided according to estimates of necessary shooting time required, cast and crew, technical resources, and materials.

Bridge music   music designed to accompany and support visual transitions in the film.

Bridging shot   any shot inserted during editing to cover a break in continuity. See also **Insert.**

Broad (also **broadside**)   a reflector light containing two powerful bulbs, creating an even flood covering an angle of roughly sixty degrees.

Brute   see **Arc.**

Budget   the overall estimated and allocated expense for the making of a film, or for any particular aspect of the process; also a daily sheet, issued to cast and crew, indicating which scenes are to be shot on the following day and which people will be required. See also **Call sheet.**

Burnt up   scenes in which set or actors are overlighted.

Busy   anything in action or setting which distracts from the intended focus of interest.

Butterfly lighting   light is placed in front of the subject and shadow reduced to a delicate minimum; used chiefly in closeups, for glamor.

Call sheet a mimeographed list, prepared by the assistant director and the unit production manager, indicating the requirements and calls for the next day's shooting; includes cast, crew, and equipment required.

Calls estimated time for various members of cast and crew to report for work.

Cameo part a bit part in a picture for which a star is cast.

Camera motion picture camera designed to take photographic images on cinematographic film; conventionally a 35 MM camera for commercial filming, but 16 MM cameras, and, occasionally, 8 MM cameras, are also used; capable of using a wide variety of lenses.

Camera angle the position or standpoint of the camera in terms of the scene and the subject being filmed; unless otherwise specified, is usually assumed to be eye level. See also **High angle shot** and **Low angle shot.**

Camera boom (also **crane**) a mobile crane with a platform for the camera which can be used for either fixed or moving shots, and allows for movement horizontally and vertically, backward and forward.

Camera operator second man of the camera crew; operates the camera physically, responsible for frame and focus.

Cameraman (also **cinematographer** and **director of photography**) senior member of the camera crew; supervises all operations of the camera and the lighting of sets and actors; with director creates the composition of the shots.

Cant (**frame** or **shot**; also **oblique angle, slant frame**) a shot made with the camera slightly tilted, to create a special effect or to exaggerate normal angles.

Cast the actors participating in a film, including **stars, featured players, bit players,** and **extras.**

Casting director responsible for keeping records of actors suitable for parts and available for work on a film.

Changing gag canvas or rubber bag, enclosed in a black cover, used for handling film in darkness when no darkroom is available.

Cheat shot a shot in which a portion of a subject or part of an action is excluded from view to create an illusion or suggest a special effect.

Cinéaste (French for filmmaker) the ordering mind of the director.

Cinema of ideas as in theater of ideas, filmmaking for ideological or social purpose, or films which probe and question intellectual concepts in the context of fiction as well as in the documentary.

Cinéma vérité (also **direct cinema**) deriving from technique of newsreels and documentary filming; deliberate imitation of style and manner of a happening; a conscious attempt to represent an unplanned, accidental filming.

Cinematography the art of recording motion photographically and reproducing it for audiences.

Cinemobile Mark IV   a single, 35-foot, bus-like vehicle, created and designed by Fouad Said, containing all necessary equipment, bathrooms, dressing rooms, and space for a staff and crew of fifty, which is rapidly replacing the huge caravans of trucks and vehicles necessary for filming on location; a self-contained unit, this vehicle has been widely and successfully used in filming recent American pictures at a variety of locations.

Clapper (also **number board** and **slate**)   a pair of hinged boards which are clapped together at the beginning of each numbered take so that sound and picture can be synchronized in editing; a slate on which the scene number and take number are written and photographed.

Clip   a short section or sequence from a film.

Close medium shot (also **close middle shot, MCS**)   a shot of indefinite distance between a medium shot and a close shot; a close medium shot of a human subject is usually a bust shot.

Closeup (**CU**, also **close shot, CS, tight shot**)   shot in which the camera, actually or apparently, is close to the subject; in terms of an actor, it usually includes area from shoulders to top of head or face only; variations are the large closeup or big closeup, focused on one part of an object or part of the face or anatomy of an actor.

Color correction   use of color filters to restrain one or more subject tones so that film will record the scene as if seen by the naked eye.

Combined continuity   a complete verbal and numerical record of the finished film, including action, dialogue, sounds, camera angles, footage, and frames, prepared by the **script supervisor.**

Commentary (also **voice over narration**)   descriptive or narrative talk in accompaniment with the film.

Composer   creates music for a film.

Composite print (British: **combined print**)   an edited, completed, positive print of the film, or strip of film, containing all sound tracks.

Composition   the arrangement and real or apparent movement of subjects in frame, shot, scene, or sequence, together with qualities of perspective, lighting, photography. The composition of a single shot is often analyzed analogously to the composition of a painting.

Comprehensive shot   a complete shot of a large area or large-scale action. See also **Establishing shot.**

Continuity   the editorial organization of shots and sequences, with transitions between them, in a film.

Continuity editing   editing which is tied to establishing definite story points; distinguished from **dynamic editing.**

Contrast   the relationship of the elements of brightness in a picture.

Contrast ratio (also **contrast range**)   range of contrast between the darkest and lightest elements of a frame.

"Cookies"   black opaque screens used to cut off light from one or more parts of the set or to shield the camera from direct light.

Costume designer   designs and creates wardrobe for a film.

Costumers   maintain clothing and wardrobe during production, assist players in dressing, and stand by on set.

Cover   the number of **setups** and **takes** used in filming a scene.

Cover set   a set in readiness for filming in the event that, for any reason, the regular filming schedule cannot be followed.

Coverage   the amount of film, the number of takes and footage, from various angles, allotted by the director in the filming of a scene or sequence.

Crab dolly   a small wheeled platform mount for the camera, which may be moved on level ground by hand; is moved by **grips;** used for easy movement over level ground or on studio sound stage floors; may be moved in any direction (crabbed). See also **Dolly.**

Crane shot (also **boom shot**)   a shot taken by a camera from a camera boom.

Credits (also **screen credits**)   the names of members of staff, cast, and crew who are officially credited, that is, recognized according to custom, contracts, and union regulations, in the film.

Critical focus   distance between subject and the camera.

Cross-cut (also **parallel editing**)   juxtaposition of two or more separate shots or scenes with parts of each presented alternately so that separate actions are represented as simultaneous.

Crutch music   mood pieces supporting scenes; principal problem is timing to end simultaneously with the scene.

Cut   (1) an individual strip of film; (2) a transition between two separate shots joined together so that the first shot is instantaneously replaced by the second; (3) as a verb, to trim and join shots together, to edit a film; (4) a shot; (5) an instruction to terminate a shot, given only by the director.

Cutaway   a shot apparently taking place at the same time as the main action of a scene; most commonly a **reaction shot.**

Cut-in (also **insert shot**)   a shot of some detail of the main action other than the faces of actors involved.

Cut-in scene   a scene taken separately and inserted into a film.

Cutout   parts of film discarded by the film editor.

Cutter   the **film editor;** also refers to his assistants.

Cutting bench   a special, vinyl-surfaced table used by film editors.

Cutting on movement   a method associated with the **match cut;** when cutting between shots of the same subject in an apparently continuous time sequence, the cut is made on the motion of the subject to reduce audience awareness of the cut.

Cutting piece   an illusory blending of widely separated locations or sets into an apparent whole.

Cutting room   room or space assigned to the editor and his assistants for editing the film.

Dailies (also **rushes**) film photographed on the previous working day, developed, printed, **rough cut**, and screened on the following day for the benefit of the director and his staff; also daily progress reports on the production.

Day for night shooting night scenes in daylight, using filters and other technical devices to simulate darkness.

Deep focus sharp focus for a **long shot** or **far shot.**

Deep focus lens a lens permitting simultaneous focus for a closeup and a long shot background in the same shot.

Depth of field the distance to and from the camera in which an actor can move or an object can be moved without becoming out of focus.

Depth of focus the extent to which a lens can focus on near and distant objects at the same time.

Detail shots shots of details, cut into the action of a sequence, usually with the effect of expanding the *time* of a sequence; for example, in a race sequence, cutting to feet of runners, crowd reactions, faces, etc., while maintaining master sequence of race.

Development (also **processing**) laboratory process for developing and fixing exposed film.

Dialing control of the sound during filming by the **mixer;** unwanted sounds can be dialed out.

Dialogue (also **lines, words**) all spoken words in a film.

Dialogue director (also **coach**) assigned to rehearsal of lines and prompting of players.

Diaphragm an adjustable ring on the aperture of the camera serving to control the amount of light entering the lens.

Differential focus photographing an object in sharp focus with rest of the shot out of focus.

Diffusion screens screens used to control light and shadow on a set. See also **Reflectors.**

Diffusor material which is used to soften a beam of light.

Direct cut a cut, but stipulated direct cut in script directions to emphasize this particular form of transition rather than to leave it optional; often used at a place where, conventionally, the editor might use another transition.

Directional movement real or apparent movement of the subjects of a shot or scene as blocked and arranged by the director as a part of his composition and **structured rhythm;** movement, within a frame, may be left (**l**) or right (**r**), towards the background (**bg**) or foreground (**fg**) of the shot; also applied to arrangements of static objects on a set which may be photographed in such a way, by moving the camera, by lens adjustment, or by changing the angle, as to make objects seem to move, as, for example, when the camera imitates the **point of view** of a moving character; also applied to the relationship of movements and motion in separate shots and scenes linked together in editing.

Director   responsible for all aspects of filmmaking from the beginning of production to release.

Dissolve (also **lap dissolve** and **mix**)   the merging of one shot into the next, produced by superimposition of the two shots and a fade out of the first and a fade in of the second; usually a laboratory process, but can be done in the camera while shooting.

Documentary film   a nonfiction film on subjects of general interest.

Dolly   a wheeled platform serving as a camera mount which can be manhandled in any direction; sometimes called **trolley** when mounted on tracks.

Dolly in (also **track in**)   moving the camera towards the subject, decreasing the distance of the shot.

Dolly out (also **track out**)   moving the camera backwards, away from the subject, increasing the distance of the shot.

Dolly shot (also **travelling shot, tracking shot**)   a moving shot, usually made of a moving subject. See also **Following shot, Running shot, Trucking shot.**

Domestic release   commercial release of a film to be shown in theaters in the U.S. and Canada.

Double   see **Stunt double.**

Double-exposure   use of the same film strip for two or more exposures to create superimposed images on developed film.

Dress extra   an **extra** reporting for work in his own tuxedo or full dress, her own evening gown.

Dubbing (also **mixing** and **rerecording**)   process of combining all sound tracks, including music, sound effects, and dialogue, into one synchronized sound track for the film; also the process of synchronizing foreign language dialogue for foreign language versions of a completed film.

Dupe negative   a negative made from a positive print.

Dynamic editing   a style of editing suitable to action scenes and characteristic of documentary filmmaking where the film is "made" in editing; its quality is rapid pace and maximum visual impact in combinations of shots.

Dynamic frame   any device or technique which serves to make the screen itself appear either to enlarge or decrease in size.

Editor (also **cutter**)   responsible to the director for entire process of editing and assembling the film, from first takes to final **work print**, including all technical aspects, optical and sound.

Effect shot   a cut made within context of a scene or sequence to another scene or shot, to comment on original scene or to establish a relationship between the two contexts.

Electric eye   light meter built into camera to set the lens opening automatically.

Emulsion   chemicals on the film's acetate base which, being sensitive to light, receive the image during filming.

Establishing shot   a shot which serves to locate the action for the scene to follow.

Exciter lamp   projector lamp which, in coordination with the amplifier, produces sound for a projected sound film.

Expressionism   in cinema refers to a filmmaking movement in post-World War I Germany; characterized by deliberate artifice in lighting, costumes, and sets, by symbolic or mime-like acting, by fantasy or strong elements of the fantastic.

Extended image   an image in which persons or objects overlap the limits of the frame, suggesting the larger context beyond the frame.

Exterior (EXT.)   shooting done outdoors, on location, or on the lot of the studio.

Extra (also **screen extra**)   a member of the cast used for background purposes and authenticity; if the extra acts or reacts in a scene, a silent bit, he receives additional pay. See also **Stand-in.**

Extreme closeup (also **extreme close shot**)   close shot of a very small detail.

Extreme long shot   shot made with the lens of the camera focused on infinity.

Eye level (also **horizontal**)   the standard camera angle, assumed unless otherwise specified by the director or the script.

Eyelight   small light used near camera to cause actor's eyes to "sparkle."

Eyepiece   viewing lens attachment to camera permitting the operator to see exactly what the camera lens will record. See also **Viewer.**

FPS   abbreviation for **frames per second.**

FX track   the sound-effects tracks.

Fade   the screen is blank (dark) with no image projected; a fade, in context of a film, usually serves as a distinct break in continuity, clearly setting off one sequence of shots from another; a slow fade calls for a very gradual diminishment of light and the image until the screen is blank.

Fade in   the gradual appearance of a picture on the screen.

Fade out   the gradual disappearance (fading) of picture and images from the screen, ending with a blank screen.

Far shot (also **very long shot, extreme long shot, distance shot**)   a shot which includes not only the entire setting, but also the details of a distant background.

Fast film   type of film with high sensitivity to light, able to record images with less light than is required by slower films.

Fast motion (effect)   see **Accelerated motion.**

Fast tempo   the overall sense of timing, of "fast and slow" scenes and sequences in a film, is determined not by the speed of photography or by the physical speed or movement of subjects filmed, but by narrative and visual context and, chiefly, by the editorial craft in cutting. The effect of fast tempo might be achieved through cross-cutting or by dynamic editing.

Favoring (also **featuring** and **centering on**) in any two shot or group shot, this direction calls for photography which will stress the significance of one or more of the characters involved.

Featured player an actor with a major part who receives screen credit (billing), but who is ranked below the stars.

Feeler print a print made from the edited negative of the work print with all effects inserted, but before final mixing.

Fill light light placed so as to control the shadows cast by the **key light.**

Film grain the size of the particles composing the light-sensitive layer of a film; a shot or print is said to be grainy when these particles are clearly visible in projection.

Film gauge the width of film measured in millimeters, as, for example, 70 MM, 35 MM, 16 MM, 8 MM.

Filters transparent glass or gelatin placed in front of or behind the camera lens to alter the light qualities or, in color filming, the tone relationships; among the standard filters used are *neutral density filters*, a gray filter uniformly cutting down on the light hitting the lens; *polarizing filters*, used especially to decrease sunlight and reflections on glass and water; *diffusion filters*, which serve to soften hard lines and are used for facial closeups; *fog filters*, which create a foggy effect; for black-and-white films, a *color filter*, which lightens its own color and darkens its compliment; and *color-compensating filters*, used to control illumination and give good color rendition.

Final negative the edited negative from which the composite print is made.

Fine cut editor's best complete version of an unfinished film, lacking **supportive elements** (see below).

Fine grains duplicate negatives of the film ordered from the laboratory for technical and editorial use.

Fish-eye lens very wide-angle lenses which, because of distortion, are sometimes used for dream sequences, fantasy and other devices of **subjective camera** (see below).

Fixed (also **static**) **camera** shooting from any angle or distance when the camera remains in a fixed position throughout the shot; distinguished from **mobile** or **moving camera.**

Fixed frame a shot in which the camera is fixed (static) and in which there is no background movement.

Fixed-focus lens a lens without focus adjustment.

Flare check a cameraman's test to determine if light is shining into the lens.

Flash cutting insertion of extremely brief fragments between direct cuts from shot to shot or scene to scene.

Flash forward shot, scene, or sequence interrupting the ongoing time sequence of a film by introducing action or events to come; it may refer forward to scenes which will be viewed or may imply future time and events outside the chronology of the film.

Flash shot a shot of very few frames and short duration, therefore almost subliminal in effect; often used as an insert within the context of an ongoing shot or scene to represent a fragment of subjective memory or an intimation or intuition of future time.

Flashback a shot, scene, or sequence, introduced into the chronological sequence of a film and breaking that sequence by referring to time past; it may refer back to action already seen or may introduce narrative elements or subjective memory of the past into the imagined present of the film.

Flip (also **flipover wipe** and **flip frame**) a transitional device in which the frame of one shot revolves 360 degrees, and flips over, ending its revolution with the frame of the next shot.

Floor any part of a studio where shooting is in progress; the ground level of any set, exterior or interior.

Focus to adjust the lens of a camera (or projector) in order to keep a sharply defined image.

Follow focus adjustment of the lens during filming to keep a moving subject in focus.

Following shot a shot in which the camera moves or seems to move to follow a moving actor or object. See also **Running shot.**

Footage a length of film measured in feet; often used loosely to refer to a shot, scene, or sequence of a film.

Foreground (fg) that part of the scene immediately in front of the camera.

Foreshadowing cinematic or narrative (or both) means of preparing the audience to accept as probable some future action or event.

Form cutting the framing in a following shot of a subject or compositional arrangement which has a shape or contour in some way similar to an image in the shot preceding it; the relationship and juxtaposition of the two can serve as a simple comparison (as in a simile in poetry), or, by association, within the context of the film, or by allusion, can be raised to the higher power of metaphor and symbol.

Frame (sometimes **still**) a single photograph in the series printed on a length of cinematographic film; in photographing a scene or shot the frame of the shot, seen through the eyepiece of the camera, or the **viewer,** determines the staging areas (background and foreground, left and right) and the composition of the shot or scene; anything which can be seen is said to be *in frame;* anything in the scene or shot which cannot be seen is *out-of-frame* or *off-frame* (of); see also **Off-camera** and **On-camera;** the average ninety-minute feature film is made up of 129,000 separate frames or 8,100 feet of film.

Frame line   the dividing line separating each single frame from the next.

Frame slant   a shot in which the camera is slightly tilted on its axis so that the image appears on the screen off center, in a tilted position. See also **Cant.**

Freeze shot   the repetition of a single frame for an extended time, done either in camera while photographing or by editing, so that, when seen in projection, the shot appears to freeze, to be a still photograph. See also **Zoom freeze.**

Front lighting (also **pancake lighting**)   the light source is from approximately the same position and angle as the camera; serves to flatten out planes and angles.

Full shot   a shot of indeterminate distance, from any angle, but fully including the subject of the shot; when applied to actors, the shot calls for the full body to be in frame.

Gaffer   the electrical foreman of the set; also may be used, loosely, to designate any foreman of any production department or crew.

Gendai-geki (Japanese)   films set in time from mid-nineteenth century to the present time.

General shot   any shot from any angle in which a complete action or a large part of the set is visible.

Ghost and glare   optical effects caused by rays from improperly placed lamps; *ghosting* occurs when faint images of the light source appear in the picture; *glare* is general veiling caused by scattered light which flattens the contrast.

Glass shot   a shot in which part of the background or setting is painted or photographed on glass or other transparent material, which is placed between the camera and the subject so that it will merge with the full-size set being photographed.

Gobo (also **nigger**)   a black screen, mounted adjustably, used to control light falling on the camera.

Goose   any vehicle designed especially to transport camera and sound equipment.

Grain   dot patterns on projected film; *fine grain* is characteristic of slow film; fast film creates *coarse grain.*

Greensman (also **nurseryman**)   charged with all trees, plants, shrubbery, and flowers not in vases on exterior or interior sets; responsible for required seasonal changes.

Grip   a skilled set laborer, general, all-purpose set assistant; the foreman is known as the **key grip** or **head grip.**

Group shot   a shot of unspecified distance and angle, concentrating upon three or more characters.

Hair check   test for line, dust, etc., in the camera aperture, made after film stock has been threaded in the camera.

Hand-held camera (HH)   use of a camera—a 16 MM camera whose film will subsequently be blown up to 35 MM—without any conventional fixed or mobile mounting; characteristic of documentary and direct cinema filming; *effect* of hand-held camera can be imitated with conventional camera mounting; though held by hand, the camera can be firmly controlled by means of body braces, shoulder rests.

Hard light   artificial lights (arcs) used to represent sunlight on a set.

Hatchet lighting   light source placed ninety degrees from the camera to create a half-shadow effect on the subject.

Head-on shot   a shot in which the action appears to come directly towards the camera; most often used in relation to **trucking shot.**

Heavy   a movie villain.

Hi hat   a small, low mount for the camera for very **low angle** shooting, or for shooting a few inches off the floor.

High angle shot (also **high shot**)   a shot taken by any means from an elevated angle in terms of the subject; sometimes referred to as **shooting down** or **looking down.**

Implicit music   music for film which, in addition to supporting the physical sense of action (see also **Kinetic music**), also serves to fit with visual image and dialogue to convey a parallel or corresponding mood, and likewise to accentuate visual techniques and transitions.

In-depth movement   movement from the foreground in a direction away from the camera or vice versa, resulting in a sense of the depth and dimension of the image.

In sequence   shooting on a schedule which follows the sequence and order of the shooting script; this is very seldom done, for reasons of economy and efficiency.

Insert slate   pocket-size identification board without a clapstick used in filming without sound.

Incidental music   music apparently coming from a real sound source in the scene, as for example, radio, jukebox, musical instrument.

Inkie   an intensely bright incandescent lamp.

Insert   (1) a shot, usually a closeup, used to reveal a **title** or any subject in detail; (2) any material cut into a scene, though not shot in the making of the scene, by the editor; (3) also a camera car used for mobile photography.

Intercut   a short cut used within a larger sequence. See also **Cross-cut.**

Interior (INT.)   any set which represents an indoor situation; distinguished from **exterior.**

Interpolated shots   see **Insert.**

Intertitles (also **titles,** distinguished from the **main title** or **titles and credits**) any shot of any written or printed material inserted in any scene or sequence of a film.

Invisible cutting (also **invisible editing**)   unobtrusive cutting by means of **match cuts** or by **motivation,** intended to distract audience attention from awareness of editing.

Iris in to open up the photographed image from a pinpoint or small portion of the frame until the whole frame is filled with the picture.

Iris out to close down the photographed image to a pinpoint or small portion of the frame.

Irising a gradual opening up or closing down of the photographed image from or to a pinpoint; can be done in camera by means of an *iris diaphragm* or by **masking;** can be accomplished in laboratory by optical or chemical means; a transitional device for linking one scene to another.

Jidai-geki (Japanese) historical and costume films.

Juicer any electrician working on the set.

Jump cut (distinguished from a **match cut**) in perjorative sense, refers to any poorly made match cut; used as a deliberate artistic device, it represents the cutting out of footage which would give the sequence a conventional continuity; also a cut in which the camera angle changes slightly on the cut, giving an impression of a jump in action.

Key light the main source of light illuminating the subject of a shot.

Kinesthetic involvement the result of artistic techniques designed to involve the audience in sharing physical and psychological feelings of the film.

Kinetic music music designed to accompany and express the actions shown in a scene or sequence.

l left; stage left or frame left.

Lap dissolve see **Dissolve.** See also **Overlap shot.**

Lay behind musical term; music to be subdued and unobtrusive in accompaniment to a scene.

Lens hood camera fitting designed to shield camera lens and film from light.

Lens turret a rotating device on the camera which carries two or more lenses which may be turned swiftly into position during shooting.

Library score a musical score created from pre-recorded music purchased from a music library.

Library shot any shot taken from a film library for use in a film; a shot not taken for a particular film, but used in it. See also **Stock shot.**

Light meter instrument used to measure intensity of light on the subject or scene being photographed; unit of measurement is *foot candles.*

Lighting the set with very few exceptions all sets, exterior and interior, in studio and on location, must be **lit,** that is, illuminated by lights and controlled by reflectors, diffusion screens.

Lip sync the synchronization of lip movements and the sound of voices.

Location any place outside a studio and its lot where exterior or interior shooting takes place; such shooting is said to be *on location; local* location is within easy driving distance of the studio; any other location is classified as *distant.*

Long lens a lens with a focal length greater than normal, therefore including a narrow angle of a scene; incorrectly called a **telephoto lens.**

Long shot (ls)   shot taken at a distance from the action or subject, conventionally not less than fifty yards and often at a greater distance; a long shot need *not* be a **full shot** including a complete setting or action.

Loop film (also **cyclic film**)   a short film with its ends joined together which can be run through a projector without interruption in continuous repetition.

Looping   process by which actors replace lines made on the original sound track, for purposes of clarity and inflection, in a studio sound recording room; a loop film is prepared and projected and the actor repeats his lines, timing (**synchronizing**) his words with his filmed lip movements; frequently used, wrongly, for **dubbing.**

Lot   any land owned by a studio and situated near sound stages where shooting may take place; also a term for the entire studio; something is located as happening *on the lot* or *off the lot*.

Low angle shot (also **camera looking up**)   the camera is situated below the subject of the shot, shooting upward.

Low key   (1) when only a few highlights are used to illuminate the subject and a large portion of the set is shadowy, the lighting is called *low key;* (2) similarly the subject may be shot in low key by stopping down the lens opening of the camera; (3) finally, a dark print, in color or black and white, is low key.

Low truck shot   a moving shot taken from a low angle.

Main title (also **title and credits**)   the title of the film; usually shown in combination with the screen credits.

Makeup artist   responsible for all makeup; except, when making up female players, union regulations confine the makeup artist's activities to area from top of head to apex of breastbone, from fingertips to elbows; also responsible for creation of all character effects, as, for example, wounds, scars, aging; and responsible for mustaches, beards, and male wigs.

Map loc:.tion   convention, established by earliest filmmakers and followed ever since, in which the frame is viewed as analogous to a map; thus right-to-left movement indicates movement east to west and vice versa, and the top of the frame may suggest north, the bottom, south; from this beginning developed more sophisticated means of directional cutting, using a rhythm of lines of movement within a shot, scene, and sequence.

Married print   see **Combined print.**

Mask   a shield or shape placed in front of the camera lens to eliminate (that is, mask out) some part of the shot.

Mask shot   shot made with lens covered to limit what can be filmed; most often used (analogous to insert shot) to simulate a shot seen through an object, as, for example, a keyhole or crack, telescope, gun sight, binoculars, or camera.

Master film the final edited negative from which all theatrical prints are made.

Master scene the overall scene, as indicated in the shooting script and by the director, considered as a unit, without regard to the breakdown of the scene into separate shots and takes or the cutting within the scene by the editor.

Master shot a single shooting or take of an entire piece of dramatic action.

Match cut a carefully unobtrusive cut designed to blend the action of two shots so closely together that the effect of cutting is minimized.

Matte shot a special effects process whereby two separately shot sequences are combined harmoniously into one print, giving the effect of being done at one time and in one location; related to **process shot.**

Meal penalty a union regulation requiring that on all location shooting the entire film company must be fed at precisely specified hours and with high quality food; failure to meet this regulation requires that the producer must pay a penalty to all workers.

Medium (or **middle**) **close shot (MCS)** or **closeup (MCU)** a shot of indeterminate distance between a medium shot and a close shot; basically a close shot in which a larger part of the subject than usual is visible.

Medium long shot (MLS) shot of indefinite distance between medium and long, tending towards the long shot but retaining the medium shot's characteristics of clear identity of persons and at least part of the immediate setting.

Medium shot by convention a shot made from between five and fifteen yards' apparent distance and including a subject or group in entirety.

Metteur en scène (French; also *réalisateur*) director, filmmaker.

Middle shot (mid-shot; also **American shot)** a medium shot which focuses on the subject from the knees up.

Minitheater a complex of two or more small, fully automated motion-picture theaters, sharing a box office, refreshment stand, and projection booth, and showing more than one motion picture.

Mirror wipe a wipe made by sliding a 45-degree mirror across the lens.

Mise en scène (French) scenery, setting, and staging; involves, for the director, direction of actors in delivery of lines and in blocking (planning) their movements; also includes planning individual camera shots.

Mixer on the set, a member of the sound crew who operates a sound console in conjunction with the camera; charged with obtaining clear and distinct sound recording during shooting; during dubbing, any one of several sound men who dial in and dial out sounds from the various tracks, creating the sound track for the film.

Mobile (also **motion**) **camera** the capacity of the camera to be changed in distance and angle between shots, or to move or seem to move during a single shot.

Model shot any shot in which a model or an object or objects is photographed.

Montage (1) term used by Sergei Eisenstein to describe rhetorical arrangement of shots (sometimes single frames) in juxtaposition with each other in order to produce or imply another unit independent of the separate elements forming it; defined by Ernest Lindgren in *The Art of the Film* as "the combination in art of representative fragments of nature to form an imaginative whole which has no counterpart in nature"; (2) French term for the editing process; (3) American term for an assembly of short shots used to indicate a passage of time and events within that time span.

MOS (also **wild picture**) any shots, scenes, or sequences taken without sound; when used in script directions it calls for a silent unit.

Motivation establishing probability or causality for anything in the film whether in narrative of script, action, and characterization of actors, or in the editing cuts and transitions.

Moving shot (also **running shot**) any shot in which the camera, by any means, follows with actors or objects moving in that scene.

Moviola originally a trade name, now used for all brands of the special projection machine used by film editors; machine allows the editor to run the film at various speeds, backwards and forwards, to stop on any single frame, and to view the film closely through a magnifying device.

Muddy scene a scene which is inadequately or badly lighted.

Multiple exposure (**double exposure**) two or more exposures made on the same series of frames.

Multiple images special effects method which produces any number of images of the same shot or subject in a frame, or a variety of separate images in the same frame and shot.

Mushroom floods floodlights used in series for general illumination.

Music editor (also **music cutter**) assigned as technical aid and assistant to the composer.

Mute negative negative of sound film not including the sound track.

Mute print positive print of sound motion picture not including the sound track.

Narrative editing see **Continuity editing.**

Negative cost the total expense of making a film.

Negative cutter a specialist at the photographic laboratory, responsible for matching the original negative, frame by frame, with the final work print created by the film editor, to create the master film.

Negative cutting the editorial work done at the photographic laboratory to match the original negative with the final work print.

Neorealism (Italian: *réalismo*) post-World War II movement in Italian cinema, lasting into the 1950s; characterized by a direct and simple style of filmmaking, and use of natural settings and unprofessional actors.

New Wave (French: *nouvelle vague*) a contemporary movement in French filmmaking, based upon the concept of the director as *auteur;* developed by critics writing for *Cahiers du Cinéma,* some of whom have since proved theory in practice, directing distinguished films.

Newsreels filmed shorts of recent news events widely shown in theaters prior to the development of television and TV news programs; significant in the development of the documentary film.

Nonsynchronous sound (distinguished from **synchronous sound** in which a sound effect is precisely matched to the visual image apparently producing the sound) the use of the sound without the visual image, the sound substituting for and implying the visual image; also applied to unrealistic sound in which the sound does not derive directly from the visual image but comments on it, as, for example, a scene showing the stockmarket with stockbrokers shouting, but the sound is of barking dogs and roaring beasts.

Objective camera by careful application of various techniques, the director seeks to divert audience attention away from any sense of filmmaking and to present the subject in a seemingly objective manner, as if the camera were merely recording events.

Obscured frame a shot in which an image or object in foreground blocks a large part of the frame.

Off-camera (also **off-frame, of,** and **off-screen, os**) any action or dialogue or sound taking place out of view in a particular shot, scene, or sequence.

On-camera (also **on-screen**) action, dialogue, or sound happening in frame, directly experienced by the spectator in a particular shot, scene, or sequence.

On the nose any aspect of a film, visual, auditory, or narrative, presented in an explicit and conventional fashion; perjoratively, a cinematic cliché.

Optical cues conventional visual devices (dissolves, montage sequences, pages of a calendar, etc.) used to indicate passage of time or change of time and space.

Optical effects any effects carried out or created in the optical department of a film-processing laboratory; in addition to a variety of laboratory effects, many effects usually created by camera or editing can be created in the laboratory by complex processes.

Optical printer a device which makes it possible for images from one film to be photographed on another film.

Optical sound track sound track made photographically during actual filming.

Optical zoom a simulated **zoom shot** created in the laboratory.

Out of sync when lip movements and other sound-producing actions on film do not synchronize with sounds on the track.

Out-take any take that is not used in the completed film.

Overlap   in sound or dialogue; a sound or words from one shot or scene intruding upon another, either carried over from a previous scene or anticipating the next.

Overlap shots   a series of shots of the same action from different angles with the effect of extending the time and distance covered by the action.

Overlap sound cut   the overlapping of sound accompanying one scene or shot with the visual transition from that scene or shot to the next.

Overlay   one sound track superimposed on another in dubbing.

Overshooting   the practice by most film directors of shooting and printing far more film of a given scene than can be used in the finished film, for the purpose of allowing maximum flexibility and creativity during editing; an average feature film, 8,100 feet, is reduced by editing from 200,000 feet of printed takes.

Over-shoulder shot   shot, sharing the viewpoint of a character, but including a portion of the character's back and shoulders in the foreground.

Package   subject of film to be made, together with basic staff, cast, and crew available and interested to work on it; and frequently including a draft of the screenplay, along with a breakdown.

Paint in   to add objects, by various means, to a photographed scene as a special effect.

Pan (also **panoramic shot**)   to rotate the camera head on its pivot or axis in a horizontal plane in order either to keep a moving subject in view or to move across a stationary scene. See also **Swish-pan.**

Pan down/pan up (British)   to move the camera in a vertical plane, down or up, towards the subject. See also **Tilt shot.**

Parallel editing (also **parallel action**)   an editing technique of presenting separately shot sequences of action happening in different locations as related to each other by shifting the audience viewpoint back and forth between the separate sequences. See also **Cross-cut.**

Peep show (also **kinetoscope**)   one of the earliest forms of motion picture involving the use of a vertically moving, sprocketed film strip, seen by a single viewer through a slit or eyehole.

Photography to playback   reversal of usual process of dubbing; here actors are filmed moving and acting to a sound track; sometimes used for musical production numbers, songs, etc.

Photofloods   small, bright lights used for general illumination.

Photoplay   in early days (1914), a euphemism for movies, result of a contest for an appropriate term; a film version of a stage play, with minimal adaptation for cinema.

Pickups   shots filmed after the completion of the regular shooting schedule and during the editing phase of production; refers to minor material, not involving extensive reshooting, but merely shots needed for transitions, continuity.

Pistol grip   grip handle at the base of a camera allowing the operator to shoot without use of a tripod.

Playback   use of a recorded sound track during shooting or in looping in order to synchronize action, sound, lip movements, and dialogue.

Point of view (POV)   an aspect of **subjective camera;** calls for the camera to simulate, by position, angle, and distance, the view of a subject in the scene of action taking place in that scene; unlike the over-shoulder shot, a point of view shot does not usually include the observing subject or subjects in its frame.

Polecats   single ceiling-to-floor poles used as mounts for light fixtures.

Position   camera position is defined as static (fixed) or moving.

Premix   preliminary stage of mixing sound tracks in which several tracks are blended together to reduce the number of tracks to be used for the final mix.

Prescoring   any music **scored** before production of a film.

Print   a positive copy of negative film; a **take** indicated to be sent to the laboratory for processing and reproduction.

Process shot (also **back projection, rear projection**)   a scene shot against the background of a moving picture, which is projected through a transparent screen behind the actions being filmed; thus the process shot joins together the two separate units of film in one unit; a conventional example is the shot of two actors in an automobile with a shot of moving traffic projected behind them for verisimilitude.

Producer   financier, and responsible overall for the making of a film, from idea through theatrical release, domestic and foreign.

Production designer   an art director with exceptional responsibility and control, including costumes, props, makeup, decorations, and style, as well as sets.

Production manager   see **Unit production manager.**

Production still   any still photograph taken of any aspect of a film in production.

Prop   any object seen or used on any set except painted scenery and costumes.

Prop box   wheeled, portable, piano-size boxes containing all materials necessary for props and their maintenance; also applied to any portable vehicle, including moving van, used by the prop man.

Prop man (also **property master**)   responsible for all objects used in the action of a film, excluding scenery and costumes.

Property   the story of subject matter of a film to be produced; or a finished film.

Post-synchronize (British; **looping** [U.S.])   recording dialogue with projected film.

Publicity still   any still photograph taken before, during, or after the shooting of a film for the purposes of publicity and advertising, including display photographs often used at the entrance of theaters.

Pull back (PB) a camera direction indicating that the camera moves, or seems to move, back away from the subject.

Put in (a special effect) to create an effect by augmenting or increasing something actually photographed; for example, flames of a fire may be *put in* a scene.

Quartz light (also **halogen**) specially designed incandescent light capable of extremely high intensity and heat; thus a powerful source of illumination.

Quick cutting editing of film in short shots for an effect of rapidity.

Raw stock film that has not yet been used, exposed, or processed.

Reaction shot a shot featuring the response or reaction of one or more characters to an action already seen or about to be seen.

Reduction (opposite of enlargement and **blowup**) process by which a film made in one width is produced in a smaller width; for example, 35 MM is *reduced* to 16 MM or 8 MM prints.

Reel a strip of film on a spool; standard reel is 2,000 feet for American 35 MM projectors.

Reflector light a light with a built-in reflector; may be either a spotlight for concentrated light beam or floodlight with evenly diffused illumination.

Reflectors reflecting boards used to control, boost, and direct sunlight or lighting.

Relational editing editing of separate shots to link them together associatively and intellectually.

Release print a film for general theatrical showing.

Release script (British) script version of the finished film. See also **Combined continuity.**

Remake another filmed version of a previously produced property.

Rembrandt lighting dramatic and shadowed lighting; term is attributed to Cecil B. De Mille upon receipt of a telegram complaining that sender "couldn't even see the characters' faces half the time" in a De Mille film. "Tell him it's Rembrandt light," De Mille replied.

Retakes takes made again of unsatisfactory material already shot and viewed in rough form.

Reverse angle shot a shot made in opposite direction, that is, *reversed,* from the preceding shot.

Reverse motion camera photographing with film running backward so that when projected the actions or movements appear in reverse sequence; important for special effects.

Riffle book (also **flip book** and **kineograph**) an early (1868) patented precursor of the motion picture in which a succession of parts of a movement are depicted on pages of a book so that by swiftly thumbing the pages, the viewer enjoys the illusion of a moving image.

"Roll it" (also **"roll 'em"**) a director's cue for the start of filming or projection of a film.

Rough cut print a first assembly of the total film in rough form and without music and dubbed sound effects.

Rough in arrangement and blocking of lighting on the set prior to shooting.

Running lines rehearsing dialogue.

Running shot a shot in which the camera moves or seems to move keeping up with a moving actor or object.

Running time the length of time a film will take to be projected at standard projection speed.

Rushes see **Dailies.**

Scenario (also **production script**) see **Script.**

Scene a series of **shots** taken at same setting or location from any number of camera angles and positions.

Scoring call assignment of musicians and conductor for purpose of recording the music track for a film.

Scoring stage special sound stage designed for scoring the music track of a film during projection of the sequences to be scored.

Screening showing a film.

Screenplay preproduction, written version of film including settings, scenes, characters, dialogue, and usually some indicated camera directions.

Scrim framed netting used in order to soften, diffuse, or eliminate light on the set.

Script (**shooting script**) a version of the screenplay as revised and prepared for production.

Script supervisor (also **script clerk**) keeps track of everything happening during shooting, that is, logs the shooting in terms of the shooting script; serves as reminder and prompter; prepares combined continuity when filming and editing are complete.

Second unit a self-contained production unit for the filming of scenes and sequences not requiring the director or principals of the cast.

Seconds assistants to the assistant director.

Sequence a number of scenes linked together by time, location, or narrative structure to form a unit of a motion picture.

Serials brief one- or two-reel films involving the same central characters, and presented on a continuing basis; traditionally each unit ending with an unresolved problem or situation (a cliffhanger) which is resolved at the outset of the next episode.

Series short films involving the same chief characters, and each film a complete episode in itself.

Set any place, exterior or interior, on location or in a studio, designated and prepared for shooting in the production of a film.

Set decorator furnishes and decorates the set.

Set dresser responsible for details of settings and locations during production.

Set painter   responsible for painting, maintaining, aging all painted parts of the set, also for eliminating reflections.

Setup   relationship between the location of the camera, the area of the set or scene, and the actors; a single camera position.

Set up shot   a shot involving little or no camera movement.

Shadowmakers   devices in many sizes and shapes used by cameramen to create shadows and to filter light.

Sharpness   the extent or relative degree in which details in a shot are presented with photographic clarity and definition; when details are clear and distinct, easily identified and perceived, they are said to be *sharp.*

Shoot   to film a shot, scene, sequence, or entire motion picture.

Shoot up/down   to shoot from a low angle or a high angle on the subject.

Shooting ratio   the ratio of film shot to the final footage of the completed film.

Shooting schedule   an advance schedule of work assignments, together with sets, cast, costumes, and equipment required.

Short   any standard film of less than 3,000 feet in length.

Shot   (1) a single continuous unit of film taken at one set and from one camera setup; (2) a single photograph or frame; (3) a notation of camera angle, distance, movement involved in one setup; (4) a printed **take;** editorially, any consecutive strip of frames; (5) **cut** is sometimes used for any shot or part of a take in editing.

Shotgun microphone   a special microphone designed to pick up and isolate particular sounds against a noisy background.

Shoulder brace   a strap and brace permitting the camera to rest on the operator's shoulder during shooting.

Skip framing   a laboratory simulation of accelerated motion; printing only a portion of the original negative frames gives effect of speeded-up action; opposite of **double framing,** which slows down action.

Slow motion   effect of slowing down natural action or rhythms; either by filming actions at faster rate than usual, then projecting at standard rate, or by optical effects in the laboratory.

Sneak preview   an unannounced trial showing of a new film before a regular theater audience.

Soft focus   effect derived from shooting slightly out of focus.

Sound   an integral part of all but silent films consisting of dialogue, music, and sound effects.

Sound boom   a boom for placing the recording microphone close to the actors in a scene.

Sound crew   all technicians on the set charged with the recording of dialogue and sounds and the dialing out of unwanted noise during shooting; a separate unit from the camera crew, but working in close coordination with them.

Sound effects editor   responsible for overseeing the preparation of separate tracks and for the final dubbing of the sound track.

Sound montage   use of dialogue, music, or sound effects to relate separate settings or sequences.

Special effects   technical tricks in photography or processing designed to create illusions; anything added to the film after shooting, in the laboratory or in editing.

Special effects expert   handles the design, mechanics, and engineering of any required special effects which cannot be created in camera or by laboratory.

Splicing   joining together separate pieces of processed film.

Split focus   maintaining sharp focus on two or more objects at different distances from the camera.

Split screen (also **half-wipe**)   frame in which two or more images are simultaneously seen.

Spotlight   any light which projects an intense and narrow beam.

Stand-in   an extra who takes the place of an actor during times of light arrangement and camera adjustment.

Star   a principal member of the cast with a leading dramatic role in the film; a major box-office attraction, not necessarily an actor or actress.

Static position   a setup in which the camera is in a fixed position and does not move or seem to move; for example, though actors move about within the frame or move out of the frame, the camera does not move with them or follow, but continues throughout the shot to shoot from an established angle, recording the same fixed frame.

Steal a shot   to photograph subjects who are not aware of being filmed.

Step outline (also **synopsis**)   a brief story outline indicating the dramatic structure of a screenplay yet to be written.

Stock shot (**stock footage**)   use of film not specifically photographed for the motion picture being produced.

Stop camera (also **stop photography**)   two separate camera operations film the same shot, the two shots becoming one shot in viewing.

Stop motion   exposure of one frame at a time.

Stop printing   the repetition of a single frame or image, created in laboratory, to **freeze** or stop action.

Story   preproduction, it is the narrative line of the script augmented by the storyboard; in filming and after, the story is the organization of shots and sequences into continuity.

Story analyst   a professional reader, preparing synopses and analyses of published material and recommending likely film properties.

Storyboard (also **continuity sketches**)   a preliminary, cartoon-strip form version, in sketches, prepared from the shooting script, breaking down action into a controlled sequence of possible shots.

Storyboard cards   graphic representation of important scenes, shot by shot, prepared in advance of shooting and including all pertinent information required for shooting.

Straight cut (also **direct cut**)   a cut called for where, by convention, another kind of editorial linking or transition might be expected.

Stretch out   a bus-type limousine for transportation to and from locations.

Structured rhythm (also **structural rhythm**)   generally applied to the overall sense of harmonious order of a film, deriving from the director's artistry and control; in film the elements are multiple, including and combining the basic narrative structure of the story, the patterns and arrangements of sound, music, and dialogue, the composition of light and shadow, the angles and movement of the camera, the editorial devices for separating and joining shots, scenes, and sequences; more specifically, structural rhythm in film refers to the purely visual aspects of the director's art, ranging from the composition of individual frames and shots to the relationships, established by likeness and contrast, of sequences, and their significance within the complete aesthetic experience of the film.

Studio driver   all-purpose professional vehicle driver; also drives cranes, fork-lifts, trucks, tractors.

Studio stock   wardrobe, props, and other materials in possession of a studio.

Stunt   any piece of action requiring the use of a professional stuntman.

Stunt coordinator   experienced stuntman who acts as foreman of any group of stuntmen.

Stunt double   a stuntman who bears a close photographic resemblance to a particular actor.

Stuntman   a professional performer of all potentially dangerous action—leaps, falls, horse falls, fights, fainting—in a film.

Subjective camera (also **subjective shots**)   shots created so that the audience views them as if from the literal or subjective point of view of a character; shots indicative of the filmmaker's feelings and attitudes towards characters, objects, events, when the process of filmmaking has been established, explicitly or implicitly, as part of the cinematic experience.

Subtitles   (1) in silent films, the insertion of printed dialogue, comment, and description into filmed scenes or between scenes on subtitle cards; (2) in foreign language films not dubbed into English, the use of white letters on some dark part of the frame to give a translation of dialogue; (3) any title other than the main title.

Sun gun   small, battery-powered unit used chiefly in documentary filming for night shooting, following a subject from exterior to interior, and as a fill light in sunlight.

Superimposition   two or more shots within the same frame, an effect achieved either by camera or in laboratory; may apply also to sounds on tracks.

Supers   direct superimposition of one scene over another, creating rhetorical effect of change which is slower than a cut but more rapid than a dissolve.

Supportive elements   the musical score, sound effects, voice-over dialogue, etc., which contribute to the primary elements (visual images and dialogue) of the film.

Survey   search for and establishment of the locations for various shots to be used in a film.

Swish-pan (also **whip shot**)   a rapid panning movement of the camera from one viewpoint or position of the set to another with the effect of blurring intermediate details in movement.

Sync dialogue track   basic sound track, consisting of all dialogue and noises recorded during filming and looping.

Synchronous sound   sound timed and simultaneous with visual images.

Tail slate   a slate held upside down, clapstick at bottom, used when it is necessary to identify a take at the *end* of shooting.

Take   each separate recording made of a shot while filming; a shot may consist of any number of takes; when any take is converted into a positive print from the negative, it becomes a **print**; also, in acting, a strong reaction.

Telephoto lens (also **true telephoto lens**)   a lens with an exceptionally long focal length, able to focus on a very narrow angle of a scene.

Tests   preliminary examinations, often by shooting film, prior to actual production, designed to check costumes (*wardrobe tests*), makeup, and talent (*screen tests*).

Theme   a musical sequence, analogous to *leitmotif*, associated in a film with a character, an action, a place; in film overall, the basic idea or subject of the film.

Thin   (1) in sound, a sound too weak or vague for its purpose; (2) in acting, a two-dimensional role; (3) in writing, a part of the narrative which is not strongly created or a character not sufficiently developed.

Tilt shot (**tilt up/tilt down**)   shot made by moving camera on its pivot or axis in a vertical plane.

Time lapse   regular exposure of single frames at long intervals in order to speed up slow action.

Title   any written or printed material used in the context of a film, as distinguished from the **main title** announcing the title of the film itself.

Titler   device for holding title cards, camera, and lights in proper relation to each other.

Tracking shots (also **trucking, travelling;** sometimes **dollying**)   shots in which a mobile camera, mounted on tracks, a truck or other vehicle, or a dolly, moves with the subject or moves towards or away from the subject of a shot.

Trailer (also **theatrical trailer**)   a short sequence of film used to advertise a feature film, and often derived from it, for theatrical showing.

Treatment   intermediate stage in development of script, basically narrative in form, between step outline and screenplay.

Trim   to cut or shorten in editing.

Trim can (also **out-take**)   a film can where marked and numbered frames, cut out of a sequence in editing, are kept.

Trims and outs   all frames of unused film left over at any stage of editing; these are stored in studio vaults for any possible future use.

Tripod   adjustable stand on which the camera may be mounted during shooting.

Trucking shot   loosely, any moving shot with camera on mobile mounting; strictly, a moving shot with camera mounted on a truck or van.

Two-shot   shot of two characters, the camera usually as close as possible while keeping both in the shot.

Typage acting   use of stock photographs from a film library of faces which, when cut into a dramatic sequence, seem to be reacting to the filmed situation and events.

Undershooting   filming sequences with too little footage to permit adequate editorial coverage.

Unit production manager   executive officer for the producer; from beginning is charged with execution of all the producer's plans, with budgeting, personnel, scheduling, picking locations, serving as manager and foreman for all crews and departments.

Ultra-slow motion   photography at a rate of 100 or more frames per second.

Unit still photographer   member of production staff responsible for taking all action, production, publicity, and art still photographs.

Utility man   lowest ranking titled member of a production crew; charged with running errands and general janitorial duties on the set.

Viewer   a small hand-held lens device with frame lines precisely fitting the subject to be shot, permitting the director and the cameraman to examine possible shots without having to move the camera; the camera operator also has a similar instrument attached to his camera.

Voice over (**VO**)   dialogue, comment, or narration coming from off-screen.

Wardrobe   department charged with all aspects of costumes and clothing.

Whip shot (also **zip pan**)   see **Swish pan.**

White out (opposite: **white in**)   opposite of a **fade out** or **in;** image becomes gradually lighter until screen goes white.

White telephone film   a type of film popular in the thirties, characterized by great luxury, opulent settings; often a musical film.

Wide angle lens   a lens of shorter focal length than is standard; creates an exaggerated perspective, increasing the apparent distance between the foreground and background of a shot.

Wigwag   an automatic red warning light which flashes outside the door of studio sound stages whenever sound is being recorded on the set.

Wild lines   dialogue not recorded on camera.

Wild sound (also **wild track**) any sound not recorded to synchronize precisely with the picture taken; may be recorded during shooting or separately.

Wild wall a removable wall on a set.

Wipe a link between two shots, both sharing the screen briefly before the second image replaces the first; there are a wide variety of possible wipes in terms of direction; a *half-wipe* is a split-screen effect; a *soft wipe* has a slightly blurred edge between the two cuts.

Work print (also **copy print, cutting copy**) any initial version of the uncompleted film used for editing, dubbing, preliminary screenings.

Wrangler a handler for horses used in a film.

Zoom (shot) a shot made by using a lens of varying focal lengths, permitting the change from wide angle to long lens or vice versa during an uninterrupted shot; camera can *zoom in* or *zoom out;* not as dimensional as an equivalent dolly shot with fixed lens but moving camera; *zoom in* effect can be simulated in laboratory with **optical zoom** in which an area of a frame can be progressively enlarged.

Zoom freeze a zoom shot ending with a **freeze,** or apparent still photograph.

Bibliography

Reference Works

Aaronson, Charles S. (ed.). *International Motion Picture Almanac* (annual). New York: Quigley, 1970.

Amberg, George (ed.). *The New York Times Film Reviews 1913–1970: A One Volume Selection*. New York: N.Y. Times, 1971.

Arneel, Gene (ed.). *The Film Daily Yearbook of Motion Pictures* (annual). New York: Film Daily, 1970.

Barnet, Sylvan, with Morton Berman and William Burto. *A Dictionary of Literary, Dramatic and Cinematic Terms*. Boston: Little, Brown, 1971.

Courtney, Winifred F. (ed.). *The Reader's Adviser: A Layman's Guide*. Vol. II. New York: Bowker, 1969.

Cowie, Peter (ed.). *International Film Guide* (annual). New York: Barnes, 1969.

Current Film Periodicals in English. New York: Adam Reilly, 1970. Lists more than 100 magazines and newspapers devoted to all aspects of film, with subscription information, description of contents, and information for writers.

Dimmitt, Richard B. *An Actor Guide to the Talkies*. Metuchen, N.J.: Scarecrow, 1967. 2 vols. Vol. 1 lists 8,000 films between 1949 and 1964 in alphabetical order. Typical entry gives title, date, and names of characters together with name of actor playing each. Vol. 2 is an alphabetical index of actors with a reference to each film in Vol. 1 in which the actor has played.

———. *A Title Guide to the Talkies*. Metuchen, N.J.: Scarecrow, 1965. 2 vols. Lists 16,000 feature films from 1927 to 1963 in alphabetical order. Typical entry gives date, company, director, and source.

Fordin, Hugh (ed.). *1970 Yearbook of Motion Pictures and Television.* New York: Arno, 1970.

Gottesman, Ronald and Harry M. Geduld. *Guidebook to Film: An Eleven-in-One Reference.* New York: Holt, Rinehart & Winston, 1972.

Greenfilder, Linda B. (ed.). *The American Film Institute's Guide to College Film Courses* (annual). Chicago: American Library Assoc., 1971.

Halliwell, Leslie. *The Filmgoer's Companion: Third Edition, Again Revised and Enlarged.* New York: Hill and Wang, 1970. A useful compendium of information listed alphabetically. Includes entries on actors, directors, individual films, etc., as well as larger topics and specialized movie terminology. Inevitably, each user will find omissions, but a very thorough listing of titles, credits, dates, awards, with helpful bibliography.

Jordan, Thurston C., Jr. *Glossary of Motion Picture Terminology.* Menlo Park, Calif.: Pacific Coast, 1968.

Kirkton, Carole M. (ed.). *Teacher Training Films: A Guide.* Urbana, Ill.: National Council of Teachers of English, 1971.

Levitan, Eli L. *An Alphabetical Guide to Motion Picture, Television, and Videotape Production.* New York: McGraw-Hill, 1970.

Limbacher, James. *Four Aspects of Film.* New York: Brussell, 1969.

McCarty, Clifford. *Published Screenplays: A Checklist.* Kent, Ohio: Kent State University, 1971.

Maynard, Richard. *The Celluloid Curriculum: An Educator's Guide to Movies in the Classroom.* New York: Hayden, 1971.

Michael, Paul (ed.). *The American Movies Reference Book: The Sound Era.* Englewood Cliffs: Prentice-Hall, 1969. Excellent illustrations. Nontechnical, but a very thorough listing of titles, credits, dates, awards, with helpful bibliography.

Munden, Kenneth W. (ed.). *The American Film Institute Catalog of Motion Pictures in the United States: Feature Films 1921–1930* (2 vols.). New York: Bowker, 1971.

Neverman, John (ed.). *International Directory of Back Issue Vendors: Periodicals, Newspapers and Documents.* New York: Special Libraries Association, 1968.

The New York Times Film Reviews, 1913–1968. 6 vols. New York: The New York Times, 1970.

Sarris, Andrew. *The American Cinema: Directors and Directions, 1929–* New York: Dutton, 1968. An entry for each director treated. Includes a list of his films with dates and brief (one to four pages) critical comment.

Schewer, Steven. *Movies On T.V., 1969–1970.* New York: Bantam, 1969.

Spottiswoode, Raymond (ed.). *The Focal Encyclopedia of Film and Television Techniques.* New York: Hastings House, 1969. Well illustrated with charts and drawings. Thorough and extremely useful.

Steele, Robert. *Cataloguing and Classification of Cinema Literature.* Metuchen, N.J.: Scarecrow, 1967.

Thompson, Howard (ed.). *The New York Times Guide To Movies On T.V.* Chicago: Quadrangle, 1970.

Wagner, Robert, and David Parker. *A Filmography of Films About Movies and Movie Making.* Rochester: Eastman Kodak, 1970.

Weber, Olga S. *Audiovisual Market Place* (annual). New York: Bowker, 1970.

The Yearbook of Motion Pictures. New York: *The Film Daily*, 1918–1957. A key source of statistics, survey articles, lists of films (with credits), awards, distributors, etc.

Zwerdling, Shirley (ed.). *Film & TV Festival Directory.* New York: Backstage, 1970.

Film Art, History

Alloway, Lawrence. *Violent America: The Movies 1946–1964.* New York: Museum of Modern Art, 1971.

Alpert, Hollis. *The Barrymores.* New York: Dial, 1964.

Altshuler, Thelma C. *Responses to Drama: An Introduction to Plays and Movies.* Boston: Houghton Mifflin, 1967.

Amelio, Robert, with Anita Owen and Susan Schaefer. *Willowbrook Cinema Study Project.* Dayton: Pflaum, 1970.

Anderson, Joseph L., and Donald Richie. *Japanese Film: Art and Industry.* New York: Grove, 1960.

Anobile, Richard (ed.). *Why A Duck?: The Marx Brothers' Greatest Scenes in Words and Pictures.* New York: Graphic Arts, 1971.

Armes, Roy. *The Cinema of Alain Resnais.* New York: Barnes, 1968.

———. *French Film.* New York: Dutton, 1970.

———. *Screen Series: French Cinema.* New York, Barnes, 1970.

Arnheim, Rudolf. *Film as Art.* Berkeley: University of California, 1957.

———. *Visual Thinking.* Berkeley: University of California, 1969.

Astor, Mary. *A Life on Film.* New York: Delacorte, 1971.

Bainbridge, John. *Garbo.* New York: Doubleday, 1955.

Balazs, Bêla. *Theory of the Film.* New York: Roy, 1953.

Balcon, Michael. *Twenty Years of British Films, 1925–1945.* Falcon, 1947.

Ball, Robert Hamilton. *Shakespeare on Silent Film.* New York: Theatre Arts, 1968.

Balshoffer, Fred J., and Arthur C. Miller. *One Reel a Week*. Berkeley: University of California, 1968.

Barbour, Alan G., with Alvin H. Marrill and James Robert Parish. *Karloff*. Kew Gardens, N.Y.: Cinefax, 1969.

―――. *Days of Thrills and Adventures: An affectionate pictorial history of the movie serial*. New York: Collier, 1971.

Bardeche, Maurice, and Robert Brasillach. *History of Motion Pictures*. New York: Norton, 1938.

Barker, Felix. *The Olivers*. London: Hamish Hamilton, 1953.

Barnouw, Erik, and S. Krishnaswamy. *Indian Film*. New York: Columbia University, 1963.

Barr, Charles. *Laurel and Hardy*. Berkeley: University of California, 1968.

Barry, Iris. *D. W. Griffith: American Film Master*. New York: Museum of Modern Art, 1965.

―――. *Let's Go to the Movies*. London: Payson & Clarke, 1926.

Battcock, Gregory. *The New American Cinema*. New York: Dutton, 1967.

Baxter, John. *Hollywood in the Thirties: A Complete Critical Survey of Hollywood Films from 1930–1940*. Paperback Library, 1970.

―――. *Science Fiction in the Cinema*. New York: Barnes, 1970.

―――. *Science Fiction in the Cinema: A Complete Critical Review of SF Films from A TRIP TO THE MOON (1902) to 2001: A SPACE ODYSSEY*. New York: Paperback Library, 1970.

―――. *The Gangster Film*. New York: Barnes, 1969; London: Zwemmer, 1971.

Bazin, André (tr. by Hugh Gray). *What is Cinema?* Berkeley: University of California, 1967.

Behimer, Rudy, with Terry-Thomas and Cliff McCarty. *The Films of Errol Flynn*. New York: Citadel, 1969.

Bellone, Julius (ed.). *Renaissance of the Film*. New York: Macmillan, 1970.

Bennett, Joan, and Lois Kibbee. *The Bennett Playbill*. New York: Holt, Rinehart and Winston, 1970.

Benoit-Lévy, Jean. *The Art of the Motion Picture*. New York: Coward-McCann, 1946.

Biberman, Herbert. *Salt of the Earth: The Story of a Film*. Boston: Beacon, 1965.

Blesh, Rudi. *Keaton*. New York: Macmillan, 1966.

Bluestone, George. *Novels into Film*. Berkeley: University of California, 1966.

Blum, Daniel, and John Kobal. *A New Pictorial History of the Talkies*. New York: Grosset & Dunlap, 1970.

Bobker, Lee. *Elements of Film*. New York: Harcourt, Brace & World, 1969.

Bogdanovich, Peter. *The Cinema of Alfred Hitchcock*. New York: Museum of Modern Art, 1963.

————. *The Cinema of Howard Hawks*. New York: Museum of Modern Art, 1962.

————. *The Cinema of Orson Welles*. New York: Museum of Modern Art, 1961.

————. *John Ford*. Berkeley: University of California, 1970.

Bowser, Eileen. *Film Notes*. New York: Museum of Modern Art, 1969.

Brodsky, Jack, and Nathan Weiss. *The Cleopatra Papers: A Private Correspondence*. New York: Simon and Schuster, 1963.

Brown, Frederick. *An Impersonation of Angels: A Biography of Jean Cocteau*. New York: Viking, 1968.

Brownlow, Kevin. *How It Happened Here*. New York: Doubleday, 1968.

————. *The Parade's Gone By*. New York: Alfred Knopf, 1968.

Bucher, Felix. *Germany*. London: Zwemmer, 1971.

Budgen, Suzanne. *Fellini*. London: British Film Institute, 1966.

Butler, Ivan. *Religion in the Cinema*. New York: Barnes, 1969.

————. *"To Encourage the Art of the Film": The Story of the British Film Institute*. London: Robert Hale, 1971.

————. *Cinema of Roman Polanski*. New York: Barnes, 1970.

————. *The Horror Film*. New York: Barnes, 1967.

Calder-Marshall, Arthur. *The Innocent Eye: The Life of Robert J. Flaherty*. New York: Harcourt, Brace & World, 1963.

Callenbach, Ernest. *Our Modern Art: The Movies*. Chicago: Center for the Study of Liberal Education for Adults, 1955.

Cameron, Ian (ed.). *The Films of Jean-Luc Goddard*. New York: Praeger, 1970.

————. *The Films of Robert Bresson*. New York: Praeger, 1970.

————. *Second Wave*. New York: Praeger, 1970.

————, and Elizabeth Cameron. *Dames*. New York: Praeger, 1969.

————, and Robin Wood. *Antonioni*. New York: Praeger, 1969.

Capra, Frank. *The Name Above the Title.* New York: Macmillan, 1971.

Carey, Gary. *Lost Films*. New York: Museum of Modern Art, 1970.

————. *Cukor & Co.: The Films of George Cukor and His Collaborators*. New York: Museum of Modern Art, 1971.

Carmen, Ira H. *Movies, Censorship, and the Law*. Ann Arbor: University of Michigan, 1966.

Carr, Larry. *Four Fabulous Faces*. New York: Arlington House, 1971.

Carrick, Edward. *Art and Design in the British Film*. London: Dennis Dobson, 1948.

Casty, Alan Howard. *The Dramatic Art of Film*. New York: Harper & Row, 1970.

————. *The Films of Robert Rossen*. New York: Museum of Modern Art, 1969.

Cavell, Stanley. *The World Viewer: Reflections on the Ontology of Film.* New York: Viking, 1971.

Ceram, C. W. *Archaeology of the Cinema.* New York: Harcourt, Brace & World, 1965.

Chaplin, Charles. *My Autobiography.* New York: Simon and Schuster, 1966.

Chaplin, Charles, Jr., with N. and M. Rau. *My Father, Charlie Chaplin.* New York: Random House, 1960.

Christian, Linda. *Linda: My Own Story.* New York: Crown, 1962.

Clair, René. *Reflections on the Cinema.* London: Kimber, 1953.

Clarens, Carlos. *Horror Movies.* Berkeley: University of California, 1968.

———. *An Illustrated History of the Horror Film.* New York: Putnam, 1967.

Cocteau, Jean. *Cocteau on the Film.* New York: Roy, 1954.

———. *On the Film.* Chester Springs, Pa.: Dufour, 1954.

Contemporary Polish Cinematography. Warsaw: Polonia, 1962.

Conway, Michael, and Mark Ricci. *The Films of Marilyn Monroe.* New York: Citadel, 1964.

———, Dion McGregor, and Mark Ricci. *The Films of Greta Garbo.* Introduced by Parker Tyler. New York: Citadel, 1963.

———, and Mark Ricci. *The Films of Jean Harlow.* New York: Citadel, 1965.

Cooke, Alistair. *Douglas Fairbanks, the Making of a Screen Character.* New York: Museum of Modern Art, 1940.

———. *Garbo and the Night Watchmen.* London: Cape, 1937.

Cooper, John C., and Carl Skrade (eds.). *Celluloid and Symbols.* Philadelphia: Fortress, 1970.

Coorey, Philip. *The Lonely Artist: A Critical Introduction to the Films of Lester James Peries.* Ceylon: Lake House, 1971.

Coplans, John (with essays by Calvin Tompkins and Jonas Mekas). *Andy Warhol.* New York: Grove, 1970.

Cotes, Peter, and Thelma Niklaus. *The Little Fellow: The Life and Works of Charlie Chaplin.* New York: Citadel, 1965.

Cowie, Peter. *The Cinema of Orson Welles.* New York: Barnes, 1965.

———. *International Film Guide, 1964.* New York: Barnes, 1965.

———. *International Film Guide, 1965.* New York: Barnes, 1966.

——— (ed.). *Concise History of The Cinema* (2 vols.). London: Zwemmer, 1971.

———. *Sweden 1.* London: Tantivy, 1971.

———. *Sweden 2.* London: Tantivy, 1971.

———. *Screen Series: Sweden.* New York: Barnes, 1970.

———. *Seventy Years of Cinema.* New York: Barnes, 1969.

———. *Three Monographs: Antonioni, Bergman, Resnais.* New York: Barnes, 1963.

Crone, Ranier. *Andy Warhol.* New York: Praeger, 1970.

Crowther, Bosley. *The Lion's Share.* New York: Dutton, 1957.

————. *Movies and Censorship.* New York: Public Affairs Committee, 1962.

Culkin, Jon. *Julius Caesar: As a Play and As a Film.* New York: Scholastic Books, 1963.

Curtis, David. *Experimental Cinema.* New York: Universe, 1971.

Curtiss, Thomas Quinn. *Von Stroheim.* New York: Farrar, Straus & Giroux, 1971.

Davies, Hunter. *The Beatles: The Authorized Biography.* New York: McGraw-Hill, 1968.

Davy, Charles (ed.). *Footnotes to the Film.* Oxford, 1937.

De Bartolo, Dick (illus. by Jack Davis). *The Return Of A Mad Look At Old Movies.* New York: New American Library, 1970.

De Mille, Cecil B. (ed. by Donald Harper). *Autobiography.* Englewood Cliffs, N.J.: Prentice-Hall, 1959.

de Mille, William C. *Hollywood Saga.* New York: Dutton, 1939.

Deming, Barbara. *Running Away From Myself: A Dream Portrait of America Drawn from the Films of the Forties.* New York: Grossman, 1969.

Deschner, Donald. *The Films of Spencer Tracy.* New York: Citadel, 1969, 1972.

Deren, Maya. *An Anagram of Ideas on Art, Form, and Film.* Yonkers, N.Y.: Alicat Book Shop, 1946.

Dickens, Homer. *The Films of Gary Cooper.* New York: Citadel, 1970.

————. *The Films of Marlene Dietrich.* New York: Citadel, 1969.

————. *The Films of Katharine Hepburn.* New York: Citadel, 1971.

Dickinson, Thorold, and Catherine De la Roche. *Soviet Cinema.* London: Falcon, 1948.

Dimmitt, Richard B. *Actor's Guide to the Talkies.* 2 vols. Metuchen, N.J.: Scarecrow, 1967.

————. *Title Guide to the Talkies.* 2 vols. Metuchen, N.J.: Scarecrow, 1965.

Dolan, Robert Emmet. *Music in the Modern Media.* New York: G. Schirmer, 1967.

Donner, Jorn. *The Personal Vision of Ingmar Bergman.* Bloomington: Indiana University, 1964.

Douglass, Drake. *Horror.* New York: Collier Books, 1969.

Dunne, John Gregory. *The Studio: A Cinéma Vérité Study of Hollywood at Work.* New York: Farrar, Straus & Giroux, 1968.

Durgnat, Raymond. *The Crazy Mirror: Hollywood Comedy and the American Image.* New York: Horizon, 1969.

————. *A Mirror For England: British Movies From Austerity To Affluence.* London: Faber & Faber, 1971.

————. *Eros in the Cinema*. New York: Fernhill, 1966.

————. *Films and Feelings*. Cambridge, Mass.: M.I.T., 1967.

————. *Luis Buñuel*. Berkeley: University of California, 1970.

————. *Nouvelle Vague: The First Decade*. Loughton (Essex), Eng.: Motion Publications, 1966.

————, and John Kobal. *Greta Garbo*. New York: Dutton Pictureback, 1965.

Eisenstein, Sergei M. *Film Form*. New York: Harcourt, Brace, 1949. Paperback by Meridian, New York, 1957.

————. *The Film Sense*. New York: Harcourt, Brace, 1942. Paperback by Meridian, New York, 1957.

———— (ed. by Jay Leyda). *Film Essays and a Lecture*. New York: Praeger, 1970.

Eisner, Lotte H. (tr. by Roger Greaves). *The Haunted Screen: Expressionism in the German Cinema and the Influence of Max Reinhart*. Berkeley: University of California, 1969.

Elton, Arthur, and Peter Bunson. *The Film Industry in Six European Countries*. Paris: UNESCO, 1950.

Enser, G. S. *Filmed Books and Plays, 1928–1967*. New York: British Book Centre, 1969.

Essoe, Gabe. *The Films of Clark Gable*. New York: Citadel, 1969.

————. *Tarzan of the Movies: A Pictorial History of More Than Fifty Years of Edgar Rice Burroughs' Legendary Hero*. New York: Citadel, 1968.

An Evaluative Guide to Films on Jobs, Training and the Ghetto. New York: American Foundations on Automation and Employment, 1970.

Everson, William K. *The American Movie*. New York: Atheneum, 1963.

————. *The Bad Guys: A Pictorial History of the Movie Villain*. New York: Citadel, 1964.

————. *The Films of Laurel and Hardy*. New York: Citadel, 1969.

————. *A Pictorial History of the Western Film*. New York: Citadel, 1969.

————. *The Art of W. C. Fields*. New York: Merrill, 1967.

Eyles, Allen. *The Marx Brothers: Their World of Comedy*. New York: Barnes, 1966.

————. *The Western: An Illustrated Guide*. New York: Barnes, 1963.

Farber, Manny. *Manny Farber's America*. New York: Chelsea House, 1965.

Fast, Julius. *The Beatles: The Real Story*. New York: Putnam, 1968.

Feldman, Joseph, and Harry Feldman. *Dynamics of the Film*. New York: Hermitage, 1952.

Fenin, George N., and William K. Everson. *The Western*. New York: Orion, 1962.

Fensch, Thomas. *Films on the Campus*. New York: Barnes, 1970.

Feyen, Sharon. *Screen Experience: An Approach to Film*. Dayton: Pflaum, 1970.

Field, R. D. *The Art of Walt Disney*. New York: Macmillan, 1942.

Films 1968: A Comprehensive Review of the Year. New York: Catholic Office for Motion Pictures, 1968.

Film Teaching. London: British Film Institute, 1964.

Finkler, Joel. *Stroheim.* Berkeley: University of California, 1970.

Fischer, Edward. *The Screen Arts.* New York: Sheed and Ward, 1960.

Five Catalogues of the Public Auction of the Countless Treasures Acquired From Metro-Goldwyn-Mayer. 5 vols. Los Angeles: David Weisz, 1970.

Flaherty, Frances H. *The Odyssey of a Filmmaker: Robert Flaherty's Story.* Urbana: University of Illinois, 1960.

Ford, Charles. *Histoire du Western.* Paris: Pierre Horay, 1964.

Franklin, Joe. *Classics of the Silent Screen: A Pictorial Treasury.* New York: Bramhall House, 1959.

Fredrik, Nathalie. *Hollywood and the Academy Awards.* Beverly Hills, Calif.: Hollywood Awards Pub., 1971.

Fulton, A. R. *Motion Pictures: The Development of an Art Form From Silent Films to the Age of Television.* Norman: University of Oklahoma, 1960.

Geduld, Harry M. (ed.). *Focus on D. W. Griffith.* Englewood Cliffs, N.J.: Prentice-Hall, 1971.

————, and Ronald Gottesman (eds.), *Sergei Eisenstein and Upton Sinclair: The Making and Unmaking of Que Viva Mexico.* London: Thames and Hudson, 1971.

Gessner, Robert. *The Moving Image: A Guide to Cinematic Literacy.* New York: Dutton, 1970.

Getlein, Frank, and Harold C. Gardiner, S.J. *Movies, Morals, and Art.* New York: Sheed and Ward, 1961.

Giannetti, Louis D. *Understanding Movies.* Englewood Cliffs, N.J.: Prentice-Hall, 1972.

Gibson, Arthur. *The Silence of God: Creative Response to the Films of Ingmar Bergman.* New York: Harper & Row, 1969.

Gidal, Peter. *Andy Warhol: Films and Paintings.* New York: Dutton, 1971.

Gifford, Denis. *British Cinema—An Illustrated Guide.* New York: Barnes, 1968.

————. *Science Fiction Film.* New York: Dutton, 1971.

Gilson, Rene. *Jean Cocteau.* New York: Crown, 1969.

Gish, Lillian (with Ann Pinchot). *The Movies, Mr. Griffith and Me.* Englewood Cliffs: Prentice-Hall, 1969.

Glucksmann, André. *Violence on the Screen.* London: British Film Institute, 1970.

Goodman, Ezra. *The Fifty Year Decline and Fall of Hollywood.* New York: Simon and Schuster, 1961.

————. *Bogey: The Good-Bad Guy.* New York: Lyle Stuart, 1965.

Gottesman, Ronald (ed.). *Focus on Citizen Kane.* Englewood Cliffs, N.J.: Prentice-Hall, 1971.

Gow, Gordon. *Suspense in the Cinema.* New York: Barnes, 1968.

————. *Hollywood In The Fifties*. London: Zwemmer, 1971.

Graham, Peter. *A Dictionary of the Cinema*. New York: Barnes, 1964.

————. *New Wave: Critical Landmark*. New York: Doubleday, 1968.

Graham, Sheilah. *Confessions of a Hollywood Columnist*. New York: Morrow, 1969.

————. *The Garden of Allah*. New York: Crown, 1970.

Green, Abel, and Joe Laurie, Jr. *Show Biz*. New York: Holt, 1951.

Grierson, John. *Grierson on Documentary*. Berkeley: University of California, 1970.

Griffith, Mrs. D. W. *When the Movies Were Young*. New York: Dutton, 1925.

Griffith, Richard. *The Cinema of Gene Kelly*. New York: Museum of Modern Art, 1962.

————. *Fred Zinneman*. New York: Museum of Modern Art, 1958.

————. *Marlene Dietrich: Image and Legend*. New York: Museum of Modern Art, 1959.

————. *The Movie Stars*. New York: Doubleday, 1970.

————. *Samuel Goldwyn: The Producer and His Films*. New York: Museum of Modern Art, 1956.

————. *The World of Robert Flaherty*. London: Gollancz, 1953.

————, and Arthur Mayer. *The Movies*. New York: Simon and Schuster, 1957.

————, and Paul Rotha. *The Film Till Now*. New York: Funk and Wagnalls, 1949.

Guarner, Jose Luis. *Rossellini*. New York: Praeger, 1970.

Guback, Thomas H. *The International Film Industry: Western Europe and America Since 1945*. Bloomington: Indiana University, 1970.

Guild, Lee. *Zanuck: Hollywood's Last Tycoon*. Los Angeles: Holloway, 1970.

Guiles, Fred Lawrence. *Norma Jean: The Life of Marilyn Monroe*. New York: McGraw-Hill, 1969.

Halas, John, and Roger Manvell. *Design in Motion*. New York: Hastings House, 1962.

Hall, Stuart, and Paddy Whannel. *The Popular Arts*. New York: Pantheon, 1965.

Hampton, Benjamin B. *A History of the Movies*. New York: Covici, Friede, 1931.

Handel, Leo A. *Hollywood Looks at Its Audience: A Report of Film Audience Research*. Urbana: University of Illinois, 1950.

Harding, James. *Sacha Guitry: The Last Boulevardier*. New York: Scribner, 1968.

Hardy, Forsyth. *Scandinavian Film*. London: Falcon, 1952.

Hardy, Phil. *Samuel Fuller*. New York: Praeger, 1970.

Henderson, Robert M. *D. W. Griffith: The Years at Biograph*. New York: Farrar, Straus & Giroux, 1970.

Hendricks, Gordon. *The Edison Motion Picture Myth*. Berkeley: University of California, 1970.

Henri, Jim. *The World's Most Sensual Films*. Chicago: Merit Books, 1965.

Heyer, Robert, and Anthony Meyer. *Discovery in Film*. Paramus, N.J.: Paulist, 1969.

Hibbin, Nina. *Screen Series: Eastern Europe*. New York: Barnes, 1970.

————. *Eastern Europe*. London: Tantivy, 1970.

Higham, Charles. *Hollywood in the Forties*. New York: Barnes, 1968.

————, and Joel Greenberg. *Hollywood In The Forties: A Complete Critical Survey of Hollywood Films 1940–1950*. New York: Paperback Library, 1970.

Hill, Norman (ed.). *The Lonely Beauties*. New York: Popular Library, 1971.

Hodgkinson, Anthony W. *Screen Education*. New York: UNESCO, 1963.

Hofmann, Charles. *Sounds for Silents*. New York: D. B. S. Publications, 1970.

Houston, Penelope. *The Contemporary Cinema*. Baltimore: Penguin, 1963.

Huaco, George. *The Sociology of Film Art*. New York: Basic Books, 1965.

Huettig, Mae D. *Economic Control of the Motion Picture Industry*. Philadelphia: University of Pennsylvania, 1944.

Huff, Theodore. *Charlie Chaplin*. New York: Schuman, 1951.

Hughes, Robert (ed.). *Film Book 1*. New York: Grove, 1959.

———— (ed.). *Film: Book II—Films of Peace and War*. New York: Grove, 1962.

Hull, David Stewart. *Films in the Third Reich*. Berkeley: University of California, 1969.

Hunnings, Neville. *Film Censors and the Law*. New York: Hillary, 1967.

Huss, Roy, and Norman Silverstein. *The Film Experience: Elements of Motion Picture Art*. New York: Harper & Row, 1968.

———— (eds.). *Focus On "Blow Up."* Englewood Cliffs, N.J.: Prentice-Hall, 1972.

Isaksson, Folke, and Leif Furhammar. *Politics and Film*. London: November Books, 1970.

Ivens, Joris. *The Camera and I*. New York: International Publishers, 1969.

Jacobs, Lewis. *The Rise of the American Film*. New York: Teachers College, Columbia University, 1967.

———— (ed.). *The Emergence of Film Art*. New York: Hopkinson and Blake, 1969.

————. *Introduction to the Art of the Movies*. New York: Noonday, 1960.

———— (ed.). *The Movies As Medium*. New York: Farrar, Straus & Giroux, 1970.

Jarratt, Vernon. *The Italian Cinema*. New York: Macmillan, 1951.

Jarvie, I. C. *Movies and Society*. New York: Basic Books, 1970.

Jensen, Paul. *The Cinema of Fritz Lang*. New York: Barnes, 1969.

————, and Arthur Lennig. *Karloff and Lugosi: Titans of Terror.* New York: Atheneum, 1971.

Jobes, Gertrude. *Motion Picture Empire.* Hamden, Conn.: Archon, 1966.

Jones, Ken D., with Arthur F. McClure and Alfred E. Twomey. *The Films of James Stewart.* New York: Barnes, 1970.

Kahn, Gordon. *Hollywood on Trial.* New York: Boni and Gaer, 1948.

Kanin, Garson. *Tracy and Hepburn: An Intimate Memoir.* New York: Viking, 1972.

Kirschner, Allen, and Linda Kirschner. *Film: Readings in the Mass Media.* New York: Odyssey, 1971.

Kitses, Jim. *Horizons West: Anthony Mann, Budd Boetticher, Sam Peckinpah: Studies of Authorship Within the Western.* Bloomington: Indiana University, 1970.

Knef, Hildegard (tr. David Cameron Palastanga). *The Gift Horse.* New York: McGraw-Hill, 1971.

Knight, Arthur. *The Liveliest Art: A Panoramic History of the Movies.* New York: Macmillan, 1957.

Kobal, John. *Gotta Sing Gotta Dance: A Pictorial History of Film Musicals.* New York: Hamlyn, 1971.

————. *Marlene Dietrich.* New York: Dutton, 1968.

Kracauer, Siegfried. *From Caligari to Hitler.* New York: Noonday, 1959.

————. *Theory of Film.* New York: Oxford University, 1960. Paperback by Galaxy, New York, 1965.

Kuhns, William. *Themes: Short Films for Discussion.* Dayton: Pflaum, 1970.

————, and Thomas F. Giardino. *Behind the Camera.* Dayton: Pflaum, 1970.

————, and Robert Stanley. *Teaching Program: Exploring the Film.* Dayton: Pflaum, 1970.

————, and Robert Stanley. *Exploring the Film.* Dayton: Pflaum, 1970.

Kyrou, Ado (tr. by Adrienne Foulke). *Luis Buñuel.* New York: Simon and Schuster, 1963.

Lahue, Kalton C. *Collecting Classic Films.* New York: Amphoto, 1970.

————. *Continued Next Week.* Norman: University of Oklahoma, 1964.

————. *A World of Laughter: The Motion Picture Comedy Short, 1910–1930.* Norman: University of Oklahoma, 1966.

————. *Ladies In Distress.* New York: Barnes, 1971.

Larsen, Otto N. *Violence and the Mass Media.* New York: Harper & Row, 1970.

Latham, Aaron. *Crazy Sundays: F. Scott Fitzgerald in Hollywood.* New York: Viking, 1970.

Lauritzen, Einar. *Swedish Films.* New York: Museum of Modern Art, 1962.

LaValley, Albert J. (ed.). *Focus on Hitchcock.* Englewood Cliffs, N.J.: Prentice-Hall, 1971.

Lawson, John Howard. *Film: The Creative Process.* New York: Hill and Wang, 1964.

————. *Film in the Battle of Ideas.* New York: Mainstream, 1953.

Leahy, James. *The Cinema of Joseph Losey.* New York: Barnes, 1967.

Lebel, J. P. (tr. by P. D. Stovin). *Buster Keaton.* New York: Barnes, 1967.

Lee, Raymond. *Fit for the Chase: Cars and the Movies.* New York: Barnes, 1969.

————. *The Films of Mary Pickford.* New York: Barnes, 1970.

————, and Gabe Essoe. *De Mille: The Man and His Pictures.* New York: Barnes, 1970.

————, and B. C. Van Hecke. *Gangsters and Hoodlums.* New York: Barnes, 1970.

————, and Manuel Weltman. *Pearl White: The Peerless, Fearless Girl.* New York: Barnes, 1970.

Leprohon, Pierre. *Michelangelo Antonioni.* New York: Simon and Schuster, 1963.

Levin, Martin (ed.). *Hollywood and the Great Fan Magazines.* New York: Arbor House, 1970.

Leyda, Jay. *Kino: A History of the Russian and Soviet Film.* New York: Hillary and House, 1960.

Limbacher, James I. *Using Films: A Handbook for the Program Planner.* New York: Educational Film, 1967.

Linden, George. *Reflections on the Screen.* Belmont, Calif.: Wadsworth, 1970.

Lindgren, Ernest. *The Art of the Film.* New York: Macmillan, 1948. 3rd ed. 1968.

————. *The Cinema.* New York: Macmillan, 1960.

————. *Picture History of the Cinema.* Chester Springs, Pa.: Dufour, n.d.

Lindsay, Vachel. *The Art of the Moving Picture.* Introduction by Stanley Kauffmann. New York: Liveright, 1970.

Low, Rachel. *The History of the British Film (1896–1906, 1906–14, 1914–18).* London: Allen & Unwin, 1948–50.

————. *The History of the British Film: 1918–1929.* London: Allen & Unwin, 1971.

Lynch, William F., S.J. *The Image Industries.* New York: Sheed and Ward, 1959.

MacCann, Richard Dyer. *Film and Society.* New York: Scribner's, 1964.

————. *Hollywood in Transition.* Boston: Houghton Mifflin, 1962.

———— (ed.). *Film: A Montage of Theories.* New York: Dutton, 1966.

MacLaine, Shirley. *Don't Fall Off the Mountain.* New York: Norton, 1970.

Madsen, Axel. *Billy Wilder.* Bloomington: Indiana University, 1969.

Malerba, Luigi, and Carmine Sinscalco (eds.). *Fifty Years of Italian Cinema.* Rome: Carlo Besteti, 1954.

Maltin, Leonard. Movie Comedy Teams. New York: New American Library, 1970.

————. *TV Movies.* New York: New American Library, 1969.

Manoogian, Haig P. *The Film-Maker's Art.* New York: Basic Books, 1966.

Manfull, Helen (ed.). *Additional Dialogue: Letters of Dalton Trumbo, 1942–1962*. New York: M. Evans, 1970.

Manvell, Roger. *The Film and the Public*. Baltimore: Penguin, 1955.

———. *Films*. Harmondsworth (Middlesex), Eng.: Penguin, 1950.

———. *The Living Screen*. London: Harrap, 1936.

———. *New Cinema in Europe*. New York: Dutton, 1965.

———. *New Cinema in the USA: The Feature Film Since 1946*. New York: Dutton Picturebacks, 1968.

———. *Shakespeare and the Film*. London: Dent, 1971.

———, and Heinrich Fraenkel. *The German Cinema*. London: Dent, 1971.

———, and John Huntley. *Technique of Film Music*. New York: Hastings House, 1957.

———. *What Is a Film?* London: Macdonald, 1965.

——— (ed.). *Experiment in the Film*. London: Grey Wall, 1949.

Mast, Gerald. *A Short History of the Movies*. New York: Pegasus, 1971.

Matthews, J. H. *Surrealism and Film*. Ann Arbor, Mich.: University of Mich., 1971.

Mayer, Arthur. *Merely Colossal: The Story of the Movies From the Long Chase to the Chaise Lounge*.

Mayer, Jacob P. *Sociology of Film: Studies and Documents*. London: Faber and Faber, 1946.

Mayersberg, Paul. *Hollywood the Haunted House*. New York: Stein and Day, 1968.

McBride, Joseph (ed.). *Persistence of Vision*. Madison: Wisconsin Film Society, 1968.

McCaffrey, Donald W. (ed.). *Focus On Chaplin*. Englewood Cliffs, N.J.: Prentice-Hall, 1972.

———. *Four Great Comedians: Chaplin, Lloyd, Keaton and Langdon*. New York: Barnes, 1968.

McCrindle, Joseph F. (ed.). *Behind the Scenes: Theater and Film Interviews from "The Transatlantic Review."* New York: Holt, Rinehart and Winston, 1971.

McDonald, Gerald, with Michael Conway and Mark Ricci (eds.). *The Films of Charlie Chaplin*. New York: Crown, 1965.

McGuire, Jerimiah. *Cinema and Value Philosophy*. New York: Philosophical Library, 1968.

McKowen, Clark, and William Sparke. *It's Only a Movie*. Englewood Cliffs, N.J.: Prentice-Hall, 1971.

McVay, J. Douglas. *The Musical Film*. New York: Barnes, 1968.

Michael, Paul. *The Academy Awards: A Pictorial History*. New York: Bonanza Books, 1964.

———. *The American Movies Reference Book: The Sound Era*. New York: Prentice-Hall, 1969.

———. *Humphrey Bogart: The Man and His Films*. Indianapolis: Bobbs-Merrill, 1965.

Milne, Tom (ed.). *Losey On Losey*. New York: Doubleday, 1968.

————. *The Cinema of Carl Dreyer*. New York: Barnes, 1970; London: Zwemmer, 1971.

Minus, Johnny, and William Storm Hale. *The Movie Industry Book: How Others Made and Lost Money in the Movie Industry*. Hollywood: Seven Arts, 1970.

Montagu, Ivor. *Film World: A Guide to Cinema*. Baltimore: Penguin, 1965.

————. *With Eisenstein in Hollywood*. New York: International Publishers, 1969.

Morella, Joe, and Edward Epstein. *Judy*. Introduction by Judith Crist. New York: Citadel, 1969.

————, Joe and Edward Z. Epstein. *Lana: The Public and Private Lives of Miss Turner*. New York: Citadel, 1971.

————, Joe and Edward Z. Epstein. *Rebels: The Rebel Hero in Films*. New York: Citadel, 1971.

Morin, Edgar (tr. by Richard Howard). *The Stars*. New York: Grove, 1960.

Moussinac, Leon (tr. by D. Sandy Petrey). *Sergei Eisenstein*. New York: Crown, 1970.

Munsterberg, Hugo. *The Photoplay, a Psychological Study*. New York: Appleton, 1916.

Murphy, George (with Victor Lasky). *Say . . . Didn't You Used to Be George Murphy?* New York: Bartholomew House, 1970.

Murray, Ken. *Golden Days at San Simeon*. New York: Doubleday, 1971.

Museum of Modern Art Film Library. *Film Notes, Part I, The Silent Film*. New York: Museum of Modern Art, 1949.

Mussman, Toby (ed.). *Jean-Luc Goddard*. New York: Dutton, 1968.

Neergaard, Ebbe. *Carl Dreyer: A Film Director's Work*. London: British Film Institute, 1950.

Negri, Pola. *Memoirs Of A Star*. New York: Doubleday, 1970.

Nemcek, Paul. *The Films Of Nancy Carrol*. New York: Lyle Stuart, 1970.

Nemeskurty, Istvan. *Word and Image*. Budapest: Corvina, 1969.

Nicoll, Allardyce. *Film and Theatre*. New York: Crowell, 1936.

Nilsen, Vladimir. *Cinema as Graphic Art*. New York: Hill and Wang, 1959.

Nitsch, Hermann. *Orgies Mysteries Theatre*. Darmstadt: Marz Verlag, 1969.

Niven, David. *The Moon's a Balloon*. New York: Putnam, 1972.

Nizhny, Vladimir. *Lessons With Eisenstein*. New York: Hill and Wang, 1963.

Nowell-Smith, Geoffrey. *Luchino Visconti*. New York: Doubleday, 1968.

Null, Gary. *Black Hollywood: The Negro in Motion Pictures*. New York: Citadel, 1971.

O'Dell, Paul. *Griffith And The Rise of Hollywood*. London: Zwemmer, 1971.

O'Leary, Liam. *The Silent Cinema*. New York: Dutton, 1965.

Osborne, Robert. *Academy Awards*. New York: Schwords, 1969.

Parish, James Robert. *The Fox Girls: starring 15 beautiful vixens and one adorable cub.* New York: Arlington House, 1971.

Pate, Michael. *The Film Actor.* New York: Barnes, 1970.

Payne, Robert. *The Great God Pan.* New York: Hermitage House, 1952.

Pechter, William S. *Twenty-four Times a Second.* New York: Harper & Row, 1970, 1971.

Pensel, Hans. *Seastrom and Stiller in Hollywood.* New York: Vantage, 1970.

Peters, J. M. L. *Teaching About the Film.* New York: UNESCO, 1961.

Perry, George. *The Films of Alfred Hitchcock.* New York: Dutton Picturebacks, 1965.

Playboy's Sex In Cinema 1970. Chicago: MHM Publishing, 1971.

Powdermaker, Hortense. *Hollywood, the Dream Factory.* Boston: Little, Brown, 1950.

Pratley, Gerald. *The Cinema of Otto Preminger.* London: Zwemmer, 1971.

———. *The Cinema of John Frankenheimer.* New York: Barnes, 1970.

Quigley, Martin, Jr. *Magic Shadows: The Story of the Origin of Motion Pictures.* Washington, D.C.: Georgetown University, 1948.

———, and Richard Gertner. Films in America. New York: Golden Press, 1970.

Quirk, Lawrence J. *The Films of Fredric March.* New York: Citadel, 1971.

———. *The Films of Ingrid Bergman.* New York: Citadel, 1971.

———. *The Films of Joan Crawford.* New York: Citadel, 1969.

———. *The Films of Paul Newman.* New York: Citadel, 1971.

Ramsaye, Terry. *A Million and One Nights.* New York: Simon and Schuster, 1926.

Randall, Richard S. *Censorship of the Movies.* Madison: University of Wisconsin, 1968.

Ray, Man. *Self Portrait.* London: Andre Deutsch, 1963.

Reed, Rex. *Conversations in the Raw: Dialogues, Monologues, and Selected Short Subjects.* New York: World, 1970.

———. *Do You Sleep in the Nude?* New York: New American Library, 1969.

Renan, Sheldon. *An Introduction to the American Underground Film.* New York: Dutton, 1967.

Rhode, Eric. *Tower of Babel: Speculations on the Cinema.* New York: Chilton, 1967.

Ricci, Mark, and Steve Zmvewshy. *The Films of John Wayne.* New York: Citadel, 1970.

Richardson, Robert. *Literature and Film.* Bloomington: Indiana University, 1969.

Richie, Donald. *The Films of Akira Kurosawa.* Berkeley: University of California, 1970.

———. *Illustrated History of Japanese Movies.* Rutland, Vt.: Japan Pub. Trading Co., 1965.

———. *Japanese Movies.* Rutland, Vt.: Japan Pub. Trading Co., 1961.

———. *George Stevens: An American Romantic.* New York: Museum of Modern Art, 1970.

Ringgold, Gene (with DeWitt Bodeen). *The Films of Cecil B. De Mille.* New York: Citadel, 1969.

Rissover, Fredric. *Mass Media and The Popular Arts.* New York: McGraw-Hill, 1971.

Robinson, David. *Buster Keaton.* Bloomington: Indiana University, 1969.

———. *The Great Funnies.* New York: Dutton, 1968.

———. *Hollywood in the Twenties.* New York: Barnes, 1968.

———. *Hollywood in the Twenties: A Complete Critical Survey of Hollywood Films from 1920–1930.* New York: Paperback Library, 1970.

Robinson, W. R. (ed.). *Man and the Movies.* Baltimore: Penguin, 1969.

Rondi, Gian L. *Italian Cinema Today.* New York: Hill and Wang, 1965.

Rosenberg, Bernard, and Harry Silverstein. *The Real Tinsel.* New York: Macmillan, 1970.

Rosenthal, Alan. *The New Documentary in Action: A Casebook in Filmmaking.* Berkeley: University of California, 1971.

Ross, Lillian. *Picture.* New York: Rinehart, 1952.

———, and Helen Ross. *The Player: A Profile of an Art.* New York: Simon and Schuster, 1962.

Ross, T. J. (ed.). *Film and the Liberal Arts.* New York: Holt, Rinehart and Winston, 1970.

Rotha, Paul. *Rotha on the Film.* New York: Oxford University, 1958.

Roud, Richard. *Godard.* New York: Doubleday, 1968.

———. *Jean-Marie Straub.* London: Secker & Warburg, 1971.

Ruesch, Jurgen, and Weldon Kees. *Nonverbal Communication: Notes on the Visual Perception of Human Relations.* Berkeley: University of California, 1969.

Sadoul, Georges. *French Film.* Falcon, 1953.

Salachas, Gilbert. *Federico Fellini.* New York: Crown, 1969.

Samuels, Charles (ed.). *A Casebook on Film.* New York: Van Nostrand, 1970.

Sanders, George. *Memoirs of a Professional Cad.* New York: Putnam, 1960.

Sarris, Andrew. *The American Cinema: Directors and Directions.* New York: Dutton, 1968.

———. *Interviews With Film Directors.* New York: Avon, 1967.

——— (ed.). *The Film.* Indianapolis: Bobbs-Merrill, 1968.

———. *The Films of Joseph von Sternberg.* New York: Museum of Modern Art, 1968.

Savary, Louis M., and J. Paul Carrico. *Contemporary Film & The New Generation.* New York: Association Press, 1971.

Schary, Dore. *Case History of a Movie.* New York: Random House, 1950.

Scheuer, Stephen H. (ed.). *Movies on T.V.* 4th ed. New York: Bantam, 1968.

Schickel, Richard. *The Disney Version: The Life, Times, Art and Commerce of Walt Disney.* New York: Simon and Schuster, 1968.

————. *Movies: The History of an Art and an Institution.* New York: Basic Books, 1964.

Schmidt, Georg, with Werner Schmalenbach and Peter Bachlin. *The Film: Its Economic, Social and Artistic Problems.* London: Falcon, 1948.

Schramm, Wilbur, with Philip H. Coombs, Friedrich Kahnert, and Jack Lyle. *The New Media: Memo to Educational Planners.* Paris: UNESCO, 1967.

Schrelvogel, Paul. *Films in Depth* (separate booklets for study, including the following titles: *An Occurrence at Owl Creek Bridge, No Reason to Stay, Overture—Overture/Nyitany, The Language of Faces, Orange and Blue, Toys, Timepiece, Night and Fog, Sunday Lark. Flavio, The Little Island, A Stain on His Conscience*). Dayton: Pflaum, 1970.

Schumach, Murray. *The Face on the Cutting Room Floor.* New York: Morrow, 1964.

Screen Greats: Hollywood Nostalgia. New York: Barven, 1971.

Seldes, Gilbert. *The Public Arts.* New York: Simon and Schuster, 1956.

Sennett, Mack. *King of Comedy.* New York: Doubleday, 1954.

Sennett, Ted. *Warner Brothers Presents: The Most Exciting Years—from The Jazz Singer to White Heat.* New York: Arlington House, 1971.

Seton, Marie. *Sergei M. Eisenstein.* New York: A. A. Wyn, 1952.

Sharp, Dennis. *The Picture Palace and Other Buildings for the Movies.* New York: Praeger, 1969.

Shelby, H. C. *Stag Movie Review.* Canoga Park, Calif.: Viceroy, 1970.

Sherman, Eric, and Martin Rubin. *The Director's Event: Interviews with Five American Film-Makers.* New York: Atheneum, 1970.

Shipman, David. *The Great Movie Stars: The Golden Years.* New York: Crown, 1970.

Shulman, Irving. *Valentino.* New York: Trident, 1967.

Silva, Fred (ed.). *Focus on "Birth of a Nation."* Englewood Cliffs, N.J.: Prentice-Hall, 1971.

Sitney, P. Adams (ed.). *Film Culture Reader.* New York: Praeger, 1970.

Slide, Anthony. *Early American Cinema.* London: Zwemmer, 1971.

Snider, Robert L. *Pare Lorentz and the Documentary Film.* Norman: University of Oklahoma, 1968.

Sohn, David A. *Film: The Creative Eye.* Dayton: Pflaum, 1970.

Solmi, Angelo (tr. Elizabeth Greenwood). *Fellini.* New York: Humanities, 1968.

Spottiswoode, Raymond. *A Grammar of the Film: An Analysis of Film Technique.* Berkeley: University of California, 1950.

Spraos, John. *The Decline of the Cinema: An Economist's Report.* London: Allen and Unwin, 1962.

Springer, John. *The Fondas.* New York: Citadel, 1970, 1971.

Stack, Oswald. *Pasolini on Pasolini: Interviews with Oswald Stack.* Bloomington: Indiana University, 1969.

Stedman, Raymond Williams. *The Serials: Suspense and Drama by Install-ment.* Norman: University of Oklahoma, 1970.

Steene, Birgitta. *Ingmar Bergman.* New York: Twayne, 1968.

Steen, Mike. *A Look at Tennessee Williams.* New York: Hawthorn, 1969.

Steiger, Brad. *Monsters, Maidens, and Mayhem: A Pictorial History of Hollywood Film Monsters.* Chicago: Camerarts, 1965.

Stephenson, Ralph, and Jean R. Debrix. *The Cinema as Art.* Baltimore: Penguin, 1965.

Stewart, David C. *Film Study in Higher Education.* Washington, D.C.: American Council on Education, 1966.

Strick, Philip. *Antonioni.* Loughton (Essex), Eng.: Motion Publications, 1965.

Sussex, Elizabeth. *Lindsay Anderson.* New York: Praeger, 1970.

Svensson, Arne. *Japan.* London: Zwemmer, 1971.

Swindell, Larry, *Spencer Tracy.* New York: World, 1969.

Tabori, Paul. *Alexander Korda.* London: Oldbourne, 1959.

Talbot, Daniel (ed.). *Film: An Anthology.* Berkeley: University of California, 1966.

Taylor, Deems. *Walt Disney's Fantasia.* New York: Simon and Schuster, 1940.

Taylor, Elizabeth. *Elizabeth Taylor: An Informal Memoir.* New York: Harper & Row, 1965.

Taylor, John Russell, *Cinema Eye, Cinema Ear: Some Key Film-makers of the Sixties.* New York: Hill and Wang, 1964.

———, and Arthur Jackson. *The Hollywood Musical.* London: Secker & Warburg, 1971.

Thomas, Bob. *Selznick.* New York: Doubleday, 1970.

———. *Selznick & Thalberg.* London: W. H. Allen, 1971.

———. *Thalberg: Life and Legend.* New York: Doubleday, 1969.

Thomas, Tony. *Ustinov in Focus.* London. Zwemmer, 1971.

Thompson, David. *Movie Man.* New York: Stein and Day, 1967.

Thorp, Margaret. *America at the Movies.* New Haven: Yale University, 1937.

Torme, Mel. *The Other Side Of the Rainbow: With Judy Garland on "The Dawn Patrol."* New York: Bantam. 1971.

Truffaut, François. *Hitchcock.* New York: Simon and Schuster, 1967.

Tyler, Parker. *Classics of the Foreign Film: A Pictorial History.* New York: Citadel, 1962.

———. *Magic and Myth of the Movies.* Introduction by Richard Schickel. New York: Simon and Schuster, 1970.

———. *The Hollywood Hallucination.* Introduction by Richard Schickel. New York: Simon and Schuster, 1970.

———. *The Three Faces of the Film.* New York: Yoseloff, 1960.

———. *Underground Film: A Critical History.* New York: Grove, 1970.

602 *Bibliography*

Tynan, Kenneth. *Alec Guinness.* New York: Macmillan, 1964.

———. *Tynan Right and Left: Plays, Films, People, Places and Events.* New York: Atheneum, 1968.

Vallance, Tom. *The American Musical.* London: Zwemmer, 1971.

Vardac, A. Nicholas. *Stage to Screen.* Cambridge: Harvard University, 1949.

Verdone, Mario. *Roberto Rossellini.* Paris: Editions Seghers, 1963.

Vidor, King. *A Tree Is a Tree.* New York: Harcourt, Brace, 1953.

Von Sternberg, Joseph. *Fun in a Chinese Laundry.* New York: Macmillan, 1965.

Wagenknecht, Edward. *Movies in the Age of Innocence.* Norman: University of Oklahoma, 1962.

Walker, Alexander. *The Celluloid Sacrifice: Aspects of Sex in the Movies.* New York: Hawthorn, 1967.

———. *Sex in the Movies.* Baltimore: Penguin, 1966.

———. *Stardom.* New York: Stein and Day, 1970.

Ward, John. *Alain Resnais, or the Theme of Time.* New York: Doubleday, 1968.

Warshow, Robert. *The Immediate Experience.* New York: Doubleday, 1962.

Weaver, John T. *Forty Years Of Screen Credits.* Metuchen, N.J.: Scarecrow, 1970.

Weinberg, Herman G. *Joseph von Sternberg.* New York: Dutton, 1967.

———. *The Lubitsch Touch: A Critical Study of the Great Film Director.* New York: Dutton, 1969.

———, with preface by Fritz Lang. *Saint Cinema: Selected Writings 1929–1970.* New York: Drama Book Specialists, 1970.

Weise, E. (ed. and tr.). *Enter: The Comics—Rodolphe Topffer's Essay on Physiognomy and the True Story of Monsieur Crepin.* Lincoln: University of Nebraska, 1965.

Wenner, Jann. *Lennon Remembers: The Rolling Stone Interviews.* San Francisco: Straight Arrow, 1971.

Whitaker, Rod. *The Language of Film.* Englewood Cliffs, N.J.: Prentice-Hall, 1970.

White, David Manning, and Richard Averson (eds.). *Sight, Sound, and Society—Motion Pictures and Television in America.* Boston: Beacon, 1968.

Whyte, Alistair. *New Cinema in Eastern Europe.* New York: Dutton, 1971.

Wilde, Larry. *Great Comedians Talk About Comedy.* New York: Citadel, 1969.

Wilk, Max (ed.). *The Wit and Wisdom of Hollywood: From the Squaw Man to the Hatchett Man.* New York: Atheneum, 1971.

Williams, Clarence, and John Debes (eds.). *Visual Literacy.* London: Pitman, 1970.

Willis, John. *Screen World 1949–   .* Annual, 21 vols. New York: Crown, 1970.

Wolfenstein, Martha. *Movies.* New York: Macmillan, 1950.

————, and Nathan Leites. *Movies: A Psychological Study.* New York: Atheneum, 1970.

Wollen, Peter. *Signs and Meaning in the Cinema.* Bloomington: Indiana University, 1969.

Woolenberg, H. H. *Anatomy of the Film.* London: Marsland, 1947.

————. *The Miracle of the Movies.* London: Burke, 1947.

Wood, Robin. *Arthur Penn.* New York: Praeger, 1970.

————. *Hitchcock's Films.* New York: Barnes, 1965.

————. *Hitchcock's Films: A Complete Critical Guide to the Films of Alfred Hitchcock.* New York: Paperback Library, 1970.

————. *Howard Hawks.* New York: Doubleday, 1968.

————, and Michael Walker. *Claude Chabrol.* New York: Praeger, 1970.

Wood, Tom. *The Bright Side of Billy Wilder, Primarily.* New York: Doubleday, 1970.

Youngblood, Gene. *Expanded Cinema.* New York: Dutton, 1970.

————. (Introduction by Buckminster Fuller). *Expanded Cinema.* New York: Dutton, 1971.

Zalman, Jan. *Films and Film-Makers in Czechoslovakia.* Prague: Orbis-Prague, 1968.

Zierold, Norman. *The Moguls.* New York: Coward-McCann, 1969.

Zimmerman, Paul D., and Burt Goldblatt. *The Marx Brothers at the Movies.* New York: Putnam, 1968.

Zinman, David. *Fifty Classic Motion Pictures: The Stuff That Dreams Are Made Of.* New York: Crown, 1970.

Screenplays and the Process of Filmmaking

Agee, James. *Agee on Film.* Boston: Beacon, 1964.

————. *Agee on Film: Five Film Scripts.* Boston: Beacon, 1958.

Agel, Jerome (ed.). *The Making of Kubrick's 2001.* New York: New American Library, 1970.

Alton, John. *Painting with Light.* New York: Macmillan, 1949.

Anderson, Lindsay (ed.). *Making a Film: The Story of "Secret People."* London: Allen and Unwin, 1952.

Aitken, Gillon, and Ronald Harwood. *The Making of One Day in the Life of Ivan Denisovich.* New York: Ballantine, 1971.

Anderson, Robert. *I Never Sang For My Father.* New York: New American Library, 1971.

Antonioni, Michelangelo. *Screenplays of Michelangelo Antonioni.* New York: Orion, 1963.

————. *Blow-Up: a Film by Michelangelo Antonioni.* London: Lorrimer, 1971.

Baddeley, W. Hugh. *The Technique of Documentary Film Production.* New York: Hastings House, 1963.

Baker, Fred. *Events: The Complete Scenario of the Film.* New York: Grove, 1971.

Bare, Richard L. ("Foreword" by Robert Wise) *The Film Director: A Practical Guide To Motion Picture and Television Techniques.* New York: Macmillan, 1971.

Beckett, Samuel, and Alan Schneider. *Film By Samuel Beckett.* New York: Grove, 1969.

Bellocchio, Marco. *China Is Near.* New York: Orion, 1969.

———. *Viridiana, The Exterminating Angel, Simon of the Desert.* New York: Orion, 1969.

Bergman, Ingmar. *Four Screenplays of Ingmar Bergman.* New York: Simon and Schuster, 1960.

——— (tr. by Paul Britten Austin). *A Film Trilogy: "The Silence," "Through a Glass Darkly," "A Winter Light."* New York: Grossman, 1968.

Bobker, Lee. *Elements of Film.* New York: Harcourt, Brace & World, 1969.

Boyer, Deena (tr. by Charles Lam Markmann). *The Two Hundred Days of 8½.* Afterword by Dwight Macdonald. New York: Macmillan, 1964.

Buñuel, Luis. *Belle de Jour: A Film by Luis Buñuel.* London: Lorrimer, 1971.

———. *L'Age d'Or and Un Chien Andalou.* New York: Simon and Schuster, 1968.

———. *Buñuel's Screenplays.* New York: Orion, 1969.

———. *Tristana: A Film by Luis Buñuel.* London: Lorrimer, 1971.

Burder, John. *The Technique of Editing 16MM Films.* New York: Hastings House, 1968.

Butler, Ivan. *The Making of Feature Films: A Guide.* Baltimore: Penguin, 1971.

Campbell, R. (ed.). *Photographic Theory For The Motion Picture Cameraman.* London: Zwemmer's, 1971.

——— (ed.). *Practical Motion Picture Photography.* London: Zwemmer, 1971.

Capote, Truman, with Eleanor and Frank Perry. *Trilogy.* New York: Macmillan, 1969.

Carlson, Verne, and Sylvia Carlson. *Professional 16/35 mm Cameraman's Handbook.* New York: Hastings House, 1970.

Carne, Marcel. *Children of Paradise.* New York: Simon and Schuster, 1968.

Carrick, Edward. *Designing for Moving Pictures.* New York: Studio, 1947.

Carson, L. M. Kit. *David Holzman's Diary: A Screenplay.* New York: Noonday, 1970.

Cassavetes, John, and Al Ruban. *Faces.* New York: New American Library, 1970.

Caunter, Julien. *How To Make Movie Magic in Amateur Films.* New York: Amphoto, 1971.

The Citizen Kane Book: Raising Kane by Pauline Kael and The Shooting Script by Herman J. Mankiewicz and Orson Welles. Boston: Little, Brown, 1971.

Clair, René (tr. by Piergiuseppe Bozzetti). *Four Screenplays: Le silence est d'or, La beauté du diable, Les belles-de-nuit, Les grandes manoeuvres.* New York: Orion, 1970.

Cocteau, Jean (ed. by Robert Morris Hammond). *Beauty and the Beast.* New York: N.Y.U., 1970.

————. (tr. by Lily Pons). *The Blood of a Poet.* New York: Bodley Head, 1947.

————. (tr. by Carol Martin-Sperry). *Two Screenplays: The Blood of a Poet, The Testament of Orpheus.* New York: Orion, 1968.

———— (tr. by Ronald Duncan). *Diary of a Film.* New York: Roy, 1950.

———— (tr. by Carol Martin-Sperry). *Screenplays and Other Writings on the Cinema.* New York: Grossman, 1968.

Coleman, H. La. *Making Movies—Student Films to Features.* New York: World, 1969.

Corry, Will, and Rudolph Wurlitzer. *Two-Lane Blacktop.* New York: Award Books, 1971.

Cross, Brenda (ed.). *The Film Hamlet: A Record of its Production.* London: Saturn, 1948.

Curry, George. *Copperfield '70: The Story of the Making of the Omnibus-20th-Century-Fox Film.* New York: Ballantine, 1970.

Cushman, George. *Movie Making in 18 Lessons.* New York: Amphoto, 1971.

De Sica, Vittorio. *Miricale in Milan.* New York: Orion, 1968.

Dreyer, Carl (tr. by Oliver Stallybrass). *Four Screenplays.* London: Thames and Hudson, 1970.

Dukore, Bernard F. (ed.). *Saint Joan: A Screenplay by Bernard Shaw.* Seattle: University of Washington, 1970.

Duras, Marguerite (tr. by Richard Seaver). *Hiroshima Mon Amour.* Picture editor Robert Hughes. New York: Grove, 1961.

Eastman, Charles. *Little Fauss and Big Halsy.* New York: Pocket Books, 1970.

Eisenstein, Sergei M. *Ivan the Terrible.* New York: Simon and Schuster, 1962.

———— (tr. by Gillon Aitken). *Potemkin.* New York: Simon and Schuster, 1968.

Eisler, Hans. *Composing for the Films.* New York: Oxford University, 1947.

Eliot, T. S., and George Hoellering. *The Film of Murder in the Cathedral.* New York: Harcourt, Brace, 1952.

Fellini, Federico (tr. by Howard Greenfield; ed. by Tullio Kezich). *Federico Fellini's Juliet of the Spirits.* New York: Ballantine, 1965.

————. *La Dolce Vita*. New York: Ballantine, 1961.

———— (tr. by Judith Green). *Three Screenplays: I Vitelloni, Il Bidone, The Temptations of Doctor Antonio*. New York: Orion, 1970.

———— (tr. by Judith Green). *Fellini's Early Screenplays*. New York: Orion, 1970.

————. *Fellini's Satyricon*. New York: Ballantine, 1970.

———— (ed. by Robert Steele). *Eight and a Half*. New York: Ballantine, 1970.

———— (ed. by Robert Steele). *La Strada*. New York: Ballantine, 1970.

———— (tr. by Eugene Walter and John Matthews; ed. by Dario Zanelli). *Satyricon*. New York: Ballantine, 1970.

Ferguson, Robert. *How to Make Movies: A Practical Guide to Group Film-Making*. New York: Viking, 1969.

Fielding, Raymond. *The Technique of Special Effects Cinematography*. New York: Hastings House, 1965.

Fonda, Peter, with Dennis Hopper and Terry Southern. *Easy Rider*. New York: New American Library, 1969.

Foote, Horton. *The Screenplay of To Kill a Mockingbird*. New York: Harcourt, Brace & World, 1964.

Ford, John, and Dudley Nichols. *Stagecoach*. London: Lorrimer, 1971.

Forman, Milos. *Taking Off*. New York: New American Library, 1971.

Fry, Christopher. *The Bible*. New York: Pocket Books, 1966.

Gardner, Herb. *Who is Harry Kellerman and why is he saying those terrible things about me?: a screenplay*. New York: New American Library, 1971.

Gassner, John (ed.). *Best Film Plays of 1943/44*. New York: Crown, 1945.

————. *Great Film Plays*. New York: Crown, 1959.

———— (ed. with Dudley Nichols). *Best Film Plays of 1939/40*. New York: Crown, 1941.

Geduld, Harry M. (ed.). *Film Makers on Film Making: Statements on their Art by Thirty Directors*. Bloomington: Indiana University, 1967.

Gelmis, Joseph. *The Film Director as Superstar*. New York: Doubleday, 1970.

Gilliatt, Penelope. *Sunday Bloody Sunday*. New York: Bantam, 1971.

Godard, Jean-Luc. *The Married Woman*. New York: Berkeley, 1965.

Goldman, William. *Butch Cassidy and The Sundance Kid*. New York: Bantam, 1969.

Goode, James. *The Story of The Misfits*. Indianapolis: Bobbs-Merrill, 1963.

Gordon, George N., and Irving A. Falk. *Your Career In Film Making*. New York: Julian Messner, 1969.

Griffith, Richard. *The Anatomy of a Motion Picture*. New York: St. Martin's, 1959.

Hamill, Pete. *Doc*. New York: Paperback Library, 1971.

Herman, Lewis. *A Practical Manual of Screen Playwriting: For Theater and Television Films.* New York: World, 1966.

Higham, Charles. *Hollywood Cameramen: Sources of Light.* London: Thames and Hudson, 1970.

————, and Joel Greenberg. *The Celluloid Muse: Hollywood Directors Speak.* New York: New American Library, 1970.

Hopper, Dennis. *The Last Movie.* New York: New American Library, 1970.

Isaksson, Ulla. *The Virgin Spring.* New York: Ballantine, 1960.

Kantor, Bernard R., with Irwin A. Blacker and Anne Kramer (eds.). *Directors at Work.* New York: Funk and Wagnalls, 1970.

Kurosawa, Akira. *Seven Samurai.* London: Lorrimer, 1971.

Larson, Rodger, Jr. *A Guide for Film Teachers to Filmmaking by Teenagers.* New York: Cultural Affairs Foundation, 1968.

———— and Ellen Meade. *Young Filmmakers.* New York: Avon, 1971.

Lawson, John Howard. *Theory and Technique of Playwriting and Screenwriting.* New York: Putnam, 1949.

Lewis, Colby. *The TV Director-Interpreter.* New York: Funk and Wagnalls, 1968.

Lewis, Herman. *A Practical Manual of Screen Playwriting.* New York: World, 1966.

Lewis, Jerry. *The Total Film-Maker.* New York: Random House, 1971.

Leyda, Jay. *Films Beget Films.* New York: Hill and Wang, 1964.

Lidstone, John, and Don McIntosh. *Children As Film Makers.* New York: Van Nostrand, 1970.

Livingston, Don. *Film and the Director.* New York: Macmillan, 1953.

London, Kurt. *Film Music.* London: Faber and Faber, 1936.

Lowndes, Douglas. *Film Making In Schools.* New York: Watson-Guptill, 1968.

Maddux, Rachel, with Stirling Silliphant and Neil D. Issacs. *Fiction Into Film: A Walk in the Spring Rain.* Knoxville: University of Tennessee, 1970.

Madsen, Roy. *Animated Film.* New York: Interland, 1969.

Mailer, Norman. *Maidstone: A Mystery.* New York: New American Library, 1971.

Mankiewicz, Joseph L. *All About Eve: A Screenplay.* New York: Random House, 1951.

Manoogian, Haig P. *The Film-Maker's Art.* New York: Basic Books, 1966.

Manvell, Roger. *Three British Screenplays: Brief Encounter, Odd Man Out, and Scott of the Antarctic.* London: Methuen, 1950.

Mascelli, Joseph V. *The Five C's of Cinematography: Motion Picture Filming Techniques Simplified.* Los Angeles: Cine/Grafic Publications, 1965.

———— (ed.). *American Cinematographer Manual.* Hollywood: American Society of Cinematographers, 1966.

Maugham, Somerset, with R. C. Sheriff and Loel Langley. *Encore*. New York: Doubleday, 1952.

————. *Trio*. New York: Delta, 1950.

Maysles, Albert, and David Maysles. *Salesman*. New York: New American Library, 1969.

McGowan, Kenneth. *Behind the Screen: The History and Techniques of the Motion Picture*. New York: Delacorte, 1965.

Menzel, Jiri, and Bohumil Hrabal (tr. Josef Holzbecher). *Closely Watched Trains*. New York: Simon and Schuster, 1971.

Mercer, John. *An Introduction to Cinematography*. Champaign, Ill.: Stipes, 1970.

Meyer, Nicholas. *The Love Story*. New York: Avon, 1971.

Miller, Arthur. *The Misfits*. New York: Viking, 1961.

Miller, Merle, and Evan Rhodes. *Only You, Dick Darling, or How to Write One Television Script and Make $50,000,000*. New York: Bantam Books, 1964.

Montagu, Ivor. *With Eisenstein in Hollywood*. New York: International Publishers, 1969.

Mosley, Raymond. *Battle of Britain: The Making of a Film*. New York: Ballantine, 1969.

Naumburg, Nancy (ed.). *We Make the Movies*. New York: Norton, 1937.

Nilsen, Vladimir. *The Cinema as a Graphic Art*. New York: Hill and Wang, 1959.

Nurnberg, Walter. *Lighting for Photography*. New York: Hastings House, 1956.

Oringel, Robert S. *Audio Control Handbook*. New York: Hastings House, 1956.

Osborne, John. *Tom Jones*. London: Faber, 1964.

———— (ed. Robert Hughes). *Tom Jones: A Film Script*. New York: Grove, 1964.

Pabst, G. W. *Pandora's Box Lulu: A Film By G. W. Pabst*.

Parker, Norton S. *Audiovisual Script Writing*. New Brunswick: Rutgers University, 1968.

Pasolini, Pier Paolo. *Oedipus Rex: A Film By Pier Paolo Pasolini*. London: Lorrimer, 1971.

Peebles, Melvin Van. *Sweet Sweetback's Baadasssss Song*. New York: Lancer, 1971.

Pennebaker, D. A. *Bob Dylan—Don't Look Back*. New York: Ballantine, 1968.

Petrow, Mischa. *Efficient Film-Making Practices: Rules, Forms & Guides*. New York: Drama Book Specialists, 1970.

Petzold, Paul. *All-In-One Movie Book*. New York: Hastings House, 1969.

Pincus, Edward, and Jairus Lincoln. *Guide to Filmmaking*. New York: New American Library, 1969.

Pinter, Harold. *Five Screenplays*. London: Methuen, 1971.

Provisor, Henry. *8MM/16MM Movie-Making*. New York: Chilton, 1970.

Pudovkin, V. I. *Film Technique and Film Acting*. New York: Grove, 1960.

Quigley, Martin, Jr. (ed.). *New Screen Techniques*. Quigley, 1953.

Rattigan, Terence. *The Prince and the Showgirl*. New York: New American Library, 1957.

Reisz, Karel. *The Technique of Film Editing*. New York: Hastings House, 1968.

Renoir, Jean. *The Rules of the Game*. London: Lorrimer, 1970.

Reynertson, A. J. *The Work of the Film Director*. New York: Hastings House, 1971.

Rilla, Wolf. *A–Z of Movie Making*. London: Studio Vista, 1970.

Robbe-Grillet, Alain. *Last Year at Marienbad*. New York: Grove, 1962.

————. *L'Immortelle*. Paris: Editions de Minuit, 1963.

Roberts, Kenneth H., and Win Sharples, Jr. *A Primer for Film Making*. New York: Bobbs-Merrill, 1972.

Serling, Rod. *Patterns*. New York: Simon and Schuster, 1957.

Shavelson, Melville. *How to Make A Jewish Movie*. Englewood Cliffs, N.J.: Prentice-Hall, 1971.

Sherwood, Robert E. *The Best Moving Pictures of 1922–1923*. New York: Small, Maynard, 1923.

Shoman, Vilgot (tr. by Martin Minow and Jenny Bohman). *I Am Curious (Blue)*. New York: Grove, 1970.

————. *I Am Curious (Yellow)*. New York: Grove, 1968.

————. *I Was Curious—Diary of the Making of a Film*. New York: Grove, 1968.

Skillbeck, Oswald. *ABC of Film and TV Working Terms*. New York: Focal, 1960.

Smallman, Kirk. *Creative Film-Making*. New York: Macmillan, 1969.

Sontag, Susan. *Duet for Cannibals: A Screenplay*. New York: Farrar, Straus & Giroux, 1970.

Southern, Terry. *The Journal of The Loved One: The Production Log of a Motion Picture*. With photography by William Claxton. New York: Random House, 1965.

Souto, H. Mario Raimondo (ed. by Raymond Spottiswoode). *The Technique of the Motion Picture Camera*. New York: Communications Arts Books, 1967.

Spottiswoode, Raymond. *Film and Its Techniques*. Berkeley: University of California, 1951.

Stroheim, Erich von. *Greed: A Film By Erich von Stroheim*. London: Lorrimer, 1971.

Taylor, Theodore. *People Who Make Movies*. New York: Doubleday, 1967

Teshigahara, Hiroshi. *Woman in the Dunes*. New York: Phaedra, 1971.

Thomas, Dylan. *The Doctor and The Devils And Other Scripts*. New York: New Directions, 1966.

Thompson, Robert E. *They Shoot Horses, Don't They?* New York: Avon, 1969.

Trapnell, Coles. *Teleplay*. San Francisco: Chandler, 1966.

Truffaut, François, with Helen G. Scott. *Hitchcock*. New York: Simon and Schuster, 1966.

Vadim, Roger. *Les Liaisons Dangereuses*. New York: Ballantine, 1962.

Vardac, A. Nicholas. *Stage to Screen: Theatrical Method from Garrick to Griffith*. New York: Blom, 1949.

Visconti, Luchino (tr. by Judith Green). *Three Screenplays: White Nights, Rocco and His Brothers, The Job*. New York: Orion, 1970.

————. *Two Screenplays: La Terra Trema, Senso*. New York: Orion, 1970.

Walter, Ernest. *The Technique of the Film Cutting Room*. New York: Hastings House, 1960.

Wanger, Walter, and Joe Hyams. *My Life With Cleopatra*. New York: Bantam, 1963.

Warhol, Andy. *Blue Movie*. New York: Grove, 1970.

Welles, Orson. *The Trial*. London: Lorrimer, 1971.

West, Jessamyn. *To See the Dream*. New York: Harcourt, Brace, 1957.

Wexler, Norman. *Joe*. Introduction by Judith Crist. New York: Avon, 1970.

Wilder, Billy and I. A. L. Diamond. *Irma La Douce*. New York: Midwood-Tower, 1963.

Wilk, Max. *The Beatles in the Yellow Submarine*. New York: New American Library, 1968.

Wilson, Michael. *Salt of the Earth*. Hollywood: Hollywood Quarterly, 1953.

Wolfe, Maynard Frank. *The Making of "The Adventurers."* New York: Paperback Library, 1970.